KINGDOM UNDER GLASS

KINGDOM UNDER GLASS

A Tale of Obsession, Adventure,
and One Man's Quest
to Preserve the World's Great Animals

❧

JAY KIRK

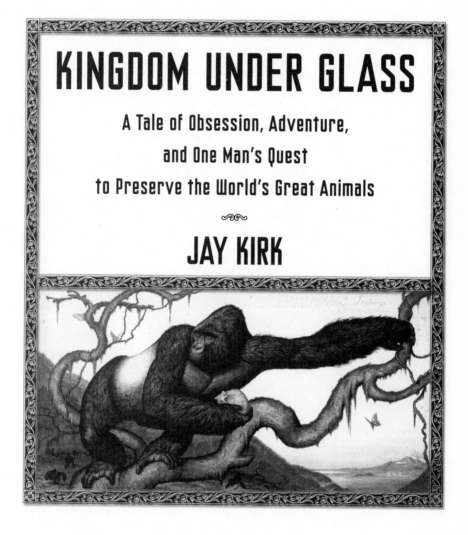

HENRY HOLT AND COMPANY

NEW YORK

Henry Holt and Company, LLC

Publishers since 1866
175 Fifth Avenue
New York, New York 10010
www.henryholt.com

Henry Holt® and ▣® are registered trademarks of Henry Holt and Company, LLC.

Distributed in Canada by H. B. Fenn and Company Ltd.

Library of Congress Cataloging-in-Publication Data

Kirk, Jay.
  Kingdom under glass / by Jay Kirk.
     p.   cm.
  ISBN 978-0-8050-9282-0
  1. Akeley, Carl Ethan, 1864–1926.   2. Wild animal collectors—United States—
Biography.   3. Taxidermists—United States—Biography.   4. Zoological specimens—
Africa—Collection and preservation.   I. Title.
  QL31.A5K57 2010
  590.92—dc22
  [B]   2009050706

Henry Holt books are available for special promotions and premiums.
For details contact: Director, Special Markets.

First Edition 2010

Designed by Meryl Sussman Levavi

Printed in the United States of America

1 3 5 7 9 10 8 6 4 2

For Julie

Works of history are first and foremost
acts of the imagination.

— Eric Foner

❧

What is your beast?

— Charles Otis Whitman

KINGDOM UNDER GLASS

BELGIAN CONGO. NOVEMBER 5, 1921

H E FELT HEARTSICK WHEN HE SAW THE GORILLA START ITS death tumble. It was coming right for him. Three or four hundred pounds of silver-backed ape slumping down the bright green jumble of vegetation in joyless somersaults. Rolling like a rain barrel, long arms flopping, ass over applecart, a furry black hogshead headed straight for the chasm below. Nothing was going to stop it now from hurtling into the void. Even if it ran him over first. Even if it took him with it. A skinny sapling was the only thing between him—between Carl Akeley, the world's greatest taxidermist—and the three-hundred-foot plummet. He leaned into it, rifle still pressed to his shoulder. The recoil alone would have knocked him off the mountain without the little tree wedged into his spine.

Technically, it wasn't a *straight* three-hundred-foot drop. Directly behind Akeley, crumbling just under the heel of his Silver & Edgington hobnail boot, was a sheer twenty-foot drop, and below that a sharp fifty-foot slide—and *then* the big straight two-hundred-foot plummet. Chances were if the gorilla kept its momentum and made it over the first drop, it was going all the way, leaving Akeley with nothing to show for the thousands of miles he'd traveled to collect it for his greatest work-in-progress.

That is, if the gorilla didn't collect him first.

His Watusi guides and gun bearer were still clinging to the steep bank, where they had frozen at varying angles after spotting the black shaggy head thirty feet or so above them. They'd first seen it from across the canyon, a black speck minding its own business, and they had spent the better part of the morning getting from the one ridge, down the canyon, and back up the other side to the crest of this one just to see if it was indeed what they'd hoped. For hours, nothing but the sound of machete. The climb alternated between strictly vertical and almost vertical, and he had to repeatedly beg the guides to stop so he could catch his breath. It was grilling work, and quite honestly he wondered if he would survive it at all. To look at him was to wonder the same thing. Here was a white man clearly done in. He was gaunt and rattle-eyed. Feverish shadows cast by the brim of his pith helmet burrowed into the crags of a face that looked as if it were literally aging by the hour. He had felt the onset of the fever before he'd even penetrated gorilla country. Despite the cool moist climate he was a man on fire. By the time they'd got to the other side of the canyon, hauling themselves up by the mutinous nettles and thistle stalk—and then out along the crest of this narrow ridge, the terrible drop just beneath—he had had almost no strength left at all. Barely enough to stop for a smoke.

Leaning against the solitary sapling, he had got an upward bead on the gorilla rustling about in the vivid welter of greenery. His gun bearer clung to the slope with his right hand, like a whaler hanging off the mizzen shrouds, holding out the second rifle if Carl needed backup. The guide who'd spotted the ape had then lain down on the ground before him, naked but for his goatskin, and waited patiently for bwana to take the shot. The explosion was only a residue now. All dead quiet except the crumpling whoosh of vegetation as it parted in the wake of the gorilla's fall.

Carl Akeley nearly sank with relief when the gorilla passed cleanly between him and the terrified guide. But then dread immediately filled in the relief when the gorilla catapulted over the first ledge.

Before his mood had given way to dread that he would lose this most rare and dear prize, the taxidermist had been filled with an almost childlike sense of awe and glee. That he was actually seeing a gorilla in the first place! That this most unknown and mythical creature was *actually* just up there, looking down at him, with an expression of passive curiosity. Its face was ugly and mild. It looked as if it were rethinking through some small but persistent self-doubt. Part of Akeley's sense of disbelief, certainly, was caused by the great heat boiling his flesh, the fever that cauterized everything passing before his eyes. He should have started taking the quinine earlier. Now, along with an evil headache, everything was distorted with an aura of unreality. It was an eerie beauty of volcanoes and misty ravines, of crooked trees dripping with moss and silvery lichen. He half expected to see fairies springing out of the lacy chest-high ferns.

Really, like a boy, he had had to pinch himself when he had seen the first knuckle print in the mud. He'd held his hand over the four impressions, curling the back of his trembling fingers above the larger mold. Then, after scrambling farther along on all fours in the ruck and jumble of vine and bamboo, they'd come to several footprints in a slick of mud. They were enormous. All but human. It was then he felt his faith slipping, and he switched from the Springfield to the double-barreled elephant gun.

Theoretically, he told himself, he did not fear the gorillas. He had even composed a sort of creed against this fear: how he had spent too much time around wild animals to believe in monsters. He knew they weren't looking for trouble. But now he felt *almost excited to a painful degree*. That was how the first white man to encounter a gorilla, Paul du Chaillu, had put it right before he'd blown the "hellish" creature straight to kingdom come. Akeley had gorged himself on these early sensational narratives before coming here. Du Chaillu believed the gorillas were so powerful they had driven out the lions and elephants from this region where they lived. Excited to a painful degree, though, was exactly how Akeley felt, even if he had tried to convince himself ahead of time that the brutes could not possibly be half as ferocious as their popular image: that of a demonic beast capable of snapping a rifle in its teeth, or ripping the head off a man with one hand, and with a penchant for abducting human females for purposes of unchaste cavorting. But when he saw the print in the mud, he'd been all too eager to hold the rifle. Then when he had finally come upon this one sunning itself on the upper slope of the canyon, it seemed a benign and gentle beast. Crouched on a mezzanine of dense vegetation, doing nothing more than regarding the day. Akeley had waited for it to charge, or to beat on its chest, as he had read in accounts, but it did nothing of the sort. It merely barked at him, like a seal. And on the fourth bark Akeley had pulled the trigger.

The truth would still bring people to the museum in droves. If only it didn't vanish into the chasm first.

After the first bounce the gorilla stopped abruptly at the very lip of the canyon. Snagged at the last moment by a wiry tree. A miraculous save, against all odds. Saved by an even scantier tree than the one Carl had used to brace himself for the shot. There it dangled, wrapped around the little tree, creaking heavily, a four-hundred-pound silverback, suspended over the very brink of the eastern Congo.

Its body was still hot.

He had only a jackknife to skin it. The guides had discouraged him from bringing any of his scientific paraphernalia. The climb was too steep to carry anything extra. He had left behind his motion picture camera as well, and he had no porters. While he roughly skinned and skeletonized the gorilla where it lay, the others held on to it where they could, and on to the American as well, clutching hold of his boots to keep him from slipping over the edge.

Wouldn't Mickie have loved that? Wouldn't that have made life easier for his soon-to-be ex-wife? End all the wrangling. Send home the lawyers. No more need to come up with epithets to call him in the newspapers. A "cruel caveman" and all the rest. No need for her to invent more malicious lies to drag his reputation through the mud.

As he tugged away at the animal's skin, he tried to keep his focus. This was no time to think about marital troubles. And yet, if he did somehow slip, if the branch suddenly snapped, and he fell to his death in the embrace of this half-skinned grizzled old ape, tumbling together through space before being smashed to bits, wouldn't Mickie have had the last laugh then? She'd be singing the hinky-dinky, parlez-vous. No doubt about it. He'd had to play all sorts of stupid games just to keep her from sabotaging this latest expedition. Lying about the date of his departure, for example. He was sure it incensed her that he'd come back to Africa without her. That all the glory was *his* this time around. But what if he lost his balance in the slippery blood? It would be in all the newspapers: Carl Akeley, the world's most renowned and redoubtable taxidermist, the explorer, inventor, resurrection artist, flenser of elephants, tailor of the integument, sculptor of the dermic membrane, had fallen to his death, pulled over the brink in the embrace of a four-hundred-pound gorilla. How sensational! Even if it paled in comparison to the sordid stuff his lawyers had told him Mickie was prepared to release to the papers.

Once again, he tried to focus on the task at hand. Carefully cutting out the gorilla's heart. Handing it to one of the men to wrap in leaves so he could preserve it in formalin later, back at camp. Ditto with the brain, liver, and specimens of skin around the pubic region—all specifically requested by the museum biologists—all the better to read into the story of their nearest living relative. He looked up at the volcano, Nyamlagira, in the near distance, near enough it made a low rumble in the air. It all looked like something from a Jules Verne novel. Who knew if at this very moment he held in his hand the skull of the "missing link"?

His boss, Henry Fairfield Osborn, president of the American Museum of Natural History, of course scoffed at the idea of any such link being discovered in Africa. In fact, he was about to send off a million-dollar expedition to Central Asia, where he was positive he'd find it.

Carl had heard some of the foolish yarns about gorillas as a guest of the White Fathers, whose mission sat at the foot of Mount Mikeno, and from where he had started his climb and got his guides as well. Shortly before his arrival a gorilla had evidently come down into a nearby village. When the men went to chase it from the banana groves, it had killed one of them, torn the man limb from limb and ripped off his head. Carl wasn't really inclined to believe the story. These Belgian friars had settled here after being expelled from Uganda. They were not entirely reliable. A day before reaching the mission, he'd passed a small cemetery where eleven Belgian officers were buried, killed during the war, the graves enclosed by elephant grass, marked with moldy wooden crosses, piled high with rocks to keep away hyenas. It was the war that had given Mickie her chance to get away from him in the first place. The Great War had replaced all their former adventures. How many years had it been since they'd stood back-to-back in a standoff against a charging dust storm of elephants? What pure exhilaration to feel her small shoulders pressed into his back, quivering with each kick of her rifle. But those days were long gone.

The White Fathers Mission was a small compound of low white-washed buildings, dirt floors, thatched roofs, and windowless shutters. (In the nearby village of Gisenyi, the local doctor used spent photographic plates for windowpanes.) At the mission the White Fathers grew vegetables and tobacco and roses. They taught the local Watusi children, conducting the spiritual salvation of the savages, and put them to work making cigars and bricks for the cathedral they were erecting here in the wilderness. The White Fathers, as overseen by Père Supérieur von Hoef, had made themselves somewhat of a welcome hostel to gorilla hunters. Most recently, Prince William of Sweden had shot fourteen. This was the same prince rumored to have divorced his wife just a few years earlier for being a Russian spy; but then it turned out the princess had simply deserted him and refused to return to cold Christiania. Now he intended to prove himself as a big-game hunter and to give his fourteen ape skins to the museum in Stockholm. The prince had taken along le Père Supérieur, who, in his long white robes, stiff cape, and fulsome beard, looked like that other mad monk Rasputin. Le Père had shot one himself and dismissed Akeley's claims that the gorilla was in danger of extinction, believing that the mountains were populated by thousands. Carl doubted there were more than a couple hundred.

This particular one he was now expertly skinning with a jackknife seemed to him like a worthwhile sacrifice—if only to preserve a likeness of what would be lost forever if a few more Prince Williams ever made their way up this mountain. Even so, doing the museum's bidding this time around made him feel like a plain murderer. He had never felt quite as sick about his job as he did now. But still, as civilization continued its rapid march across the last of the earth's hidden worlds, there was really nothing else he could do but preserve a snapshot of this near relic.

If only he'd been able to preserve what he'd had with Mickie. It was the grounds of cruelty that really ticked him off, he thought, as he severed the gorilla's head. He kicked aside the pile of innards and watched them slide down the grassy slope. That he had tied her to their bed and turned on the gas in their Upper West Side apartment. Threatened to cut her throat with a razor. Abandoned her to die of blood poisoning after her infernal pet monkey had bitten her on the leg and damn near cost her her life—of all things, that *he* had abandoned *her*. Well, she had deserted him first. Not the other way around. They were all stinking lies. It was outrageous, especially now that he had found out the truth. That she meant to ruin much more than his good name. That all along— or at least in the end—it was *she* who had planned to murder *him*.

Or at least that's what the psychiatrist said.

She was batty. Completely insane. But, still, if she was prepared to go public with her mad ravings, it wouldn't just be ruinous to his reputation but would besmirch the museum as well. He pried off the finger-

and toenails one at a time with the blade, carefully numbering each like a rare beetle, tucking them into his breast pocket.

He felt incredibly weak and tried not to think whether he'd be able to get back to camp on his own. His fever radiated around him like a box. He could have lain down right here and fallen asleep; but he would rather do anything than resort to the humiliation of having his men carry him back like a child. He was far too old to be doing this kind of work anymore. The sapling bowed under the weight of the half-skinned gorilla. A vulture floating out over the canyon banked an invisible current. Even if Akeley didn't fall to his death, Mickie might get her way regardless. He could tell by the troubled looks of his guides that he must have appeared grave indeed. More like a sickly seventy-year-old than a man three years shy of sixty. By his own estimate, he'd lost twenty pounds in the last three weeks. His clothes barely hung on his frame. He looked like the first draft of one of his own manikins.

He worked till the point where his fingernails felt sore and loose—a hazard of the trade; arsenic made it all but impossible to keep one's fingernails.

After they had skinned the gorilla, his guides packed up the bones in their baskets, and with Carl following behind at a determined limp, they began the march back down to the base camp.

Somehow he made it on his own before dusk.

As he prepared a batch of plaster to make a mold of the soles of the gorilla's feet and the palms of its hands, the mist shuffled through the trees and wrapped around the camp. His men were busy cleaning its skeleton, and he kept a close eye on them while they worked; he had already taken all the necessary measurements and preserved the organs in jars of formalin for the trip back to New York. One of the men was attempting to build a fire. In this weather, in the constant fog and rain, it was a struggle, and everything—tents, guns, chop boxes—was covered by a green spidery mold. Just to protect the unexposed film for his motion picture camera, each reel was kept in a sealed tin. Five reels then went in a larger tin box with the lid soldered on. Then four of *those* packages were sealed inside a corrugated cardboard carton and packed in a tin-lined cedar box. The whole shebang was carried in a galvanized iron box just heavy enough for one porter to manage on his head (while keeping his balance with a spear).

He held the gorilla's head in his lap, studying its face, as he stirred more plaster for a death mask. The gorilla was an older male, no doubt in the twilight of its peaceable life, even if, in death, he could see the vague indentations of worry in its dilated creased face, its uncertain eyes. It was deeply unsettling to recognize such distinct *character* looking back at him. There was no other word for this quality. This old ape had had its own dilemmas. It made him feel like a murderer, not just because in a distorted way it looked humanish—and no doubt that distortion was caused in part by the fever—but because, unlike a zebra or hippopotamus, it had that vaguish quality of personality. Zebras had fierce spirit, but they did not have individual character.

Akeley poured the white gloop over its face, letting the plaster seal in all the inscrutable furrows, concealing, for now, any doubts about what he had just done.

Later that night, to the utter disgust of the native guides, out of some irresistible curiosity, he would cook and eat some of the flesh of the old gorilla. He was depleted and ate it for strength. The unmarinaded meat was surprisingly sweet. It did not taste taboo. But then, in the middle of the night, he woke in a cold sweat, convinced he had hallucinated the entire thing. The trip across the sea. The hunt. The terrible climb. The reality of the gorilla. He could not be convinced otherwise until he stumbled out into camp and saw the old male's skin hanging there, flapping in the cold wind.

Its skeleton creaked at him on the rack.

He could hear a hyrax in the trees, making its eerie screech, just like a child shrieking in pain. However pitiful, the cries of this strange shrewlike creature did nothing to elicit the sympathy of its enemy the leopard. The cat's tracks were visible on the ground around their tents come morning. In the distance the cauldron of Nyamlagira was spitting lava and glowing under the scud of clouds drifting across the night. In a way he envied the old gorilla. He would have gladly exchanged roles. Given it his steamer ticket back to New York, let it deal with his wife, the lawyers, pick up his god-awful lecture circuit. Just leave him here to die in peace. Let the volcano be his funeral pyre.

But then, he would never have lived long enough to give the gorillas reason to thank him. For truly, even these ones here, the dead and dismantled, would have risen from their vats of formalin to thank the taxidermist if they could have seen what he was about to do. His next act. Even if he didn't know yet himself, it would change everything.

~∾∾∾~

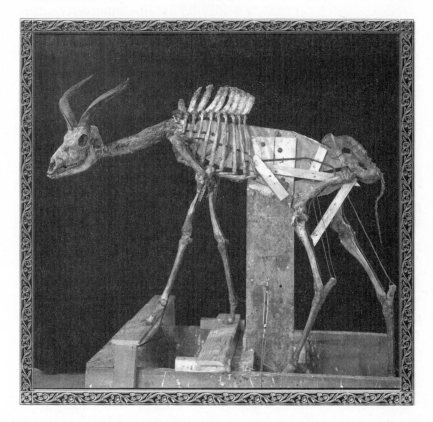

PART ONE

The Resurrectionists

CHAPTER ONE

WINTER, 1883. BROOKLYN

WAS THIS REALLY IT? BEFORE HIS LIFE HAD EVEN BEGUN, TO BE cast out and condemned to sit day in, day out in this basement dungeon before a great pile of dead birds? It was like a bad dream. The pile, heaped on the table, never got any smaller. He might think for a while that it was shrinking. He'd work his way into one corner for a while, skinning birds in one particular quadrant, digging a small cave, chipping away at the side of the mountain one dead bird at a time, but then another plume hunter would arrive in his muddy hip boots with a sack over his shoulder, stinking of gunpowder and bird shit. Then Wallace, the ogre who owned this dismal chop shop, would step out of the shadows to negotiate a price, and another sack of terns and egrets and robins and warblers would come tumbling out on the table, and the work would be just as daunting and endless as before.

He had really flubbed his one great chance to have ended up here. One day you've got your whole life ahead of you; the next you're condemned for an eternity to keep pushing yourself back up a mountain of dead birds. It was the most barbaric work in the world, skinning birds for ladies' hats. It was a world away from the future he'd been promised at Ward's Natural Science Establishment in Rochester, New York. There he might have eventually seen his own handiwork end up in the world's greatest natural history museums. But then there'd been a kind of misunderstanding. He'd been too ambitious. He'd been too careless, and yes, possibly even arrogant. Mistakes were made. And then Professor Ward—the great maestro—had gone and cast him out of the only Eden he'd ever known. He'd been fired.

And now Carl Akeley was a virtual prisoner in this dank basement of a moldy warehouse below the Brooklyn Bridge, where he could barely hear his own gloomy thoughts over the screech of tugboat whistles and the drone of the oil barges and naval vessels that crowded the East River. The sickening stench of the workshop, lit by the sallow light of gas jet lamps, was ghoulish. John Wallace was a short, intense man with a cockney accent often thickened by beer as he lorded it over his underground realm, dealing brashly with the hunters who brought him birds by the sackload daily, and the boys who worked for him, turning the flightless lumps of feather into cash.

Carl and several other young men came in the morning before sunup, hung their coats by the door, and sat on wooden benches around a large table heaped with the day's work. The hunters came in from the rookeries on Long Island and the forests of New Jersey, bringing in as many as four hundred birds a day. They were dumped onto the table— bluebirds, sparrows, grebes, waxwings, all mixed together in a welter of beaks and bloodied plumage. Carl would reach into the heap, where it was sometimes still warm in the center, take hold of a bird, skin it, quickly shape it into something that might look chic on a lady's head, and then move on to the next. The boys' fingers were nicked and scratched and bled from the sharp talons and sewing needles. Loose feathers dusted the floor in drifts. At best, the work was a sort of assembly line: One boy skinned a bird, passed it along to the next, who wound tow for the body. Another bent wire for the necks; another cleaned wings with turpentine. Another might poison skins all day long. In the end they were dried, boxed, and shipped off to the milliners in the fashion district of Fourteenth Street, where they were affixed to ladies' hats for J. Gurney & Son, the New York Millinery Supply Co., and others. Given how this peculiar fashion was at its absolute zenith, Mr. Wallace had earned a reputation as the most prolific stuffer of birds in the long and sordid history of taxidermy. He always had need for skilled and semiskilled boys.

Akeley had had no trouble getting the job.

To sit before this avalanche of dead birds that would never grow any smaller—this was his punishment for having had the temerity to try to make something of himself. The worst part was the stinging regret that never went away, that never got smaller, that stared back at him out of a thousand cooled eyes. If only Professor Ward had given him a chance to explain himself! Working at Ward's Natural Science Establishment had been the closest he would ever get to serious museum taxidermy. His only crime had been youthful ambition. Well, that, and falling asleep on the job; but Carl felt certain Professor Ward would have been kinder if only he'd known about the late-night experiments he'd been conducting, if he'd only bothered to ask before giving him the boot. If only whichever envious snake hadn't destroyed his experiments before he'd had the chance to show the professor. He'd actually thought he was on the verge of reinventing the art of taxidermy. How stupid he'd been. There was nothing artful about this work. It was brutal and disgusting. He was no sculptor, like he'd boasted. He was a nobody. That was all there was to it, and all that was left was to accept the fact that he'd been sentenced to a lifetime of utter insignificance— *skinning birds for ladies' hats.*

Things could have turned out so differently! He thought of all the countless hours he'd spent as a boy cloistered in his room, studying the spattered copy of the taxidermy manual ordered from the back of *Youth's Companion*—he'd passed right over the ads for the Velocipede and the Reading Machine, even if he did go in for the adventure stories where explorers faced off against rabid panthers and savage Indians, the serialized features like "Cast Away in Japan"—the ad had been right there between the flexible rubber mittens and a kit for becoming a licensed telegraphy operator. Price one dollar. As small as a chapbook of poems, the book was bound by a dark brown cloth cover with gold embossed letters that read, simply, *Taxidermist's Manual*. The author was a Professor J. W. P. Jenks. Taking heed of the manual's first and primary admonition to work in secret so that "none may know the mysteries of the art," he had hidden himself in his room to begin his experimentations. Under his bed and crowding every free surface, splayed on sheets of newsprint, were the victims of his education. On his window ledge rested the frail skeletons of chipmunks, robins, and defleshed wrens bleaching in the sun. His desk was littered with awls and thread and scissors and pins—much of which had been pilfered from his mother's sewing basket. In the summer, flies thrummed outside his open window but seemed to know better than to light on any of the still lifes inside; however tantalizing they may have looked, the poison that preserved the illusion of life had a tendency to ward off intruders.

PREPARATION.

To ½ pt. of 60 per cent. alcohol add an ounce each of arsenic, camphor, alum, and two drs. strychnine. Shake it well and let it stand 12 hours. It is then fit for use. Label "Poison," and keep the bottle well corked.

(Ingredients easily obtained from Bishop's Drug Store)

To Carl, this was more than a hobby. It was liberation. An escape from the pall that hung over the house, cast by the ghosts of his three dead infant brothers and his mother's grief, which kept her trapped in its dark weeds. Something "unnatural" had happened to this house, to this family. A friction had grown over the years, and his mother, more and more, put the blame on Carl's father, turning all her bitterness toward him, castrating him for failing to give her a life as good as her well-to-do and puritanical sisters'. Even though it had been she who refused to go west, as her husband wanted, to make a better go, to be free of their "clay slab" of a farm. But she did not want to leave her sisters, her family. She'd already lost enough. Blaming her husband only got easier once he'd lost his nerve and made the foolish mistake of paying another man a thousand dollars to go fight in the Civil War in his place. The substitute survived the war and lived long enough to collect interest on the debt for many years, further sinking them into poverty, and each season the farm grew more crabbed and worn-out.

Perhaps his mother had become so numbed by her own melancholy, which now trailed from her pores like a noxious gas, that she didn't notice the stench that had taken over the upstairs of her home. But at some point one of the sisters, Carl's aunt, who lived just down the street, became alarmed at the way the boy was turning into a pale, unwholesome thing, and how his mother was doing nothing to stop it. A thirteen-year-old shouldn't spend all his time hiding in his bedroom, she said, doing God knows what to those poor animals. Young Carl had heard the whispers, eavesdropping at the top of the stairs, while his aunt conspired to rob him of his chief pleasure in life. It was an unnatural obsession. A disgusting habit. Other children taunted him now for his queer hobby. Did she know that? Yes, his mother knew, she knew, but what could be done?—the boy's father would not lift a finger. Well, of course not, her husband had no backbone. (This was not said so much as it hung in the air: his father's failures commingling with the odor of the child's playthings.) The aunt was scared for his future. Frightened for his soul, too, since the boy didn't even have the decency to quit his unholy labors on the Sabbath. The county insane asylum was only half a day's buggy ride from their hometown of Clarendon, New York. Surely, there, the boy might be cured of his morbid whims.

Who knew? Perhaps he'd have more freedom to do as he pleased in an asylum. At the very least, he would have escaped, like his father had tried. Carl resented his mother for what she had done to his father. For the constant nagging. For wanting his father to suffer for his poor choices. For destroying his morale.

His mother did not suffer the shame of her husband's cowardice with grace. But still she wasn't going to ship her son off to an asylum. Truth be told, she was fond of the white rabbit Carl had mounted for her birthday. It was perched on a stump in the front yard. His aunt would soon enough change her song, too, after the boy worked his magic on her pet canary—this, after she'd forgotten to put the drape back over its cage one freezing winter night.

In any event, he'd been happy to finally move away from home. Lucky to get away.

He could still remember the first moment he'd seen the outside of Ward's Natural Science Establishment; it was as if he'd arrived at his true home at last. He'd learned of its existence from his first employer, an interior decorator named David Bruce, who managed to earn quite a tidy living off the current nature craze, painting wildlife murals in the parlors of Brockport, New York's most well-heeled citizens, the sort who spent their leisure time chasing butterflies with silk nets, collecting snails at the beach, or stomping through the woods in high-button shoes in quest of the latest fern de rigueur for their terraria. The obsession with collecting, some might have said, fit the country's growing acquisitiveness. Bruce happened to live just a few miles down the road from Carl's family's farm. Before hiring Carl as his assistant, he had taken him out for an oyster dinner, but as the shells piled up on the older man's plate, he could see the boy was only ravenous for information about the business of stuffing animals and whether it was true a person could make a living doing something so much more edifying than growing potatoes. He could see the boy had an almost feverish air about him, as if he had a true calling. After a few weeks it was clear Carl had no knack for mixing paints or cleaning brushes or sketching starfish or seashells— or anything for that matter that didn't involve a flensing knife. On the other hand, whenever the chance arrived to stuff a bird or chipmunk for one of the cabinets Bruce assembled for his clientele, the youth's display of talent far surpassed that of his employer's. Ultimately, Bruce had had to let him go—the kid was never going to make it as a decorator—but in so doing suggested he might look into getting a position at a place in Rochester called Ward's Natural Science Establishment.

That would mean moving away from home. Rochester was twenty miles away from Clarendon. But he was almost eighteen, and at Ward's, he would be working for the country's premier supplier of specimens for the new natural history museums popping up everywhere. For a young aspiring taxidermist, it would be the equivalent of enrolling in the École des Beaux-Arts. There, Bruce assured him, he would meet other young men similarly afflicted with his zeal, and he would earn a good dollar doing what he really loved.

So there he'd found himself, standing outside the jawbone of a blue whale that served as the front gate to Ward's Natural Science Establishment, trying to screw up the courage to knock on the door. To walk off his nerves, he'd wandered around Rochester, pacing along the busy Erie Canal, and up Buffalo Street where the deafening steam-powered flour mills, whirring and grinding, generated a mist of pulverized flour, which hung in the frigid air like fine snow. (If he had wandered along the canal long enough, he might have taken notice of a skinny young man just a few years older than himself by the name of George Eastman, who was conducting his own dubious experiments with odd-looking glass plates that glistened with a transparent chemical skin.) Finally, Carl ended up back outside the whale's jawbone. It was an all-or-nothing moment. This was the only place where he conceivably belonged. But to think: that he could knock on the door, and this man whom he'd never met, this Professor Ward, could take one look at him and snuff out his young life by simply saying *no*.

For one afternoon in a person's life to have such freight. Everything until now had been mere preparation for this moment.

After lingering for what seemed like an eternity on College Avenue, gaining and losing his courage with each passing carriage, he finally built up his nerve to walk under the looming jawbone. Inside the court-yard was like a peddlers' village, or the campus of a New England pre-paratory school, if stranger. There were fourteen white frame buildings in all, adjoining an orchard. One had a moose skull dangling from the gable. Where you might expect a weather vane on another building was what appeared to be a giant gastropod shell, or maybe a prehistoric snail. Skeletons and bleaching bones were scattered on the ground outside what was evidently a converted bowling alley.

When he stopped to ask a man carrying what looked like a stiff, giant anteater where he might find Professor Henry Augustus Ward, he was directed to the building where a stuffed ape sat propped on the front porch. Above the door was a sign. COSMOS HALL. A distracted-looking older man answered his knock and acknowledged, after Carl's stammered introduction, that he was indeed Professor Ward, upon which Carl mutely presented the handmade business card he had hast-ily prepared the night before.

CARL E. AKELEY
ARTISTIC TAXIDERMY IN ALL ITS BRANCHES

The professor was a balding man with a trim silver beard, a noble alert face, and oddly squarish ears. He took the card and looked it over, while his free hand rummaged in the pocket of a well-worn Prince Albert frock coat overflowing with newspaper clippings and crumpled letters, and, amid the rustling, Carl could have sworn he made out the sound of metal bits jinking about. He later learned that the professor had the habit of picking up and pocketing stray nails off the shop floor, a custom which caused his wife endless grief, given how it mangled his clothes.

As disheveled as he may have seemed, Professor Ward was a highly esteemed man who'd helped many of the country's best natural history museums get off the ground. He had no interest in the spiritual or reli-gious view of nature—the prevailing belief at the time that if only man peered deeply enough into Nature, he would see its inner Design, and how the divine watchmaker had precision-engineered all of creation to benefit humankind and its works (a belief echoed from the pulpits and from most best-selling natural history authors)—but believed that all of the major fields of science (geology, paleontology, mineralogy, botany, and zoology) were interconnected and revealed the true nature of existence as a sort of interdependent mechanism. That there existed a kind of fragile wovenness between the world of organisms to the spheres they inhabited. An animal was not separate from his habitat but was in fact part of a larger relationship. This was a fascinating new concept. It had even spawned a new term: *ecology*. Part of the reason this notion was taking root, no doubt, was that some people were gradually waking to the realization that what they had formerly perceived as limitless— namely, that is, America's supply of natural resources—was finite indeed. Wilderness was the one commodity the nation had always believed it possessed in inexhaustible abundance. It had shaped America's image of itself. Defined the boundaries of its potential—that is, there were no boundaries. But by the mid-1880s not only was the frontier conquered, it was *closed*. The world had become smaller. Yet inside that smaller world everything was tied together in a fragile union. This ecumenical philosophy would ultimately become the model for all museums and was reflected in the arrangement of Ward's cabinets, whereby the spectator could move from one realm easily into the next: stones, birds, trees.

Whether you were a geologist who wanted a rare gem, a paleontologist in need of a *Glyptodon* skull, or a museum in need of a *Megatherium*, Professor Ward was the dealer you sought. His business prepared exhibits representative of every natural kingdom—animal, plant, and mineral—and he had agents and collectors working for him all over the planet. As a young man he'd gotten his start collecting specimens for Louis Agassiz, who was then still cobbling together his Museum of Comparative Zoology at Harvard, but as natural curios became increasingly in fashion Ward quickly realized he could make a killing selling prepared fossils, gemstones, and mounted animals to private collectors, colleges, and the upstart natural history museums. There were great profits to be made. To meet the demand, he had traveled to Persia to collect meteorites, climbed Mount Vesuvius for volcanic rocks, collected mummies and inscribed scarabs in Egypt, and had even brought back the skeleton of a Siberian mammoth. He had gone in search of fossils in Abyssinia, minerals in India, and skins in Zanzibar, Java, Japan, Borneo, New Zealand, Patagonia, and Zululand. When he was twenty-five years old, on a collecting expedition along the Niger River, he'd come down with blackwater fever and was left to die on a small island by his riverboat crew. He was taken in by a native woman named Calypso, who nursed him back to life in the idyll of her grass hut, and for a time tried to make a husband of the professor, but once he'd regained his strength, he left the heartbroken Calypso to continue his life of rock collecting. By the time he was twenty-seven years old, in 1861, he had the best geologic collection in America. The truth was, Carl was lucky to have found the professor himself actually on the premises. He was a man in perpetual motion, constantly dashing off to one corner of the world or other to track down an exotic fish skeleton or to purchase the meteorite collection of a Russian noble.

The company he kept was as legendary as his travels. He had hob-nobbed with David Livingstone, even given the older man advice on how to proceed up the Niger, having made the trip himself before the famous missionary. Darkest Africa had given Professor Ward a pecu-liar and priestly aura himself; it was as if he'd visited the mythical cen-ter of the earth and returned to tell about it. A missionary of divine curiosities. He counted among his friends Buffalo Bill and P. T. Bar-num, a collector of natural wonders himself, even if many of the show-man's artifacts were as unnatural in the extreme as his Feejee Mermaid or his Elephantus-Hippo-Paradoxus. Barnum's most recent and favor-ite acquisition, however, had not been a hoax, but an African elephant named Jumbo. Ward had promised to mount Jumbo, the largest *Loxodonta africana* in captivity, in the event anything ever happened to the circus impresario's biggest crowd-pleaser.

By the time Akeley arrived, in 1883, Ward's emporium had become a virtual assembly line to the museum world, and an Ivy League train-ing camp for all types of naturalists, many of whom would go on to become among the most prominent curators and scientists in the field. Frederic Lucas, the future director of the American Museum of Natural History, had himself started at Ward's skeletonizing pigs. It was foul and backbreaking work, and the hive of resurrectionists Ward kept busy filling his orders for the new "temples of science" were vulnerable to a host of diseases like anthrax, rabies, sarcoptic mange, even the bubonic plague—just a few of the occupational hazards faced by those who played with dead animals for a living. Arsenic powder was stored in barrels like cake flour. The lethal yellow motes swirled in the shafts of sunlight that fell on the studio floor.

Nonetheless, Professor Ward was used to turning away eager young men with trilobites in their eyes. Yet when he looked at Carl's little homemade card, foremost in his mind, no doubt, was the enormous contract he was now in the middle of fulfilling to supply the American Museum of Natural History with a specimen of every known bird and mammal in North America. That would have been enough, but then a second contract had followed to supply the museum with a specimen of every known *monkey* in the world. More than fate, Carl Akeley had the luck of good timing on his side.

Ward absently pocketed Akeley's card, where it was swallowed by the other detritus, gruffly let him know that "anything he might already know about taxidermy would be more of a liability than an asset," and, fiddling with his clumsily knotted black silk string tie, told him that he would report at 7:00 A.M. sharp, work a twelve-hour day, earn $3.50 a week, minus room and board, that there were no holidays and no sick days, and upon penalty of being stuffed and mounted himself he was to refrain from smoking in the studios. Ward had already suffered one fire in 1869 and lost every damn last thing, so smoking was strictly verboten. And so was sleeping on the job. Therefore, when Carl was discovered six months later taking a nap on a pile of skins in the attic, he was called back down to Professor Ward's office and promptly fired.

❧

IT WAS THE tedium of the Brooklyn dungeon that would kill him faster than all the arsenic in a herd of elephant skins. At Ward's at least there had been a splendid variety of animals. Here the monotony was as rigid as each stiffened little wing. Carl himself might skin a hundred or more in a single shift, though he couldn't help but put as much art and care as possible into each bird. Hunched over the table, bluebird firmly in hand, he would first press his thumbs under the armpits to dislocate the wings, snip off its feet, and then pluck out its eyes—stuffing cotton into the empty sockets, its beak, and, using a small pair of forceps, its miniature cloaca to prevent unwanted leakage. Drawing the tip of his blade from its breastbone to its tail, his ankles crossed beneath his chair, concentrating, careful to push, rather than pull with his thumbnails, he degloved the bird, dropping its rib cage and innards in a pail. Every few moments he stopped to daub away with a damp rag a spot of blood that had seeped onto the feathers. Despite the gory nature of the work, he tended toward fastidiousness.

Once a skin was scraped clean, he sprinkled it with the camphor-scented arsenic powder, rubbing it liberally into the feathers, in and around the intricately hinged and interlocked quills and carpal joints of the wing, fanning out the secondaries to work the poison into every barb and vane.

The last thing he did before handing it off was to sever the bird's head, scoop out its little dollop of brain, and stuff the hollowed cranium with cotton before impaling the skull on a short stem of wire. The next boy—or Carl, when he worked this station—then unspooled a length of medium-gauge wire, the full length of the bird plus a third, bending back and curving the wire so it conformed to the contour of the bird's body: a dipper-shaped armature around which twine was quickly wound until it resembled (roughly) a flaxen tuber with the dimensions of the original bird. The skin was then affixed with sewing pins to the string manikin, stitched on, and then passed off to the last boy, who pierced a thinner-gauge wire through the bird's shoulders, carefully lacing on the wings under the coverts, bending them into the semblance of flight. Then the pins were removed, stray feathers straightened to hide the artist's hand, arsenic brushed off, and glass eyes glued into the empty sockets. When Carl worked this end he tried his best to give the eyes a look of believable consciousness. Even if his own were blunted dull by the repetitive nature of the work.

It was devoutly uninspiring. Oh, how he missed the exciting buzzy atmosphere of Ward's. Whenever he pictured his old workstation, or his first tour of the maze of studios, through rooms filled wall-to-ceiling with shelves of lizards and fetal pigs afloat in jars, the workshops where men assembled cabinets resembling alien dollhouses filled with ammonites, mollusks, and cephalopods; the Invertebrate Rooms; the Zoological Museum; the osteology shop, where beet-faced Germans stood over vats of boiling bones; and, of course, the taxidermy studio itself, which shimmered with saws, cleavers, and fleshing knives—that chaos of brightly colored feathers and furs and exotic beasts in various stages of disassembly and reassembly that filled his heart with joy, oh, how it stung to remember. How he missed the giant snakeskins that hung like kites from the rafters! The skins of colobus and chimpanzees, golden monkeys and vervets slowly leaching out their essence in great mounds of salt on the floor. He had been right there, one of the young men in a leather apron, one of Ward's boys, surrounded by a reeking halo of preserving alcohol, ankle-deep in crimson blood-soaked straw. In his memory all of it was as sparkling as the gems below them in the Mineral Department, from which now and then through the spattered floorboards came the sharp whine of a steam-saw cutting sections of a meteorite.

Not that after a while he hadn't noticed a certain lack of artfulness in the taxidermy done at Ward's. When it came down to it, no matter how happy he had been there, he'd still been disillusioned to learn how crude the art of professional taxidermy really was. There was hardly much more to it than what he'd learned in the manual out of *Youth's Companion*. The work primarily consisted of turning a skin upside down and unceremoniously stuffing handfuls of sawdust into its deflated pelt until the animal resembled a clownish effigy more than the living thing it had once been in the wild. It required hardly any knowledge of anatomy whatsoever. The misshapen, lumpy monsters, literally stuffed like empty bags, embarrassed Carl. The salt and alum tanning left the skins stretched and uneven and generally so distorted they almost looked immoral. The blank-eyed corpses were no more expressive than parlor room sofas. In truth, the art of taxidermy was still indistinguishable from the craft of crude upholstery.

Dissatisfied with the limitations of his trade, Carl had begun independently studying anatomy in his spare time and conducting experiments at night. He thought he might have a few ideas for bringing their craft into the modern age. But because Ward didn't want employees using company time in pursuit of pipe dreams, Carl had to stay late to develop his new techniques, using the studio after hours, sacrificing sleep and meals to save money to buy his own lantern fuel and supplies.

He wasn't the only one at Ward's who had ever tried to improve on the old methods. William Hornaday, who'd left a year before Akeley's arrival to become chief taxidermist for the United States National Museum in Washington, D.C., had created, in 1879, a family of orangutans cavorting amid the canopy of a durian tree, using clay to render more realistic, natural attitudes. Others had tried excelsior as a substitute for muscle, and even Charles Willson Peale, who had built the very first natural history museum for the public in Philadelphia back in 1786, had experimented by carving the musculature of his manikins out of wood. But these were the most significant advances since the discovery of arsenic, and since Ward frowned on wasting time, taxidermy had not progressed much further within his august halls.

Before he began to tinker around with the manikins underneath, Carl was determined to attack the problem of removing the skin itself. If only it could be done in a way that the finished mount didn't look like a wharfside indigent stitched together by a hasty and tremulous coroner. He had been thinking a lot about sculpture. How materials like bronze or clay could be used by a sculptor to capture the animal's true spirit—its deeper animal essence *beneath* the skin. Why, then, did they, who worked with the animal's *actual* skin, do no better? A true artist would no sooner butcher the skins the way they did than a painter would mount his canvas with roofing nails. His first experiment was to see if he couldn't peel the animal more discreetly and harvest the skin intact. Or more nearly intact, with a minimum of incisions. It was not an easy challenge and called for his deepest stores of patience. Using a zebra he'd shanghaied one night, and working on it through dawn, he had carefully removed the zagged skin, laboring to make his cuts less conspicuous.

He would trick it out of its skin if necessary.

Without resorting to a single extra incision, he had managed to slowly inch off the leg skins, working with the patience of a Zen monk—shoulder-deep in its belly, his clean-shaven cheek resting against the zebra's bristled haunch, only dimly aware of the sound of its hoof clopping against the floor—until he had finally slipped each off like a stocking. Once he had the zebra husked, it truly looked as if the animal had stepped out of its skin voluntarily, and he hung it to dry. But when he returned the next day, his eyes yoked with dark circles, he found that his work had been cruelly sabotaged! Slashed from leg to abdomen, his perfect skin hung in ribbons.

Indeed, someone seemed to have it in for Carl. No doubt, some of the others had begun to think of Akeley as nothing more than a loafer. After working all night he tended to spend his days at his cluttered desk staring into space, making weird sketches of vivisected animals, and overzealously studying anatomy textbooks. Repeatedly he was sabotaged. Each time he'd get so far, he would find his skins cut to ribbons, or his molds of the animal smashed and left in the trash heap out back. Certainly he wasn't the only one who saw there was room for improvement at Ward's. But the issue turned moot the day the foreman found the young apprentice asleep on a pile of tanned hides in the attic, exhausted from his nights spent spelunking zebra carcasses, and went and finked him out to Professor Ward. If only he'd been able to make Ward listen! On the other hand, maybe he should have just kept his daydreams to himself. They were what had got him exiled to Brooklyn. Even if he knew taxidermy could be done better, now it was too late. He would never have the chance to prove himself. Each of the little birds mocked him for having flubbed his one chance at greatness.

C ARL RENTED A ROOM IN BROOKLYN FROM DR. ISAAC KAUFMANN Funk, a lexicographer and publisher of religious books, who in a few short years would partner with Adam Willis Wagnalls to form a publishing house to provide the country with a cheaper version of *Encyclopaedia Britannica*. But in these days, Dr. Funk was mainly committed to his work as a "spiritualist detective," and to this end held frequent late-night séances in his brownstone.

Night after night the parlor filled with mediums, clairvoyants, and other paranormalists committed to the "scientific" investigation of psychic phenomena, reincarnation, telepathy, crystal gazing, coincidental dreams, oracles, spirit paintings, and other animistic inquiries into the possibility of consciousness beyond the grave.* In an era when the known world seemed to be shrinking under the microscope, the country was rife with spiritualists eager to relocate the cosmically unknowable, to redefine the boundaries of mystery. While his landlord was busy laying telegraph lines across the great unknown, though, Akeley's

---

*After his own death, Dr. Funk himself would report back via a medium that he was still peeved about slanderous remarks made by the editors of the *Sun* and the *Brooklyn Eagle* regarding his paranormal experiments and how surely now—ipse dixit—he would have the last laugh. He also expressed irritation that his campaign for phonetic spelling had still not been picked up, despite the difficulty of getting his ideas across clearly when he seemed to have trouble coming up with the right words. This despite the fact that, as the befuddled spirit confessed, he had once "fathered a dictionary."

own interactions with the dead, working for the wretched soul of John Wallace, were much more mundane.

He worked from eight in the morning until six at night with a half-hour break for lunch, spent his evenings scrubbing the smell of dead bird from his hands, and then lay in bed, kept awake by the spirit rappings and other desperate means by which his landlord and lonely guests attempted to make contact with the countless souls trapped between Brooklyn and the afterworld.

On his rare days off, Carl moped around the city, hunched against the cold wind, sidestepping immigrant children dressed in rags behind wheelbarrows full of frozen potatoes and bricks, his ears assailed by the polyphony of Polish, Yiddish, Italian, Russian—a universe of languages which reminded him of the many tongues spoken at Ward's and which now only made him feel all the lonelier. Horses, hoary with ice, snorting steam, crunched through the snow like pack dogs. Most young men of a certain creative temperament would have been exalted to find themselves in New York City—the closest thing to Paris in America—but Carl's heart was in Rochester. As he brooded, he was oblivious to the bustling piers outside his place of work, the spars and masts and ice-sheathed rigging of the brigs and barks and other ships moored along the docks, even the pleasure boats and steamers trailing black smoke on the East River, schooners hauling white pine from Nova Scotia, sugar-cane from the Caribbean, oil scows bringing coal for the kerosene refineries. Here was one of the busiest channels in the modern world.

Just across the cold river from Wallace's shop you could see the crowded tenements of the new immigrants of the Lower East Side, who now made up almost 40 percent of the population of the city. Over thirteen million aliens had come to America in just the past couple decades, and their numbers continued to grow, each year outpacing the last. It was the largest migration in human history, and the presence of those teeming hordes sent a shock deep into the hearts of the city's oldest and most respectable families. To many in the Anglo-Saxon Protestant establishment, it was nothing short of a massive human catastrophe in the making. How long, they asked, before the barbarians penetrated the delicate membrane surrounding polite civilization? How in the face of this invasion could they preserve their way of life? Their favorable balance of power?

To get into Manhattan Carl hopped the elevated rail, but stuck in his gloomy thoughts barely noticed as the "Eighth Wonder of the World" clattered into view. Completed just months before his arrival, the Brooklyn Bridge, spanning 5,989 feet, emerged from a shroud of swirling snow. Its two stone Gothic towers loomed over the East River—the tallest man-made structures in the Western Hemisphere. To prove the safety of the longest suspension bridge in the world, P. T. Barnum, master of bunkum and Professor Ward's old friend, had walked twenty-one of his elephants across it, with Jumbo in the lead, as thousands of bystanders crowded the banks, holding their breath as the slow-motion stampede sent thudding echoes shuddering across the river.

He took the trolley up Fifth Avenue, mesmerized by the sight of barons in brushed silk toppers with gold-tipped walking canes, climbing in and out of shiny black phaetons, a pair of kid gloves clutched lightly in their pink fists, and all the women swaddled in furs, their elaborate hats trimmed with the tiny embalmed hummingbirds, wrens, and titmice that he himself had likely confected. The mansions of the rich looked like European castles. No matter how they walled themselves off, though, these lords of the Gilded Age could not shake a common creeping fear at the sheer number of alien newcomers crowding the southern tip of their island. Indeed, the immigrant was regarded with the same suspicion as that felt by bird-watchers who would soon begin to witness that other rapacious nonnative, the European starling, evicting the more timorous native species from their Central Park nests.

But, truly, for your average blue blood, it was the purity of his superior race plasm that was most at risk through a gradual diluting of the bloodline. It was as if somehow Nature itself had turned on him—and it was this fear in part that explained the motives of some of the wealthy patrons and trustees of the American Museum of Natural History, founded in 1869, to shape that institution's role as a sanctuary, where the city dweller might regain his senses, recover his serenity, and where the immigrant himself might also go to observe the neatly laid boundaries of species and race. And perhaps, so informed, be dissuaded from committing the sin against nature of miscegenation. That there was so much fear of the commingling of plasms was ironic at a time when America itself had begun to vigorously export its own unsolicited brand overseas—all in the interest of *expansion*, of expanding its newfound power, and spreading its superior culture to the unenlightened, a goal that was widely shared by the general public, who agreed with Reverend Josiah Strong that it was our God-given duty to bear the White Man's Burden and "civilize the savages." In general it was a time when partitions were breaking down, when nations were jumping back and forth across each other's membranes and bloodstreams. Even if the world was not quite yet symbiotic it was a thriving time for opportunistic infection.

Carl would find no sanctuary at the natural history museum. Only an annoying reminder of the work he'd been doing at Ward's before he'd been fired. Instead he spent his time at the Metropolitan Museum of Art. But here, too, everything spoke to him of his failure. For a while he studied the sculptures of Michelangelo, Rossellino, Bernini—or at least the plaster casts of the famous masterpieces, since the Met had not yet begun acquiring the actual originals—but then he stopped going altogether. It only stirred his resentment. He had to face the facts: his life as an artist was finished. He would never produce anything as beautiful as Barye's *Theseus Fighting the Centaur Bianor* or William Hunt's *The Horses of Anahita*. He sat gazing at the majestic Percherons for hours, desponding.

Back out in the dread daylight it was almost as if all of womankind had conspired to come out with the express purpose of mocking him by donning their most outrageous bird hats. Almost every female, young or old, wore a hat upon which was pinned a bird that glowered at Carl like a badge of shame. There were ostrich plumes, tufts and sprays of white heron, birds of paradise, dashes of robin, scarlet tanager, and bluebird—bizarrely shaped hats, but more bizarrely ornamented not only with feathers but parts of birds, just a wing or a feathered breast, and in many instances the entire bird itself perched upon these giant brims half as wide as the sidewalk. Here was a whole gull, coquettishly perched in a nest of taffeta. A ring-necked pheasant snuggled in the crown of a touring hat, plump and alluring. As if there were no more natural habitat; as if woman and bird lived in some sort of symbiotic relationship akin to that of crocodile and plover. Some looked as if a tragic collision had taken place, as if the bird had crashed into the hat and was just stuck there, wings crucified, by a magical suspension of gravity; other birds looked as if they had fallen out of the sky, or lay etherized, slumbering, on the brim.

They were in practically every shop window that lined Fifth Avenue, put on display like elaborate winged pastries or brightly feathered cakes. Truly, the only boundary was the milliner's imagination. How, one wondered, did these women hold aloft such aviaries? There were hats with eight or nine warblers huddled like Christmas carolers; hats accessorized with whole nests and preserved eggs; birds ensconced in dramatic tableaux of roses and silk. One trend was to affix just a pair of wings to one side of the hat, or cocked on either side, as if the hats would lift the women up, whereby they would steer themselves to their next tea party via the rudders of their tortoiseshell-handled umbrellas.

How did this bizarre trend catch hold? Was it a sign that civilization itself had really gone mad after all? After decades of mindless expansion, with Nature on the verge of collapse, the Pyrrhic victors had now gone and begun adorning themselves with the actual corpses of the vanquished. No matter how trifling it seemed, wasn't fashion always symbolic of society's deepest underlying anxieties? The birds were talismans, fetishes. Really, no less bizarre than what one heard of savages in Darkest Africa decorating themselves with the body parts of wild animals to ward off evil spirits. And yet, women of the civilized Western world were doing so at the rate of some two hundred thousand birds a year. Clearly, to banish such anxieties as they bore would require industrial-strength levels of voodoo.

Of course, at this rate, the birds would run out. That fact alone had begun to worry people in some circles, bird lovers, clergymen, women's groups, and some scientists—people who didn't necessarily feel that gobbing up your wardrobe with dead animals was haute couture. A few magazine stories had snuck out about the depredations of the plume hunters—of birds slaughtered, stripped of their fashionable crests and tail feathers, and left in heaps like so much rubbish, the survivors abandoned to die an agonizing death with their backsides flensed and exposed to the sun. Many species (most notably the egret) were on the verge of extinction. Rookeries all along the East Coast were being wiped out. In general, there was a dawning sensitivity to the plight of wildlife—after all, the bison and the passenger pigeon were not coming back—but it was the millinery industry in particular that caused the most moral outrage. In part, perhaps, because the results were so visible. But it was also because women in Victorian culture were supposed to be paragons of virtue and morality, and how could a woman be moral who wore a dead bird on her hat?

This was a definite turning point in America's relationship to nature—a dawning awareness that maybe God had not intended every creature great and small to serve as a limitless supply for humanity's every last whim. There was a sudden urgency to preserve what felt as if it were slipping between people's fingers.

The only thing Carl Akeley was concerned with preserving, for the time being, however, was his fragile sanity. He wasn't thinking about the big picture, but rather questioning how many more days he could work in the dungeon skinning birds to satisfy the vanity of society ladies. He considered returning to his parents' farm and then despised himself for entertaining such craven thoughts.

But then, come spring, having surrendered to his dismal fate, he was fitting a glass eye into the hundredth socket of the hundredth fox sparrow he'd stuffed that day when his employer shuffled down the steps and in his usual gruff manner handed Carl a letter. The return address was only partly obscured by the gore-stained print of John Wallace's hateful thumb. *Rochester!* Carl set down the sparrow and tore open the envelope. It was from Professor Ward. His former employer had belatedly realized Akeley's creations were earning more money than those of his other taxidermists on staff. He had also discovered that the reports regarding Akeley's poor workmanship had been in error. (Presumably, his phantom nemesis would now be looking for work elsewhere.) In any event, whatever Carl had been doing was paying off, and Ward had changed his mind and wanted him to return at once.

As he cast off his leather apron and fled the basement chop shop into the bright midday sun, which billowed white in the mainsails of the procession of schooners headed out to the Upper Bay and from there to the mighty Atlantic, he could not help but feel a little smug in his sudden freedom. He was no longer a captive in John Wallace's dungeon. No, he was already dreaming about how he might get his next zebra.

CHAPTER THREE

JUST AS THE LAST OF THE ANIMALS WERE BEING LED BACK TO their boxcars for the night, and the brass band continued playing inside the big tent while the "towners" filed out into the chilly September air, redolent of roasted peanuts and waffles, a train whistle rose above the music and murmur of the departing crowd. The night's most memorable, if unscheduled, act was yet to come, however. Given the way the animals and props were loaded and unloaded—a new town per day— the circus manager had carefully checked the timetables for St. Thomas, Ontario, September 15, 1885. No trains were supposed to come this route until nine o'clock. But here it was, half past eight, and there was Special No. 151 coming around the bend, bound for Detroit, its yellow headlamp illuminating the line of thirty elephants still lumbering single file down the tracks.

Bringing up the rear was Jumbo, P. T. Barnum's star attraction, his greatest and most popular acquisition by far, a seven-ton, twelve-foot-tall, fourteen-foot-long African elephant, who now sauntered along with his diminutive compatriot, Tom Thumb, a pygmy elephant attired in top hat and striped trousers. Each night the two elephants—big and small— were the last to leave the ring. But now they were trapped. The other elephants had had time to clear the tracks, but Jumbo and Tom Thumb were caught in the narrow chute between a fence running alongside the steep embankment to their left and the stationary train of circus cars. In a hurry the roustabouts tore down a section of fence and the elephants' handler tried his best to get the beasts to come down the embankment, but the elephants were too confused or frightened. As the train bore down on them, its light swept across the lions and giraffes and ostriches behind the bars of their painted compartments of the Greatest Show on Earth, and then picked up Jumbo's immense shadow, shuffling it across the side of the train like one of Eadweard Muybridge's primitive motion pictures. When the engine tried to stop, the iron wheels stuttered on the rails. But it hardly mattered; hydraulic brakes would not come along for another two years, and the train flew toward the retreating elephant in a screeching spray of sparks.

IF ELEPHANTS SEE their lives pass before their eyes at the moment of death, is it possible Jumbo might have wondered whether his own had been real or just some conjured dream of a merchandising wizard? Had he been flesh and blood or merely the brooches and ice cream cones and stickpins and extralarge hot dogs sold on the midway? The hats, cigars, pies, even walking canes—the inanity of it all—to which his name had been plastered? Or had he been even less than that? A hollow, elephant-shaped balloon batted back and forth across the ocean in a game of imperial badminton?

Because even before he had joined the Greatest Show on Earth, traveling across America, town to town, trailing along with half a mile's worth of boxcars crammed with the natural and not-so-natural wonders of the world, he had been a naturalized British citizen. Originally, he'd been picked up by a German big-game hunter collecting African animals to sell to European zoos, purchased as an infant from a group of nomadic Hamran Arabs—descendants of the Roman Elephantomachoi, or Elephant Fighters—who had probably killed his mother for ivory; then he was sold to the Ménagerie du Jardin des Plantes, in Paris, in 1861, before ending up at the Royal Zoological Gardens in London after a hasty swap for a rhino.

In London, Jumbo's main responsibility was to give British schoolchildren rides, often as many as half a dozen at a time, and he quickly became the most popular attraction at the zoo. He seemed perfect for the job, given how docile he was, even if, sadly, his gentle demeanor was most likely attributable to the way he'd been beaten as a juvenile, neglected in a squalid Parisian sty where rats had chewed on his feet until he was almost hobbled. However, for nearly twenty years, the humble elephant was the kingdom's most beloved plaything and seemed content.

But when Jumbo turned twenty, his gentle demeanor began to dissolve. At first, the changes in his personality were subtle. He was moody and disagreeable. He did not eat the sweet buns the children fed him with the same relish as he once had. He seemed distracted, as if he were mulling over some hopeless riddle. Sometimes a look of contempt flitted across his eyes.

But then the changes became more fearsome. He began to throw temper tantrums at night in his pen, banging his head against the wall and charging at the zoo's staff. Worst of all, perhaps, he began to undergo several unbecoming physical transformations. A black sticky goo began to suppurate near his ears, a frightening musky smell filled his living quarters, and—a most unwelcome sight to the British mothers who brought their children to ride on the leviathan's back—he began to rouse more readily and in a most grotesque fashion. Jumbo's penis—which, when erect, was four feet long with an agile tip that groped about blindly like a Brobdingnagian inchworm—turned a sickly greenish color and dribbled urine continuously.

Unsurprisingly, the zoo superintendent decided it might be prudent to keep Jumbo out of sight for a little while.

Now that he was confined in his stall, the tantrums grew into uncontrollable explosions of wrath. Like a seven-ton madman, he hurled his bulk against his cell, ramming himself over and over into the walls, until he smashed the door. To keep him from tearing down the building or stampeding into crowds, his pen had to be reinforced with sheets of solid iron. A new door was secured with eight-inch-thick oak beams, and yet as Jumbo continued to go berserk he even splintered a couple of those.

The worst was still to come: one day, while in a blind rage, he drove his tusks through the iron-plated wall and snapped off his tusks at the jawbone. Because an elephant's tusks don't stop growing, this quickly led to more pain and a massive infection, when his tusks began to grow outward through the flesh in his cheeks, just below his eyes, which required an impromptu surgery. The general consensus, at the zoo, was that Jumbo had gone insane. Civilization—or rather, life in captivity—had done him in.

What they did not know was that, most likely, Jumbo had entered the state called *musth*. During musth, the bull elephant prepares to mate, which, in the wild, is often accompanied by extreme and often fatal combat between male rivals. It has been said that an elephant in musth is the most dangerous animal in the world.

Given that Jumbo's main function was giving rides—an estimated 1.25 million piggybacks over the course of his sixteen-year career to children who included royal princes, a young Winston Churchill, and a pudgy, asthmatic Teddy Roosevelt—his career as a suitable playmate for England's schoolchildren was finished. In fact, the zoo's superintendent was actually giving serious thought to having Jumbo destroyed when he got a surprise telegraph from P. T. Barnum, offering ten thousand dollars for the mad elephant.

Barnum had eyed Jumbo with envy for a long time. Despite the fact that its wild reaches were shrinking, America was expanding. Coming into its own as an empire. It only seemed right that the biggest mammal in captivity become an American citizen. But unaware of the elephant's altered personality—not to mention his green dribbling penis—he did not expect to have any luck. So he was as surprised as he was delighted when the British quickly took him up on his offer. Yet the elephant's extradition would not come easily. The British public didn't know about Jumbo's outbursts when it learned the Americans were stealing their Jumbo, and the country nearly rioted. One letter in the *Pall Mall Gazette* expressed the general consensus: "After all the children Jumbo has so patiently carried, all the buns he has so quietly and graciously received, is he to be turned out at last to tramp the world homeless and unbefriended, the mere chattel of a wandering showman?"

In a word: yes. And to that end, Barnum had sent several of his agents to the London zoo, where a massive padded oak crate, reinforced with iron, was quickly constructed and a departure date set for the cross-Atlantic trip. But after a week they had still not managed to persuade their chattel to enter the box.

News of Jumbo's imminent departure, and stories of how he was being tricked into the crate with figs and buns appeared in the London *Times* almost daily. After a first, and then second, rendezvous with a steamship to New York passed, without the elephant being persuaded to get in his box, Jumbo grew into a jingoistic cause célèbre.

In thousands of letters, children begged Barnum to set aside his cruel heart and please not take away their Jumbo. Petitions were signed. Prayer vigils held. Citizens demanded that Jumbo not leave British soil. The English were concerned that the circus lifestyle would be too stressful for poor Jumbo, that the American diet would prove deleterious. Living in America would damage Jumbo's self-respect and put a "Yankee twang in his trumpeting." The House of Commons debated whether America was deliberately swindling them out of their greatest living monument. Queen Victoria herself grieved over the issue, as if P. T. Barnum were Rumpelstiltskin come to collect the castle's firstborn. Zoo officials complicit in the struggle to lure the stubborn elephant into his giant packing crate received death threats. British intellectuals took umbrage. John Ruskin wrote that the decision of the Zoological Society to rid itself of Jumbo was "disgraceful to the City of London and dishonorable to humanity." James Russell Lowell, the poet and American ambassador, said, "The only burning question between England and America is Jumbo."*

---

*Curiously enough, not that much earlier, another battle between Europe and the United States had been fought with similar animal proxies. Shortly after the French and Indian War, in 1766, the remains of an unknown creature of immense proportions, including a jawbone, two tusks, and molars the size of Cortland apples were excavated along the Ohio River. Its discovery mystified naturalists in Europe and America. It seemed to bear resemblance to the "eliphant," but how on earth could such a tropical creature survive in Ohio? Some naturalists opined that it was the fossil of a giant hippopotamus, while others speculated that its tusks and femur resembled the remains of the Siberian mammoth. For the time being, it was classified as the American *incognitum*. Rumors of such a monster had been reported as early as 1705 by Cotton Mather, who believed the discovery of several gigantic molars along the Hudson to be evidence of a race of giants erased by the biblical Flood. But it was the political impact of the giant's appearance in the New World that had the greatest significance. At the time, it was the belief of many Europeans that most species found in America were somehow inferior to those of the Old World. This view had been laid out by Georges-Louis Leclerc, comte de Buffon, the leading naturalist of his day, in his popular *Theory of American Degeneracy*. As Buffon had it, American animals were weaker in size and strength due to the cold weather and "noxious exhalations" produced by the overly dense forests. Buffon even went so far as to suggest that this same feebleness extended to the Native American ("He has no hair, no beard, no ardour for the female"), and his followers surmised that this degeneracy would naturally infect the colonists' virility as well. The theory put Americans on the defensive and ignited jingoism on both shores. But now America had the ultimate refutation—America had, as the naturalist-minded president Thomas Jefferson said, "the largest of all terrestrial beings." In fact, Jefferson, who kept bones from an 1801 excavation spread out in a spare room of the White House, believed that this creature still roamed the West, and when he dispatched Lewis and Clark to chart the great unknown beyond the Mississippi, gave specific instructions that they keep an eye out for such a beast. Jefferson would also attempt to rebuff Buffon's theory when he presented fossils of the *Megalonyx* to the American Philosophical Society in March of 1797, claiming that the bones belonged to a giant tiger which also likely continued to stalk the American wilderness. Clearly, either animal could annihilate any creature the French or British had roaming in their bosky heaths. Comparative dentistry would eventually classify the *incognitum* as the American mastodon, a relative of the woolly mammoth. The *Megalonyx*, on the other hand, would turn out to be a giant sloth.

Indeed, Barnum could not have been happier over the controversy surrounding his latest acquisition. After all, as British outrage grew louder, future American ticket buyers were becoming increasingly curious about just exactly what it was Mr. Barnum was snookering out of the British. When the editors of the *Daily Telegraph* telegrammed Barnum to say that HUNDREDS OF CORRESPONDENTS BEG US INQUIRE ON WHAT TERMS YOU WILL KINDLY RELEASE JUMBO? Barnum replied that a HUNDRED THOUSAND POUNDS WOULD BE NO INDUCEMENT TO CANCEL PURCHASE.

The case finally ended up at Chancery Court, but the judge ruled there were no grounds for an injunction against the zoo for selling the beast.

"Jumbo's fate is sealed," the *Daily Telegraph* wrote. "We fear, however, that Jumbo will never come back to us alive. His mighty heart will probably break with rage, shame, and grief; and we may hear of him, like another Samson, playing the mischief with the Philistines who have led him into captivity, and dying amid some scene of terrible wrath and ruin. We hope Mr. Barnum fully realizes what ten and a half tons of solid fury can do when it has a mind."

But, still, during this whole fiasco, Jumbo wouldn't move. The longer Jumbo declined to walk into the crate, the more public outrage mounted, the more the Zoological Society schismed, and the greater anticipation grew in America to see the great mastodon. Barnum's agents telegraphed the boss: JUMBO IS LYING IN THE GARDEN AND WILL NOT STIR. WHAT SHALL WE DO?

LET HIM LIE THERE A WEEK IF HE WANTS TO, Barnum wired back. IT IS THE BEST ADVERTISEMENT IN THE WORLD.

The only one who seemed capable of calming the elephant at all, or getting anywhere near him, was his longtime keeper, Matthew Scott. Scott, a small shy man who wore a bowler that had a way of making his head look diminutive, had been Jumbo's guardian for seventeen years. The elephant and Scott were best friends and even shared the same sleeping quarters. When Scott was present, Jumbo's temper mellowed, and the handler never feared the elephant, even at his most psychotic. Each night, in Jumbo's stall, they would split a quart of beer before bed. Indeed, Jumbo was a renowned tippler. Along with his daily two bushels of biscuits, two bushels of oats, two hundred pounds of hay, one sack of onions, three loaves of bread, and five buckets of water—plus numerous apples, candies, and figs—Jumbo consumed a bucket of beer a day, and sometimes, when feeling poorly, a couple gallons of whiskey.

Scott was very protective of his "Jummie," and not just because of the natural bond that had grown between man and beast over the years. To ride the whiskey-guzzling pachyderm was free, but it was also customary to tip the handler. But if Jumbo was too dangerous to give kiddie rides anymore, Scott's source of income was dried up, and the handler had no more reason to help the Americans than anyone else.

That is, until Barnum offered him a handsome salary if he would woo the beast into his crate and then join his Jummie in America. Scott conceded and within a day had secured Jumbo in his box.

On the morning of his departure, thousands came to the zoo to bid Jumbo farewell. Women and children wept as the sedated elephant, clad in chains, was ushered into his box. Mobs clamored outside the gates, heckling the zookeepers and cheering on Jumbo. Sixteen horses were hitched to the six-ton crate, and as it slowly made its way to the harbor, a crowd of bereaved citizens followed it like a tumbrel to the gallows. As they crossed the ocean, Scott administered whiskey as needed, never leaving the elephant's side. On April 9, 1882, Easter morning, thousands of jubilant New Yorkers received Barnum and his prize as if he were a homecoming general with spoils of war. The crowd, in a drizzling rain, accompanied the elephant from Pier No. 1 as he was paraded up Broadway on his way to join the rest of the circus animals at the Hippodrome, Barnum's New York home base. Some of the public was surprised, even disappointed, by his stumpy tusks, which weren't half as grand as those of the smaller Asian elephants Barnum already owned. But it was hard not to be duly impressed by his overall enormousness.

It had cost Barnum an estimated thirty thousand dollars to procure Jumbo, including the fees he was forced to pay for the fifty tons of freight his special delivery had displaced on the ship, and steerage for some two hundred emigrants who would have otherwise been aboard. But over the next three weeks alone, as Jumbo joined the mayhem under the big top, as crowded with the bizarre as any painting by Hieronymus Bosch, Jumbo earned Barnum three thousand dollars a day. Fortunately, by the time Jumbo had arrived in New York, his fits of rage had subsided, and he had returned to his former gentle self. Perhaps it was the oversea journey spent in solitary confinement that had finally broken him.

As the circus began its yearly rail tour, Jumbo and Scott were chauffeured from town to town in the elephant's own special, private Jumbo Palace Car, as if the elephant were the very mascot of the Gilded Age. The Palace Car was forty feet long, eighteen and a half feet high, with giant doors painted gold and red. America now had twenty-six thousand miles of track for the Prince of Humbug to travel, much easier than in the early days, when he'd started out, moving from town to town by horse and wagon. Much more precise, as well, in terms of making schedules. In fact, Barnum had mastered the difficulties of mobilizing his army with such clockwork efficiency that the German Kaiser himself had induced the showman to allow his quartermaster general to travel with the circus to learn better strategies for improving his military's rapid deployment. Even if, of course, now and then, there was a glitch in a timetable.

WHEN SCOTT SAW the train, he started rushing Jumbo and Tom Thumb forward, but they were already too far down the tracks. Trapped. His only chance was to try to get them to the end of the line of cars. When he saw they would never make it, he jumped down the embankment at the breach in the fence the quick-thinking roustabouts had torn down. Jiggling his lantern, he called for Jumbo and the little one to follow. It was only a short drop, eight feet, but both elephants stood frozen, trumpeting hysterically. The train whistle blotted out their panicked bellows and Scott was still begging them to come down when Jumbo suddenly turned tail and began running down the tracks back toward the big top. It all happened in an instant. The train hit Tom Thumb first. The cattle catcher swept up the little elephant and tossed him down the embankment. He was thrown clear twenty feet into the field, breaking a leg and crushing his top hat, but otherwise left intact.

The way a collision like the one that followed is usually described is *sickening*. Not that there have been many similar collisions by which to compare. But the sound of this collision—of seven tons of flesh and thirty tons of diamond-stacked steam-powered locomotive—did in fact send an *ill-making* shock wave through every being unfortunate enough to have been within earshot. The tender and first boxcar buckled and jumped the rail, and the entire train twisted and flipped onto its side, releasing a deafening hiss of broken steam. Amazingly, there were no fatalities among the passengers, who, soon enough, were crawling out of the wreckage, wandering about in a daze, their confusion worsened by the unexpected sound of lions roaring in the dark. When Scott ran through the cloud of scalding steam to his friend, the elephant was still barely alive, moaning, and leaking buckets of blood. Scott stroked his face and held his trunk, comforting him as best he could, but the elephant did not live long. To remove his body from the track, 160 men, using hawsers and cables and long-handled crowbars, heaving and dragging, rolled the slain elephant down the embankment. Unwilling to return to the Palace Car alone, Scott crawled up on top of Jumbo's corpse and, weeping, fell into a deep sleep, while local men with flaming torches and boys with pocketknives moved in for souvenirs.

CHAPTER FOUR

Barnum didn't get the news until the next morning, while eating his breakfast at the Murray Hotel in New York. The first thing he did, after setting down the telegram, was have a wire delivered immediately to his old friend Henry Augustus Ward in Rochester. They had already prearranged a plan in the event of Jumbo's demise. Always thinking ahead, Barnum had been plotting from the very beginning how he would continue to profit from the animal even after it was dead. Ward soon replied that he personally wouldn't be able to attend to the crisis, but he would honor the promise and send his best taxidermists at once. Barnum would have been happier if it were Ward, but Henry assured him that the young men he was sending were of the highest qualification. In any event, it was a relief. There was no time to lose.

Since he knew the newspapers would be knocking on his door by lunchtime, the next thing he did was begin concocting a more daring and heroic end for the elephant, where, instead of fleeing in a panic, Jumbo had picked up Tom Thumb with his trunk and tossed the smaller elephant to safety, pushed Scott out of the way, and then, realizing it was too late to save himself, faced down the "leviathan of the rail" and charged the oncoming locomotive head-on—nature versus machine, et cetera, et cetera—dying nobly.

The story would, more or less, stick.

It would also make it all the more poignant once Jumbo was stuffed and mounted and leading the parade again, in death as he had in life, with little Tom Thumb limping alongside his mummified hero. Barnum was already thinking how he might dress up one of the other elephants, Alice, in a black veil, so she could play Jumbo's grieving widow. God! It was almost better than it had been while Jumbo was still alive. Of course, he would have to decide whether to keep Scott on the payroll. It was a strike against him that he'd failed to protect Barnum's property from that mob of souvenir hunters. They'd cut Jumbo all to pieces. It was really going to be a hell of a job for Ward's skinners. He just hoped they'd hurry. There was no telling how long Jumbo could hold out. The corpse had already been exposed for nearly twelve hours. "If I can't have Jumbo living," he said, as if to reassure himself, "I'll have Jumbo dead, and Jumbo dead is worth a small herd of ordinary elephants."

❧

As FAR AS Carl knew—rushing toward Canada now on the night train from Rochester—he was headed toward what would be his life's greatest single adventure. The one amazing story he would keep for years to come, the one he'd be able to tell his grandchildren, how he had picked up the pieces of Jumbo the elephant! There wasn't another single animal that walked the earth half as famous. Very few taxidermists would ever have such a legacy—taxidermy being not the sort of work you pursued if you desired fame and fortune. But to be able to say he'd had the great P. T. Barnum as a client—that alone would be enough of a résumé to start up his own business one day if he wanted. Only one opportunity like this might come along in a lifetime. He better not botch it.

For sure, the stakes were high, so he really couldn't help but be nervous. There was no telling what shape Jumbo would be in by the time they got there. But Carl was determined more than ever to show Professor Ward once and for all why he hadn't made a mistake by hiring him back. There was nothing as sweet as getting a second chance, and since Carl had come back to Ward's he had not taken his good luck for granted. He intended to never take anything in life for granted again. He looked out the window at the darkness that masked the speed of the train. Only once in a while did he see the outline of a barn door scooting by, lit within by lantern, a farmer up early milking his cows. For Akeley, this trip to Canada was the first time he'd ever been out of the country. Unless Brooklyn counted as a foreign land.

Ward had called Carl and Bill Critchley down to his office late the day before, where they'd found him fiddling with his string tie, speedily untying and retying it into an equally botched knot. (Since returning to Ward's Carl had learned that these ties were special ordered from Paris in batches of twenty, but because Ward had never figured out how to tie them properly, they were always uniquely tangled, depending on the frustration level of the day.) After a moment Professor Ward gave up and waved a telegram at them. It was the message from Barnum. While he waited for them to absorb the shock, he stuffed the telegram back into his pocket among all the other papers and bits of tack and nails, then told them they would be going to retrieve the corpse on the next train to Ontario. They barely had time to collect the equipment they would require before getting to the station.

Now on the train, Akeley looked at Critchley slumped over in his seat, sleeping under his foolish little wool hat. Despite the mustache, he had a somewhat dainty, almost effeminate face, with brown wavy hair and soft hands. It was strange to see him carving up and skinning dead animals when one expected him to be folding ascots and picking lint off top hats at Wanamaker's. One wondered if it had been Critchley who'd sabotaged his zebra skins. But there was no sense in dwelling on that now. It really didn't matter. He was back at Ward's, and that was reason enough to be happy. It was just good to have escaped John Wallace's dungeon of dead birds. When he looked out the window he now saw just the faintest splice of light, like a seam coming undone at the horizon, and he lit another cigarette as the conductor passed quietly through the darkened car carrying a lantern with the wick turned low. Carl could feel the rails humming beneath his feet, clacking in the soles of his brogans. Of course, Critchley was technically in charge, since he held seniority over Akeley. But Akeley already felt that this job somehow belonged to him. In his bones, he knew he had to make it his; he had to give everything he had to it. To be good at anything in this life you couldn't ever stop proving yourself. Not ever.

※

COME THURSDAY MORNING, a day and a half after the accident, the massacred elephant still lay on the embankment, rotting in the hot September sun.

"This stench is enough to gag a maggot," Akeley mumbled, with the stem of his pipe clenched firmly in his teeth. He refilled the bowl and lit it often to ward off the heavy fumes of decay.

The elephant was in sorry-looking shape. There were large gashes in his feet and hide, and the blood-burned skin was already disintegrating and drawing thick droves of flies. The souvenir hunters had really done a number, too, despite the fence the circus had put up to protect the corpse. They had clipped his hide, nicked his ears, pulled out hairs, and chipped away at his already truncated tusks. The train had crushed his skull in over a hundred places. Putting him back together would not be easy. But first they had to take him apart, and to that end, six local butchers waited by to assist in the dismantling.

Standing in the crowd, as the taxidermists approached the elephant's corpse on the embankment, were Bearded Lady Annie Jones and Chang Yu Sing, the Chinese Giant, in his silk robes and clog shoes, standing mournfully beside Major Atom, the dandy midget with his cane, top hat, and fob chain, a few Zulu warriors, and Jo-Jo the Dog-Faced Boy. Elastic Skin Man stood by, tugging at the skin of his elbow nervously.

The tents bellied in the warm air on the quiet lot.

Despite the overwhelming stench, and the butchers' growing impatience, Akeley worked with a calm assurance, taking his time, making elaborate sketches and measurements, being careful to adjust for missing chunks and divots, before he would allow anyone to touch the carcass. Even Critchley seemed to yield to the younger man; everyone at Ward's knew that Akeley was Ward's star pupil now. He was the prodigal son returned. Critchley was in fact more than happy to let Akeley take the lead. The size of the job was as gargantuan as the stench.

Once they opened Jumbo's stomach, among all the half-digested buns, Akeley and the butchers salvaged several hatfuls of British pennies, along with a handsome collection of nails, keys, rivets, metal screws, gold and silver coins, pebbles, gravel, and one very well masticated policeman's whistle.

It took two solid days to do the job. The butchers hauled away the fat and blubbery flesh by the wheelbarrow, piling it on a funeral pyre where the remains burned on a bonfire fueled by four cords of wood that would waft over the town of St. Thomas for days, thick enough so bystanders who came seeking souvenirs went home not only with British pennies in their pockets but with the rich smell of burned elephant deep in their clothes. When done, they packed the epidermis—the skin alone weighed 1,538 pounds—in a tank filled with warm water spiked with alum and salt. In all, there were 2,400 pounds of bone. The forty-six-pound heart, which would go on display at Barnum's museum, was preserved in a barrel filled with alcohol.

※

BACK IN ROCHESTER, a separate building big enough to work on such a huge specimen had to be built, even if Akeley would begin working on Jumbo before the roof was finished. Ward had promised Barnum that he would have the elephant ready in two months, but right away it became clear it was an impossible deadline. For one, Jumbo was the largest animal in the history of taxidermy ever to be mounted. In addition, they were not simply preparing the elephant to stand motionless in a museum. This mount would have to be sturdy enough to endure afterlife travel by land and sea and, of course (ironically, perhaps), by rail, in a Palace Car modified into a sort of whistle-stop mausoleum.

Under the clatter of hammers, while the mastodon's skeleton macerated in a brick tank the size of an aquarium, Akeley directed the construction of a manikin with Trojan horse dimensions. It would fall apart if it were just stuffed in the usual way. Instead, Carl would build a pedestal of heavy oak beams, and bolt the elephant's feet to six-by-nine-inch crossbars, and then construct a massive internal truss that, using beams bound by rods, bars, and bolts, with the enormous defleshed skull mounted by an iron bar to the giant oak armature, would support the burden and simultaneously describe the elephant's rudimentary shape.

Another complication was that Barnum himself—when he discovered that the skin could be stretched out—wanted to know if Jumbo could be mounted even larger than he had been in real life. Ward told him yes, it could be done.

"By all means let that show as large as possible," Barnum said. "Let him show like a mountain."

When Ward conveyed Barnum's wishes to Akeley, Carl only shrugged, and ordered the tanners to stretch the skin out more. After all, this was P. T. Barnum, the same man who had showcased an attraction dubbed the "Happy Family": a tense menagerie of live birds and cats, bunnies and snakes, and other mismatched predators and prey all sharing one cage. He was not altogether concerned with scientific accuracy.

But the delays couldn't all be blamed entirely on the showman's whims. Despite Barnum's exaggerated specifications, Akeley still meant to re-create the truest image of Jumbo possible, and this kind of perfection would take time. First, he built up the shape of the body around the beams, using planks cut to form, angled and planed down, so, for starters, he had a giant elephant-shaped keg. Then, for finer detail, he covered the surface with two-inch basswood lathing, steamed and curved to fit, and then, using the tedious measurements he'd made before skinning Jumbo, honed the surface to reproduce as accurately as possible the animal's subcutaneous musculature. The longer he took, the more Barnum, who was worried that Jumbo wouldn't be ready in time for the upcoming circus season, threatened Ward over the contract. Ward put pressure on Akeley, but he would not be pushed into turning out more hack work. If he was going to do the job, he was going to do it right. Bringing an elephant back to life was not a labor one hurried. It was an epic. He had to follow the slow pace of intuition.

Before he had even put on the skin, the finished manikin was an uncanny sight. The ghost of Jumbo made of wood; Pinocchio a moment before inhaling the fairy dust. And then the skin itself—which had been shaved down to half an inch thickness—was painstakingly tacked onto the manikin with 78,480 countersunk nails.

When Jumbo was finally rolled out of the workshop, half the population of Rochester turned up at dawn, before the flickering streetlamps had yet been snuffed, just to catch a glimpse of the resurrected corpse slowly passing by on its short journey to its waiting private railway car. As it did, the crowd broke into applause. Not only had Akeley successfully rebuilt the circus elephant in all its enormous grandeur, but he had captured the essence of Jumbo's personality in the fine, uncanny details. The people saw it at once. Jumbo's spirit preserved before their very eyes! Madame Tussaud could not have done better.

P. T. Barnum officially unveiled the mounted elephant, February 26, 1886, at a memorial banquet at the Powers Hotel, in Rochester, where a legion of reporters and high society had been invited to feast their eyes, as well as their palates, and to be entertained by the Prince of Humbug himself. After a sumptuous spread, including plenty of "grape juice and corn elixir," Barnum surprised his guests by announcing that they were all in fact—and this was no hoax—now eating Jumbo! The chef had ground up 1.5 pounds of his ivory and served it as a kind of jelly. They were all eating Jumbo for dessert! Wasn't that just bully?

If any of the society women present that evening expressed their curiosity as to how Mr. Barnum had ever managed to conjure such a stunningly convincing monster—they whispered giddily among themselves, as if frightened that the stuffed elephant, lit under the ballroom chandeliers, were, in fact, still alive, holding its breath, just waiting for the right moment to stampede the guests—they would have found their attention directed toward a twenty-one-year-old young man, alone at a table across the hall, who himself looked stuffed into his borrowed tuxedo. How could such a charming, shy young man have created something so absolutely terrifying? The young illusionist, perhaps noticing that people were staring at him, glanced up, blushed, and then quietly turned his attention back to his dish of tusk-flavored aspic.

CHAPTER FIVE

ONE OF THE FEW FRIENDS CARL HAD MADE AT WARD'S WAS A coleopterist named William Morton Wheeler. Wheeler was a handsome, cerebral young man with wavy blond hair and a light blond mustache who was always impeccably groomed, in contrast to the chronically mussed Akeley. One of Henry Ward's most promising students, capable of reciting the Greek and Latin poets as readily as he could hold forth on the topics of conchology or the mating patterns of the golden fungus beetle—or any beetle, for that matter—Wheeler was from Milwaukee and had returned home shortly after Akeley's tour de force with Jumbo to take a job at the Milwaukee Public Museum. Once established, as curator of invertebrates, he soon persuaded Akeley to move to Milwaukee to work part-time in the taxidermy department. It wasn't a difficult choice for Carl to make. After Jumbo, there hadn't really been anywhere left for him to go at Ward's. Little there had changed. He was sick of the mediocre results that came of stuffing skins with sawdust, and the atmosphere remained hostile to experimentation. No matter how well Jumbo had come out, there had to be a better way, but he was only going to discover it if he ventured out on his own. It was time to take a risk in life. A part-time job would allow him to continue exploring his own techniques in his hours off.

Wheeler's mother took him in as if he were her own son, and the two friends converted a run-down old carriage barn on her property into a studio for Akeley. It was where he would hang his first business sign.

C. E. AKELEY'S

STUDIO OF SCIENTIFIC AND DECORATIVE TAXIDERMY.

COLLEGE AND MUSEUM WORK A SPECIALTY.

The studio had a potbellied stove and a cobwebbed window above his worktable where he could watch birds flit in and out of the elms. After a while he got used to the constant sound of the horse-drawn trucks from the brewing companies clopping along the cobblestones day and night. He worked his hours at the museum during the day, which mostly consisted of fighting to keep its older collection free of bugs, and then pursued his own goals in the evening, taking on whatever odd jobs he could to establish his business. Getting work wasn't hard; there was still a healthy demand for dead animals as decoration, as fashion, and even as advertising. A not uncommon sight in drugstore windows was a stuffed cat arched on a tree stump, hackles spiked, facing off against a taxidermied dog frozen midbark. The animals were advertising collodion, a familiar bite and scratch medicine—oddly enough, the same solution of pyroxylin used by Eadweard Muybridge to coat his plates for his Zoopraxiscope, the first primitive motion picture camera, with which he had filmed the staggered movements of animals in locomotion, and which would inspire Edison in kind to begin developing his own instrument.

Late into the night, while Akeley scraped skins, Wheeler would sit in the big overstuffed chair they'd salvaged from his mother's attic, reading aloud to him by the blazing light of a kerosene lamp. The freethinking Wheeler had set himself the task of enlightening his younger friend, who often seemed as if he could think of nothing but work. With a stein of ale on his knee, Wheeler read aloud from Schopenhauer, Shakespeare, Tolstoy, or Rousseau, frequently stopping to make sure Carl was listening, or to elaborate on the theme at hand, whether it be the impossibility of man to directly experience the world as it really was, or the ontological implications of the noble savage.

Since Carl always tried to have an animate version of whatever species he was skinning around as a model—or *the thing in itself*, as Wheeler would have put it, *das Ding an sich*—his studio eventually began to resemble a small zoo. Cages with squirrels and raccoons were stacked on his workbench. For a time, he even had an opossum with eleven babies that played around him as he worked, scampering over his piles of stained notebooks, or napped in Wheeler's lap as he turned the pages.

Carl was in the midst of staging a couple of minks fighting on a log—for a furrier's window display—when, one evening, Wheeler showed up at the studio with a black eye, his face swollen and cut, his shirtfront covered in blood. He'd been distracted on his way home, mulling over a new collection of beetles he'd been sticking on pins earlier that day, when he'd wandered smack into the middle of a labor riot and got beaten up by a pack of ruffians. His assailants, most likely, were boys from one of the rowdy "law and order" leagues, militias hired by industrialists to keep down union leaders and mobs. This sort of thing was going on a lot lately. In May, Governor Jeremiah Rusk had given his militia permission to fire on one thousand Polish workers who'd had the temerity to march on the Milwaukee Iron Company. It was the same week as the Haymarket riots in Chicago.

But by the time Wheeler staggered back to the studio, he wasn't so upset about what had happened, except it meant Carl would have to give up skinning for a night to read instead, picking up where Wheeler had left off the night before in *Anna Karenina*, where Vronsky first meets Anna at the train station—just before the train backs up, crushing the drunken guard—while Wheeler listened, sitting in the chair with a damp cloth to his face.

No, despite the riots, and the fearful talk of Jacobin-style revolutions and "carnivals of revenge," the two young naturalists spent their free hours wandering around the city, blissfully oblivious to the union leaders hectoring for fair wages in Washington Park, the armed packs of vigilantes patrolling the streets, and the air of suppression which hung like the thick and ubiquitous stench of hops. Wheeler and Akeley preferred not to dwell on politics; it was too crude a subject for the taxidermist and the beetle impaler. Their minds bubbled with a different kind of ferment. The only revolution that stirred their hearts was the one where they would overturn the fusty reign of old-fashioned museum exhibition.

During their endless walks, along the promenade where they had to hold their hats against the frigid winds off Lake Michigan, or sitting in the beer gardens, drinking in the German Kultur amid the discontented murmur of German émigrés whose revolution against their own monarchies had failed, they discussed Charles Darwin, and the comedy of watching religious leaders continue to tie themselves in knots trying to refute his theory of evolution. The national attitude toward nature itself was enduring an anxious transformation. The underlying reason for the popularity of natural history, aside from giving the bored middle class a way to fill their leisure hours, had always been the spiritual payoff. Through the prism of nature, and the contemplation of God's fecundity, Victorians had believed they were able to see His Design. But now they were asked to believe that the abundance of life was evidently not only without holy design but *random*. There was much for the young naturalists to discuss. Perhaps even, on occasion, to mock:

"Did you hear the one about the country boy who was asked where the Ten Commandments came from?"

"No, where, Carl?"

"From Sears, Roebuck, where else?"

One of Darwin's books in particular drew their attention, *The Expression of the Emotions in Men and Animals*. To draw his conclusions Darwin had studied thousands of pictures of infants, great works of art, and photographs of the insane who were "liable to the strongest passions." He had also gathered data from missionaries and others who worked with aborigines and natives—from the Maoris of New Zealand to the "wildest tribes" of the North American West—all to determine whether emotions such as anguish, disgust, joy, and surprise were expressed in similar fashion to those of the European with whom they had little or no contact. That they were identical only further confirmed Darwin's belief that all the races of man shared a common progenitor. The skin might conceal such truths to the holder of the basest (if common) prejudices, but it was also the medium that best revealed the universality of those reflexes beneath the surface. Darwin concluded that both expression and the *recognition* of expression were among the most instinctive of all traits. Expressions such as the bristling of hair follicles under extreme terror or the baring of teeth in a fit of rage were also evidence that man shared qualities readily observed in the lower animals. Beneath the skin of man or beast were the same delicate muscles. The same sensitive machinery of mood, an elaborate contraption of twitches, depressors, levators, and corrugators signifying state of mind. The facial muscles of apes were not limited to mere expressions of "rage and fear," as some anatomists had it, but encompassed the same range of emotions as humans'. Grief was grief, whether you were an orangutan or a pharmacist. Certainly, animals experienced life much as *Homo sapiens* did. Even if it was hard not to suspect sometimes that they inhabited an entirely different and unknowable consciousness.

It was also in Milwaukee where Carl would first discover the cyclorama. Created by German émigré artists fleeing the potato blight and the iron fist of King Frederick William III—only now to endure the iron fist of Frederick Pabst—these monster illusions dotted the city. As tall as fifty feet and as long as a football field, the cycloramas were huge paintings that engulfed the viewer in the center of a Civil War battle, the crucifixion of Christ, or panoramic scenes of ancient Rome in flames, overrun by barbarian Ostrogoths. The canvas screens revolved around the viewer on a series of mechanical rollers, giving the audience the mesmerizing, if slow and squeaking, impression of what some had come to call *moving pictures,* a term Edison hadn't yet appropriated. The elaborate attention to detail, the lighting, the smell of pigment, the grand scale of it all lulled in the taxidermist's hungry imagination. He too wanted to make something that would conquer an audience this way, a suspension of disbelief.

Nearly as mesmerizing was what he encountered at the dime museum on Grand Avenue. There Akeley and Wheeler saw the same sort of sensationalist wonders to which Barnum was treating the world: shrunken heads, fake mermaids, and erotic tableaux of young girls in flesh-colored tights posing as nude paintings. They would also come across the live savage exhibit, which no doubt gave their talks about Rousseau a certain new urgent slant. Carl had never come face-to-face with an actual aboriginal before. At the dime museum, the savage's station was by the front entrance, near a giant mud anthill, inside of which visitors were presumably led to believe the native ate and slept after museum hours. Etched with war paint, dressed in a barkcloth robe, and dandling a whale-bone spear, this lone ambassador from some far-flung primitive nation stared out from behind a glass partition with tired eyes. A label on the wall by the exhibit revealed that he was from a tribe called "Earthmen."

❧

ONE NIGHT WHEELER was reading *Through the Looking Glass* while Carl worked on the skin of an orangutan which the museum had recently acquired from Borneo. When he reached the part where Alice encounters Humpty Dumpty, he paused to make a joke, asking Akeley how he thought he might go about mounting an egg of such absurd dimensions for the museum? But Akeley was not paying attention. He was standing back from his workbench, regarding the primate's skin with a lost-looking gaze, his pipe loosely clenched in his fist.

Wheeler set the open book across his knee.

"Are you really thinking, Carl, or are you just thinking that you're thinking?"

It was a question he often put to his friend.

But this was not one of his usual spells of absentmindedness. He was thinking, all right. But he would not solve the problem he saw before him—not a problem, per se, but a deeply embedded question—until a few nights later, after Wheeler had gone home, when he again brought out the orangutan.

He had already built the usual armature. The leg and weirdly long arm bones were clamped to the wood-block pedestal, the skull bolted down, a slapdash skeleton that looked like some Mexican Day of the Dead parade float. As much as he had tried to hone his powers of observation and to get as close as possible to re-creating exactly how the animal really looked—despite whatever Wheeler had said about Schopenhauer's pessimistic view on the matter of the representation of reality (i.e., how any effort to experience the world as anything more than shabby representation was doomed to further *distort* and distance man from the true thing)—he still felt his creations lacked a vividness he knew must be possible.

He was preparing to stuff its skin in the usual way when he began to think. What he wanted was a more subtle medium—more expressive, a more convincing way to impress the skin with the muscle beneath. The essence that did not so much lie on the surface but somehow came from somewhere deeper. Something he would have to see and find with his hands, the ape's unseen essence—the pongid's noumenon, as his philosopher friend might have put it—concealed and revealed simultaneously by the deception of its outer skin. That was it; in order to truly bring it alive, what was underneath would have to come to life first. He moved the corncob pipe from one side of his mouth to the other and looked at the sawdust clenched in his fingers. Then he let it fall to the floor, wiped off his hands on his pants, and started pacing around the creaky floorboards of his studio.

At Ward's, using clay had not been an altogether new idea. The staff kept it around to rough out and bulk up the armatures for larger mammals, and before he had left they had even begun using clay sometimes to finish the surface of a manikin, to give it a bit more natural look. Naturally, Akeley himself kept a spare bucket of wet clay on hand. Maybe that's all he had in mind when he picked up the first lump and weighed it in his palm. Massaging the clod slowly in his fist to soften it, he stood with his free hand on his hip, leaning forward toward the ape, twisting the clump behind his back, like a pitcher contemplating whether to throw a curve or a knuckle, and then he tore off a pinch and pressed the clay under the zygomatic arch of the monkey's skull. He built up the skeleton, packing clay around the pelvic bone, its legs, working slowly and following the intuition of his hands. He tried to be mindful of the details at every layer and stopped frequently to check his progress against the original measurements taken by the explorer before he'd skinned the animal.

When the sun set, the gas lamps hissed to life out on the street. The only other sound was the tick of the clock and the occasional half-conscious mutter of satisfaction from his own lips. Then it gradually dawned on him. What he was doing. That he was finally doing what he was meant to do. He was actually sculpting. Why had he never tried this before? He looked at the clay embedded in his fingernails, smiling. Nothing had ever come so naturally.

He stayed up all night, surrounded by a blue haze of pipe smoke, in an ecstatic wide-alert haze himself. He only stopped now and then to relight his pipe, or flip through his notebook to consult the explorer's sketches, to double-check the width of a haunch, the circumference of a bicep, a photograph of the monkey's dead but still smirksome face. When he went to bed, at last, the birds were singing, and the tobacco smoke swirled around the clay ape on its pedestal like a golem awaiting the spell of life. That would come the next day, once Carl awoke after only a few hours' sleep and cautiously tried on its waiting skin. The fit was perfect. By following his sketches to the final detail, he had captured each indelibly unique trait, each nook and plane of the animal's outer surface, every undulation, mole, scar, and wrinkle, so that—like a reverse suit—the manikin was perfectly tailored to the skin. There was an eye-tricking sense of motion under the skin. As if something like *will* was surging forth from within. Indeed, the ape looked as if it might leap off the table and jump out the window.

CHAPTER SIX

IN SEPTEMBER 1888, TWO YEARS AFTER HE HAD BEGUN WORK-
ing for the Milwaukee Public Museum, Akeley suddenly found himself with much more creative leeway. His friend Wheeler, at the ripe age
of twenty-two, was promoted to director when the previous director,
Carl Doerflinger, who had not been a particularly visionary man, except
when it came to a keen eye for dermestid beetles for his underlings to
quash, had left due to health issues.

Shortly after Wheeler took the reins Carl hatched his most ambitious plan ever. At first, Wheeler might have thought his friend was
being a bit excessive, as if Carl had only had one too many cups of German coffee that morning, but he kept listening. After all, more than
anybody, Wheeler recognized his friend's genius. How he had begun to
give each of his creations something akin to personality—almost in the
way Renaissance artists had been the first to render human subjects
with anything like true *individuality*. But once he'd heard him out,
Akeley's plan—or vision, if you wanted to go that far—struck him as
prophetic. A glimpse of the museum of the future. If he could only convince the trustees that it was remotely doable.

As they were now, wildlife halls were nothing more than glorified
curiosity cabinets. Trophy rooms with the heads of slain animals hung
on the walls. A few hundred bird heads pinned, in profile, above a name-
plate with their Latin moniker and locality of execution. Glass cases of
monkey paws and bat wings. Skins had the mangy pelage of old towels.

They were not meant to be entertaining. Aesthetically speaking, little had changed since the dull exhibits of the eighteenth century. If anything, there was more art in the hand-carved cabinetry than the animals themselves. On one occasion Akeley and Wheeler were examining a particularly hideous mount—so terrible you could hardly tell whether it was a cat or a dog or whatever—when a ray of sunlight pierced one of the demented glass eyeballs and the two men fell to hysterical laughing. If natural history museums were going to accommodate popular taste, they needed to spice things up, and Carl's plan would do just that. In a nutshell, he proposed collecting and mounting the *entire* spectrum of mammal life that skittered and burrowed across the great state of Wisconsin. As if that were not enough, he also proposed creating each creature's habitat; not to just stuff them in a cabinet but to actually reproduce the animal's environment—its own personal ecosystem—with as exacting a level of detail as he would reproduce the animals themselves.

Wheeler and Akeley had spent many hours over the past few years discussing the relatively new concept of ecology—the study of the interrelation between organisms and their environment—and in fact it had probably been Wheeler who had first explained it to Carl. And now the young taxidermist had come up with a dramatic way to showcase the idea itself by building an elaborate set of worlds populated by whole family groups interacting with their habitat and each other—mating, foraging, fleeing—complex *dynamic* tableaux rather than simple portraits stuck in a glass vacuum. Ultimately, it would be a grand peepshow into the inner world of Wisconsin's woodland fauna. Carl intended to start with muskrats.

Against the initial wishes of the museum trustees, Wheeler soon arranged for Carl to get money to go ahead with the scheme. After all, it was going to cost a lot of bullets. The only remaining question was who would actually go out and collect all these animals?

❧

AROUND THIS TIME, Akeley stopped off one afternoon to visit his friend Arthur Reiss for a snip. Arthur owned a small barbershop near Carl's studio, though, truth be told, Carl's hair was already thinning on top, and it tended to frizz out on the sides, so whatever Arthur could do for him was provisional at best.

It must have been while Arthur clipped away that Carl got to talking about his upcoming project, and the barber might have mentioned how he himself had done some hunting, now and then, and asked if Carl might like a hunting partner for his expedition.

That would be mighty handy, Carl said.

As his hair dribbled to the floor, they got to talking about possible areas in northern Wisconsin where they might start. As Arthur stropped the razor to shave Carl's face, a petulant-looking girl came in through the back, gave Arthur a halfhearted kiss on the cheek, and plopped herself in the empty chair. Absentmindedly, she began to swivel, kicking off with her feet, and attempting to catch glimpses of herself in the mirror on each passing turn. Akeley must have taken the spinning girl to be the barber's daughter or maybe kid sister—she couldn't have been more than fourteen. He watched her swivel out of the corner of his eye. Her arms were red and chapped as if she'd been doing laundry. Just looking at her, you could tell she had to be a handful.

The following weekend, when Akeley met up with Reiss to hunt, the girl was there. It was then that he discovered the girl was not Reiss's daughter but his wife. Reiss introduced her as Delia, but he never called her anything other than Mickie. A little over a year ago, she'd apparently just shown up out of nowhere, a girl with wild hair lost in the city, hungry and confused, and still fuming mad at the poor stupid parents whom she'd left behind on the farm. Reiss had taken her in, given her a haircut, listened to her story of running away, which, truth be told, didn't altogether make a lot of sense, but he'd gotten her a job washing dishes and then, shortly before her fifteenth birthday, made her his wife.

Akeley did not care about any of that. He only worried the girl would get between him and his muskrats.

He had not hunted since he was a boy, when he'd gone to collect birds and chipmunks, with the aid of Professor Jenks's manual. Now, in the bleak October woods of northern Wisconsin, the gun had the sorry heft of nostalgia. As they walked through the woods, he was aware of the presence of the girl between himself and the barber, who carried his rifle upside down over his shoulder, hand around the barrel. She wore her hectic mass of wavy brown hair stuck, pell-mell, under a slouchy hat. When Carl stopped to squat and inspect a pile of scat, the girl squatted too, curious, and when he glanced up at her he could not help but notice—along with the fact that she had burr reeds caught in her hair—that her eyes were extremely blue.

She carried their basket lunch and chatted haphazardly about whatever came to her mind, the unadulterated observations of a teen girl, as they mucked through the early winter marsh in pursuit of muskrats. When Carl finally shot one in the midst of repairing the roof of its stick and mud hut, it flopped in the water with a cold splash, and Mickie clapped with delight as he trudged through the stiff bulrushes to collect his first specimen. Ordinarily, he told her, taxidermists didn't go out to fetch their own subjects. But given the importance of this project for the museum, he wanted to have complete control over every detail. Even though she was just a girl, she seemed to understand this, that his intentions were somehow loftier than most, even if it had the air of bragging.

Back at his studio, while he and Arthur cleaned their guns, thawing their feet before the coal-burning stove, Mickie cooed over his collection of eerily lifelike animals that seemed to look back as if trapped behind their beady eyes. She had already begun to think of Akeley as some kind of mild-mannered sorcerer.

Soon she was visiting his studio, frequently, without her husband. At first, she just sat in the overstuffed chair, watching Carl work. She could watch him go at a muskrat for hours with a sort of menacing intensity just to get its jaws just right around a willow branch, until he had achieved, with great expenditure of sweat, the most convincing and dynamic *gnaw* possible. She talked incessantly, asking lots of questions, and though he was quiet in general, he was happy to provide answers, and to show her what he was doing, even the parts you would not have thought a girl would care to stomach. Otherwise, for the most part, she was like an ordinary girl as far as he could reckon, telling him stories, complaining about her husband and about washing dishes, and how bored she was cooped up, and how watching his work was much more interesting than watching her husband cut hair. While she talked, she would poke food through the bars of the cage where the muskrat Akeley had trapped also watched the taxidermist at work, though with notably less enthusiasm.

Whenever she stopped by, Carl let her play assistant, arranging the foliage collected during their hunting trips, cleaning his pipes, sweeping the studio, and keeping his scaly-tailed web-footed study aids happy in clover.

It must have gradually dawned on him that the girl seemed to be making herself more and more at home—even if, by letting her, he knew he was probably making trouble for himself with the barber. But there must have been something flattering about having such a pretty girl around who wasn't disgusted by what he did. It wasn't a job that typically drew admirers. Finally, the day came when she asked if she could try to skin something herself. He would have started her out with something small, like a wren or titmouse. Standing by her side at his workbench, he would have first shown her how to hold the scalpel, where to draw the first incision, and when she wasn't utterly revolted by the sight of the intestines squirming out, he went around behind her, maybe holding her wrist to help guide the blade under its jaw, showing how to gently flick open the tendons, explaining where to put her thumbs inside the animal's warm pulp, how to gently pull away the skin. She held it up, admiring her own handiwork, spreading out the wings like a paper doll. Laughing, he told her about when he was a boy and he'd presented the canary to his aunt; when he had boasted, "It can almost sing!" He didn't bother to add that the same aunt had thought he should be put in an asylum for his morbid preoccupations.

She told him her own story about how she'd once put on her father's boots and gone out in the night to stomp all the drying bricks in a neighboring bricklayer's yard after the men had teased her earlier that day just because she was easy to tease.

Who even knew if the barber knew she was here?

Soon, he had an apt assistant who was able to do more than clean his pipes and feed his pets. She was like his own personal elfin helper. A gift from a fairy godmother. Except instead of helping him cobble together shoes in the middle of the night, she stitched porcupine hides. Or churned away at the tanning vat with a broomstick. He would look up now and then to notice, almost with surprise, that she was still there, hunched over his desk attempting to husk the skin of a grosbeak—struggling not to sever the thin membrane between the skin and intestines—with the most adorable look of concentration crimping her furrowless brow. He could not help himself if he soon began to experience a soft tenderness under his rib cage whenever he saw her there. She was a lovely girl. It was impossible not to feel the slightest swoon at the sight of her delicate hands, even with the grime of his macabre workshop under her nails. If anything, to him, she was even more precious with her smooth arms flecked with blood.

He soon came to know everything about her. How her father was a brutal man who had treated her like a slave. Like Carl, she'd grown up on a farm, in Beaver Dam, Wisconsin. The ninth child in a family of Irish immigrants, she was the youngest daughter, born when her father was in his sixties. A stubborn, hot-tempered girl, she found life on the desolate high prairie lonely and hard. The only ostensible purpose of her existence was to wash dishes, make beds, and clean up after her older siblings. The last straw came when she was thirteen and refused to bring water to the hateful field hands as her father had ordered and she had run away instead. She didn't say why she'd refused to bring them water—as if she'd been carried away on that fifty-mile walk by forces she did not completely understand. Who knew what kind of pain had burned in her mind to keep her feet going all the way to that faraway city?

Carl sympathized with her more than she could know—or maybe Mickie did know, surely sensing how his mother had poisoned a part of him, with her depressive puritanical moods, her toxic dissatisfaction with life, and the shriveling scorn she heaped on his father for his helpless, if many, failures of character. In any event, when she reached Milwaukee, she'd burned off the tantrum, or whatever spell of madness had taken over the girl inside, but she had no intention of returning. She'd wandered around the city for a few days, hungry and bewildered that everybody seemed to be speaking German, until the barber had found her huddled outside his shop. She'd married Arthur Reiss but soon grew bored. And then one day she'd found herself in the cold northern woods following a strange man who wanted to kill muskrats only to bring them back to life.

AKELEY LOST HIS CHAMPION AND FRIEND WHEN WHEELER LEFT the museum to accept a fellowship at Clark University. The new director, lacking his predecessor's vision and affection for the taxidermist, promptly demoted Carl to the task of tending to the legions of dermestid beetles infesting the museum's decrepit Victorian exhibits. Akeley was insulted, and for weeks Mickie had to listen to him fume. She was now seventeen, having long ago left Arthur Reiss. She must have felt sorry for the barber, for leaving him the way she had, but her heart had told her to follow this other man. Despite his outbursts and fragile moods he was easy to love.

Didn't they know he was more than just an exterminator? Hadn't they heard of Jumbo the elephant? No, of course not, because he'd never gotten proper credit. He knew that the world looked down on his chosen vocation. That it was not considered a legitimate art in any sense. It was a trade for rough, uncultured brutes. Taxidermists ranked just a few notches below undertaker. But he had not been born into this world only to take skin beetles out of it. He would strike out on his own, and they would struggle, but in the end his ego had no other choice. His dream of a mammal hall was abandoned. The fur-bearing creatures of Wisconsin would all breathe a collective sigh of relief when Carl tendered his resignation on September 20, 1892. Had he known the nation was on the verge of an economic panic, he might have done otherwise. Either way, he would have to resort to more commercial work to get by now.

But at least he had Mickie. They had found in each other a kind of sanctuary. It was almost as if they were orphans. She took him seriously. In her eyes he was a great sculptor, and more. It was as if she didn't smell the stink of decay that surrounded him like a halo. And even when they were living in absolute poverty, he still had a way of making things light. When he wasn't in a wretched mood he had a funny sense of humor that snuck up on you. She had never felt more comfortable with anyone else, even if he had a way of looking at her sometimes, as if he were trying to determine what kind of animal she was beneath that pert upturned nose and stubborn mouth. She was muse and pupil rolled into one. Carl finally had to admit he loved the girl. But sometimes he felt like he wanted to know her better, to really know her, the way he wanted to get to the bottom of everything.

They were lucky to have found each other. They shared a kind of self-doubt about their place in the world; she felt like a dunce around some of Carl's university friends and colleagues, and he too had his own issues of illegitimacy, of not being accepted as an artist. She took care of him, of their living necessities, while he slaved away repairing torn mink stoles, tippets, and muffs, mounting pheasants, and even meeting the demand for inane novelties in furniture, like deer-leg coatracks and other fur and feather bric-a-brac. If things got really bad, he could always go back to work for Henry Ward. His former mentor had repeatedly asked him to return, especially now with the deluge of orders for the upcoming World's Columbian Exposition in Chicago. But Carl preferred to remain a free agent, even if it meant going hungry from time to time.

Actually, it turned out that he had made the right decision by leaving the Milwaukee Public Museum. Because soon, Akeley would receive his own commission for the exposition. It seemed the whole world was getting geared up for it. People talked of little else, and the newspapers reported on each minute step of the fair's construction along Lake Michigan, as if the people of earth were preparing for the arrival of the Kingdom of Heaven itself. The fairgrounds would spread over 700 acres along the lakefront, a neoclassical metropolis of 150 glittering palaces built by leading architects of the day: a vast manorial estate housing the greatest collection of industrial and cultural exhibits ever assembled, a living museum to beat all museums, a curiosity cabinet of cosmic proportions, landscaped with statuary, opulent gardens, artificial lagoons and canals traversed by electric-powered gondolas. It was an unreal outsize fairyland of Colonial Revival plaster castles that would give it the sobriquet the "White City."

So when Carl received a letter from the United States National Museum in Washington, D.C., asking if he would prepare a mount for its exhibition in Ethnology Hall, he and Mickie put everything they had into the job.

The World's Columbian Exposition, or Chicago World's Fair, would be held the following year, in 1893, to celebrate the four hundredth anniversary of Christopher Columbus's discovery of America, and—more to the point—to showcase the manufacturing marvels of Western civilization. During the industrial revolution, expositions like this were the debutante balls for developing nations: giant meretricious pavilions where the booty of scientific progress—that is, science in the service of industry—was put on parade. This one would be bigger than the World's Exposition at the Crystal Palace in London in 1851, and the Paris Exposition, in 1889, when the French had erected the Eiffel Tower as a soaring monument to the steely spirit of the mechanical age. With its slaughterhouses and stockyards, its glass and iron towers, and its clanging railyards, the city of Chicago was the perfect backdrop to show off America's burgeoning industrial power. Come nightfall, the White City was illuminated with over two hundred thousand incandescent lightbulbs provided by the Westinghouse Corporation. The display would burn three times the wattage as the entire city of Chicago. It was a stunning, electric hymn to Progress shimmering on Lake Michigan. A beacon of the New World's liberation from the savage wilderness, out of which it had forged itself and then tamed to do its bidding. The largest of the palaces, or "halls," as they were called, located in the Court of Honor, were curiously reminiscent of the gilt-lobbied mansions of the Astors and Carnegies which blotted out the sun along Fifth Avenue in New York, and Prairie Avenue in Chicago, except that these palaces hummed with the dynamos that now drove the pistons of an accelerating world day and night. The nobility of the world were the victors of capitalism, the captains of industry, and this was to be their coronation. Despite the endless array of machines, the theme of the exposition was "Not Things But Men." Asked by the National Museum to prepare a mount, upon which the wax likeness of a Comanche warrior would sit bareback and meekly view the competing riches of America's Gilded Age, Akeley provided the low-tech contribution of a stuffed horse. Specifically, a white bronco.

The great show of prosperity inside the White City belied the economic situation in the rest of the country, where, by 1893, layoffs were endemic, banks were closing, and a handful of businessmen had already jumped to their deaths—a grim harbinger of the depression settling over everybody who didn't live on Millionaires' Row. Akeley was happy to have the work. He would be paid $115 and was given an additional $75 for expenses.

There was only one problem. Carl's new method had a fatal flaw. Despite the thorough tanning, the repeated salt and alum immersions, and enough arsenic to kill a stampede of broncos, the moisture of the clay beneath was causing his skins to rot. However, he was not about to go back to the old upholsterer's methods of sawdust and rags. He needed to find a new method—and quickly. Even though they weren't married yet, he was determined to provide for Mickie. Somehow he needed a way to transfer the perfection of detail in his clay models to a more stable medium. Perhaps it was all the enthusiasm for classical forms that pervaded the architecture of the fair that got him thinking. Instead of shaping clay with his hands, perhaps he could work more like a stone sculptor. Why not use the same infinitely malleable material that the White City itself had been sculpted from—plaster? For his purposes, it would be eminently more easy to handle than marble.

He began to work in the usual way, attaching iron rods for the legs and neck to a wooden pedicel, then roughing out the horse's dimensions with a light framework of steel supports and lathing. But instead of bulking up the armature with tow and clay, this time he wrapped it with a medium-gauge wire cloth, crimping and bending the unwieldly mesh, hammering and snipping it into place. When he had what looked more or less like a horse-shaped birdcage, he mixed a large batch of plaster in a giant tub, retarding the mixture with flour-paste glue. Then, with Mickie's help, he began to dip strips of burlap in the goo, bandaging the mesh horse with the sticky white poultice, and building up a thick uneven cocoon. After a few days, once the hollow, four-legged—if somewhat abstract-looking—mass had dried, with one eye on the diminutive clay model he'd made before skinning the horse, Akeley painstakingly began to *carve*. He had never been much of a whittler as a boy, but he proved as able and intuitive with the chisel as he had with his bare hands. As he etched away at the hardened block, the Carrara-white shavings gathered at the feet of his ladder like drifting snow.

As the exposition came closer, Akeley's commission would jump to three horses for two more Indians. After the National Museum contacted him in mid-January to request the two additional mounts—a bay and a spotted horse—Akeley found himself depending on his mistress more than ever. Fueled by anxiety and fear of the poorhouse as much as creative ambition, the lovers worked night and day, weeks on end, eating little, barely sleeping. Although unable to find a spotted horse right away, they soon acquired the bay. And as Carl began to build up another manikin, Mickie herself—as imperturbable as if she were baking a ham—donned the leather apron to shave down the hide with the double-handled cleaver, before paring it down to the requisite quarter-inch thickness with the small knife until her thumbs were blistered and her childlike features speckled with gore.

While the second plaster cast dried, they went in search of the spotted horse. The museum had requested the three horses be ready by March 1. Right off, Akeley knew this to be impossible. However, he had informed Washington that the white bronco could be delivered by mid-February, and the other two, he was sure, by the beginning of April. But finding a spotted horse—not just a decent specimen but any spotted horse—was more of a challenge than he'd imagined. It didn't seem like it should have been so difficult. He'd probably seen hundreds of spotted horses in his lifetime. But now they were nowhere to be found. For days at a time he and Mickie hunted all over the city and then in neighboring towns. Still failing to turn one up, they went to the country, scanning fields and pastures, stopping at farmhouses, glancing in every paddock. It almost began to feel as if they were searching for an animal that did not exist. But they kept at it despite growing doubts and the encroaching deadline. They kept their eyes open on the street, leering at every passing carriage, under every yoke. They made inquiries at the rendering plant, the police barracks, and to every and any approachable teamster they met. On weekdays they visited the racetracks, where, biding their time, Carl sketched thoroughbreds doing laps—studying the way their flanks moved, committing to his mind the kinetic fluid motion of living trotting muscle—while Mickie ate roasted peanuts, her collar flapping in the manure-tainted breeze.

Even after he had completed the bronco and nearly finished the bay, he still had not found his spotted horse. By April 14—two weeks past his deadline—he had to write the museum to say he could have the bay and bronco delivered by the following Tuesday, but that, alas, he had not got his hands on a spotted horse . . . quite yet. Though, he wrote, "we have heard of one and are in hopes of securing it in a day or two." He promised to have it delivered in time for opening day, May 1.

Given how close the fair was now, the museum wanted Akeley to ship the horses directly to Chicago. Since he had evidently located a spotted horse—even if it meant he would have to work double-time to complete it now—he should wait and deliver all three in the same shipment for efficiency's sake. But the spotted horse he thought he'd secured had failed to materialize. And once again, he found himself scouring the streets, peering into dimly lit stables, until three days later, when he had to admit defeat and wrote back to the museum saying that he would be shipping the two finished horses alone.

On April 17, he had the two horses delivered to the train depot. Then a most propitious thing happened. Between that Saturday morning and the next day, just hours after seeing off his freight, he somehow, miraculously, stumbled upon what he'd been looking for all along.

It was hard to believe. But where did he find it? Perhaps—that is to say, no one knows for sure—on his way back from the train depot, on that cool April evening, after personally seeing to it that his horses were safely nailed up in their temporary coffins and carefully loaded onto the waiting boxcar, and then strolling back down the narrow streets, Mickie wrapped under his arm, passing the taverns and the rowdy candlelit faces within, they came by the Bergmann & Maier Ice Company on Mitchell Street—as they would have passed it a hundred times before—but on this most hypothetical night they both stopped dead on the slushy cobbles outside the open stable and stared in disbelief. There, standing beside the blocks of ice piled in straw, still in harness, was a shivering dray horse, its muzzle clumped with dirty icicles, but its hide a pure white with the exception of several black splotches that marked it as auspiciously as the spots on a rolled die.

Once their eyes had fully adjusted to what they were seeing, would Akeley have approached the owner of the icehouse? How readily would the proprietor and the taxidermist have come to an agreement? Did it cross the iceman's mind that this man who claimed to be a "sculptor" and his squirming nymph were trying to put one over on him? Gruffly, he mulled over Akeley's queer proposition, regarding his piebald pony in an entirely new light. After what seemed like an interminable amount of hemming and hawing, and near rebuffs by the iceman, who remained skeptical—that is, again, if this is how it all went down—yet who was no doubt softened by the sight of the young girl suffering in his cold barn, an agreement was struck. The horse would enjoy one last meal of oats that night. Its corpse was to be delivered to Akeley's studio the next morning on a sledge.

Regardless of the spotted horse's true provenance, Akeley completed the job in ten unprecedented days and delivered his third and final horse to Chicago by April 29—with just two days to spare before the exposition's opening ceremony. When the curators from the National Museum uncrated this equine triptych (taking extra caution with the spotted horse, since it hadn't had adequate time to properly dry), they were dazzled by the absence of any visible seams in the hide. But that was only the half of it. Walking around each horse, they noted the extravagant attention to detail, running their hands along the muscled haunches, the taut tendons, the breath-tensed nostrils, a raised vein appearing to pulse with hot blood under the smooth, deceptively cool pelage. The impression was that the manikins had actually *grown* into their skins. Carl Akeley's technical skill, as a master of illusion and sus- pender of life, was in a class of its own. What they could never know was the influence of the little muse at his side, the eighteen-year-old girl with the flinty eyes and the wild hair, who had in fact helped to shovel out the damned horses' guts herself.

❦

WHEN MICKIE AND Carl went to visit the expo themselves, with Wheeler in tow, perhaps the most stunning spectacle was not the fair itself but the sight of hundreds of people carrying around the little black boxes called "Kodaks." At times the constant clicking noise of the cameras grew frenetic, as if the spectators could not believe what they were seeing with their own eyes. They were astonishing little machines. The Kodak needed no tripod to be supported; nor was the operator required to confine herself under a stifling black curtain to shield out unwanted sunlight. George Eastman's own experiments back in Roch- ester had paid off handsomely. Having done away with the conventional heavy glass plates, the new celluloid film he'd invented could be wound on spools inside the Kodak, itself a simple-looking contraption, no bigger than a small birdhouse with a leather strap. Fully loaded, with enough film for one hundred exposures, the first handheld camera in the world weighed four and a half pounds. And at two dollars a day, nearly anyone of relative means could rent one, making the World's Columbian Exposition the first mass-photographed event in history. Overnight, Eastman had turned America into a nation of amateur photographers, preserving everything in sight in a million little boxes.

Pressed together, Carl and Mickie pushed forward along with the crowd through the octagonal Administration Building, gawking up at the 275-foot-high dome, taller even than the dome of the U.S. Capitol, this being the gateway through which 27.5 million people would enter the fair over a six-month period, pulling in almost seven hundred thousand on its best day. To look across the Midway was to behold a sea of bowlers, with the occasional feathered tern or gull bobbing on the waves. Keeping close to his friends was Wheeler, who was getting ready to go off in a few weeks for Würzburg, Germany, to study insect embryology, but who wanted to see the marvel of the fair first.

The fair itself was not unlike a hive. A giant buzzing show-and-tell. A demonstration of how the modern world had come into its own. In each massive hall were dozens of smaller pavilions, where the process of electrometallurgy, or modern dentistry, or demonstrations of how rock could be crushed and pulverized now to a more exact scree, or gold extracted by chemical lixiviation, or otherwise useless gems plucked from the deep could be polished and put to good use, were celebrated alongside the endless new machines. The terrible whine of dynamos and turbines and the rapid-fire chuff of pneumatic pumps, traction engines, and motorized tools drilled and hammered and stamped until the noise was so great one had to hurry through with hands over ears or spend the day wandering about in a deaf haze.

In the Exhibit of Manufacturers, where visitors and their snapping Kodaks rode by overhead in observation cars suspended from ceiling-mounted cranes, and where one might see the latest doings at the Pavilion of the Liquid Carbonic Acid Manufacturing Company, one's senses were cauterized by the varnishes and eye-stinging dyes, or vaporized by the smell of tanned hides in the leather trades exhibit where the air literally vibrated from the shoe-stitching machinery, benumbed yet again by the endless bombardment of new earth-digging tools, new weapons, new refrigerators, rubber tires, pharmaceuticals, hydraulic oil wells, ceramics, plumbing marvels, textiles, clocks, banking exhibits, prosthetics exhibits, the latest in this, that, and the other, not least of all new ways to rot in hell, as seen in the undertaker's exhibit, where modish coffins, urns, and mausoleums were as shiny and polished as a showroom of this year's latest model phaetons.

Outside, the Midway was just as chaotic if not more so. Here, between the moving sidewalk, the full-scale model of St. Peter's Church, and Hagenbeck's Circus—where lions pulled chariots and Bengal tigers climbed ladders that teetered above the passersby—was the "caravansary of nations," a hubbub of ambassadors from the Old World crowded one on top of another in the Irish Village, the Chinese Village, the Javanese Village, the brightly tiled Tunisian Village, the East Indian Bazaar, the tenebrous cliff dwellers' habitations, and even a re-creation of Egypt's Temple of Luxor, complete with seventy-foot-tall obelisks and a fleet of noxious-smelling camels on Cairo Street.

At one point, passing through the Palace of Fine Arts, the trio stopped to study a sculpture of a grizzly bear mauling a loincloth-clad Native American. The bear had the Indian's arm clamped in its jaws. The suggestion was that the bear was protecting its cub, which huddled beneath the man and bear, both of whom were standing upright. The expression on the savage's face was sheer terror. As they stood looking at the sculpture, Carl and Wheeler began to discuss the probable sensations of such a predicament. Even though he was an anatomist, Wheeler couldn't say for certain what it would feel like to have one's flesh torn into like this poor devil's. To be gnawed on like a bone. Did the man feel any pain or merely fear? Fear itself, however well wrought by the sculptor here, of course, was only necessarily a symptom of the mind. Not an accurate measure of physical pain. They wondered if some kind of natural anesthetic defense would kick in? If only the victim could tell us what it was really like! Alas, the sympathetic power of art could only evoke so much. Mickie laughed at their morbid banter, and then they were off again.

Navigating through the totem poles and kiosks, weaving their way through the plaster casts of famous Greek sculptures, the virtual refugee camps of tepees, yurts, bark houses, and skin lodges, bumping against German castle guards, half-clothed men carrying war canoes, and other nearly naked souls in masks wielding rhino-skin shields, bustling Sudanese women in veils, Eskimos with harpoons, Japanese samurai, and a few stranded-looking Laplanders standing on the hot gravel pathway in snowshoes and tending to their equally estranged looking reindeer, they could not have been any less dumbfounded by the cacophony than any other ticket holder or, for that matter, the displaced global villagers themselves.

Pausing to regain their senses in the shade of the palm trees planted outside the Moorish Palace, where they could hear Vienna waltzes pulsing from the nearby *Aeschenplatz*, and the smell of the strange bitter tobacco wafting over from the Turkish Corner, the naturalists surely consulted their map and concluded that Wheeler need not travel to Germany when it was right here, right next to the Amazonian Warrior Village. Indeed, why travel at all now? Not when the fair, which, if anything, was a kind of time machine that had conveniently compressed the entire contents of the world until all things worthy and unworthy were of equal value and equally accessible and therefore positively irrelevant. What was the point of adventure at all? Ah yes, Wheeler might have said, but what about the insects? The fair organizers had not thought of everything, after all.

TO MOMENTARILY ESCAPE the chaos of the Midway, the three friends ducked into Electricity Hall. Once inside, after viewing a few of the more kinetic exhibitions, they would have found themselves on the other side of a heavy curtain partition. They had entered into a parlor of some sort. The room was thick with cigar smoke and murmurs, and the men and women already there were packed in tightly around some evident object of interest.

As they shoehorned themselves in, they saw how everybody was waiting on a man in the middle of the room, bent over, with his back turned, peering down into what looked like a plain cabinet. The cabinet stood about four feet high, was shaped something like a coffin—or half a coffin, at any rate, planted upright—but with some sort of viewing device mounted to the top. After a few moments, the man laughed, straightened himself, shook his head in disbelief, and then encouraged the next person in line to step up. Somebody said the cabinet was a machine called the Kinetoscope—the latest invention by Mr. Edison, the Wizard of Menlo Park, who'd created the phonograph, the telegraph, and an earlier version of this contraption called the Zoetrope. Of course, he'd also invented the electric bulbs which lit up the White City at night.

The way people giggled after looking into the peephole, you might have guessed that whatever it was was just going to be some kind of tawdry lark at best. That is, except for the look of complete befuddlement—or was it fear?—that accompanied each departing face. Still the crowd moved forward.

If only because he was eager to get on to Ethnology Hall to see his horses, it would probably not have crossed Carl's mind that whatever was inside the cabinet was unsuitable for the eyes of his female companion; he gave Mickie a nickel to go first. Handing Carl or William her hat, she bent over as tactfully as possible, peering down into the box's innards, which rattled and creaked surreptitiously, without giving away the merest hint of what it revealed to its audience one solitary witness at a time. When she looked back up her expression was of utter bafflement. *Carl, you'll never!* Beseeched to look and make sense of it himself, Carl dropped a coin in the slot and lowered his eyes to the viewfinder, resting his hands on his knees, a cigarette still burning between his fingers. As he stared down into the dark, waiting, he was only aware of the sensation of the brass portal, still warm from Mickie's face. After a moment came a *clunk* and the grinding of a motor and then the soft creak of reels starting up. Then, suddenly, the light hit his eyes.

In the next moment, he would find himself staring at the figure of a rotund little man: with a black walrus mustache, wearing a broad silk tie, a tweed blazer, and a flimsy white paper shirt collar. The warmth of the lantern and the hot smell of the cellulose nitrate—not entirely unlike the odor of chemicals Carl had used himself to de-pest exhibits at the museum—was oddly soothing. The man in the box had a mildly facetious expression, as if self-conscious of being observed. Against a background of pure black, he held a white handkerchief in his right hand, twiddling his nose with his left. He blinked a few times as if something were about to come over him, and then his nose began to crinkle. As soon as whatever it was had passed through him he reared back, hands rising in feeble protest, eyes pinched, until his head suddenly lunged forward and in one spastic motion he sneezed into the tightly clutched handkerchief. In an instant it was over.

Despite the jostling crowd behind him, Carl dropped another nickel in the slot and waited. Inside the box the motor hummed and the soft clack of the sprockets started up as forty feet of celluloid began its short squeaky safari around each of the eighteen velvet-covered wooden spools. As the cells flickered to life once more, shutters clicking away, the man reappeared and twiddled his nose and sneezed exactly as the first time. When the light went out, it was hard not to wonder what the man did next. Not that it could have been all that interesting, but, still, the desire to see what happened next was there all the same. Did he pocket the handkerchief? Did he sneeze again? Regardless, for Carl, his first encounter with motion picture technology would have left his mind reeling. What if one could preserve the world this way—*actually moving*—to trap an image, to observe it repeatedly, this intimately, as often as one needed until you got it right.

Carl let the cigarette go cold between his fingers. If he was of a fatalistic temperament, he might have entertained the uneasy notion that this technology could potentially obviate the need for his own chosen art altogether. If one wanted to observe a wild animal, to really capture its essence, with such an instrument you would no longer have to kill it first. The future would need no taxidermists. But Carl Akeley was of no such temperament. Even if given to sulky moods, he was ultimately an optimist. And being a man of his time—that is to say, optimistically inventive—why wouldn't he use this very technology to *improve* his art? If nothing else, he had found a new tool. He was as happy as if he'd discovered the recipe for arsenic itself.

CHAPTER EIGHT

A T FIRST, MICKIE HAD BEEN DREAMING OF PARIS. ALMOST AS if she could still smell the freshly baked baguettes from the French Pavilion. She dreamed of croissants and cafés, of wine and snails, of artists in puffy shirts painting at easels. If she'd known any French, she would have practiced under her breath, as she pressed out each wax leaf and let it cool between her fingers. They were working on a new deer group, and she was making the artificial foliage. The idea had been to go to Paris for Carl to formally study sculpture, and then maybe submit this new installation—if they could finish in time—to the upcoming Paris Exposition. It had all been her idea; she had practically talked him into it. It was just so dreamy. To picture him up on a ladder against a block of marble, with his sleeves up and suspenders down, chipping away with hammer and chisel. She knew how badly he wanted to be considered a real sculptor. To be taken seriously. In Paris he would have studied with the best while she wandered the city, visiting museums and galleries, floating along the esplanades and allées, learning the refined things in life. Then when they came back, she wouldn't just be a simple little farm girl anymore. She would be world traveled. She would have acquired for herself that most subtle aura of *l'expérience*. And so they'd thrown themselves into the work. It was a special job, one Carl was doing at his own expense and in great secrecy. A piece where he hoped to bring together a number of his novel ideas, a piece that would bring it all to the next level. Talk about a labor of love; this was it. Mickie had done everything to help. To gather accessories, she had even made several brave trips alone to the woods of northern Wisconsin, hiking through the forest with a heavy backpack, taking photographs of trees, stopping now and then to gather up moss or lichen, or to make a plaster mold of a leaf or flower. But the harder they worked, the harder it got to make ends meet. Already two years had passed since they'd begun the deer group, and it was still nowhere near being done. Too much of Carl's time was spent patching fur coats just to pay their rent.

And then Paris somehow fizzled.

It was disappointing. Carl had been as far as Toronto and New York City. She had been nowhere but Chicago. Which had been such a dingy town, at least outside the White City. Everything hung under a pall of coal soot. The clean new buildings clashed with the mountains of rotting garbage in the alleys below. The everywhere smell of horse manure. The slums and canals clogged with floes of trash and the clockwork shriek of hogs from the mechanized slaughterhouses. And those eerie edifices called skyscrapers—you had to crane your neck so. It was hard not to be afraid they'd fall right over on you as you walked underneath; people said one was actually ten stories tall! You couldn't step out in the street without being run over by a dozen wagons going thirteen different ways, and the sound of saws and hammers and steam-powered rivet guns practically cut you in half. How did people who lived there manage to keep their heads from exploding? You could almost feel the city growing up around you like a hive being built before your eyes—clanging trains and trolleys and chuffing steam and everyone working like mad to make everything as tall as possible, as if a flood were on its way that very night. Telegraph wires going every which way made it nearly hard to tell which was up and which was down; they looked like a tightrope walker's net strung upside down overhead. Passing from the train station to the fairgrounds, if she'd caught a glimpse of herself in one of the panes of plate glass bound to a dray, destined for one of those rising towers, she would have seen the comical look of an awestruck girl gripping her hat, caught in the tide of a nation on the cusp of empire.

Paris was dead. But then another opportunity arose.

It turned out that Carl's old friend Wheeler, who was over in Germany, had met the director of the British Museum, and he had told him all about Carl, how he was the greatest unrecognized genius of his time. And so an invitation had arrived—the British Museum asking Carl to come help resurrect its own moldy collection. It wasn't Paris, but it would be steady, dignified museum work. Carl couldn't afford for them both to travel, but once in England he would get the money to send for her. In the meantime she'd stay and keep working on the deer.

She stopped for a moment to wipe the sweat from her upper lip. To keep the wax pliant, she had to keep the room blazing hot. She blew on a leaf before setting it down alongside the others. Then she cut a square of the thin cotton batting and lay it across the plaster mold. Like the fossil of a beech leaf. For each tree she had made six or so molds for variety of size, then the mold was fitted into a vise like a lemon squeezer. She cut a short length of thin copper wire and held it where the central vein and stem would go, then poured melted wax from the double boiler bubbling on the stove. When she clamped down the vise, the wax oozed out the sides, and then she plunged the whole works in a pail of cold water.

The room was so hot she was able to work practically naked. Her knees were spotted red, and the floor was spattered with hot wax. Drips smoking on the stove made the studio smell like church. Like snuffed candles.

Half-finished deer lurked around her in varying degrees of genesis.

She gently lifted out the cast, trimmed the batting with a pair of snippers, and, twirling the leaf, slowly inspected it. Even colorless, a pale translucent white, it had all the filigreed detail of the veins. She would consult her color notes later before painting. After a while the work became hypnotizing. A pleasant repetition. All in all she'd done how many thousand? You lost count after a while. Sometimes she must have felt like she was turning into a tree herself. As always, Carl had invented and patented the method. For more complex things, like pinecones, or maple keys, or delicate flowers, he cast metal dies from the plaster molds. They were assembled one petal at a time. She set the wax leaf down on the newspaper with the other few dozen already finished that morning. She wouldn't have bothered to read the headlines. What business was it of hers whether the new income tax would or wouldn't be overturned by the Supreme Court? Better to focus on the trees than the forest. Best to focus on the leaves than the trees. At the end of the day she would have a hundred or more surrounding her on the studio floor. Each individual leaf and sprig of clover as detailed as the deer themselves. Exact replicas. No one yet had seen this piece they were working on. But this was the level of mimicry Carl was after. As if they weren't taxidermists but counterfeiters.

Her blistered fingers were proof of the painstaking work already done. Lord knew how many years it would take to finish the whole thing. Not just one diorama but four giant dioramas set together like four rooms. In each suite a scene of the same family of deer—though, of course, not really the same four deer but sixteen different deer playing the same parts—arranged over each season. Like four time-lapsed portraits, taken at intervals of the same square of forest at different times of year. In spring, the deer seem to be just coming to, sniffing at the thaw in the air, the trees studded with light green buds and flowers nubbing up through the damp earth. Summer would find the family at the bank of a lush stream, the buck stepping into the water, antlers covered in sparkling velvet. Not only did the foliage change in each diorama, but the deer had been collected at the peak of each season to show the accurate phases of pelt and antlers. In autumn the grazing deer have lost their reddish brown coat to a bluish gray. The buck's velvet hangs like a molting spider. The fall leaves would be the most complex to reproduce. She would tint the wax first and let the reds and yellows bleed together. By winter the buck's neck and shoulders are fuller. His antlers hardened. The doe nibbles at a sprig of mallow poking through the artificial arsenic-laced snow. The fawn nestles down in it. Hundreds of pounds of confectioner's sugar blanketing the ground, caulked over the bare branches. This was the one season where she wouldn't have to make so many leaves.

She could not really picture London. But Carl was on his way now, and she would follow as soon as possible. Carl had told her about Mr. Bruce, his first employer, the man who'd told him about Ward's, and he was British, and very nice from what Carl had said, and besides England *was* very close to France, wasn't it? Thinking of Mr. Bruce would have naturally led her to think of Mr. Ward and how Carl's old boss had gone bankrupt after the World's Fair. Ward had barely been able to save himself at the last minute. He'd had to sell all the wonders he'd shipped to the exposition—thirty cars of crystals and dinosaur fossils, meteorites and all sorts of stuffed things—to the department store man Marshall Field. Mr. Field had bought Ward's collection to put in his brand-new natural history museum. The museum itself was being converted from what had been the domed Palace of Fine Arts—the same building where she remembered Carl and Wheeler dwelling over that horrible sculpture of the bear eating the Indian—its collection built up from all the artifacts left behind after the rest of the White City was dismantled.

Among those artifacts was Carl's own bronco, with its mounted warrior chief. Carl was actually planning to stop in Chicago on his way to New York, where he was supposed to catch the boat to England. Just to take a look. After all, it wasn't every day he got a big piece put in a big city museum.

She looked at the winter deer. Maybe the British Museum would buy the entire piece when it was finished. How cold a place was England? She had certainly wondered how she'd dress. She'd probably need a whole new wardrobe. But she shouldn't be thinking about clothes when they didn't have money for her passage yet. Even if he never made a cent, though, they had each other—or at least they'd be together again soon—and that was enough. She wasn't the kind of girl who was going to whine to her man about needing a whole new wardrobe. She didn't want Carl to think she was foolish the way so many other girls were. More than anything, she wanted to be taken seriously. Maybe that's why she came off as stubborn. Not looking frivolous took a lot of energy. It was okay when she was with Carl. He didn't make her feel like she was just a twit. He said they would get married as soon as he could afford it—and that was partly what kept her going, building this forest one leaf at a time, as if each leaf were a penny for her dowry. The sooner they finished, the sooner they could sell it.

Of course the work kept her mind off being alone too. It wouldn't have been hard to feel abandoned if she'd let herself. Who knew when he would send for her, or if he'd decide once he was there that he liked the London girls better than the simple farm girl from Beaver Dam. On the other hand, was he really going to find another girl willing to do the sort of filthy things she did for him—skinning rodents, reaching her hand back into the hard-to-reach places inside a deer where Carl's wouldn't fit? A girl who'd go off on her own for days at a time all by herself to the bleak forest to gather up leaves and sticks and to fetch bags of moss and dirt because he was a fanatic about getting everything just right?

No matter what, England would have to be better than Milwaukee. Here your clothes always smelled like stale beer, which was maybe worse than dead animals. If he abandoned her here, where would she run away to next?

❧

BUT THEN SHE'D heard from Carl. Sooner than expected. Much sooner. He had made it as far as Chicago, where he'd gotten sidetracked. He'd stopped over at the new Field Museum to see where his horses had ended up, and while there, he had met a most pleasant individual.

He'd been standing in the grand hall, admiring their broncos, which looked as stately as anything displayed in a real museum, when he'd heard the click of footsteps approaching and had turned to see a distinguished-looking gentleman with a meticulously groomed beard and long walrus mustache. The man introduced himself as Daniel Giraud Elliot, the new curator of zoology. But, of course, Carl would have known the name right away. This was one of the great men responsible for establishing the American Museum of Natural History. As adviser to the museum, in its early years, he had persuaded the trustees to purchase the Verreaux collection from Paris—some 220 mounted mammals, 2,800 birds, 400 skeletons of birds, fish, and reptiles—and he had personally donated over 4,000 animal skins himself. He had also been part of the American Museum's first expedition, in 1888, to collect endangered bison from North Dakota. But it was the eminent naturalist who was now gushing over the younger man's work. Elliot was more than aware of Akeley. In fact, he seemed to have been expecting him.

When Carl told Professor Elliot that he was en route to take a position at the British Museum and had only stopped over in Chicago on a lark to look at how his broncos had been put on display, Elliot clasped his hands behind his back and lowered his head, which he gently shook while frowning at the marble floor. It was a shame for America to lose such talent, he said. Especially when the staff right here at the Field were searching for somebody with his type of gift to help build up their new collection. Someone capable of creating the sort of dynamic exhibits Akeley had developed. And then, as if the idea had just occurred to him, he asked by chance whether Carl had thought about staying in America? If the right opportunity arose? What if, in fact, he could persuade him to stay and join them at the Field? He lifted his head and looked Carl in the eye. Perhaps as their chief taxidermist?

Akeley was stunned. But he had to wonder if he took on the job whether they'd go for anything as radical as what he and Wheeler had dreamed up for the Milwaukee Public Museum. Though, of course, that would mean having to adapt his plans from collecting all the mammals of Wisconsin to all the mammals of Illinois, which couldn't be all that different really. But Dr. Elliot had nothing like that in mind. Surely, one priority would be to repoison the skins of the enormous collection inherited from Ward's. It needed sprucing. There was a lot of work to starting up a new museum. But, no, Carl was far too valuable an asset to just tend to their skin beetle woes. In fact, Elliot hoped he would help him begin to procure *new* collections as well. More to the point, Elliot said, his long mustache rising with his smile, how would Carl feel about joining him on an expedition to Africa?

PART TWO

~⚬~

Ahab on the Veldt

CHAPTER NINE

Nothing short of Dante's description of the Inferno could do it justice. Without any wish to swear, but as merely stating a simple fact, it is a veritable Hell on earth.

—Daniel Giraud Elliot

THE CITY OF BERBERA SMELLED OF FRANKINCENSE AND MYRRH. The incense curled lazily upward from smoking copper pots, intoxicating the street bazaar with its resinous aroma. The air in the ancient seaport was hot enough, it could have smoked on its own. A sultry breeze off the Red Sea rustled through the lonely palm trees growing along the white beaches where urchins collected coconuts near the crumbling Portuguese and Arab fortresses that had served the slave trade—from the sixteenth and seventh centuries, respectively—only until the very recent past. Now, instead of slaves, Africa's vast stores of untapped resources (rubber, copper, tin, cotton, and diamonds) had brought back the Western powers in search of raw materials to stoke the fires of Industry. Great Britain now controlled this impoverished blister of a town. The rest of Somaliland was, more or less, however tentatively, in the hands of the Italians.

Out on the water, in the Gulf of Aden, a lateen-rigged dhow rolled in the waves, while several white-robed fishermen labored at the long bow hauling in a dripping net. Arab merchants hawked pottery and jewelry from Mozambique, cloves from Zanzibar, and Indian traders sold ostrich feathers, incense, coffee and honey, ivory, and rhinoceros horn brought in from the interior by German hunters. Somali women in long black robes carrying skins filled with water or soured goat's milk milled about the yellow dirt streets. The scene was like something out of the Old Testament. All that was missing were camels. Not that there should *not* have been camels. On the contrary, the place should have been crawling with them. Under normal circumstances, it would have been nearly impossible to walk down the street without stepping in the sun-baked piles of dung. The distinguished Daniel Elliot would have liked nothing better than to dirty his new boots with a gob of dromedarian slobber.

But there were few camels to be found for the party from Chicago. The Italians in their incompetent and belated attempt to join the scramble for colonies had used up the lot of the beasts in their recent, catastrophic military foray into Ethiopia. A defeat which would earn them the opprobrious honor of being the only European power to be routed by an African nation.

The rest of the European powers had already managed to slice up the entire continent among themselves. The French had the fatter parts of the western continent; the British controlled Egypt and the Suez Canal, the Red Sea, South Africa, and the happy hunting grounds of Maasailand; the Portuguese had Angola and Mozambique; the Germans had German East Africa, South-West Africa, Cameroon, and Togoland; the Belgians possessed the rubbery heart of the continent, the Congo—which, since Édouard Michelin's patent for the pneumatic tire in 1891, was turning out to be one of the only colonies that was actually paying for itself, however murderously; the Spanish had their token outpost in Rio de Oro and a fingernail with a scratch of gold clinging to the tip of Morocco; and then the Italians, in a secret deal with the British, who desired only to keep it out of the hands of the French, had nabbed the desolate and profitless minicolony of Eritrea and, with it, most of coastal Somaliland. Now, in their haste to catch up with the other European nations, Italy had gone and attempted to extend its paltry imperial holdings into Ethiopia with bogus treaties.

General Oreste Baratieri, the governor of Eritrea, had secured his treaty with neighboring Ethiopia, that more verdant and arable landscape the general had long envisioned as an idyllic locale for Italian settlers to grow olives and wheat and coffee, by courting its supreme sultan, Emperor Menelik II, with five thousand modern rifles and two million lire's worth of ammunition to defend his empire against rival warlords. All of the European powers accepted Italy's claim, except for the French and Russians, who continued to supply rifles and ammunition to Menelik once he realized how he had been deceived.

In fact, Baratieri had presented Menelik with a different treaty altogether. One that failed to clarify the key point whereby Italy would now legally hold the entirety of his country as a protectorate—a particularly galling sticking point when Menelik believed all he had given away in exchange for the guns was a small scrappy province to the south, which, technically, belonged to a rival sultan and was therefore no more desirable to him than that other wastrel of a colony, Somaliland.

To Carl Akeley, Somaliland hardly resembled the lush jungly Africa he'd imagined. It was arid and waterless and devoid of vegetation. It was nothing more than a miserable desert. In fact, to evoke the popular metaphor of the period, if Africa was a cake that had been divvied up between the major powers of Europe—a *magnifique gâteau africain*, as King Leopold II of Belgium liked to say—and the Belgian Congo was a big rich moist banana cream pie, and German East Africa was a Black Forest cake (with Kilimanjaro's glaciered peak as frosting), if the British and French holdings were an assortment of madeleines, mincemeats, and Yorkshire puddings, then Italian Somaliland, that crusty excrescence on the Horn, where Elliot and Akeley found themselves come April of 1896, sans camels, sans clue, was as slender and dry as a week-old biscotti.

※

THE PARTY FROM Chicago had not originally planned to come to Somaliland. In fact, to say they had any real plan at all would be an overstatement. It was almost as if they had boarded their ship in New York Harbor on March 4, 1896, waited until they were halfway across the Atlantic, and flipped a coin to pick their destination. At first, Elliot thought perhaps they would go farther south, to the verdant plains of Mashonaland, but in London they were told it would be unsafe, considering how the Ndebele were in revolt against their British protectors, still miffed, it seemed, at Cecil Rhodes, who'd caught them off guard in 1893, rolling in his machine guns and seven-pounder field guns while the natives were in the throes of a smallpox epidemic and too weak to fight back. Even after looting their country, killing thousands, slapping a "hut tax" on the survivors, and introducing the concept of forced labor, the British were still caught wholly unaware when, three years later, the Ndebele started hacking settlers to pieces with machetes, shooting white officers, spearing women and children like antelope in the street, and generally "making breakfast" of every white face they saw.

"A small party like mine," Elliot explained to his boss, "probably would have been exterminated in short order."

On second thought, he briefly considered going into German East Africa and hunting in the more clement zone around Mount Kiliman-jaro. But there, too, the Masai—a notoriously brutal race of warriors—were in revolt against their Teutonic overlords. It would not do to put themselves in the vicinity of that mess either.

Elliot, meanwhile, had tucked away in the back of his mind a chat he'd had before leaving with a seasoned explorer by the name of A. Donaldson Smith, who, as it happened, had traveled to Somaliland only a few years earlier, in 1893. Though Smith had been in search of a pas-sage to Lake Lamu, he remarked to Elliot how, passing through the Ogaden, a region which straddled the border of Somaliland and Ethio-pia, he had seen good-sized herds of kudu, a majestic species of elk-sized antelopes the Field Museum hoped to acquire.

That was good enough for Elliot. He needed to make a decision, and quickly. Though they'd planned on an eight-month expedition, Elliot discovered to his chagrin, en route, that he only really had enough funds for two months.

Everything—from camels to porters—was going to cost more than planned. A headman alone would cost $120 a month. He calculated that he'd need $4,000 more; and since he was still waiting to hear back from Chicago in reply to urgent wires he'd already sent begging for more money, he did not want to further muddle his prospects with a lack of certain destination. Disregarding rumors of growing friction between Italy and Ethiopia, he quickly decided Somaliland would have to do.

What Elliot couldn't have known was that, just before his own arrival, General Baratieri, sensing his countrymen's growing lack of confidence in the way he had so far handled the conflict, would go ahead and invade Ethiopia. Having no reason to fear going up against a bunch of savages armed with sticks and weapons they wouldn't even know how to use—he had cleverly made sure the bullets he'd given them didn't fit the rifles—he bragged to Italian newspapers that within a few days he would bring back Menelik "in a cage."

Perhaps he had not taken into consideration the fact that the French ammunition actually fit the weapons. Nor that Russian artillery specialists had been helping to train the growing Ethiopian army for months. Nor, of course, did it help Baratieri's campaign that intelligence reports he'd received prior to advancing three battalions into the rugged hills of Adowa had wildly underestimated by half the number of the enemy now gathering in said rugged hills of Adowa—so that as his men tried to create flanks on the awkward escarpment, they were doing it with a mere thirty thousand enemies in mind, when, in fact, the unified tribes of Ethiopia had risen to seventy thousand, outnumbering Baratieri's forces five to one.

"These enemies have advanced, burrowing into the country like moles," Menelik said. "With God's help I will get rid of them."

General Baratieri would chew on his hubris right up to the fatal moment when the clatter of swords and war drums and buffalo hide shields began to thunder and echo in the stony canyons, and a stampede of barefoot warriors surged up out of the dry gorges, rising like a sudden flood, agleam with crimson war paint, a torrent of spears and daggers and finely tuned French and Italian rifles pouring out of the ravines, down and up and over the warped scarp, clambering over boulders, led forward by priests in full liturgical regalia bearing processional crosses, and Emperor Menelik himself astride a horse bedecked in a scarlet saddlecloth (his regal head shielded from the midafternoon sun by a golden parasol born aloft by a nimble servant), cavorting above the smoking mayhem, and urging the Abyssinians to fight to the death or until the stupefied children of Romulus were smote.

Helplessly, the Italian general watched as his battalions were vaporized in a dazzling scrum of spears and cannon fire. When the dust cleared, the rocks were strewn with the mangled corpses of 4,133 of Rome's finest soldiers. Another 2,000 had been led away on a five-hundred-mile march to Addis Ababa as prisoners. In addition to these casualties, another 4,000 *askari,* or native soldiers conscripted from Eritrea, were killed or captured, the prisoners subjected to the ritual amputation of their left hand and right foot. Not since the Battle of Adrianople against the Visigoths of A.D. 378 had Rome suffered such a humiliating defeat.

❧

As they steamed down the Red Sea, Elliot's vessel would pass retreating Italian naval ships going in the opposite direction, the blood-swabbed decks crowded with the wounded and dead. By this point it was too late to turn back. He had received the money from Chicago. And then, once halted in Berbera, he was soon too obsessed with the difficulty of mustering up enough camels to worry about anything else. After several weeks, they had only been able to scrounge up thirteen camels—sixty-seven fewer than Elliot calculated he'd need—making up the difference with a motley assortment of mules, donkeys, and extra foot porters, enough, at least, to get started. They would pick up more camels later. By the end of April, it was time to begin their long southern trek toward the Ogaden, the very region over which Italy and Emperor Menelik had come to war. But Elliot had waited long enough. They were tired of delays and, quite truthfully, could no longer afford them now that the trustees had grown impatient. Besides, there was important work to do now. They were headed into the interior in hot pursuit of *Equus asinus somalicus*. Otherwise known as the African wild ass.

❧

Mickie herself wouldn't have recognized Carl as he set out on this first leg of the trip. On the boat ride over, he had let a beard unfurl from his still boyish face, and he had grown morbidly skinny, having vomited half his body weight into the Red Sea. "Akeley is a new man or ought to be," Elliot wrote in his diary from aboard the SS *Britannica*, "for there is not much left of him but his outside skin. Neptune has the rest."

Now, as he headed into the desert on his mule, his clothes hanging off his shriveled scarecrow frame, he looked like a mystic from some order of castaway mendicants. That is, except for the porkpie hat he had inexplicably chosen over a proper sun helmet, one that might actually have protected his thinning pate from the scorching rays.

Riding alongside him, on a strained-looking pony, was the portly Edward Dodson, a taxidermist with a fondness for marmalade whom they had picked up along the way from the British Museum. The two taxidermists, one bone-thin, the other a butterball, were a comical sight as they cantered side by side into the desert, trailing after their Somali guides. Dodson, who had accompanied Donaldson Smith on the 1893 trip to Lake Lamu, had survived a number of scrapes on that gentlemen's expedition, including several skirmishes against natives armed with poison-tipped arrows, a near attack by an enraged elephant, and a capsized dugout canoe that had left the poor man dangling above the river from an overhanging tree branch, squealing and kicking while an alligator snapped at his fat ankles, his porters laughing from the bank. Dodson had also learned a number of hard lessons about the rigors of performing taxidermy in equatorial climates which he would pass on to Akeley.

After they had ascended the first steep escarpment, thirty miles inland from Berbera, they leveled out onto a stark vast tableland, nearly featureless except for the occasional clump of desert grass or dwarf shrub. The few trees they saw looked skeletal, and their pack animals carefully avoided the lethal-looking spiked aloe called "Spanish bayonet." They rode parallel to the faint outline of the rugged mountains to the far north until these too diminished and all that was left to anchor the traveler's eye was the sight of his own loping shadow. To break up the blinding monotony, Akeley fixed his gaze on the bony ridge protruding from his donkey's misshapen skull. The heat radiating from beneath its hooves was so intense it was a wonder the beast did not spontaneously combust and leave him straddling a pile of smoking ash.

Where were the jungles and natives with bones sticking out of their noses? Where were the cannibals and elephants? The Africa of storybooks. What you read about when you read about the interior of Africa. Wherever they were, however, was not the interior of anything. It was a place of banishment, some purgatory on the outskirts of nowhere. If they ever arrived, wherever they were going, Carl had to hope, the interior would be a different story. Anything would be preferable to this endless boredom. Possibly even being boiled alive in a pot and eaten by cannibals.

When Elliot stopped over in the desert village of Mondeira to try to secure more camels from local tribesmen, Akeley and Dodson continued the search farther out into the arid plateau for that other ruminant which had so far eluded their detection. Not only had the Italians made it next to impossible for Elliot to recruit the camels they needed, but their troops had imported with their own livestock the rinderpest virus, which, in seven short years, had wiped out 95 percent of the indigenous cattle along with most of Somaliland's warthogs, giraffes, antelopes, buffaloes, and elands—all species that the museum hoped to obtain. *Equus asinus somalicus,* already the rarest species of the horse family in Africa, could have succumbed to extinction by now for all they knew.

But the Somalis seemed to know where to go. To avoid the heat of the sun, one day the party rose at three o'clock in the morning, ate a small breakfast of oatmeal and coffee, and then started out into the cool desert night. As they traveled, the Somali guides chewed khat leaves to keep themselves awake and sang snatches of songs passed down in the oral tradition for thousands of years, songs about camels and war and love, and songs that grappled with the difficulties of astronomy as they tracked their progress by the shift of stars across the dome overhead. The Somalis had a remarkable memory for poems, memory being crucial for a people without a written alphabet and who lived in a vast featureless landscape where a muddy waterhole or patch of forage might be a day's walk or more. The songs were metrical—a chantlike, alliterative poetry—and the more khat they chewed, the faster and more incoherent became the recitations. Like blind men or dead souls, Akeley and Dodson let themselves be led out into the dark, as if the turbaned men walking alongside the white men's mules were escorts to the next life.

At first, the only sense that they were moving through the dark at all was the swaying warmth of the animals beneath them and the sound of shuffling hoofbeats. As their eyes adjusted, the desert took on an almost subaquatic quality. Here and there they saw the scuttling shadow of a lizard and scorpions the size of small lobsters skittering across the sand. Every once in a while a shadow broke off and flitted across their path, gradually resolving itself into the shape of a hyena or fox. Occasionally, one of the creatures stopped to watch the men pass, hidden but for a pair of green eyes.

As the first glimmer of sunlight trickled over the flat horizon, and the cool breeze of night burrowed back beneath the sand with the other nocturnal creatures, the Somalis unrolled their prayer rugs and knelt toward Mecca, but not before first tucking fresh pinches of khat inside their cheeks. The psychoactive leaf—the leaf of Allah—quickened the Koranic verses on their way to Heaven. Their chanting finished, they rose, clapping sand from their robes, and fixed a small fire out of dried camel dung to boil water for tea. After preparing another breakfast for the white men, cooking biscuits by baking the dough between two sheets of tin over the fire, the guides themselves crouched at a distance to eat their own breakfast of rice and ghee and dates, spitting stones into the pinkening light of the morning desert. It was not until they had traveled three more hours, when the sun had grown higher and more threatening, that one of the Somalis spotted something that looked like a wild ass.

At first, Carl didn't think so. Anyway, it was a long way off, at least four hundred yards, too far to tell. Unable to make out any distinguishing features, he wondered if it wasn't just a stray mule. When they got closer to three hundred yards they could make it out better: an unextraordinary-looking animal with striped legs and a black bristled mane. It was, in fact, the animal they sought. Still, it failed to impress Carl. Even so, as far as he knew, it was the last remaining wild ass in Africa and was therefore now rightly property of the Chicago Field Museum.

With no cover to hide behind, the hunting party approached directly; even when it became aware of their presence, its long ears flipping suspiciously, it did not seem overly alarmed, or perhaps it had only been pretending, because when they got within two hundred yards, the donkey suddenly bolted, disappearing in a clatter of dust up a hillside. At the top, it stopped and looked back down, as if waiting for them to follow. So they climbed up the low rocky hill in pursuit. When they encountered it again, the ass stood a mere one hundred yards away. It appeared to have forgotten about them, and seeing them rematerialize now did not appear to raise any concerns for the animal. This lack of defensiveness on the part of his quarry unnerved Carl, and his first shot sent up a spurt of rock dust well over the animal's shoulder. It didn't even bother to glance up. It kept grazing on a clump of thorn scrub as Carl's wayward bullets continued to reel and crack off the hillside. When he reloaded and fired again—this time remembering to hold his breath as he squeezed the trigger—he heard the tight thump of the bullet against the hide. The blood sparkled like garnets on the rocks. But instead of falling over, the ass merely turned its head from its breakfast and looked at him with a pitiful expression of disbelief. Carl fired again, this time opening a trench in its belly. Still, the ass stood fast. There didn't seem any point in firing again. But, figuring it wasn't going to die properly as long as it remained standing, Carl finally strolled up to the ass and, planting one foot behind its hind leg, gave it a shove, tripping the fool thing onto its side. When it hit the ground it was dead. He was disgusted with the whole ordeal and thought, if this was going to be the life of a museum collector, there wasn't much sport to it.

Soon enough, however, they would have an entirely different battle on their hands. Because after they finished the work of skinning and skeletonizing the donkey, they noticed that their guides were acting shifty. By now, though, they would have grown accustomed to the fidgetiness of their khat-addled friends and shrugged it off. They would not discover the true reason for their porters' agitation until they stopped, a short while later, in the shade of a rock face, to clean their guns. Akeley asked his man for a canteen. Skinning the ass had left him parched, and he also wanted to rinse the gore from his fingers. He must have known right away from the miserable look on his guide's face. They were out of water. The canteens were dry.

It was approaching midmorning, when the sun would soon grow intolerable. Their guide had assured them that there would be plenty of sources of water along the way, but there hadn't been, and by the time they'd finished with the wild ass, and gotten it packed up on the camels, they still had a five-hour return trip to camp. To go on now without water would be perilous. But after a hurried conference among themselves, which Akeley and Dodson could not understand, one of the guides came back to say he knew of a well that was only an hour's walk. So, with no other choice, they started out, the skinned carcass of *Equus asinus somalicus* draped over one of the camels, its numbered bones packed up into boxes that rattled and shifted against the camel's lopsided sway.

After traveling for much longer than an hour—and in the opposite direction of camp—without coming across anything resembling a well, Akeley and Dodson began to protest, but the Somalis seemed unperturbed. For a while, they trod through a narrow defile, closed in on either side by high stone walls that acted as a tunnel and which drove the hot wind and sand into their eyes, further eroding their resolve. Still, they had no choice but to follow the Somalis; they were not sure they could have made it back to base camp on their own. It was not until four hours later that they came upon the promised well.

It was underneath a half-dead coconut tree; the tattered gray leaves rustled thickly like papier-mâché. The well was just a ditch in the ground, a small crater hewn out of the limestone earth, a broken stone wall surrounding its perimeter. Because there were no other people or animals at the well, they did not have to wait. When one of the Somalis jumped into the hole, with a dirty hollowed gourd clutched to his chest, the others waited to hear the splash. But there only followed the thump of bare feet in the pit. Then the dry scratching sound of the lip of the gourd scooping sand. The guide scratched away like this for an hour. And then he climbed back out of the hole and gave the worn-down gourd to the other guide. They worked in shifts, chipping away, cutting deeper into the sand. But it was hopeless. The well was dry.

God only knew how far from camp they were. It was early afternoon, the most treacherous time of day. The Somalis were used to going for great lengths of time without water, were in fact rumored to be able to go for days without drinking, but Akeley and Dodson were now starting to grow delirious. Their lips were blistered, their tongues were swollen lumps of chalk, and their skulls ached violently. Dodson's pursy face was pink and boiled-over. The porkpie hat Carl wore gave him no protection, and he was still coated in gore which he hadn't been able to wash off, except by rubbing handfuls of sand against his skin.

A few more hours in this heat without water, and they would be goners. They knew they were too far from camp to make it without water, yet there was no direction to go now except back, which they did, but before long they were met by a sandstorm. It came up suddenly as if it had been stalking them and had sprung just at the point when they had grown too weak to resist.

When one of his guides shouted over the wind and flying sand, Akeley could not hear the man, whose voice was further muffled by a muslin scarf. When Akeley fell off the mule, and the guide stood over him still exhorting incoherently, he could have reached up and murdered the man, if only he had the strength in his hands. Finally the Somali succeeded in shouting that he'd remembered another well where they might find water. This one, like the last, was only an hour away. Akeley and Dodson weren't having it. Without the energy to stay upright in their saddles, they unbuckled the girth straps and sought out the leafless shade of a solitary mimosa tree and, using the leather saddles as pillows, covered their faces with the woolen saddle blankets while they awaited the return of their guides.

For all they knew, they were being abandoned. They were stranded at least a day from camp without water. But they did not have the strength or the will to do anything about it. Moaning under his blanket, Dodson looked like an overfed shrouded corpse, already half buried in the blowing sand. Each time Carl peered out, to relieve himself from the stifling hot air under the mule-stinking blanket, or to see if the Somalis were on their way back, the sand singed his eyes. So, with the blanket pulled back, in the twilight of his woolen cave, and the sandstorm whistling eerily outside, he pulled the locket Mickie had given him before he'd left from under his shirt to look at her gently mocking blue eyes, then fell asleep.

There was no telling how much time had passed when Akeley felt a nudge in his ribs and lifted back the blanket to see one of the guides standing over him. The sandstorm had subsided, but it was much, much hotter. The Hamite still had the same forbidding look he'd had after climbing out of the first well. There was no water at this one either. After telling him the bad news, the Somali shrugged, as if that closed the affair, and Akeley let the blanket fall back over his face. There was nothing now but wait to die. He was too tired to do anything else. As he felt his innards slowly cooking, he smelled something foul and looked out from under his blanket to see the Somalis, sitting cross-legged before a small crackling fire, roasting a lizard. A little while later Akeley felt himself being prodded in the ribs again.

His gun bearer stood over him with a stick and a wild giddy expression on his face. He was animatedly pointing out in the desert. Akeley turned his head and saw several vaporous figures approaching in the distance. As the figures emerged from behind the scrim of heat, he saw it was a caravan. In another moment the wide horns of cattle came into focus, and he could hear the faint timbreless clink of a cowbell. Akeley told the gun bearer to go negotiate with the nomads for water, then put his head back under the blanket. It was only a while later that the Somali poked him again with his stick. This time he jabbed him hard. The man was shrieking and waving his arms and pointing at the caravan, which Akeley, sitting up with difficulty, saw was actually now receding. As it passed them by, the wagon's spindly wheels creaked in the sand. The ensemble of overburdened animals clattered by with bowls and misshapen wooden utensils. On the camels' backs, Carl saw, were several skins swollen to bursting, beaded with moisture. The Somali was jabbering and near tears. He said that the nomads had said the white men could die for all they cared. *Could die for all they cared?* Akeley, cursing and spitting sand, hoisted himself against the skinny bole of the mimosa and picked up his rifle. He dug around with weak fingers for a cartridge from his gun belt, shunted one into the chamber, and yanked the bolt. He took his aim at the back of the nomad holding the reins, trying to steady his bead on the man's ratty turban—his arms were shaking—and gave Dodson a kick. Dodson stuck his boiled turnip face out from the blanket and rasped, "What the bloody hell is it?"

He told him to pick up his gun.

"I've got the one on the left," he said. "You take the other."

Did he really have it in him? To murder in cold blood?

As they were about to fire, his Somali went berserk and started screaming at the departing nomads, who, upon seeing their situation in a new light, decided to negotiate, and soon their guide was returning with one of the filthy dripping skins. It turned out to be not water but soured goat's milk. It was warm as blood and tasted not faintly of dung, but all that mattered now was that it was gloriously wet.

❦

AFTER A MONTH, Elliot had finally managed to buy enough camels to carry the many barrels of salt that would be needed to cure all the skins they planned to collect. However, after traveling with Akeley and Dodson a hundred miles deeper into the desert, as they got closer to the Ogaden, he had to abandon most of his caravan, including the armed Somalis, in Adelah, since they didn't have enough camels to carry both water and salt, and since salt was almost as important now to their purpose as water was to their survival. Thanks to southern monsoons, a fierce wind had picked up and would not cease for many weeks. It was a constant battle to keep the tents from flying off, and for days at a time conversation became pointless as their words were ripped from their mouths and cast away like tumbleweeds. The camels, for the most part stoic, moved forward against the grit-filled wind with their long wincing faces turned sideways. Somewhere between Baferug and Deregodleh Akeley turned thirty-three years old.

Once they reached the Toyo Plain, come mid-June, Elliot felt the onset of malaria. He had chills and could barely stay on his horse. Even with an ample supply of quinine tablets, Elliot was an old man and more vulnerable than his colleagues to the sporozoan parasites curdling his red blood cells. He urged the others to go on with the work they had come to do, and to leave him be; he would recover soon enough. After a few days, he couldn't get up out of his cot, and while his tent boy stayed behind to nurse him, Akeley and Dodson went hunting for hartebeest. In general, by now, the rinderpest had already weakened the hartebeests enough that any native so inclined—and many were inclined—could approach the dying animals by foot, kill them with their bare hands, and take their hides. It was not that much more difficult for Akeley and Dodson.

Akeley had also begun to experiment with the camera that he'd bought in Chicago for twenty-eight dollars. An Empire State No. 2. It was a favorite among professional commercial photographers, made of hand-polished mahogany, and looked like an accordion on a tripod. In the catalog Carl had marked the 5×7 for \$23 "sow"; the $6^{1}/_{2} \times 8^{1}/_{2}$ for \$25 "pig"; and the 8×10 for \$28 "hog." In the end he went whole hog. The camera was a way for him to make extensive studies of the animals' anatomy—vivid postmortems—prior to skinning. Considering the state of the technology, it was a pioneering thing for him to do. "Field photography was in its infancy," as Frederic Lucas, a fellow graduate of Ward's, and later director of the American Museum of Natural History, wrote, "in the stage when it was not so difficult to photograph a bird in the open as it was to find the bird in the photograph." Just six years earlier, in fact, at a meeting of the American Ornithologists Union, a member had "pointed with pride to a photograph of a gull, stating that it was his one success in 150 negatives."

Well into the night, while the others relaxed around the campfire, drinking whiskey and listening to the Somali storytellers recount the day's adventure in elaborate pantomime and song, Akeley would be in his tent developing the glass plates. He was an obsessive and tireless worker, to the point that Elliot, hardly able to care for himself, worried about the younger man's health. Long after the others had gone to bed, they could hear the clip of his shears as he sat by the dying fire, with the skin of a boar's head in his lap, bristles turned inside out, trimming and flicking gobbets of fat into the sizzling coals.

※

ONE AFTERNOON, WHILE Elliot was still sick, slumped in his canvas chair, taking up the only square of shade for forty miles, and Akeley was in the middle of skinning out a male hartebeest he'd bagged on the morning hunt, they saw an army of horsemen appear on the ridge. They were just a small band of men now: Akeley, Dodson, and Elliot, who looked like a scarecrow propped up in his chair, though one who instead of deterring birds had drawn the attention of a black ring of vultures wheeling slowly overhead. They had retained just a few porters, who now sat up nervously and watched the spears gathering on the hillside. There were only half a dozen or so guns between them, but these were not readily available at the moment, since the gun bearer in charge of cleaning them still had the necessary parts disassembled and laid out on a rug in the shade of the cook's tent. Not that it would have helped much. On the ridge, there were at least three dozen horsemen, maybe more.

Finally, one of the horses broke from the line and raced down the slope, raising a cloud of sand in its wake. Akeley wiped his knife and waited. The horse came to the edge of camp, and its rider spoke with one of the tent boys and then galloped the short distance over to where Elliot sat lifelessly under his tree. The messenger's horse was adorned with colorful knotted tassels dangling from its saddle and bridle, looking strangely festive in the barren landscape. Without dismounting, the messenger began to chant—while the tent boy calmly translated for Elliot—before turning and galloping back to the top of the ridge. By this point Akeley and Dodson had come over to Elliot, and as they did so, a cry went up—*Mot!*—and the riders on the hill suddenly started at once down toward their camp. Akeley looked at the oncoming cavalcade—at the warriors bearing two spears each over their heads, some with clubs and swords jouncing at their sides—and asked Elliot what the messenger had said. In a weak voice, Elliot said that the messenger had informed him that they were in the land of the Habr Yunis, who were ruled by Sultan Nuir, and that this would be the sultan and the royal family coming to bid them welcome. To look at the descending horde, however, Carl was not entirely inclined to dispel the possibility that they were about to be hacked to pieces.

The cavalry pulled up just short of Elliot's chair, sending up a plume of sand. In the center of this band of nomadic warriors was the sultan, a harrowed-looking man of at least sixty, very tall and spare, sitting erect in his saddle throne and holding a long spear in his fist. Akeley and Dodson stood stiffly behind Elliot. For what seemed a long while, no one made a motion to dismount, the riders looking over the men of science and the men of science looking over the king's menacing escort. Then the messenger started a new chant. Again, Elliot's tent boy translated, letting the white men know that the sultan welcomed them to his country, that as soon as he had learned of their presence he had hastened to make this visit, and that the Europeans and his people must be firm friends; only in this way would they be invincible and fear no one. Carl couldn't help but wonder what would happen when they found out they had no guns to trade. But this did not seem to be what the sultan was after. For the lengthy duration of the sultan's speech, the royal escort sang in a loud rhythmic chant. After a while it had a trancelike effect on the listeners.

When the song was finished, the sultan dismounted, and with some difficulty, Elliot was helped to his feet so the two men might shake hands. Then Elliot ordered that a pot of coffee be made and for his tent boy to bring the king a seat. The only high-back chair in camp was brought out and placed in the shade under the thorn tree beside Elliot's. As soon as the sultan was seated, Elliot drooped back down into his own chair. When the coffee was poured, though, he rallied enough to fulfill his duties as host—or guest; it was unclear. Because once they were comfortable, Sultan Nuir clapped his hands, at once dispersing his retinue, who rode off and entered into the formation of a circle. Then, with a shout—*Mot!*—the horses began a sort of orchestrated prancing: the circle broke, and they faced off against each other in mock battle, the warriors unsheathing their double-edged swords, and clanged blades as they passed each other. Then the horses came back into their circle, and the carousel quickened, with the riders spinning faster and faster, swords flashing, until a rider or two at a time would break from the circle and suddenly charge toward Elliot, turning sharply at the last second before his chair, and vaulting the horse up on its hind legs so that beast and man towered over him, and when it seemed the horse could stretch no higher into the air, the rider cried *Mot!* In this way each of the horsemen extended his formal welcome. The pageantry would have seemed absurd if not so terrifying.

When the reception came to an end, the sultan regaled Elliot with tales of the ongoing battle in which he was engaged with his rival clan of the Mijjertein. Evidently, they had been at war forever, and his men had the scars to prove it. The sultan himself was not too proud to show his own scars to Elliot, the nastiest of which was on his right leg, above the ankle, where it appeared to Elliot the injury itself had been made more grisly by its cure, a horrible distortion of skin where a red-hot iron or, more likely, a spear held to the coals had cauterized the wound. Elliot leaned over the sultan's leg, peering at the scar, and declared it a veritable "doosey." He told his new friend that he must be sure to take better care of himself, saying how, after all, like Elliot himself, he was no longer a young man, and at this the sultan laughed, the steam from his coffee tickling up over his ancient Hamitic features. It was true. He would have to try to take fewer knocks, but what was one to do? he sighed; such was the life of a desert warlord.

Just before departing, the sultan took notice of the half-skinned hartebeest which Akeley had left off working on upon the Habr Yunis' arrival. Curious, he approached the unfinished animal, gazing at the other striped and spotted skins of gazelles, hyenas, kudus, oryxes, and even the skin of a lion that hung drying around the taxidermist's tent like barbaric pirate flags. Seeing the sultan's interest, they attempted to explain their true purpose here in his land: that the man with the unruly beard and hartebeest blood on his hands was like a magician of sorts, who, when they returned to their own native country, would make the dead animals reappear just as they had in life, suspended for eternity, in something they called a diorama. The sultan seemed perplexed. If their purpose was to make the animal appear alive, why kill it in the first place? Perhaps too confused to object, the old warlord remounted his horse and disappeared back over the ridge, onward to his next battle.

❧

COME AUGUST, AFTER Elliot had recovered sufficiently to travel, they had reunited with the rest of their caravan in Hargeisa, replacing the camels that had either dropped dead or grown ill, and collected enough men and water and more salt—twelve hundred pounds—for the remaining four-month excursion across the border and into the Ogaden. Before embarking on the longest stretch of their journey, Elliot sent a telegram to Frederick Skiff, director of the Field Museum, saying,

MY COMMUNICATIONS TO YOU AFTER THIS WILL
BE VERY IRREGULAR, BUT IF YOU HEAR NOTHING

FROM ME YOU CAN TAKE IT FOR GRANTED THAT ALL IS WELL, FOR EVIL NEWS TRAVELS FAST EVEN IN SAVAGE LANDS.

To REACH THE Ogaden, now, they had only to cross the one hundred miles of forbidding landscape known as the Haud. They slept by day, traveling at night, to avoid the sun. But it would not be the sun that would trouble them here, nor lack of water. It had not rained in the Haud for two years, yet they were met by torrential downpours. The earth turned to a river of slush, bogging down men and animals alike, and as the thunder growled around them, and orange stalks of lightning flared on all sides, the camels simply lay down and refused to budge. There was nothing to do but wait out the storm in their soaking tents, which collapsed around them like boggy skins.

When the rains ceased they continued southeast, until one late morning they came abruptly to the end of the plateau that they had been traveling across for three months and found themselves looking out over the edge, where fifteen hundred feet below, stretched as far as the eye could see, were the yellow plains of the Ogaden.

As bleak as the plains seemed at first, they were not entirely devoid of wildlife. There were rhino tracks near their campsite, and deafening choirs of lions at night. It was one afternoon, here, after Akeley had been hunting for days without luck, that he shot a warthog and then unthinkingly left it in pursuit of an ostrich that he'd seen dash into the tall grass. (He meant to simply collect the warthog on his way back to camp.)

He tracked the bird's fat-taloned prints for several hours, until he figured out that he was actually on the trail of a male and female. A hell of a lucky break. If he could get them to lead him to their nest, and there were any good-sized chicks, he could collect a whole group in one fell swoop.

He followed their strange booming calls and less frequent glimpses of their heavy round behinds trotting ahead through the dense grass. When he lost sight of them, he climbed up onto a nearby termite mound, scanning the grass with his binoculars and waiting. Then, all of a sudden, a tufted blob appeared in his lens. He fiddled with the knob until the bird's skinny rat-head came into focus, and he unslung his rifle, but it was too small a target. Then the other bird poked up its head, and figuring he stood a better chance of hitting at least one, he decided to take the shot, but by the time he took aim, the damn things had ducked out of sight. After repeating this several times, he tired of the game and decided to climb down off the termite hill and go back into the grass after them.

All he found was an empty nest in a small clearing. The sandy ground was so scratched up with tracks, he couldn't tell which way they'd gone off, and for a minute he stood there wondering what to do next. Then he heard a sound, a rustling in the grass, and the ostrich cock came running out. Akeley half aimed and took a wild shot. But before he could chamber another round, the hideous bird vanished back into the bush and again he was alone.

When he saw that the last bit of the day's sun was beginning to flare against the horizon, he started back. But, on his way, when he returned to the spot where he'd left the warthog, he found to his naive dismay only vulture feathers and hyena tracks scattered in the dusty red soil. The entire day had been a complete waste.

He had not gone much farther, however, when he saw a hyena duck ahead into the grass with what he was pretty sure was the head of his warthog in its jaws. He cursed when it slipped away before he could get in a shot, and decided to think about the stiff drink he'd have when he got back to camp. But then, a few steps later, he saw another shadowy figure in the grass and—in the mood to take vengeance for his loss— thoughtlessly fired.

In reply, a high chilling yowl came from the grass. It was not the cry of a hyena at all. Scared now, he fired two more shots and then felt the dry click of the trigger on the third. His rifle was empty. Sensing that he had only wounded whatever he'd just blindly shot at, he ran up a nearby hill, trying to jam a cartridge into the magazine. He jumped over a bank into a dry, sandy riverbed and turned to see if he was being followed. But by the time he registered the black spots and long switching tail springing from the grass it was too late. The leopard knocked the rifle from his hands.

Then lunged for his throat. But, instinctively, Carl twisted—and just in time—as its jaws clamped down on his shoulder instead. Screaming and doing his best to dodge the giant cat's scrambling hind claws, he managed to fall in the right direction and by dint of this accident pinned down the cat with the weight of his body. The cat struggled to right itself in the loose sand, but Carl kept the advantage for the moment. With his knees on its chest, and his elbows jammed in the cat's armpits, he kept its flailing front claws spread clear of his face. If only because Carl's first shot had injured the cat's hind foot, he was still alive. On the other hand, his left arm was still stuck in its jaws.

With no weapon—his rifle and the cartridge now lay in the sand out of reach—all he could do was grip the cat's throat with his free hand and squeeze. He squeezed until he could feel the quick hard pulse tapping under its silken fur. The rapid breath from its nostrils was hot on the skin of his arm. When the cat gagged and gasped for air, its bite slackened momentarily enough for him to slide his arm a few inches before its fangs clamped back down. He squeezed again and slid his arm another inch. Each time, its jaws snapped shut. In this excruciating way Carl progressively dragged the length of his entire arm through the cat's teeth down to his wrist.

It seemed only a matter of who would hold out longer, and since it was he, not the leopard, who was doing most of the bleeding, he resigned himself again to the likelihood of dying. It was growing dark. As he wrestled with the leopard, the stars above seemed to dart and squiggle dizzily. He listened to the crunching of his own flesh, of the fibers of his muscles being shredded, and he suddenly recalled the bronze sculpture in the Palace of Fine Arts he'd seen a few years before at the Chicago World's Fair, of the bear with the Indian's arm in its jaws. He almost laughed, thinking how he'd be able to tell Wheeler exactly what it felt like now. Unfortunately, he probably wouldn't survive the experience, and therefore Wheeler would have to remain in the dark. *Carl, are you thinking, or do you just think you're thinking?* There was not really any pain at all. Only the sound of the crunching of his flesh. And in the midst of the struggle he felt a strange sensation—he thought the word was *joy.* At least the joy of a good fight. The fear and adrenaline had given way to an almost dreamy feeling. He looked deep into the cat's face. Close enough to feel its rumbling purr in his sternum. The cat's shining kohl-lined eyes held his gaze with an eerie patience. Though beneath its terrifying surface the leopard was clearly suffering too. They were suffering together.

He did not feel particularly sorry for himself, except that the whole ordeal made him homesick for Mickie. To anyone walking by, the sight of the young man and leopard entangled, limbs entwined, gnawing and strangling each other to death, and evidently taking their time about it, would have looked as surreal as it must have felt for Akeley, whose consciousness floated in and out in a terrorized daydream until after some untold amount of time he sensed the leopard's campaign was flagging. With the last dregs of his energy, Carl climbed on top of the cat and steadied his knees on its chest. Then he forced down with his full weight and felt a satisfying give, followed by a crack. The cat lurched and let out a muffled whimper. He did it again and felt another rib snap. As he continued strangling the cat with his free hand, he rammed his ensnared fist farther down its throat. The leopard spit and hissed and gurgled violently, but in the end its jaws went limp.

After Carl slid his mutilated arm free, he lay on the ground under the stars until he was convinced he wasn't dead. By the time he got back to camp, blood-drenched, his clothes in shreds, and dragging the leopard's carcass, it was well after dark. At the sight of his arm, his companions looked as if they might be sick. But Akeley was wide-awake. He had quite possibly made the most intimate set of observations of a subject he would ever record.

CHAPTER TEN

H E COULDN'T HELP BUT NOTICE THE OTHER PASSENGERS STAR-
ing. He was on the streetcar, back in Chicago. Rumbling down Michigan Avenue. It was a warm spring day, 1898, his sleeves rolled up, so of
course people were going to stare. Who could help but stare? God, the
man's arm looked like it'd been dragged over by a spike harrow. In spite
of that, in spite of the leopard, his arm hadn't actually been the reason
they'd returned early from Africa. It was Elliot's malaria that had cut
the expedition short. Carl would have gone on with his arm plastered
up, injected full of Borofax, and in fact he had gone on for a while like
that, collecting a dik-dik, a gerenuk, and a few more black-backed jackals, all one-armed. Nobody knew how he'd managed.

Who could blame him if he never wanted to go back to Africa again?
At least, along with thirteen species altogether, he'd collected a lifetime's
supply of dinner party material. Stories he could tell his grandchildren.
Even if he never set foot outside Chicago again—even if he never left his
studio—he had had more than enough adventure to last a lifetime.

The trolley approached Van Buren Street, and people shoved their
way off through the push of new passengers coming up the steps. When
a little girl stared intently at his arm, he buttoned down the sleeve and
scratched at his wrist self-consciously.

Of course if there were going to be any grandchildren to scare with
his stories, he'd have to marry Mickie sooner or later. Just as soon as

things settled. When he had enough money. Maybe, when they did get married, he would take her someplace special. For now he bounced back and forth between the museum and the studio he'd rented on Harper Avenue, where they continued work on the deer project. (And where in a shed in the back he kept several live deer as study models.) The deer had been his experimental lab, where he hoped to work out some of the answers to the problems that kept cropping up with his work, namely that when he got back from Somaliland, some of his animals were starting to go south. The horses he'd done for the World's Fair were already splitting. Other sculptures had begun losing their form. The plaster underneath had dried and cracked. The skins were starting to warp like jack-o'-lanterns. What he needed, he realized, with some terror, was an entirely different medium. Plaster was too heavy—far too heavy if he was ever going to mount anything larger than an ass or an antelope. The thing was to find a substitute—some way to copy the plaster manikin, to make a cast of the cast. Whatever medium he used had to be pliable enough to capture the finest details of the clay model—that subtle topography of the animal's surface—yet sturdy, waterproof, and lightweight.

He watched as a gust scattered a flurry of loose newspapers, some carrying news of Commodore Dewey's squadron moving toward the inevitable showdown with the Spanish in Manila Bay, others bearing the headline "Chris Merry Is Hanged." Merry had gone to the scaffold at the county jail a few days earlier for murdering his wife. He'd beaten her to death after a "family quarrel," he confessed to his guard over a last meal of ham and eggs. As Carl absentmindedly watched the swirling paper, his own mind returned to his problem with the deer.

How to fix his family tableaux for maximum preservation? He'd been held up for months now, tortured, but he needed to figure it out once and for all if he was ever going to populate Mickie's enchanted forest.

Maybe it was when he saw loose newspapers spiral up on a squall from the lake, seeing them hanging there, fooling gravity, that the answer struck him.

Paper? *P*apier.

Papier-mâché.

It jolted him out of his seat as if the trolley had run over the idea itself lying in the street. Such was the force of this idea that he actually stood up and shouted, *I've got it!* People were staring at him now, though not because of his arm. But he didn't care if he looked like a maniac. This was a real eureka moment. If it hadn't been the swirling papers, it would have been something else. It could just as well have been the sight of a doll in the lap of the girl across from him, the kind with a papier-mâché head and painted eyes, painted lips, shiny lacquered cheeks. Wherever the thought had come from, without pausing to yank the cord, he stepped off the moving car and started running back to the museum on foot. He was lucky he hadn't broken his ankle or gotten run over for the price of revelation.

As far as eurekas went, admittedly, it was a bit dull. After all, what better to recall the sticky doldrums of childhood than the scent of paper and glue on a miserable afternoon? But to Carl, papier-mâché was a miracle. Mâché, he knew, would not crack. Its slow-drying nature would be perfect for modeling the most difficult, the most delicate features of eyelid, nostril, lip. The fine details that would give the animal its final beatific expression. In order to make the manikins durable—as well as light—he would layer the mâché with wire mesh, and for bigger animals like the kudu he would use three, four layers. A rhino might require five layers. An elephant, six. (He was thinking back to Jumbo.) He would eventually work all this out. The only hitch now was simple mechanics: how to keep the papier-mâché from sticking to the plaster mold?

It was easy to transfer from clay to plaster; clay was water-soluble, but mâché stuck to the mold like concrete. The question was one of a barrier. A firm prophylactic. But sensitive enough to reproduce the plaster impression—the living fossil—onto the mâché. A skin *between* the skins. He would solve that riddle too before he was halfway up the museum steps. *Muslin!* What could be more perfect? It was delicate, impressionable, and cheap as apples.

Back at the museum, he knelt before the finished plaster mold of a gazelle and began to brush the recessed cavity with glue. Then, over the next few days, with barely an hour of rest, he gingerly worked the diaphanous fabric into each and every crease and fold with his fingertips, patiently shaping the muslin into every muscular contour, every inverted tendon, every wrinkle, every wart, dimple, or protruding systolic vein. If nothing else, going to Africa had given him a new way of looking. Maybe the leopard had transferred something aside from the bacteria under its claws into his bloodstream after all.

When he came back a day later and the muslin had dried—looking something like a gazelle-haunted shroud turned inside out—he sat down and began to mix a batch of papier-mâché. He churned the paste and shredded paper in a bucket. It smelled like the racetracks. Like wallpaper. When it was ready, he began to repeat the process with the gloopy strips, going over the mold again with the same tedious, painstaking attention to detail as he had with the muslin. His arms were starched up to the elbows. He continued bandaging the gazelle's interior, overlapping the wet strips, until his knees ached and his legs went numb. When the effigy was completely dry, after three or four days, he submerged it in a tub to dissolve the glue, to slough the plaster mold, the internal pleura of mâché itself being waterproofed with shellac. When he fit a crowbar down the middle seam and began to pry, bubbles flocked to the surface. Then, with his assistant, he dragged the waterlogged gazelle out of the tub, and the plaster clumped off in their hands like wet bread.

As he beheld the gazelle within, a tight clenched feeling of being on the brink hooked him by the stomach. He had accomplished something like the lost wax method used by sculptors of bronze. A perfect papier-mâché replica of the original clay model. A dewy bone-white gazelle. The skin fit like a wet glove.

How, after this, could he ever again feel like the mere practitioner of some bastard art? He was a sculptor, fine, yes, he had proven himself there. He was an artist. But more important, now he was a *taxidermist*. Finally one deserving of the name. No longer would it seem as if the animals were only trapped in a parallel universe; he now would give his beasts the souls of objects everlasting. He was, in a way, their bard. Who else had ever spoken more eloquently on their behalf?

❧

THREE YEARS LATER, on September 1, 1901, Carl returned to the museum after an errand one day to find everyone in a dither. Something tremendously exciting had clearly transpired. He'd missed whatever it was, but the staff were all eager to tell him about it. Evidently it had some bearing on him personally. Or, more specifically, on his deer. After all, when he'd finally completed the Four Seasons, as he'd named his secret masterpiece, and revealed it to the museum's board, they had purchased it, and were now having it installed in the West Court. It looked like an excavated fairy tale. You could practically hear the cicadas in the summer diorama, smell the moss and wet leaves at the water's edge. No reproduction of nature had ever been made with such specific detail. Nearly five years in the making. It wasn't open to the public yet, but Carl learned that there had been a special visitor that day. *Carl, you won't believe it. He wanted to see you. He was asking for you, Carl.*

Who, who was asking?

The vice president.

Ryerson? Or Ream? The Field Museum had two vice presidents.

Roosevelt.

Who on earth?

Roosevelt. Teddy Roosevelt. He was here looking at the deer.

The vice president. TR. The colonel. Quite possibly the most beloved war hero—no, the most beloved *man*—in America. *Theodore Roosevelt.* He was *here*?

Where were you? Where the hell were you, Carl?

Roosevelt had stopped in Chicago on his way back from a trip west, where he'd delivered an address in Colorado for the state's quartocentennial, waxing evangelical about the bravery of the pioneers and their Restless Quest for Metal Wealth, et cetera, before spending a stormy afternoon here on Lake Michigan, standing stout and stolid on the deck of the naval trainer *Dorothea.* As one officer after another went belowdecks, TR stood fast, talking to whoever would listen, not about politics but about literature, about the poetry of Longfellow and Whitman, and the Norse sagas. He was there making an official inspection of the vessel—an honor of sorts given his former role as assistant secretary of the navy, a position from which he'd famously resigned during the Spanish American War to lead a brigade of volunteer cavalry in Cuba. On this stopover in Chicago, he'd also reviewed the Illinois National Guard, some of whom had likewise served with Colonel Roosevelt at Santiago, when he and his Rough Riders had made their famed charge up San Juan Hill. That he had fought alongside the common men, leading them with saber and pistol, had earned him not only victory but near-universal admiration. Everywhere he went men were eager to shake his hand. Just to get a glimpse of this great war hero.

Here was an immense force of character. A moral turbine. A man who more than embodied his times. He consumed them, chewed them up with his large clapboard teeth, and the people stood in awe of his heroic eructations. It was an unusual voice, not manly per se, but like a viola played on the upper register, strident yet commanding, a voice with "more than a suspicion of falsetto," and so it sounded as it filled the austere halls of the Field Museum, as he strode through with his attendants, one wrist pressed behind his back, taking note of this or that bird or mounted lynx, testing his memory for the Latin of the species, dazzling the staff with his own commodious knowledge of the natural world, then gazing up in awe at the dinosaur (a plaster cast of *Hadrosaurus foulkii*), asking what the latest thinking was regarding the mass extinction of the dinosaurs, and then musing aloud about how much longer this or that species might have until it went extinct— pointing to the relatively unthreatened looking Somali wild ass—the subject of extinction being so much on the public mind that, the same day as his visit, the *Tribune* had published in its joke section:

> "Well," said the oyster. "You're up against it. You are going to be extinct in about twenty-five years."
>
> "I know it," gloomily responded the lobster, "but when I go I won't leave any measly vegetable substitute behind me, and that's more than you can say."

As he took everything in, he regaled the staff with stories about hunting panthers in the Rockies on his recent trip, and how in one instance after the dogs had treed a lion it had leaped thirty feet out of the tree and tried to make a break for it, and then how he himself had jumped from his saddle into the scuffle of hound and lion and stabbed the cat in the heart.

Carl, if you'd been here, you could have shared your own leopard story! How damnably similar! But you missed him. Indeed, Carl was disappointed. Inasmuch as he had a personal hero, TR was it. Carl too believed in the "gospel" of work. He was a farmer's son, after all. Yet, unlike his own father, here was a man who would never in a million years have paid another to fight in his place. Anyway, it was too late. The vice president was on his way back east, on his way to deliver a Labor Day address at the Minnesota Fair, before going on to Vermont, where he would give another speech at the Vermont Fish and Game

League on Lake Champlain. Boring, typical, unvital business of the vice president. But whatever task he took on, he took on completely. Just as he had as police commissioner of New York City, rooting out corruption, just as he'd performed the drudgery of civil service commissioner under Grover Cleveland's administration. People admired the way he did not hesitate to act. He leaped in and did whatever needed to be done without overthinking. As he himself would put it, overthinking was the timid way of the overcivilized man, the price we paid for living in the modern world, but if only your overcivilized man would get outdoors more—pick up a gun and go hunting—he might overcome the "tameness and monotony all too common in our lives."

But you should have seen him when he saw your deer, Carl's colleagues marveled. He'd stood right here, right before the winter group. He asked to meet you; he wanted to meet the artist. TR went from season to season, pausing to admire how you'd done the young buck scraping the bloody velvet from its spikes, preening itself for the reign of winter. Staring at those deer as if something had turned the man back into a boy, as if reminding him of the woods he'd played in, when in innocence he had still imagined an infinity of never-ending trees, even if now he knew it had all been illusion, like the painted background beyond those deer; that storybook frontier of the child's mind was already closed, a mirage that had vanished along with the bison and the elk. No, America was as fixed as the cubits inside these glass crates. There was nowhere left to escape.

Amazingly, Roosevelt's visit to the Field Museum was just six days, *six days exactly,* before the slugs from Leon Czolgosz's revolver would fell President William McKinley. Roosevelt himself would receive word shortly after a chicken pie dinner at the Vermont Fish and Game League in Isle la Motte. Just, in fact, as the steamboat ferry was coming into dock; his belly still warm with food; the nip of the lake air. Czolgosz, a man who claimed to be an anarchist, perhaps just to claim something, had approached the president at the Pan-American Exposition, in Buffalo, New York, inside the Temple of Music. It was so hot, so filled with perspiring humanity, no one in the reception line thought a thing about the handkerchief wrapped around his hand. That is, until it caught fire. At the time of the shots, the organist was playing Schumann's *Kinderszenen* (Scenes from Childhood). For a week McKinley held on. The doctors were positive he'd survive; he was eating toast and in fine spirits.

But then gangrene set in, he began to deteriorate, and at 2:15 A.M. on September 14 Theodore Roosevelt was already hurrying back to Buffalo bearing the telegram that read ABSOLUTELY NO HOPE.

✂

ROOSEVELT DIDN'T RETURN to Chicago until two years later. In the minutes approaching 2:00 P.M., on April 2, 1903, the city was momentarily suspended in time. Trolleys on Grand Boulevard were frozen in place. The streets were closed down from Michigan Avenue all the way to Lexington and Fifty-eighth. Automobiles had been banished. No carriage, horse, or bicycle was permitted to move. The streets were swept within an inch of their lives. The docks outside the slaughterhouses were hosed. The air was bright with the smell of shoe polish and Brassoline. Even the rain that seemed on the cusp of menacing the day's excitement was in abeyance, as if in deference to all the silk top hats beginning to come around the corner. Lining the street for as far as the eye could see were nearly two thousand police officers. Decked out in dress blue uniforms, white gloves, black bow ties, and standing collars, they held back the heaving mob, craning to see the mounted police now clopping into view, followed by the first of the carriages glossed to the spokes and bearing the city Brahmins—the mayor, county congressmen, business leaders, council members, members of the Union League—all sashed in maroon and Prince Albert frock coats, and gleaming toppers that tilted in the southwesterly wind. Then, as the cavalry detail came into view, the mass surged. Boys perched in the trees peered down the parade route with hands cupped to their mouths and shouted *Hip! Hip! Hip!* And then appeared the carriage they had all been waiting for, escorted now not only by a cavalry detail and police but by several anonymous-looking men in dark plain attire, whose eyes never stopped frisking the crowd. The corpulent figure in the pince-nez waved and smiled as the carriage continued toward Thirty-third, where the procession would then turn east to South Park Avenue.

Roosevelt, on his first great western tour as president, had stopped in town to receive an honorary law degree from the University of Chicago. And now as the procession was winding its way through the packed streets toward Hyde Park, on its seven-mile journey, he silently rehearsed what he was going to say later that evening about the Monroe Doctrine, including the new gem he had about carrying a big stick and speaking softly—though perhaps he would not relate how it was a proverb of West African origin. He'd become more wary when it came to the color issue ever since he'd invited Booker T. Washington to the White House for dinner—the first black man ever to receive such an invitation. The public reaction, at least in the South, had been explosive and violent. Death threats had overwhelmed the White House.

In the carriage with President Roosevelt was the chairman of the citizens committee, Charles S. Deneen, Professor George E. Vincent from the University of Chicago, and a nervous-looking Secretary William Loeb. They were followed by carriages bearing, among other luminaries, Secretary of the Treasury Leslie Shaw, Surgeon General Marion Rixey, Senator Albert Hopkins, and H. N. Higinbotham, president of the Field Museum.*

After turning south on Grand Boulevard to Oakwood Boulevard, the parade continued east to Drexel Boulevard, then south to Drexel Square. It had been argued whether to allow the president the privilege of walking a portion of the drive, but this was finally decided against, for security reasons, but also due to the notoriety of his vigorous stride and the lack of daring volunteers to keep step with him. Security was always an issue, but perhaps at the moment even more so. Details had emerged regarding a new plot on the president's life. The source of this information was a gentleman by the name of J. C. Fremont, who had been involved in the Back-to-Africa movement after the Civil War. Fremont's information was shaky—the details of the supposed plot kept changing—and he was considered by some to be nothing more than an elderly Negro of some disrepute, but any rumor of a threat had to be taken seriously.

Now as the procession came to the east side of Washington Park, it made a final turn south along the Midway, before arriving at the university, where awaited the faculty in maroon and sable hoods, and the wives wrapped in Japanese silk and kilted chiffon, though with notably fewer birds adorning their headwear—decent progressive women having more or less stopped wearing such hats now.

---

*The same Harlow Niles Higinbotham who would brag just a few years later, at an annual meeting of the American Association of Museums (May 5, 1908), how not twenty years earlier the spot where they had erected the Field Museum had been "nothing more than a wilderness, a morass inhabited only by wild birds, lizards, snakes, and frogs," and yet they had successfully "transformed [it] from the wilderness to a thing of beauty that as memory refers to it cannot but be a joy forever."

This, no doubt, was in part because of the president's fervent support of measures to put an end to the fashionable slaughter. A whole new movement was growing. It had started with the bird hats—a less repulsive target would be difficult to imagine—and out of that, a wave of sympathy to save the rest of nature. An awakening of sorts had begun to prod America's collective, if drowsy, conscience. The first federal legislation to protect wildlife, the Lacey Act, had been passed largely thanks to a klatch of well-to-do ladies in Boston who had formed a group called the Audubon Society. Their first order of business was to put a stop to the plumage trade and persuade other respectable women to join their boycott.

Likewise, the ink was still drying on Roosevelt's executive order of March 14—signed just two weeks earlier—creating the first national bird reservation, on Pelican Island. A month from now he would be clambering down into the redwood forests of the Yosemite Valley with John Muir, the nation's most outspoken prophet for wilderness protection and the founder of another grassroots organization, called the Sierra Club.

Muir would urge Roosevelt to make Yosemite a federally protected forest—and he would get his wish, plus protection for Glacier National Park in Montana. Over the course of TR's administration, a total of 230 million acres of national wildlands would find protection too. Though different in temperament and ultimate ideals, Muir and Roosevelt shared a general belief that modern man had become effete and *over-civilized*, and that the cure for this materialistic disease resided in a return to the great outdoors. Both agreed that the urban dweller must go to the wilderness to slough off his artificial skin, burn himself down to the elements, and find moral renewal. One sure way to cleanse oneself of the "cobweb cares" of modern life and to awaken from the "stupefying effects of the vice of over-industry and the deadly apathy of luxury," as Muir put it, was to give oneself over to panting "whole-souled exercise" through glade and dell. Both men were given to savage outdoor exercise. TR would drag along cabinet members and ambassadors on endless hikes along the tangled rugged gorges of Rock Creek Park, until his entourage was slicked in mud, clothes tattered, or collapsed on the bank while the president stripped nude for a bracing dip in the torrents. Muir once climbed the tallest pine he could find during a summer thunderstorm and bellowed with joy as he was batted about by the flashing rain and winds. It was a matter of "getting in touch," as Muir said, "with the nerves of Mother Earth."

Roosevelt's urgent measures to protect the wilderness, however, were not driven by motives as wholly spiritual as Muir's. (Muir openly criticized the president by asking when he was going to "get beyond the boyishness of killing things.") The president didn't think much of the back-to-nature movement. Muir was more in the mold of the transcendentalists. A wild-beard, like Thoreau, he believed nature possessed a divine spirit which must be saved if humanity itself were to be rescued from the soul-shrinking materialism of the age. TR, on the other hand, was a pragmatist. If he had grown up believing, as did most of his countrymen, that America was limitless, brimming with an everlasting supply of forest and coal, he now knew otherwise. Yet as the country grew, it still needed that wealth of resources that had fueled America's power into the twentieth century. Without them, America would collapse back in on itself like a paperboard box left out in the rain. More than anything else, TR stood for expansion. But to keep charging up the hill, he knew Americans would need to manage those resources carefully. Even if he personally had a deep and sentimental connection to the outdoors, his first consideration was for the country. He did not believe in anything so "goo-goo" as nature for nature's sake. *Conservation* was a matter of survival. A matter of well-regulated, efficient plundering.

To *not* do something would be to woo the end of civilization. TR was well aware that most species were not necessarily intended for the long haul. Unlike Thomas Jefferson, that other great naturalist president, who had hoped to find mastodons roaming alive and well in the West, TR and his contemporary scientists understood why the earth was a seeming graveyard of creatures that belonged to the realm of myth. No, those species had not died out because of a biblical Flood. The evidence showed history was one giant boneyard of extinct species. That everything living today merely existed on a bright and smoldering fringe of eternal eclipse. For many, it was a hard idea to swallow. Here today, gone tomorrow? But this new awareness—this new fear—was linked to the urgency about preservation in general. Even at the Boone and Crockett Club, a guild whose primary requirement for membership was having slain a species of big game, and of which TR himself was a founder, all the members seemed to discuss over afternoon brandies anymore was the imminent demise of the elk and mountain lions they so enjoyed hunting. Who ever thought a species could *disappear forever*? It was sacrilege to think God would create something only in order to let it peter out.

But science—the fossil record—said otherwise.

And like TR's friend Henry Fairfield Osborn, director of the American Museum of Natural History and one of the nation's most prominent paleontologists (who also happened to have been boyhood friends with Teddy's brother; they had all grown up playing in the same woods along the Hudson), Roosevelt worried mightily about the more existential specter of extinction. The most overwhelming proof, of course, was the dinosaur fossils Osborn and Andrew Carnegie were bringing back by the trainload. Quite a race had been set off between the natural history museums to plunder the quarries in Montana and Wyoming for more and bigger sauropods, hadrosaurs, apatosauruses, et cetera, a competition that, thanks to Osborn's uncle and museum trustee J. P. Morgan, and his monopoly on the railroads, New York was winning handily.

The sight of these defleshed monsters sent a current down the spine. Even more than the dread wonder of being dwarfed by the skeleton of a giant lizard, the fossils presented the terrifying idea of extinction itself.

This was where Carl Akeley stepped in. The man with the impossible job. Like the prehistoric artist charged with the task of crawling back into the deepest, hardest-to-reach chamber, with nothing but a lump of charcoal, just to depict the animals that would be gone once the ice cap withdrew. His job, in a very real sense, was justified by extinction.

For what else could they do but preserve images while they could? When the alternative—to protect the actual species themselves—was like trying to stop time or the rotation of the earth?

It wasn't just the finitude of the dumb creatures that was so worrying, but the very notion that this evident madness on the part of their Creator (i.e., the cosmic indifference whether an entire species slipped away) might extend to their own species as well. TR himself felt this threat keenly—this potential for "race suicide," as he put it, whether it would come about by the toxin of overcivilization, from a loss of vigor and striving, or from a reluctance to breed on the part of the "English-speaking people," or "American stock," which, after all, was the only race TR and his friends were really worried about.

"If the processes now at work for a generation continue to work in the same manner," TR wrote in the *Outlook*, a popular magazine, "the future of the white race will rest in the hands of the German and the Slav. Are Americans really content that this land of promise, this land of the future, this abounding and vigorous Nation, shall become decrepit in what ought to be the flower of its early manhood?"

In a sense, the animals were a projection for their own fears of extinction.

And Akeley's dioramas were only an unwitting allegory for the most deeply felt, if selfish fears of the time. The fear of impermanence. Not to say, of course, that the year 1903 had a monopoly on such fears. In the end, though, all Carl Akeley could offer was the cold consolation of the eulogist. The wistful illusion of immutability. If nothing else, his time capsules might signal to some future sentient species questions worth pondering. If only: who built these marvelous tombs and why?

※

AFTER THE CEREMONY in Kent Theater, and the conferring of the degree of LLD upon President Roosevelt, the crowd gathered outside around a ribboned-off construction site where the new law school was to be erected. The honor of laying a cornerstone had been requested of the president. After a series of articles had been placed in the copper-lined box inside the stone—among them a photograph of President Roosevelt, a photograph of the founder of the university, photographs of the members of the law faculty, a photograph of the building itself, a list of students in the law school for this, its first year, a copy of the regulations of the university, and the student newspaper, the *Maroon*, of Wednesday, April 1, 1903—the block was lowered as the crowd stood watching, and, according to the *Tribune*,

> the president seized the official trowel, which streamed with maroon ribbons, and turned in to help out the masons. Unlike the usual official dabs which lay ordinary corner stones, the president's efforts were serious and vigorous. He trimmed the mortar out to the edge of the stone, patched up a bad spot left by the workmen, and then stepped back with an air of pride as the stone fell into place. The official mallet, likewise streaming with maroon, was then thrust

into his hands ... He swung the implement as if in judgment of his strength, and then he hit the stone a light clap.

By now there was a swarm of some ten thousand come to hear the
president, including many students crowded onto the balconies of the
surrounding dormitories, all straining to hear his speech. "It is of vast
importance to our well being as a nation that there should be a foundation deep and broad of material well being," he said, his bullish arms
pumping under the wind-flounced gown. TR flashed a grin—as sunny
as an acre of Illinois cornfield. "It was one of our American humorists,
who, like all great humorists, was also a sage, who said that it was easier
to be a harmless dove than a wise serpent ... Of course it is essential
that you should not harm your fellows, but if, after you are through
with life, all that can be truthfully said of you is that you did not do any
harm, it must also truthfully be added that you did no particular good."

Then there was a commotion from the crowd. Several women
screamed. Several bodies were seen to fall over. This followed by shouts
of *STOP THIEF!* Police were running from every direction into the
crowd, truncheons flourished, and for an instant general mayhem
reigned, before police apprehended a man, who, in his hurry to escape,
had knocked down a number of women and a few gentlemen as well.

But the man was unarmed. This was no assassin. No anarchist, no
barbarian ready to crash down the gates. Only a pickpocket who'd
attempted to liberate the diamond stud from the tie of a gentleman
overly absorbed in TR's words.

Alas, if only the president's schedule had not been so jam-packed—a
dinner and yet another speech after this and then rushing off to take
a midnight train—he might have stopped by the museum again, but
it was not to be. Carl would have to remain disappointed not to meet
his hero for a second time. But, thank God, at least the plot against
Roosevelt's life had been foiled. Or at any rate remained a rumor. The
details of which were forgotten in the mind of Mr. Fremont, along with
his long-quashed plans for getting back to his ancestral homeland of
Africa.

Speaking of which, the Field Museum had begun planning for its
own return trip to the dark continent. If Chicago couldn't keep up with
New York's dinosaurs, it was still the only museum to have sent an

expedition to Africa—where, even better than fossils, were enormous creatures still roaming the continent. This time the quarry would be elephants. Elliot, too old to lead such an odyssey again, would help persuade the trustees to send Akeley in his place. It would be a much more organized expedition, aimed deeper into the interior, by way of the railroad the British had recently completed. He would set off in August 1905. Akeley, as chief taxidermist, felt his methods were ready to be applied to something as large as an elephant. Now it was only a matter of convincing Mickie to join him. It would be the honeymoon they'd never got around to since getting married, on December 23, 1902. And, besides, Carl would need an extra hand to collect accessories, like flowers and leaves, something at which she'd already proven herself, a thousand times over, to be so capably talented.

CHAPTER ELEVEN

IN THE GREAT EMPTINESS OF THE VELDT, THE LOCOMOTIVE HAD come to a stop. At first the passengers did not know why, but word eventually filtered back that a herd of elephants was crossing the tracks. It was dark out, so no matter how she narrowed her eyes, Mickie could only make out the vague adumbration of a tree here and there in the cloudy moonlight. There was no sense in waking Carl. Earlier in the day, as they had come up into the highlands, a hundred miles from Mombasa, someone had spotted a black sable antelope and tried to get the conductor to stop—a service evidently done often enough, even when it meant holding up the train for a whole day just so first-class passengers could go on an impromptu hunting spree. Fortunately, this time, they hadn't. Later, passing over a river, they had seen hippos crowded together, mouths like fanged bathtubs. And crossing the bridge at Tsavo, there had been morbid whispers. This was the place where those awful man-eating lions had devoured 140 coolies while the British were still building the railroad. Once the lions had gotten a taste for human blood their thirst could not be slaked. No wonder in the end the British nicknamed the train the "lunatic express."

Mickie wondered what the animals thought, if they had thoughts, when they saw this train clacking across this landscape that only a few short years earlier had been a complete wilderness—how its occupants must have looked all stuffed inside their compartments, arranged just-so behind pane after pane of window, a giant diorama on wheels. It was probably not a metaphor that would have occurred to the native Kikuyu; to them, the train resembled a great iron serpent. Their witch doctors had presaged its arrival long before the first rail was laid.

It *was* funny and not a little bit preposterous to think how the only reason the settlers were here in the first place was to make the train pay for itself. Unlike on the American frontier, the settlers here had actually followed the train and telegraph lines, rather than the other way. The original purpose of the train being not to ferry big-game hunters onto the savanna but to insert an imperial presence in Uganda. Not that Uganda itself—the railroad's final destination—was any more imminently desirable than the no-man's-land across which the train must first pass, an area of some quarter of a million square miles now known only as the Eastern Protectorate, but because in Uganda was Lake Victoria, and from Lake Victoria issued the headwaters of the mighty Nile.

Because the Upper Nile nourished Egypt, and Egypt was host to the Suez Canal—England's shortcut to India by some seven thousand miles and forty days—Uganda was now of great strategic importance. After all, whoever controlled the Nile controlled Egypt. For a time the French and British had managed the canal under dual control, but when Egyptian nationalists had threatened to dynamite it in 1882, and the French blinked, the British had gone ahead and invaded the country on their own—an event that would prove pivotal in the Scramble for Africa and catastrophic to the entente with France. As for Uganda, the Germans had gotten there first, but because the Kaiser hadn't bothered to enforce his treaties, the British had simply gone in and delivered their own treaties at the point of a Maxim machine gun. But even in victory the British worried about improbable threats to their trade route with India. In order to dismantle their economy, all their enemies would have to do would be to somehow tamper with the flow of the Upper Nile. The French would do it if they could. The Germans would sabotage them too, they were pretty sure. What if the Germans occupied the Soudan? What if a dam were erected? What if the canal were bled dry? It seemed insane but what if—all great modern terrors began with a what if— *what if* their enemies somehow sabotaged the Nile itself? The only thing to do was secure the entire length of the river. How else assuage this natural tendency of empire toward paranoia? A six-hundred-mile railroad from Mombasa would get them to the starting point. The idea at the Foreign Office to persuade settlers to come to Africa to plant crops of tea and coffee for trade had only been an afterthought once it realized the cost of the railroad—£5.5 million—was sinking the nation into debt. All of this for the canal. All this complexity and indirection, this imperial legerdemain. And for what? Because, all along, it was passage to India, not Africa, which the British Empire sought to protect. India was the colony that mattered most: for all those delectable, exquisite textiles. For its calicos from Calcutta, for its Indian silk moths, for its wool from Himalayan mountain goats, and its cashmere harvested from the soft chins of the pashmina goats of Srinagar. Here was the driving force behind imperialism: feathers, fur, and fleece.

In any event, Mickie could still not see the elephants blocking the train. But earlier that evening, at dusk, before Carl had fallen into his slumber, they had seen a herd of giraffes just as Kilimanjaro had come into view. Carl had pulled down the sash, and they'd pressed together to look out into the great expanse with the wind and the fading light rushing against their faces. The massive ice-tipped dome—nineteen thousand feet above the veldt—was surrounded by a halo of bluish mist. How fabulous it was to see the moon for the first time from Africa. And the giraffes were so graceful and alien. The way they ran they almost looked as if they were moving in slow motion, running in a long aquatic gallop, like giant sea horses.

Once the elephants had moved on, and the train got moving again, she turned to Carl, but he had slept through the entire thing. Drooped over in his seat, he still wore his dust goggles, which gave him a slightly ridiculous, if endearing, appearance. Everyone on the train, practically, wore them on account of the bloodred dust that billowed through the cars—it being infinitely preferable to keep the windows open than risk breathing the unventilated air of the closed-up compartments. God knew what diseases you might get. Instead, everything was covered in a thin layer of fine grit. It blew through the train and worked inside your ears and nose, even collecting in the Spode china soup bowls in first class, in the carefully laid out silver spoons and ladles like powdered rouge.

She reached into Carl's pocket and took out his cigarette case. His head bobbed with the steady motion of the train, and his broad hands were loosely entwined, his sleeves rolled up so the purplish scars on his forearms were visible in the shadows cast by the guttering oil lamp carried by the conductor as he passed through their rattling car. It was nice to see him doing nothing for a change. Practically the only time he'd stopped to take a break from work was when he'd taken those few emergency days off on her behalf, in the winter, just six months before they would leave for Africa, when he'd escorted her to California for a few weeks' rest from—well, nobody really knew what her problem had been. But he had been such a dear love to take care of her like that. Now she was just content to see him resting.

The museum demanded everything of him, and as each success raised the stakes, the more intense and frenzied their lives became.

Everyone wanted to know what the Akeley Method was—that's what they were calling it now. The American Museum of Natural History in New York had offered him a job, but he hadn't been ready to move; he still felt the Field Museum would give him what he needed. But then some kind of arrangement had been made with the director of the American Museum to at least send out one of its own taxidermists—a handsome young fellow named Jimmy Clark, fresh out of art school, just a few years younger than Mickie, to stay a few months to learn all the secrets Carl was willing to share. Some of Carl's friends thought he was crazy. He shouldn't give it away. They badgered him to write up something in a science journal, to lay claim to the Method before somebody else took all the credit. There were museums going up everywhere, they said. One in Pittsburgh, another going up in Brooklyn, and they were *all* going to use his techniques. But Carl never had anything to fear. Everybody already knew who was behind them. Mickie herself didn't pretend to completely understand the Akeley Method. All she knew was that everyone was talking about it. Or, at least, everyone in the museum world. What other world was there now?

She lit another cigarette and watched out the window: at this other, strange new world passing by, where the telegraph wires were strung on poles extrahigh on behalf of the giraffes. When the sun began to come up, she watched the flattish landscape trundling by out the window. In the far distance were rumpled green hills, but for the most part it was an eternity of long coppery grass pocked here and there by a venous tree that resembled, as much as anything, a burst capillary. Out on the plains, every once in a while, she saw a settler plowing his field. Crops of coffee and tobacco ricocheted by. The occasional water tank or telegraph station. Here and there the flash of a disk plow, a bit of sun snagged on the shiny new barbed wire. The land was so fertile it yielded two harvests a year. There was something amusing about the way these new landed gentry looked—especially to her eye, having grown up on a farm—struggling behind a team of oxen, turning over the red soil. Most of them, after all, had never done a day of hard labor in their lives. They were aristocrats drawn by the government's lure of a new life. Spurned lovers, nephews who hadn't sized up, men eager to cast aside the yoke of life under Victoria, fugitives from respectable society seeking adventure. They made no bones about wanting to shape the savage wilderness into their own version of a civilized world. And here they were, cultivating land that had never been broken, living in mud-wattle huts with grass roofs, a tribe of arrivistes given to champagne and silk garters.

She tried to look for lions, but they were all hidden in the tawny grass. Somewhere in the middle of nowhere, she saw a group of natives, half naked and carrying long withy spears and shields painted crimson. How did they walk on that hot-looking earth in their bare feet? Though, by now, she was certainly good and ready to take off her own boots. Hers were still new-tight. She'd gotten them in London, along with the rest of their provisions, at Silver & Edgington, Ltd., before they'd set sail from Dover. Never in her life had she seen such an emporium. It was almost like Field's department store, with that same inviting smell of boot cream, except that everything was geared to colonial officers destined for far-flung outposts of the British Empire and, increasingly, your modern explorer. Carl said it was the same establishment that had kitted out Henry Stanley. And if not for the gracious interference of one of that establishment's most solicitous experts, a tweedy wisp of a man named Mr. Little, they would have been lost.

After a few pleasantries, whereby Mr. Little had ascertained the duration and nature of their business in Africa, he took them first to look at tents. Without a proper roof over their heads, they probably wouldn't last more than a day where they were going now, would they? Naturally, all of the tents for sale were waterproof, made of light green rot-proof canvas, with the ground sheets sewn in, and red-lined against the tropical sun. But they must keep in mind, it was going to be their home as well—their home away from home—so it wouldn't do to just pick out the first triangle of canvas and head off into the bush. Just because they were going to be living in the heart of savagery itself, he assured them, there was no reason one couldn't enjoy every bit of elegance to which one was no doubt accustomed. And saying so, Mr. Little ushered the

Americans in awkward awe through a maze of upholstered leather armchairs, caned mahogany sofa beds, Regency mahogany game tables, carved elm writing desks, oak sideboards, brass-mounted escritoires, settees, canopy beds, bookcases, cut-glass vases, walnut chiffoniers, and ornately framed pieces of art suitable for hanging from canvas walls. With the right amenities, there was no reason the tent belonging to an officer of His Majesty's Foreign Service, whether pegged down in the sands of the Soudan or perched on a wind-battered crag in the Himalayas, couldn't be furnished every bit as elegantly as a drawing room in Henley-on-Thames.

Set up around a hearth, where a few logs crackled invitingly, was a gentlemen's social table, a cozy parabola of polished oak facing the fire, yet another item that could make their evenings that much more companionable. It all gave one the feeling that for many of these colonists, the whole global domination thing was just one big, very well-catered picnic.

Perhaps he saw their expression and realized that they weren't in fact looking for the Henley-on-Thames package.

To be quite honest, sir, since the difficulties of the Boer War, some of your campaigners were moving toward a more *modernized* approach. Early on, the British had been able to engage the enemy while maintaining a certain degree of comfort, but then, given the appurtenance-free, savagelike way in which the Boers had chosen to fight—not entirely unlike the guerrilla tactics of the Americans, if you'll beg my pardon—there was now an understandable view for making things more travel-worthy. After all, the empire had to remain mobile now, didn't it? Certain sacrifices had been made. Given the necessity for increased mobility, they had developed a number of truly remarkable devices, "knock-down" or "metamorphic" furniture, all configured to fold up and collapse in the most unusual ways, as he now demonstrated, fumbling with the new X Compactum, a popular bedstead model, which after just a few tries did in fact resemble something a person might reasonably consider lying down on. Next was a combination bath-and-washstand that virtually disappeared before their eyes, a collapsible butler's tray-in-stand, and the extremely popular Roorkhee chair—with leather strap arms and a canvas back and seat, it was by all means the sine qua non of campaign furniture. If it's good enough for the British major general, it ought to suffice for anyone's needs, sir.

Taken next to the clothing department, they were exhorted on the advantages of breeches over trousers. Trousers being too hot and not to mention tending toward a nasty habit of collecting mud. But at the same time, one must protect the legs, so the solution was combining breeches *with* stockings. He recommended leather leggings for snaky country, then demonstrated on a mannequin how to properly wind a puttee around the calf, and how to fix the garter just below the knee. Now, how about we try on these mosquito boots, ma'am. Snug? Not too snug, I hope.

As for your outer garments, I cannot recommend highly enough the Aertex line of nonactive cellular clothing, which, given its special design, will protect you from the well-documented peculiarities of the sun prevalent in that part of the world.

If he saw their lack of comprehension, he patiently went on to explain how it was the actinic rays of the sun, or, in the vernacular, the *blue* rays, which had been found to be most prejudicial. Especially virulent at the equator, these rays were perilous in the extreme to members of the white race, as medical science now universally understood, having recognized the tendency for these beams to descend vertically upon the head, which could lead to all manner of harm, including insanity. The actinic rays were the cause of sunstroke, Mr. Little assured them, and the red rays, or nonactinic, had no harmful effect whatsoever. And so they had developed the Aertex fabric, which, being dyed red, blocked out these injurious actinic blue rays. It was even used to line the tents. Well worthy of trial, sir, well worthy of trial. All the best solar topees, or sun helmets, were now similarly lined with this nonactive cellular material, sometimes with an added layer of protective foil. As were the spine pads, sir, another item I would be deeply remiss to see you enter onto your voyage without. One must protect the head and spine at all costs. The Aertex will also help protect your skin from prickly heat and boils, a most common ailment in the tropics, especially considering how much more *freely* the skin acts in such a climate. Mickie did not understand it all entirely, but it wasn't the sort of thing to question of course.

But, oh, it did make picking out a hat more difficult. There must have been at least a hundred different styles! There were topees and pith helmets and terais and Bombay Bowlers. Was one to get a White Drill and Khaki Canvas Shikar Helmet or the Cawnpore Tent Club? The Viceroy or the Minto? The Pith Tent Club, the Mayo Felt, the Princess, the Malta Felt, the Curzon, the Wolseley, the Monarch, the Kitchener, the Soudan, the Leader, the Pigsticker, the Rhodesian, the Leopold, the

Jodhpur, or the Metropolis? A good fit, that one, ma'am. The Lady's Pith Bombay. The Brisbane, sir, a good choice, excellent ventilation. Or, if you'll try this one, the Viceroy Felt? If you don't mind my saying so, sir, that does look fetching. That one's nice too. Ah yes, the Prince of Wales. By all means, sir. A much-vaunted item of headwear.

Now, shall we consider the topic of your bedding, sir? Of course, you'll want your bedstead to be iron or brass to avoid vermin chewing away at it while you sleep. But, if not, sir, a piece of advice? At night put the feet of your bed in bowls of water to keep away white ants. Either way, may I kindly recommend against the low camp bed, on account of snakes? Oh, and might I inquire whether any children will be attending the expedition? He directed their attention to several mahogany cribs. They both shook their heads.

Now will you have enough stationery, sir, for filing your reports? We have a very fine selection of journals. One for the lady as well. Oh and here's an inkwell. And here are our toiletry requisites. Will you be requiring a boat, sir? No, then, how about sports and games requisites? How about an extra case of candlesticks? Brandy tub? And how about a portable Gramophone, sir? Soda siphon for making sundowners? A bidet for the lady? These are the little things that can make life under canvas so much more pleasant, sir. So much more *endurable*. Mincing machine? Suet scraper? Flesh fork? A good supply of pocket handker-chiefs? And don't forget a tin opener, sir. Have you considered how much whiskey you'll be bringing with you? It's every bit as important as a well-stocked medicine chest. Speaking of which, you'll need one of those, won't you? Here's a fine portable chest of japanned sheet iron, or this more ornamental one in metal and teak; both come complete with lancets, serums, gauze, castor oil, sal volatile, saddle soap, soda mint tablets, chlorodyne, collapsible tube of Borofax, bismuth subnitrate, ipe-cac, and permanganate crystals—for snake bites—and an ample supply of peristaltic persuaders. *Very* much recommended, sir.

The best cure for sunstroke, sir, if I may say, is a direct hypodermic injection of whiskey—mixed with equal parts water. Speaking of which, have you had the chance to look at our esteemed wine list? Before we do, though, let's take care of the matter of your chop boxes. Chop boxes, sir, that's right, to carry your food.

And so another hour spent in the grocery department, down aisles of Bird's custard powder, Robinson's groats, Franco-American Hungarian Goulash, gooseberry jam, Cream of Wheat, and tins of cheddar cheese, potted pheasant, brandy peaches, curried lobster, and pigeon stewed in mushrooms. Mr. Little was now making up a list of foods to be packed and prepared for their voyage in zinc-lined airtight watertight tin trunks. Cocoa, tinned fish, beef tea, Worcestershire, egg in powder, malted milk. And don't forget enough marmalade, sir. Two chop boxes should be adequate for a twelve-month expedition. Bring enough for the natives as well. Better than beads. The chop boxes, as well as your other trunks, you'll notice, are cork-bottomed for the comfort of the native's head—each packed with no more than sixty pounds, as per the merciful regulations of the Colonial Office—humane, but not *too* native-friendly, sir, if you'll catch my meaning. He fondled the padlocks and tittered into his fist with an air of complicity.

Of course, if you ever ran out of food and were in a tight spot, you could always just find a village and help yourself to whatever was needed. Half the time the natives will run away terrified anyway—but there's absolutely no reason not to just walk into their huts and take whatever is needed. As the eminent author of *The Art of Travel*, Sir Francis Galton, said, "It was absurd to be over-scrupulous in these cases."

Now this might seem like a silly question, but did the gentleman have a tuxedo? A morning coat suit? An evening dress suit? While they might now be prepared for the harsher elements, sartorially speaking, they also might want to consider attire for more formal functions: introductions to district officers, imperial administrators, dinners in Nairobi, or perhaps just to spruce oneself up for an evening when the *savagery of it all* began to wear down one's morale, as it no doubt would. He showed them an assortment of cummerbunds, a most useful article of clothing, which, if too hot, did away with the need of a waistcoat, and also protected the vital abdominal organs. As you'll soon see, in the tropics, there's a most disagreeable tendency for temperature fluctuations, and a cholera belt like this one—do you find it comfy, sir?—will ward off the dysentery. He showed them how the cummerbund could be worn outside or under the shirt. If you value your life, sir, you won't remove it day or night. Would you like to try on this gabardine Burberry jacket, ma'am? The rain absolutely flecks off it like quicksilver. Puts a regular mackintosh to shame.

And then, after picking out a few more last-minute practical items, including stockings, pajamas, bloomers, and wool riding breeches,

Mickie let her husband know, that for fear the *savagery of it all* would very likely imperil her sense of femininity, he would be well advised to indulge her and purchase at least two sets of the peach silk underwear adorning that mannequin in the corner. It was promptly packed into one of the tin-lined trunks for later purposes of improving morale.

※

THEY ARRIVED IN Nairobi on October 18. After the bustle of waiting for their luggage—dozens of brand-new trunks and zinc-lined chop boxes piled up on the platform—and seeing to it that it was all stowed until Carl could arrange to hire enough foot porters, they made their way from the depot to the hotel in a rickshaw pulled by a native child in a white skullcap and rags. He was barefoot and wore an anklet of bells that chimed as he ran. As they staggered along, one had to wonder why there was a town here at all. It was more like a stage set of tin shacks and provisional-looking sheds reminiscent of an old Wild West frontier village. The town, only a couple of years old, was named after the small stream that passed through which the Masai called Uaso Nairobi, meaning "cold water," and until the train had arrived, it had all been nothing more than a mosquito-infested swampy outlier, a flat stretch of papyrus in the middle of nowhere.

The short answer could be found by glancing to the west. In a mere twenty-seven miles, before continuing on to Uganda, the train would have to ascend two thousand feet before reaching the summit of the Kikuyu Escarpment, where it then dropped fifteen hundred feet to the Great Rift Valley, a sublime and vibrant trench in the earth's crust running four thousand miles from Jordan to Mozambique. As marshy as Nairobi was, it occupied the last flat stretch before this geologic disruption, and so the base of operations that had been built here during construction of the railroad, where the engineers could figure out the tedious problem of laying track on the sharply pitched escarpment, had grown and festered into a town.

As they cantered up Victoria Street, the main road, they passed the dingy Indian markets, known as *dukas*, and the tailor shops where old Chinese men worked outside on their porches at treadle-driven sewing machines, and the squalid little hovels with prostitutes standing half concealed in doorways behind burlap curtains, and at the west end of the street they trotted through the rat-infested melee of the bazaar, where the smell of hashish bittered the air, no less intoxicating than the exotic banter of Urdu and Swahili, Kalenjin, English, Mandarin, and German that lashed their ears. Crisscrossing the road were Masai cattlemen prodding along their noisy dewlapped bulls, and Arab ivory traders with giant tusks cantilevered on their shoulders. Steering around clusters of pie-faced missionaries, and rubber merchants from Uganda, their barefoot chauffeur dodged clucking ostriches and mules, Boer farmers and coffee speculators from German East Africa, diamond hunters, empire builders, and the many native women who somehow managed the feat of carrying atop their heads enormous bunches of bananas, or baskets piled high with yams, baobab seeds, and cassava, and others bent low like medieval peasants under a hut's worth of sorghum thatching strapped to their backs. Sheep, pigs, chickens, and goats wandered the streets; there were domesticated breeds of cattle, brought from Europe, with redwater tick fever and blue tongue, sheep with rot foot, and the faces of some of the animals were swollen and dripped with pus, having found themselves unwitting hosts—though guests to the land themselves—to colonies of sinus-burrowing grubs which slowly devoured the inside of their skulls. The farmers were experimenting: learning how to raise livestock that could survive in this place. Now and then a herd of zebras or wildebeests would stampede through the middle of town and raise a cloud of red dust that would stay in the air for days. Lions and leopards prowled the streets at night, dragging off the occasional unsuspecting drunk. Nairobi was only six years old but had already become, inadvertently, the busy metropole of the ever-expanding white man's universe.

After turning onto High Street, around a team of oxen pulling a giant tumbling roller that sloshed with water ballast as it crunched over the dirt, they took another turn up Government Road, just past the police barracks and jail and the offices of the district commissioner and provincial commissioner, and all the other supernumeraries of Great Britain's imperial presence—housed for the time being in a cluster of corrugated iron sheds—until they arrived at the cool, white veranda of the Norfolk Hotel.

ONCE IN HER room, Mickie was unpacking her things—only a few items for the few nights she expected to be in the hotel—when there came a timid knock at the door. It was already open a crack, and when she turned she saw a young boy staring back at her. He was no more than nine or ten, a native boy. Behind him stood the hotel manager, who told her that the boy had seen Mickie and Carl arrive on the train and wanted to join their safari.

It was the local version of running away to join the circus, he said, laughing.

She looked at the child. He had the most gorgeous black eyes she had ever seen. Her husband was trying to drum up enough boys now—wasn't that what they called them?—so why not this one? She would probably be doing Carl a favor, and, besides, she liked the looks of the child right away. In fact, she felt a real desire to possess him. The boy was staring at her hair with a look of amazement, but she could not have blamed him. She knew how odd it must have looked. Even though she'd just turned thirty in December, her hair had begun to turn white and, no question, on a woman as young as herself, it did look peculiar. She gestured for the boy to come inside, and handed him the mirror she'd just taken out of her portmanteau. He held it uncertainly and began to examine himself suspiciously. Honestly, the boy did have a lovely face. He was not that much younger than Mickie had been when she'd run away from home.

She asked the manager the child's name. The manager spoke to the boy in Swahili, and after a moment he mumbled an answer to his reflection.

His name was Gikungu Mbiru. He was from around Fort Hall. Probably his parents were dead, given the recent trouble there lately.

When she went downstairs to meet her husband, the boy hid behind her as she entered the lounge, where she found Carl at the bar with another gentleman, who, it must be said, had a rather wild appearance, with an unkempt mane of black curly hair and a big black beard and crinkly—was the word *ironical*?—eyes. He looked as though he'd been raised by lions.

Carl introduced him as R. J. Cuninghame, and when she stepped forward to let him take her hand, she could not have failed to notice that he smelled nearly as feral as he appeared. Carl said that Mr. Cuninghame was the most famous elephant hunter in British East Africa, and that he was going to teach them everything there was to know about the creatures. Mr. Cuninghame gave her a sparkly lopsided smile, one which must have given her some indication of how long the two men had been at the bar before she arrived, then nodded at Carl and said, to the contrary, it was her husband's fame that had preceded him—after all, he'd never strangled an animal, let alone a leopard, with his bare hands!

Where he wanted to take them was up Mount Kenya, that's where the really good-sized tuskers were, unlike anything left around here, but they were going to have to be patient and wait a while because the Brits were not yet done putting down the Kukes who were making an awful fuss of things up there. In the meantime, he said, they could go hunting in the Athi Plains and maybe farther up the rail line in Kijabe.

Mr. Cuninghame screwed his face into a grin when he saw the boy hiding behind Mickie, and he leaned back against the bar on his elbows, as if to say *speak of the devil, who's your Kuke?*

She wouldn't have understood. *Kuke?*

Kuke. Kikuyu. The little one there.

She wanted to introduce the child properly but couldn't remember his name, and decided that she would have to give him one she could remember.

"This is Bill," she said in her most measured voice, as if she were a schoolteacher introducing a new pupil. "Bill would like to work for us, on our expedition." After all, they did mean to hire local boys, didn't they?

The elephant hunter and her husband laughed. He's too small, they said. And, besides, they didn't plan to use Kuke porters. If they brought him along, how did she know he wouldn't cut off her head in her sleep?

What a preposterous idea. She looked at the boy, then back at the elephant hunter. He had a commanding Scottish brogue, but otherwise he was a wire of a man, and somehow in his ratty stinking bush jacket and giant sheathed knife dangling off his rhino-skin belt, he looked like a little boy playing dress up. She didn't know too much about the natives, he could see that, and very likely he took this opportunity to give her a little history lesson. If she hadn't heard, the natives weren't always so friendly. They poisoned the settlers' water. Ambushed caravans. They made raids on camps and work parties along the railroad. The buggers even ripped up parts of the railroad itself—fishplates and sections of track and so on—then forged them into spears and other weapons which they used to kill off the whites! This was no story to tell a lady, but only a year ago, if she really wanted to know what they were like, a group of Kukes had killed a settler by staking him to the ground, wedging open the poor bastard's mouth, and then letting every man, woman, and child in the village urinate down his bloody throat.

No, it wasn't a story for a lady, but she needed to know the truth. Africa was no place for daydreamers. This was all fine and well, but Mickie still insisted on keeping the boy. She was not going to be talked out of her own instincts.

In any event, Cuninghame would have said, he's not allowed in the bar. And neither, for that matter, were women.

This was made plain by the hard stare of the bartender, whose name also happened to be Bill. Bill Pickering. This Bill had made his way to Nairobi after getting discharged from the Royal Artillery, in South Africa, and was innocently on his way to the new colony to make his fortune when he'd accidentally shot and killed another passenger while showing off his revolver. It had just gone off. A bad bit of luck. He'd done three months in jail, and now he was working as a barkeep. It was a good job, working at the Norfolk. You got to meet a lot of fine, adventurous people. Crazy, funny things happened: like the time Lord Delamere rode in on his horse and destroyed a few bottles of whiskey with his pistol. On the other hand, working at the Norfolk could start to give a fellow ideas. You saw so many other men making their fortunes. Why should he be stuck pouring gin fizzes when others were getting rich? Little did Bill Pickering know, but in a few months' time, these thoughts would nag him until one day he would throw down his rag and head out for the Congo to try his hand at the ivory trade. Unfortunately, his enterprise would be cut short when he came across one elephant more reluctant than some to give up its tusks. Despite years of negotiating with drunks, poor Bill's experience would not help him this time. The adventure came to a grisly end when the elephant plucked off his head and flung it into the jungle, where, no doubt, it made a fine meal for a hyena that evening.

Mickie looked out the window at the beeches and the little grass-roofed gazebo in the garden behind the hotel. Mr. Cuninghame and Carl had turned back to the topic of elephants. The shame was, the same thing that had happened in South Africa would happen here. The tuskers would run out of habitat, that is, unless they weren't all killed off by every duke who wanted to prove his salt first. Extinction, to Cuninghame's thinking, was already a foregone conclusion. The elephant was doomed as surely as the Cape warthog, Burchell's zebra, the blue antelope, the red gazelle, and the Barbary lion. In the same miserable queue of species as the giant sable, the bongo, the roan, the eland, the klipspringer, and the white rhinoceros—all in limbo, all on the verge of being snuffed out. That's why he admired what Carl was doing. But he shouldn't dally if he wanted to get any elephants for his museum. At the rate things were going, between the ivory trade and the settlers razing the land, the elephant *would* go the way of the quagga. No, the wildlife here wasn't inexhaustible like the old-timers thought. But, having learned to be wary of men in pith helmets, they were much more difficult to track. Now hunters had to travel farther into the bush to find them, which meant hiring more porters. Really, the best place to hunt them would be up on Mount Kenya. The elephants that lived up in the old timber forests below the peaks were huge old tuskers, the biggest Carl and Cuninghame would find anywhere. They would just have to wait for the Brits to settle their business with the Kikuyu first.

Cuninghame looked at the boy behind Mickie without saying anything.

The Akeleys had really picked a hell of a time to come over. He looked again at the Kikuyu boy, at Gikungu Mbiru, at Bill. *That's right, it's your people who are holding up nice Mr. and Mrs. Akeley here.*

But Mickie stepped in on the boy's behalf. She already felt enough affection toward him to defend her decision, despite this ridiculous opposition, and so leveling her gaze, and setting her fists on her hips, she asked her husband if he didn't think she might require an assistant when it came to collecting snakes and insects and birds and whatever else it was he wanted her to do while he was off chasing elephants, or did he expect her to work alone?

That seemed to settle it. Her husband didn't want to cross her, not at the beginning of their journey. And what did it matter to him if another set of hands, no matter how small, came along? As far as she was concerned, she had adopted the boy.

If you thought about it, Cuninghame said, sighing, it was no great surprise the little ones wanted to join their safaris—it was no wonder *any* of the natives might decide joining up with the whites was safer. It had to be better than living in one of the crowded, pestilence-ridden reservations. In any event, the elephant hunter told the Akeleys, they ought well make themselves comfortable for the time being. There was no telling how long it might take for the Brits to get things under control again.

In fact, they would be stuck at the hotel for over a month. But they'd learn soon enough that this was the way safaris went: intense periods of death-defying adventure bracketed by weeks or even months of purgatorial waiting.

⚘

CARL AND R.J. had been gone now for two weeks. They'd taken half the porters with them up the mountain, up to where their Wandorobo guides had found the feeding grounds, eight thousand feet up, into the old mountain forest just below the bamboo belt. It was strange for Mickie to have come all this way with her husband—all the way across the world—only to be left alone, with nobody but their native porters for company. Luckily, they were a very friendly sort. All during the day they went about their chores, sewing clothes, cooking, collecting firewood, and in their free time drinking banana beer and playing cards. Among the things she had learned about her companions was that they were inveterate gamblers. Even Bill—the youngest—had already lost the new khaki shorts and shirt she'd given him. He had literally bet his shirt! Not that any of them really had much use for clothes in the first place, but that was the sort of thing you got used to as well.

During the day, she collected flowers and grasses and other bitsy things that would later be used as background scenery for the dioramas. On occasion, as well, she went hunting meat for their party. Even though she was a lone woman, she was still a lone *white* woman and therefore the only one in camp licensed to use a firearm. Except in extreme emergencies where he might be called upon to save his employer's life—say, a charging rhino combined with an unconscious bwana—the native was forbidden to fire a white man's gun. A gun bearer, naturally, could carry it right up to the crucial moment, but to discharge a bullet under anything other than the most extraordinary circumstances was to invite twenty lashes, a punishment dealt out by the *askari*, the native soldiers who were an obligatory member of any safari, there mainly to keep the porters in check. And so the task of collecting meat fell to her. She was not enthused about this job at first. But she soon found she wasn't such a bad shot, and since it gave her a sense of contributing to the daily existence of their little tribe, it was one she learned to like.

Playing the part of anthropologist, she also visited the Kikuyu *shambas* at the foot of the mountain, where she tried to obtain curios for the museum. At the doorways to their huts, the women ground corn and pounded sugarcane. Most of the women had mangled their ears to one degree or another—pierced, if you could call it that, so savagely that the lobes were distended like taffy. Large metal hoops dangled from the riven lobes, and even the upper cartilage was perforated, strung with beads and other colorful gewgaws. The bangles around their upper arms flashed in the sun as they hoed their plots of sweet potato or weaved each other's hair—or what remained of it, since most of the women shaved the better parts of their heads, leaving only a choppy pug at the back of the scalp. Unlike the Kikuyu men, the women could enter the forests of Mount Kenya at will without fearing the elephants. The elephants seemed to know that men were their natural enemy. It was safer for the women to collect firewood.

If she'd attempted to visit these same clusters of beehive-shaped huts only a few months earlier, she would most likely have been killed. At first, Carl had been reluctant to leave her here alone while he went off hunting, but in the end Cuninghame convinced them that she would be completely safe, the British having finally taken control of the situation, and besides, it was the expedient thing to do. She'd serve the expedition better with a butterfly net than by trying to keep up on the long slog of the hunt.

It must have given her comfort to have the Kikuyu boy, Bill, with her when she went to visit the villages. And since he was not getting along so well with the other porters, as it turned out, most of them being Swahili and Nyamwezi, or Kamba, she had noticed that he seemed to feel more comfortable sticking close to her besides.

For trade, Mickie had brought a number of knickknacks, salt and pepper shakers, a few glass cologne bottles, and the like, objects sure to merit commerce with local tribespeople. But the easiest barter, she had found, was to win them over with a show of her shocking white hair. She had gone prematurely gray and the locals were so taken by the sight of it, and they clamored so for her to take it down, it seemed perfectly fair to charge admission. If she were to be their entertainment, she would demand in exchange a bracelet or piece of handicraft—and in this way she had started to accumulate quite a collection of artifacts for the museum.

But for the most part, she busied herself collecting diorama accessories. She never went alone but was always attended by Bill, as well as a gun bearer, and sometimes one of the *askari*. Carl insisted on it for her safety. Bill was enthusiastic about helping her find different kinds of things, coming back to her time and again with an elephant shrew or a lizard cupped in his hands or a dragonfly, which she would then let him drop into the relaxing box.

While she looked for flowers, attempting to identify the familiar ones—gladiolus, torch flower, myrtle or something that looked to her like myrtle, chrysanthemums, and little blue flowers that looked like miniature Gramophone horns—or while she waited for one of the boys to come back with something new, she often stopped to watch a group of monkeys in the branches. They always seemed to be there, especially along the riverbank. They were the same kind of monkeys that sometimes appeared in camp and hung around the cook's tent until they were either thrown a scrap or chased off. They were long and spidery, with a dunnish gold fur and the most curious little black elfin faces whose expression always seemed frozen in timid surprise. They struck her as endlessly comical. And yet, as they jumped from branch to branch, she often had the funny feeling of wanting to climb up into the trees and frolic with them, to follow wherever it was they went to when they disappeared.

Later in the afternoon, when it was too hot inside her tent, she had one of the boys place her worktable on the edge of camp, somewhere with a bit of privacy, where she could daydream while she cast her discoveries in plaster. Her tent boy, Ali, would bring her a cup of tea, only to find her staring off at the peaks where Carl was hunting.

She remembered, when they had still been in the Aberdare Mountains, biding their time until they could go on to Mount Kenya, before the Kikuyu uprising had been put down, looking at these same peaks from afar, and Bill telling her about Kirnyaga, what the Kikuyu called Mount Kenya, and how Ngai lived up there, an entity she eventually came to realize must have been these people's impoverished idea of God. This had been back in the spring. They had been forestalled for nearly six months before they'd finally been able to come to Mount Kenya, but in the meanwhile they had tried for elephants in the Aberdares. And in late December, on their anniversary, near Kijabe, she and Carl had beheld the Great Rift together for the first time, standing on its ledge, looking out over the great gulf, from the Mau Escarpment. An infinite meadowed ravine inhabited by the most wondrous creatures one could ever dream up. Zebras, wildebeests, oryxes. Great swift clusters of impalas, juking and dashing across the plains like flocks of barn swallows. Galaxies of topi, hartebeests, and antelopes. Her heart burned like a filament that surely might snap. The entire valley—the moment itself—radiated with an aura that was downright electromagnetic! In February they had moved on to Lake Elementia, where they hunted flamingos and other waterbirds, and where they had shot a hippo. Who had ever seen such a fantastic creature? The boys had jumped into the water to drag it up by its mouth. Dead, it floated surprisingly well.

Before dinner, her tent boy, Ali, would reappear to shyly inform her that her bath was drawn, and she would put away her work, go back to her tent and undress, peeling off the sticky puttees, and then slip into the tingling water, where, left alone to soak, with the happy sounds of the cooks preparing the evening's meal outside, she watched the rising steam curl around the tent's ridgepole.

Nighttime was always a little bit lonely without Carl, or any dinner companions, for that matter, but even that was not so bad, as each night the porters made a roaring campfire and then joined her after dinner for what she had come to think of as their nightly "forums."

The natives excelled at storytelling. Especially Ali, who held all of them in rapture with even the most mundane recounting of their day. For instance, how Memsahib, for that is what they called her, which they would soon enough shorten to Bibi, had shot an antelope that morning. At one moment he might have his crowd in stitches over a bit of slapstick, how Bibi had snagged her skirt on a branch, or slipped in buffalo spoor, then bating their breath with melodramatic suspense when the antelope appeared on the scene, miming Mrs. Akeley now with exaggerated movements, holding the invisible rifle high in the air with one eye comically widened down the barrel, and lifting his knees high in a ridiculous pantomime of the stealthy approach of the huntress—then suddenly whacking his bare foot on the coals so sparks flew heavenward when he barked out the report of the rifle and finally, deft thespian that he was, moving the more tenderhearted individuals in his audience to tears, as he played the part of the faltering doe.

Two weeks had passed when a great commotion signaled the arrival of a runner from her husband's party. The messenger approached her tent, followed by the entire camp. *Memsahib must come now!* The message was from Carl. He wanted her to come at once and to bring her rifle. It was late morning, approaching lunch, and for a moment after the messenger finished she just stood there dumbfounded with her basket of flowers and snippers. Bwana Carl was a two-day hike away. She was terrified. What was wrong? Was her husband hurt? Had he shot an elephant? It wasn't clear. *Memsahib must come now!*

In no time, they had broken camp and were off up the mountain, Mickie still wearing the mud-spattered skirt she had gone out collecting in that morning, a pair of binoculars on her hip, and her bundle of hair shoved under a slouchy beaverskin hat (actinic rays be damned).

She felt lost suddenly heading into the forest, carried along with this small army of men, the extra skinning supplies, and the extra salt, in case Carl had gotten an elephant. For hours they climbed along scantily lit paths choked with bracken and vine. Woods so dark and dismal the urge to turn back was great, but her husband needed her, so she tried to focus on not tripping. When they came to a river, the men held their boxes high to wade across, even carrying Memsahib herself, who held her hat with one hand, upon their shoulders. After a while, Carl's messenger brought the party to a tunnel of sorts, a forbidding cave of trees, which Mickie was informed was an elephant trail. It would lead them up to the feeding grounds and to her husband's camp.

As she entered into this primeval subway, the dimmed light made it feel as if they had suddenly leaped ahead two hours in the day. A queasy claustrophobic fear settled in her stomach, as if they were trespassing, as if they were following an ancient path never intended for their eyes, passageways that got so narrow in places the tree trunks were polished to a high gleam from where elephants had squeezed by for decades or even hundreds of years. Large rocks that shone like rubbed bronze. Otherwise, the forest was an impenetrable tangle.

They showed her where to watch out on the path, where to mind suspicious vines that might trigger the weighted, poisoned spears hidden overhead. And then there were the elephant pits, dug by the Wandorobo, nine feet deep, and spiked at the bottom.

Come dusk, the porters began to make a clearing with their machetes, or pangas, but it was too damp to start a fire. With nowhere to pitch tents, when it turned dark, everyone lay down on the hard ground to try to sleep. Mickie wrapped herself in a blanket, keenly aware of the still presence of the men around her. In the morning, when she was woken by the shrieks of colobus monkeys, her blanket was stiff with cold, and her companions looked like huddled corpses, naked but for the fetishes they wore to protect themselves from the elephants, their bare skin covered in a thin film of ice.

Later the next afternoon, after another day's grueling hike, the messenger began to chatter excitedly and then ran ahead when they were within shouting distance of her husband's camp. When they got closer, Mickie could hear the busy sound of men and what sounded like the splashing of water from a paddlewheel. The first thing she saw was not a steamboat stranded in the forest, however, but a flurry of porters dashing about in what looked like a poorly organized, old-fashioned bucket brigade. Using cooking pots, teapots, rubber basins, and enameled bedpans as improvised pails, a line of them led off into the woods toward whatever stream or mountain spring they were drawing their water from, but instead of a house on fire, the last man in line tossed his bucket onto the hulking carcass that was the center of everyone's attention.

It took her a moment to realize that it was actually an elephant. It did not seem *all* that large. But, to be fair, it was already half skinned, and yet what there was of it, she noticed as she got closer, was diminished by the fact that it seemed to be stuck in a hollow. Everyone was splashed with blood from head to foot, and strips of bright red elephant meat were strung about on branches, giving the otherwise gray forest scene an oddly festive look.

When she found her husband, he was actually halfway inside the elephant. He stepped out from under a bulky flap of skin, as if stepping out from a sagging circus tent. Though he made an effort to greet her warmly, she could easily see he was in a horrid mood. Given his evident state of mind, and that his clothes gave off the strong mulch of death, any attempt to embrace would have been pointless anyhow.

Right away he began to rant. The elephant was rotting quicker than he could keep up. When he'd shot it, it had come on them without warning, and then fallen into this damn ditch. There was no way to move it with the few porters he had, so he'd sent for her and the others as soon as possible. It was a narrow spot here, and they'd barely had a chance to see it come around the corner. These trails didn't give you any room for error! It had been like coming face-to-face with a train in a tunnel. But the skin was already rotting, that was his problem now, so he'd come up with this idea of a bucket brigade to try to preserve it with salt water. The porters were mixing the salt in their pails by the stream. The last two weeks had been exhilarating but a hell of a time, Christ Almighty, if that wasn't putting it mildly. Before they'd been charged by the elephant, they'd already been nearly killed on two other occasions—once when a buffalo had charged and then again when a whole herd of elephants stampeded. They'd been extremely goddamn lucky on both counts. And then several mornings ago the guides had found spoor, and they'd tracked it to this bull—a huge bull, ten feet at the shoulder, and with a fine set of tusks. They'd only got one brief glimpse, but R.J. estimated the ivory was a good ninety pounds per tusk. This bull would be perfect for the museum. So they'd tracked it for several days, and that had been a hell of a thing. Just working through this, this—he held back another curse—*terrain*. After a few minutes, Cuninghame wandered over and stood off to the side.

The elephants had gone higher than they'd guessed, Carl continued, almost into the bamboo belt. It had taken them forever to find the feeding grounds. Then, finally, one day they had got close, they were sure it was close, but all their attention must have been focused in the wrong direction because the damn thing had snuck up on them and charged from the rear. It was almost as if while they'd been hunting the elephants, the elephants had been hunting *them*. There hadn't been a second to think. They'd been completely taken by surprise. So he'd taken the shot. At first he was sure he'd killed the one they'd been tracking all along, but it was not the same bull. He rubbed irritably at his forehead with the back of a begrimed forearm. It was not the bull he'd wanted at all. *This* bull only had one tusk. Not that he'd had time to notice that particular detail given the circumstances. It had been self-defense, he said. He'd had to shoot it. R.J. stood listening to Carl telling his story, just grinning at Mickie.

There was a bit of gore on Carl's forehead, which she wanted to wipe away, but he was so livid she resisted the temptation. Poor man, she thought. He looked crushed. It wasn't certain whether he felt worse about killing the elephant or because he'd botched the job. A month earlier, when they'd been hunting in the Aberdares, he had shot his first elephant under similarly trying circumstances. A cow had rushed them from around a blind bend in the trees. He had claimed self-defense for that one too. In Carl's eyes, that one had been far too small, and they'd left it behind to rot. Of course, Cuninghame had talked him into taking the ivory; there was no sense in not taking it.

Anyway, Carl said, this elephant was useless. But he wanted to keep the skin, because at this point he had lost hope of getting anything better. The splashing kept up behind him. All he could do now was forestall further damage. He turned to look at the porters dousing the skin with bucket after bucket; the water trickled down the grooved maze of wrinkles in a thousand briny rivulets.

The real problem now, however, was that he'd expended his quota for elephants. This was why he'd sent for her in such a hurry. Even though it had never been the plan for her to use it, her own hunting license included the same two elephants as his did, and even if Cuninghame was willing to look the other way for the sake of science, Carl was too ethically upstanding to do so. Basically, what he was telling her was that she was going to have to shoot an elephant. She alone would have to complete their mission.

As soon as what he had said began to sink in, she felt almost sick with fear. But there was nothing to worry about, Carl said. Cuninghame would be there to tell her what to do. He must have seen the blood draw from her face. Regardless, they wouldn't start hunting for another week, so she didn't need to start getting worked up just yet. There was plenty of time for that later, after they had finished with this elephant. For now they only had to worry about getting it skinned and ready to ship back to Chicago. And so that's just what they did. But they were working against the clock of decay, so they worked late into the jungle night, their gruesome labor lit fitfully by jostling torches. Mickie herself did the ears, using a small paring knife to patiently scrape the cartilage and fat until each resembled a giant velveteen purse. As small and insubstantial as Carl made this elephant out to be, working this close, sitting on a stool right alongside its head, next to its gargantuan face, Mickie thought, it did not seem the least bit lacking for sheer presence.

CHAPTER TWELVE

ONCE THEY'D FINISHED THE SKIN AND SENT IT BACK DOWN THE mountain with a group of porters, off on its way to Nairobi for safe-keeping along with the skull and tusks and most of its skeleton, they set out again up the mountain, up into the bamboo where the daylight fell in sheaves of green and green-gray. As they climbed higher in the early morning, a mist descended from the glaciers and shrouded their party until you could barely see the two Wandorobo guides ahead. The taller of the guides reminded Mickie, in spite of his monkey-skin cape, or perhaps because of it, but more because of a certain aristocratic air about his carriage, of a British statesman. For some reason, they had dubbed him Joey. As for his companion, the shorter Wandorobo, since he wore a band of gold bark around his head and a rusty panga from his waist, they called him Julius Caesar. Caesar liked to sit at Akeley's haunches in the evening and wait for puffs on his pipe.

It was Joey who looked for signs of spoor, while Caesar kept his eyes in the canopy above, looking for poisoned spears, now and then testing a suspicious patch of ground for elephant pits. As they crept ahead, tense and alert, searching for danger above and below, it was easy to imagine how at any moment any one of them might suddenly be swallowed by the ground, or yanked into the trees by a sprung snare, or stopped dead in his tracks by a spear. Mickie came up behind her husband and Cuninghame, and in the greenish crepuscular light her skin looked as blanched as her hair. Her skin flushed cold and then hot, and she felt sick to her stomach. Every time she heard a noise off in the woods, strangely amplified by the mist, she felt she would faint. It was unsettling, to say the least, to have been put into a position like hers with practically no warning. Of course, she had had a week to mentally prepare herself, waking each morning to the sound of the elephants' trumpets, near and far, but nothing could have prepared her for the actual hunt. Her nerves were running rampant, and sometimes she felt she would collapse, or wanted to collapse, to go to sleep until the nightmare of anticipation was over.

Carl tried to encourage her with his own excitement. At night, when they were finally alone in his tent, he told her about the things he'd seen the last couple of weeks, and his fascination with the elephants made her feel less fearful. He shared everything that Cuninghame had already taught him. For instance, had he told her what they sounded like? They made this peculiar rumbling in their stomachs that sounded as if they were maybe talking to one another. It was funny, because it always seemed the moment the elephants became aware of their presence the rumbling went silent. It was much louder than you'd think. He was under the impression that it was the sound of their digestion while eating, but it almost sounded like a high-powered electric motor grinding away. He tried to imitate it—a disgusting noise that made her laugh— and she snuggled closer to him under the blanket.

But in the morning, when she was woken by the trumpets, and remembered why they were there in a freezing cold tent snapping in a frigid wind, the whole ordeal seemed so unreal, as if she were Little Nemo in Slumberland waking from a dream where she would never measure up. And yet, there was her gun bearer, waiting outside the tent, in the first sobering wisps of dawn, with her rifle cleaned and ready.

They had seen no actual elephants so far, but there were tracks everywhere. The earth was plowed up with the great stamped holes, deep as barrels, filled with scummy ponds of ice water. Cuninghame told Mickie to keep alert; despite its enormous girth, an elephant could turn on them as nimbly as a startled rabbit. The elephant, he said, courteously holding back a liana vine for her, was really an elusive and surprisingly silent creature, which, being the same color as the shadows of the forest, easily disappeared into its surroundings. An elephant could be completely invisible until it was too late. To keep at bay the persistent and overwhelming urge to turn back, she reminded herself that they were here not only to test the boundaries of their personal fear, but to carry out an important and prestigious errand for one of the great scientific institutions of the world. But each time she heard a loud sound she thought she would die. Somehow the amulet of their mission was losing its power.

By late morning the guides reported back that they had picked up the spoor of what looked like a good-sized bull. When Cuninghame crouched to probe its generous droppings with a stick, the cartridge belt slung around his hips clinked softly. Julius Caesar knelt and inspected it alongside him. His eyes were bright and darting. *"Tembo,"* he said. *"Tembo kikubwa."*

"What did he say?"

"An elephant," Bill said. "A big one." The elephant was close, and by the look of the footprints—inside of which Bill could have easily curled up and taken a long, cool nap—they were indeed on the trail of a beast. Mickie felt somewhat dizzy, as if pulled down by the gravity of the hole in the ground at their feet.

"Feeling all right?" Carl asked.

"Yes," she lied. But she let him hold her arm until the feeling passed anyhow.

After a moment, Carl went to Mickie's gun boy, took the Mannlicher, checked it over, and handed it to her. "You'll do fine," he said.

It seemed they had barely come around the next corner, just out of the thick of the woods, and up along a ridge facing a forested ravine, when they saw the herd on the other side. There they were—the elephants—just across the valley. Maybe it was the lack of immediate proximity, for it would take some doing to climb down the steep side of the valley and across before they could actually reach them, that made it feel somehow anticlimactic.

For a while, Carl and R.J. and the two guides studied the herd intently. And as the message was sternly passed back, the burble of the porters gradually hushed, and she could hear the shift of the crates and luggage as they paused and momentarily set down their loads. When R.J. lit a match, to see whether the wind was in their favor, all watched the flame tremble briefly until the wisp of sulfur wafted back toward the line instead of out over the canyon, and the headman began ordering his men to remount their loads and prepare for descent.

It was just as the first of the porters began clambering down the steep slope that there was a sudden commotion in the line to the rear. And then an incoming tumult and crashing in their direction, loud cracking pops of wet bamboo, and screams all around of *Tembo!* As the elephant came charging into their midst there were crashes of boxes and the clank of kettles and breakfast plates flying helter-skelter along with tins of sardines and Edward's Desiccated Soup and Horlick's Malted Milk as the porters threw aside their burdens and ran into the trees for safety. Over the chaos, Carl was shouting at Mickie to shoot, and the headman was screaming in Swahili for those who had already begun the descent to turn back. And for a moment, Mickie found herself facing the most enormous creature she'd ever seen—and in that same moment it let out a blare of such shrill fury it sounded as if the forest itself had trumpeted. The noise echoed across the canyon and hovered in the trees. And then, in an eyewink, before anyone could get off a shot, the bull heaved itself over the canyon ledge with a massive thud and spray of earth and splintering wood and went crashing into the valley below with the grace of a boulder strapped to a toboggan.

All that was left was a giant trench, and a smattering of leaves fluttering out over the chasm. They stood at the top of the hill, dumbfounded, looking down into the gorge, where, far below, they could make out the treetops shaking and trembling in the wake of their escapee. The sound of it crashing across the valley floor lasted for some time, but there was no sense in shooting now, and even less in chasing after. By the time they reorganized, and got all of the shaken porters back out of the woods, and sorted out the mess, it was nearly dusk. There was nothing to do but set camp for the night, there on the elephant's impromptu trail, with a couple *askari* on guard after dark. But early the next morning, before Mickie had even fallen asleep, it seemed, Carl was hurrying her out of bed. She found her gun boy, half asleep himself, already dressed and standing outside her tent.

"Memsahib fight elephants today," he said, while she lingered as long as possible over her biscuit and tea.

They followed the steep detour the elephant had blazed, downhill, and then across the valley, and then up the other side where the bull had merged onto one of the preexisting trails. Here, its tracks joined with those of the herd they had seen the day before, but after a short time the guides were able to decipher it from the others without too much difficulty, their bull being so much the larger. They followed its tracks all day, trudging onward in a forced march, until they came to a glade where they lost its trail again in a confused gathering—at a rotary of sorts, a muddied frenzy, between migratory paths leading to the higher feeding grounds—and after a few frustrated hours they were ready to give up. Their bull had been swallowed by the forest. But then one of the guides found an impression which they were certain was where it must have lain down for a nap. They could make out its girth, its head, and even where its enormous tusks had left their seal on the duvet of vegetation.

It was midafternoon when Cuninghame abruptly gestured for Mickie to crouch behind a brake of ferns. The guide was signaling silently ahead with a wild expression. As she stopped, she felt Bill, the nearest behind her, stop as well. When she heard the heavy crunch of wood she looked to where the guide was pointing and saw a patterned chink in the trees suddenly darken. She saw its heavy gray bilge and a single hind leg as wrinkled and stout as a beech, its ivory glowing like an obelisk in the woods. For motivations unknown, the elephant was demolishing a tree, tearing off a heavy branch, and the sound of the wood being slowly crunched by the vise of its trunk was terrible, if not as terrible as waiting to see how soon it would notice them, but they did not have to wait long. As soon as it alerted to their presence, the elephant trumpeted. This close, the sound carved a canyon beneath her feet. But then the hulking figure came slowly around the copse of bamboo, as big as a coal car, its enormous trunk searching the breeze. It was hard for Mickie not to think of its trunk as some vulgar intelligent member, the valve at its tip groping wantonly in the air.

"What a monster," Carl gasped.

She wanted to turn and flee, but Cuninghame pushed her forward. He doesn't have our scent yet, Cuninghame whispered, but once he does he's certain to charge. He touched her elbow lightly, and his voice, urging her on, was almost inaudible. She had the perfect shot.

She had seen elephants in zoos in America, of course, and she'd seen the stretched-out effigy of Jumbo, but neither experience had been nearly as imposing as meeting this live one face-to-face, in its own realm, especially now with her being urged forward like a sacrificial virgin. Here, it was not king of the circus but overlord of the universe, and if it chose, she knew, it could crush her like a pulverette of aspirin. Set in its broad mammoth head, its gaze was forlorn and resentful, and its wrinkled hide, right down to the pendulous folds between its hind legs, looked like vulcanized rubber. Its yellowed tusks were each as long as a man.

She had a clear shot, but she was not yet ready to pull the trigger. As the elephant ripped another branch off a tree, and swatted it against its side like a tired flagellant, she remained paralyzed. She held the bead on its ear, a straight brain shot if only she pulled the trigger.

"*Shoot!*" Carl said.

"Yes, shoot," Cuninghame said. "Now, do it now."

But she could not, not just yet. She was too overcome by the petrifying beauty of this animal. It dropped the branch now and returned her gaze as if challenging her to approach. Lacy light seeped through the trees, playing across its skin as if across a breathing movie screen, and a duet of butterflies flitted about in the gravity of its immense stillness. The elephant's presence was sublime and seemed to dwarf the small, human notion of time itself, as well as any memory she might have had of all the preceding moments that had brought her here. She remained deaf to her husband's pleas to pull the trigger for the sake of God, until the elephant turned away and the spell was broken. The moment was over. It had vanished into the trees.

Once she realized what she'd done—or what she hadn't done—she felt terrible. Her husband was pacing in helpless circles, too furious to speak. He looked as if he might be sick. After letting her gun boy take back the Mannlicher, she went and put her hand on his arm.

"I'm so sorry, Carl. I promise I'll do better next time. I promise I will."

Anyone could see that he was trying his best to contain his disappointment.

"Come along, Akeley," Cuninghame said, running his pipe through the pouch of tobacco he'd withdrawn from his hip pocket, not once taking his eyes off the spot where the elephant had stood only a moment before. "We'll follow him and give her another chance."

But by early dawn the next day the natives were no more enthusiastic about being back on the climb than Mickie. The porters at the end of the column had been dragging, and holding up the rest, so it was no great surprise when word arrived at the front that they had lost their tail end. Carl had to stop the hunt in order to send a few others back to locate the lost ones. Only after they were reunited with the group was the hunt resumed. And then, after several more confounding and tire-some hours, when it became clear that the guides had been leading them in circles, and Carl realized that this was the case, he lost his tem-per, sent the guides to the rear, and fined all the porters a week's wage.

It was not yet late morning.

As they climbed higher, swampy whorls of mist seeped between the moss-draped trees. In such conditions, and with Carl acting as guide now, navigating with a compass, and looking for pits and trip wires at the same time, Mickie was terrified. After a while, though, once Carl had calmed back down, he redeployed the guides to the front, to the relief of all. They had gone another hour or so when Julius Caesar came running back out of the fog wagging his arms with a demented look on his face. They had finally caught up with the bull.

It was hard for Mickie to see where he was pointing. Cuninghame crouched behind her and whispered to look into the fog bank to the left, behind the bushes, and then after a long while she could see it. At least its ears and its back—just faintly adumbrated in the mist. They crept closer, under cover of the vine-draped trees. She could hear a rumbling, but then the noise ceased, and the elephant started to amble forward, its black-tipped trunk fishing for the intruders' scent. It was forty feet away. She stood as firm as her trembling legs would allow, clenching the rifle, sweat dripping down her sides, and waited as the elephant emerged from the cold mist in its entire majesty.

"Shoot right above the shoulder," Cuninghame said. "You've got a straight shot to the heart."

She raised the gun to her own shoulder and tried to steady the wavering sight by holding her breath and shutting out all feeling once and for all. Tiny beadlets of cold dew freckled the rifle barrel. The ele-phant's ears stirred the mist around its massive head. As she squeezed the trigger, calmly, as if she had all the time in the world, she saw down the barrel how the elephant stared back at her with a kind of extreme patience, right up to the instant when fire flashed from her muzzle. A clap of pinkened dust burst off the elephant's hide, and it staggered for-ward, leaking blood, and then crumpled onto its heavy front legs. The vacuum left in the wake of the explosion was sucked up immediately by the surrounding soft, softly waving tops of the cedars and ferns, then filled by a pitiful dying bellow, and then straightaway silenced by her second thunderous shot.

When she saw the elephant on the ground, heavy and dead by her own hand, or by the extension of the weapon in her hands—there was little difference now—the fear and second-guessing she had felt for the many days leading up to this hour abated. Her heart was beating wildly. The certainty of it all was exhilarating.

At first, they approached with caution. And then only began exploring the felled elephant with confidence once they were quite sure it was dead, walking around its perimeter, slowly taking in its immense dimensions, its musk-metal scent, feeling with their hands the intense heat it still put off, seeking out the bullet holes, and fingering them as the hunter does almost unconsciously. One of the guides pointed out a festering wound on its back where a spear had pierced the elephant but failed to kill it, and they probed down under its skin with their knives and retrieved the iron point lodged between the leviathan's ribs. The two Wandorobo guides climbed up onto its side, taking in the view from its heights, proudly surveying all below, and even posing for a few photographs before Bwana Carl began to document the animal in earnest. Cuninghame said, without a doubt, it had to be one of the biggest bulls he'd ever seen bagged on Mount Kenya, if not in fact the largest. But the more he looked at it, the more excited he got, convinced now that it was without question the biggest he'd ever seen. It looked like Mrs. Akeley had set a record.

After an hour's rest, and a picnic lunch in the shadow of the dead giant, they began the long process of skinning it, while the porters set up camp and began to build fires to smoke the meat into jerky. But before this, the Wandorobo cut out the mighty tusks, which stood end to end twice as tall as the tallest man among them. Nine feet of tusk. With his back turned to Mrs. Akeley, Cuninghame then cut out the nerve from the ivory's stump end. Mickie stood beneath the arched tusks, now buttressed on either side of her by the two guides, and Cuninghame before her like a priest with the bloody pulp in one hand. Invoking the ancient Arab ritual by which he himself had first been initiated, he anointed her with the tusk nerve, making a mark on her forehead, so that the blood ran down her nose.

For a moment, the forest stood silent.

"Mrs. Akeley, hearken, Allah christens you Elephant Hunter."

Back in Chicago, Carl would mount Mickie's bull with one he had shot, the two bulls posed as if fighting in the rotunda of the Field

Museum. It was a stunning accomplishment, and once again Carl had seized the attention of the museum world. Not least of all, the attention of the new president of the American Museum of Natural History, Henry Fairfield Osborn, who had already begun thinking about building some kind of hall that would focus exclusively on elephants.

CHAPTER THIRTEEN

Henry Fairfield Osborn, president of the American Museum of Natural History, stepped off the elevator at the fourth floor of the museum and into the din of construction. The sound of hammers and the gripe of an electric-powered drill echoed down the southeast wing to his right, from the Hall of Fossil Reptiles. To his left, past the iron gleam of spears and rhino-skin shields in the fledgling Hall of African Anthropology—soon to be augmented by a generous addition of Congolese artifacts courtesy of King Leopold II of Belgium, gifts no doubt meant to butter up his uncle, and museum trustee, J. P. Morgan—a separate army of carpenters and masons and cabinetmakers raised their own din on the new wing going up now on Columbus Avenue.

He had come down from his office on the fifth floor to see how their latest pièce de résistance was coming along. He himself had given this one its name. *Tyrannosaurus rex.* They had scratched it out of a stony matrix as hard as Bakelite in Montana. Like the *Allosaurus*, it had almost dainty forelegs, absurd in contrast to its enormous fanged skull and its massive razor-taloned hind legs. The largest teeth in its four-foot jaws were a full six inches from the socket. The tyrannical lizard king, the museum's new mascot. This was the one that would bring the public in droves and dazzle them speechless. Perhaps even put the fear of God into their hearts.

Just today—March 21, 1909—the *New York Times* had reported on perhaps the museum's rarest discovery ever: that of a mummified *Tra-chodon*, even if it had buried it on page four, after the news that Vice President James Sherman was *not* ill as had been rumored, or that Colonel William Tucker still refused to submit to his wife Elizabeth's demands for divorce. The thing was that it was a three-million-year-old dinosaur skin.

Not a skeleton but a *skin*.

As Osborn stepped into the corridor and paused before the wall case of a few smaller recent finds—two mastodon teeth, the skull of an extinct beaver from Nebraska, a narwhal tusk—the dimmed reflection of his well-brushed mustache, stiff white collar, and the firm and redoubtable Nordic brow floated briefly over the artifacts. He moved briskly toward the clamor of hammers and saws, into Tertiary Hall, now going back in time, into the Age of Mammals, past the fossilized bones of the great Irish elk, the woolly rhino, pygmy hippopotamus, prehistoric deer, giraffe camel, and cloven-hoofed skeletons of all persuasions. Bones chipped from the frozen mud, wrenched from the rock itself, salvaged from an eternity of silt. Of course they weren't really bones but meticulous fakes crafted over the course of millions of years, one molecule surrendered at a time, the original slowly and painstakingly converted into carbonate of lime or silicate.

Speaking of meticulous, the other great acquisition he had made this year was the one he'd poached from Chicago—his new master taxidermist, Mr. Akeley. In his mind, no artist compared. You half expected his creations to jump out and bite your thigh. There was something so immaculate and uncanny about them. An ability to get across the meaning of an animal with just the tilt of an ear, the strain of a tendon pulled taut as a lute string. Even William Hornaday—the former master—had conceded that he was the finest in the world now. Truly, he had done for taxidermy what Michelangelo had done for sculpture and painting. But Osborn likened Akeley more to Phidias. The great Greek sculptor who had carved statues of Zeus and of Athena inside the Parthenon. Just look at the two elephant bulls he'd mounted for the Field. They were like gods, yet as nimble as a couple of fighting minks! How had he mastered such a scale? Osborn had got an idea from the reports sent back from Jimmy Clark, who had picked up quite a lot on his trip. But why not bring Phidias himself to New York? Chicago had grown too small for this taxidermist's ambition. The word was the Field's new director wanted to focus more on birds! He did not have the same vision, the same willingness, or perhaps just the same appetite (or maybe it only came down to money) for extravagant acquisitions as Osborn. Here in New York, Akeley's talents would be given room to breathe.

As for Osborn's planned Hall of Elephants, it was to be as comprehensive as possible. A Parthenon devoted to the mighty Proboscidea. One showing the progression of the species—from the smallest six-foot-tall *Palaeomastodon* (which Osborn himself had collected in Fayum, Egypt) to the endangered elephants of the Indian and African continents. Akeley himself would create the dominant centerpiece: a full-size, fully realized habitat diorama. It would be an enormous project, of course, but Akeley felt it was entirely feasible. It was hard to believe the Field could be so stupid, but it was to Osborn's advantage now, wasn't it? And so he'd commissioned Akeley to return to Africa now, four years after his last trip. He would do for the African elephant what he'd already done for the white-tailed deer.

Uncle Morgan didn't like the idea at first. He thought it was too many damn elephants for one hall. Naturally, J.P. had always been a great benefactor to the museum—he practically kept it afloat with his subscriptions, and he'd provided free shipping for hundreds of tons of dinosaur bones from the quarries out West. Osborn didn't want to oppose him, but most of the other trustees—Cornelius Vanderbilt and Cleveland H. Dodge, for two—were enthusiastic about the project, and in the end he got the necessary funding to send Akeley back to Africa.

And now that it had all been arranged so Akeley would be meeting TR over there as well, it was just too perfect. Teddy Roosevelt was out of office, taking a holiday, as it were, going over to shoot big game to his heart's content, and collecting on the Smithsonian's nickel. (In fact, Osborn was thinking about asking Teddy to be a trustee himself when he got back—he needed close friends on the board.) TR would be embarking for the dark continent in just a matter of days. He understood why TR was clearing out: he was no more constitutionally capable of not meddling in government affairs than a turkey vulture was capable of not meddling with carrion, as TR put it himself. After such a presidency he *had* to step out of the limelight if his successor was to stand a chance.

Even though the Smithsonian was paying Teddy's way, he had agreed to meet Akeley and to bag a couple of elephants for their new hall in New York. The then president had much availed himself of Ake-ley's expert advice during the planning stages of this trip, and had even invited Akeley and his wife to the White House for dinner. The taxider-mist and the former president were planning a rendezvous on the Uasin Gishu Plateau to go hunting together. It would be great publicity for the American Museum—the kind that wouldn't get buried on page four.

Even so, as far as Osborn's own studies into the larger questions of human origins were concerned—a topic to which he was more and more lately devoted—Africa clearly wasn't a candidate for serious study. The climate alone ruled that out. Whereas it may have proven suitable for the primitive races who had taken to the less demanding, more luxuriant niches of the temperate and tropical zones, Africa lacked the requisite northerly clime to have ever spawned the more adapt-able races—those being, of course, "the Aryans, Nordics and Anglo-Saxons."

To have ever evolved into such a highly developed species, with its more complex civilizations and higher moral character, he theorized that his own ancestors must have originated in a harsher, colder envi-ronment where the struggle for existence forged them in ways the decadent tropics of Africa could not. It was the "struggle for existence" that had given the superior races their winning edge. They had paid their dues in the Pleistocene, while the darker races had lived out lives of relative ease. This was why Professor Osborn was positive the Dawn Men could never have come from anywhere like Africa.

He passed the cabinet of horse teeth, the horses themselves—the paradigmatic skeletons illustrating their canter through evolution: *Eohippus, Orohippus, Mesohippus.* All evolving, in the professor's mind, with an orderly and purposive progression into the future, toward some unknown but irreversible and perfectible end. By and large, he agreed with Darwin, but he could not accept the idea of a random universe. If anything, he believed in predetermined mutations. Mutations with the faint, reassuring air of Presbyterianism. The universe had to have a *plan.* Just as he himself had a plan for the museum.

When he came to the skeleton of the titanotheres—a caricaturist's version of the rhinoceros with perversely large horns—he mused that it was a superb example of how specialization could go astray, leading the animal down the road to its own demise. Here was a lesson the modern citizen would do well to heed. The more specialized modern man became in his factories and universities, the less prepared he would be for adapting to the rapid changes already threatening to capsize civilization. If unprepared to defend himself, to defend against the corruption of the species that was taking place right now under his very nose, survival was doubtful.

Stepping back another fifty million years or so, he continued into the Southeast Pavilion, where workers clambered around on a large scaffold, and the sweet garlicky stench of oxyacetylene singed the air from a welder's gun. The sunlight slashed through the wooden slats and on the strange apparatus beneath—part bone, part steel—as a giant pulley slowly heaved one of the unwieldy sections of skeleton heavenward, squeak by squeak, while below a crew of preparators patiently affixed an infinite number of attenuating vertebrae to the steel armature that itself was like a twisted truss of a skyscraper. The *T. rex* was like part of the new skyline, soaring overhead, the massive skull like a steam shovel.

In the middle of the hall was the *Brontosaurus,* stretched out voluptuously—sixty-six feet long, sixteen feet high, and thirty-five tons—only one ton less than the meteorite Admiral Robert Peary had discovered in Greenland, "Ahnighito," the heaviest in the world, which now rested three floors below on a concrete pedestal.

In the corner was the vicious tableau of *Allosaurus* feasting on the remains of another, fallen *Brontosaurus*. It was just as his paleontologists had found it at Como Bluff—predator and prey resting together in adjoining graves. The teeth marks on the *Brontosaurus* matched the teeth of the *Allosaurus*. Here was another lesson the public might take away. The most basic law of nature: the very ruthlessness and struggle of survival. It was why he sometimes depicted his dinosaurs in combat, to dramatize the great battle for survival.

The dinosaurs brought people in droves, of course. Especially on Sundays, when the working class had their day off. The *T. rex* was sure to become the museum's drawing ticket. But the mystery of the day—at least according to the *New York Times*—belonged to the decidedly less regal, goonier-looking *Trachodon*. There were already two of the duck-billed skeletons here, grazing on wax seaweed in a mock swamp from the Cretaceous. He thought he might place the mummy in a low case beside the others. The mummy was too crushed to mount erect. But it didn't matter. All the viewer needed to behold was the miracle of preservation—the oldest known skin in the world.

The fossil hunter who had found the dinosaur had discovered it curled up, in a grave of soft sandstone, its forelegs stretched out imploringly, as if fending off intrusion.

The entire purpose of the museum, of course, was preservation. Preservation of the past, preservation of the facts. Preservation of the correct order of nature. Now, more than ever, the curators felt that they must preserve specimens of the rapidly evaporating flora and fauna across America's dwindling wilderness. As Osborn's sometimes difficult curator of ethnology, Franz Boas, had said, they were the last generation to be in a position to do so.

At the same time, the museum was now in a better position to collect and preserve artifacts from the rest of the world. In the nineteenth century, as the nation had grown—expanding west—so too had the museum, filling up with specimens (and curious ethnological artifacts, such as those from exterminated native tribes). And now as U.S. markets expanded worldwide, the museum was building halls to accommodate all of the corners of the globe where it would be seeking artifacts. You could say that its own work was enabled by the extension of American interests, in particular by TR's strenuous efforts to secure America as a young imperial contender. Just in the last year the museum had sent expeditions to the East Indies, the Arctic Ocean, Alaska, Japan, Korea, New Zealand, Nicaragua, Tahiti, the Philippines, Samoa, Trinidad, Venezuela, Egypt, Hawaii. They went in tandem with the expansion of American power overseas. Osborn thought this only fitting—he often thought of his work in terms of conquest.

Such work came naturally for the museum trustees—most of whom were bankers, brokers, railroad tycoons, elite businessmen of all stripes—they were all in the business of acquisition. But given the new anarchic threats at home, they were also now in the fearful business of preserving their own status quo. It wasn't just sequoias and black-footed albatrosses that needed saving.

The natural social hierarchies—those gentle but powerful laws dictating where each kind took its place in the Kingdom of America—were under threat now. For Osborn's kind, in a way, owning the dinosaur bones was to possess a kind of bewildering and terrifying knowledge. The most elite, moneyed individuals in New York should perhaps feel an uneasy sympathy with these great, powerful lizards. In the end, nothing had been able to save the dinosaurs—those uncontested aristocrats of the Mesozoic. But what had done them in? Had it been an asteroid? A nasty virus? Or could it have been that the dinosaurs had made the fatal mistake of mixing with the wrong species? Commingled with an alien "race plasm" on the Lower East Side of the Jurassic? It all concerned Osborn deeply. Why did modern man not know better? The cavemen knew (as he'd written in one of his screeds to *Collier's*) that the Neanderthal had not mixed his blood with the superior, more artistic and cultured Cro-Magnon. The evidence was in the caves near Les Eyzies and the sophisticated animal drawings found there by Abbé Henri Breuil.

Why should negroid mingle with caucasoid? Jew with Christian? Pole with Nord? The thought made him shudder. A *Trachodon* may as well couple with a merganser! There was nothing more revolting to him than the trope of the melting pot. Who had come up with this disgusting metaphor? A more apt comparison could be found in the common latrine. "Put three races together," he often said, "and you are as likely to unite the vices as the virtues."

Walking by the windows in the tower, facing out over Central Park, he could see governesses bundled up in the chilly March air, pushing wicker prams down the crushed-gravel paths, bicyclists and horse-drawn carriages vying against the taximotor cabs coming off the transverse, rattling up the paving stones, and onto a freshly macadamized Central Park West. The smell of their belching engines (burning the drilled-up remains of *Trachodons* so far as he knew) stained the air. It was a typical weekday morning. A peanut vendor steaming his wares outside the park entrance at Hunters' Gate. Matrons headed for the Ladies Refreshment Pavilion. He could see the top floors of the new Plaza Hotel twenty blocks south, and over the tops of the oaks and larches he could make out the cast-iron cresting and weather vanes adorning the mansards lining Fifth Avenue—Mrs. Astor's place, the Payne Whitney mansion, the Byzantine-Moorish dome of Temple Beth-El on Seventy-fifth—and all of the new towering apartment buildings climbing up around the park like brownstone castles.

You could hear foreign tongues in the park now. Yiddish, Italian, and German blatting like starlings from behind every shrub and park bench. Long gone were the days of the carriage parade; the park was no longer the rendezvous of polite society.

But at least up here, on the Upper West Side, he was far enough removed from the disease-ridden tumult of the huddled masses. It pained him that thousands of children were born to these slums. This was the evil of the industrial revolution come home to roost. His city, his New York, had been completely transformed. The lower orders were practically taking over the city. His own race was eminently adaptable—innately ingenious—characteristics which made it the natural governing class; but how could anyone adapt to the arrival of *two million* immigrants a year? How many millions now had passed through Ellis Island and gone no farther? Eighty percent?

At some point, of course, the state must intervene. To defend the purity of the race plasm. One couldn't expect the average citizen to think in these terms. These things would ultimately have to be regulated for the welfare of the species. "As science has enlightened government in the prevention and spread of disease," Osborn wrote in the journal *Science*, "it must also enlighten government in the prevention of the spread and multiplication of worthless members of society."

He had given a fair amount of thought to the topic. Things could be done. To eliminate an unwanted trait, for example, one need only prevent that person from procreating. Alcoholics, degenerates, and Bolshevists should simply be barred from entering the country; however, for those beyond redemption (the feebleminded, the deaf, etc.), there were certain techniques—entirely scientific—that could be used to make sure the inferior germplasms did not perseverate.

These were hard questions, and science must answer them, as well as the serious questions surrounding race. But not with prejudice. No, they had to remain open-minded. If only they could have such a discussion with some of the other races and expect them to keep an open mind as well! Even if they weren't technically all of the same species (as he believed each race had originated separately and grown in parallel, but untouching, lines of evolution), even the lowest races, Osborn thought, possessed at least a modicum of the divine force and were therefore capable of improvement. Science could determine what the virtues of each were, and how they could best be put to use in a modern civilization.

He believed that it was race first and foremost that had molded the destinies of man, but allowed that education and free will—that nurture, in a word—could play a role to a degree as well. Otherwise why bother to instruct? Why bother to lead the city's mongrels to the museum, to the one place where they could get a firm lesson in the laws of nature, and by so learning, return to the world inclined to do it less harm?

Osborn hoped his exhibits could serve as a reminder, a lesson, an antitoxin. To make the museum of some use to society, a bulwark against the rising tide of ignominy. In this time of crisis it was the museum's highest purpose. Its entire mission was to provide the opportunity of direct experience with nature. For the museum to provide spiritual regeneration. As escape and salvation from urban-industrial degeneracy. To improve people's minds and hopefully stave off anarchy or revolution.

If he could show the morality of evolution—demonstrate that "evolution simply confirms morality," as his predecessor, Morris Jesup, had put it—impress upon the mind of each patron the importance of obedience to the higher laws of nature, well, then, all the more reason to hire artists like Mr. Akeley to lure in the public with his vivid illusions. Otherwise, if they failed, at the rate things were going, you had to almost wonder if they shouldn't build an extra hall just to preserve the likeness of Henry Fairfield Osborn's own supreme genus before it too was extinguished. Put it on display in a gilt-frame diorama for the contemplation of future species. Sealed off behind a pane of glass, in the meantime, he and his monocled friends might be safer from the invading hordes.

CHAPTER FOURTEEN

THE STARTLED EXPRESSION ON HIS WIFE'S FACE GREW SMALLER as the balloon slipped farther away. At the sound of cable winding out, Carl must have wondered if he'd ever see her again. If it were to set loose, there was no telling where the balloon might come down. She would be just as likely to descend on a village of Pygmies and be proclaimed a god as to drop into a den of hungry lions.

But despite a bit of initial turbulence, and a scrape across the trees, the contraption seemed to be holding steady. Carl could still faintly make out Mickie's nervous grin; she was waving and holding on to her sun helmet—and for good reason, too, since for the moment she appeared to be on a collision course with the sun itself.

They were on a small hill overlooking Nairobi. A fairly good-sized crowd of onlookers from town had come out to watch in the early morning. Everyone stood around, holding their hats and looking up, gasping in unison each time the balloon swerved on its moorings. Off to the side, standing next to Akeley—who was cranking away at his own new tripod-mounted contraption—the corpulent impresario of this inflated spectacle, W. D. Boyce, seemed to be enjoying his first test.

"Isn't this a crackerjack!" He waved his hat in the air at Mickie, his most fetching guinea pig yet.

Though, of course, the real test would come once they'd mounted the movie cameras to the balloons and floated them out into the bush. This was just a momentary diversion, a publicity stunt. The real business of W. D. Boyce's African Balloonograph Expedition had yet to begin—that business being to capture the first aerial photographs and motion pictures of the dark continent. What real conditions would be like out there still left a number of questions upon which W.D. mused for the few newspapermen who cared. "If the mosquitoes are bad," he said, "we can sleep high in the air in our balloons. Out of reach of disease carrying mists and poisonous reptiles and insects!"

Standing with his fat fists on his girlish hips, he gave his man at the windlass a sharp order to let more cable out, and Mickie grew smaller still. Akeley was trying to keep Mickie's flight framed in the viewfinder of his own motion picture camera, which he'd brought along for the purpose of filming elephants. The camera was just another modern tool for making better taxidermy as far as he was concerned. It was a difficult machine to operate, but not as difficult as following the meandering thoughts of the balloon tycoon.

Akeley had met Boyce during the seventeen-day voyage from Naples to Mombasa, aboard the German *Adolph Woermann*, and the man had been talking Carl's ear off ever since. Of course, Carl knew who he was. Boyce was a well-known fixture in Chicago, a bigwig publisher and all-around muck-a-muck. He owned half a dozen newspapers, a paper mill, and a power company. He was said to be worth twenty million dollars, and lived in a mansion with fifteen fireplaces, and yet, to Akeley, his attempts at small talk must have sounded decidedly idiotic. To wit: "I should enjoy greatly being up in a balloon in a thunderstorm, wouldn't you? It must be a great sensation!"

Boyce had found his niche by copying the basic format—not to mention the stories—of Joe Pulitzer's *New York World* and then repackaging it for rural readers in a weekly he called the *Saturday Blade*. He'd also put out a women's magazine called *Boyce's Monthly*, with its ads for Swift's Wool Soap and flannel-lidded bedpans, and the *Chicago World*, a sporting weekly. He had deployed a formidable army of some six-thousand-odd newsboys across the country to deliver the *Blade*, the largest circulating weekly in the country.

Boyce boasted that it was a family paper, but Carl no doubt recalled how the man had run for Congress only to lose after a scandal that had led to accusations of printing obscenities and corrupting the youth.

In the wake of that kerfuffle he and his wife had divorced, and he had latched onto the Balloonograph adventure as a way to keep his mind off his troubles. He needed to get out of the country for a spell, and he was looking for the right kind of publicity. Fortunately for him, he had chosen the right continent at the right time, since Teddy Roosevelt was also a guest here now, on his own well-publicized big-game hunting trip. For the time being at least, the world's attention was turned to Africa. In fact, Boyce had deliberately chosen Africa with the aim of placing himself squarely in the former president's limelight. Boyce was the sort who would throw ideas against the wall until one stuck and made him rich, no matter how daft. If nothing else, the highland airs had overstimulated his capacity for daft ideas.

He was in the midst of hatching another one this very moment: "I am also thinking about a system of wireless telegraphy to be attached to the balloons for communication with stations to be established at cable ports on the coast," he said, giving the balloon carrying Mickie an odd look. "I shouldn't care to use it, though, if the sparks from the apparatus were likely to set fire to and explode the balloon."

Below the launch site was an assortment of box kites, motion picture equipment, and wooden tanks of sulfuric acid which had been blended with scrap iron to make the necessary hydrogen gas.

The night before, Boyce had played a few of his own motion pictures on a large screen outside in the square. Confused, excited dogs had repeatedly attacked the flickering images, causing great bursts of laughter in the audience. The movies were ones he'd made on the voyage down the Red Sea by suspending a cinematograph from a box kite. It was thrilling for the guests in the audience who'd been passengers on the same ship to watch themselves, snatched out of recent memory. There was a bird's-eye view of the sundeck, and of the first-class swimming pool, and plenty of the passengers moving about below, like birds themselves, dressed in white pants and straw hats and short black ties, taking choppy strolls around the deck. The best footage was of passengers playing deck sports. This is how they bided their time on the brutal, sultry crossing. The Germans did not join in these games, but the British played them avidly. The Germans rudely kept to themselves, played solemn rubbers of bridge, or laid out in their chaise longues with their sunburned children, while the British had all the fun. There was one favorite where all the men had to dash across the deck and then kneel at the feet of their female partner, who then had to knot their man's necktie as quickly as possible and light his cigarette, all in a gale of spitting sea wind, before each man ran back to the starting line. There was another variation of this game where the man had to thread a needle. It was harder than lighting a cigarette. Except for Akeley, who, nimble as he was with needle and thread, excelled magnificently.

Boyce's blimplike appearance wasn't helped any by the soft, spreadable face, nor the polka-dot bow tie and meandering inspirations. Akeley could not have objected to his enthusiasm, but this man's passions seemed almost idiotically whimsical, as if he had just taken up with the next idea that happened to float, unbidden, through his mind. To wit, did Akeley happen to know anything about the mountain gorilla?

Boyce had read or heard something about these creatures, and he found the prospect of their actual existence fascinating. Only a handful of white men had ever seen these rare apes, but from what he understood, they were reputed to be absolutely ferocious. There were reports of the beasts ripping off men's limbs and snapping rifles in half with their teeth. This was just the thing people wanted to read about! Exactly the type of story the rubes who bought his papers went in for! According to the most reliable accounts, this half man, half beast lived deep in the jungle in the Belgian Congo, where it dwelled on the slopes of ancient, fire-spitting volcanoes. Not that long ago gorillas had been thought mythical creatures, solidly in the same category as unicorns and mermaids. The German officer Captain Robert von Beringe had made the first sighting just seven years earlier. (And the French-American explorer Paul du Chaillu had only made the discovery of the lowland gorillas in 1855.) And now with people so riled over the origins of man, and where these alleged Dawn Men might have come from, these apes were looking like an even better story to W. D. Boyce. Their uncanny, if monstrous, resemblance to human beings had really stirred up the whole Darwinian can of worms! Man descending from apes and all that. While that was all surely piffle, Boyce assured Akeley, these creatures were still something that would grab the public's attention. Would it, boy! Snakes *al-ive*! Had Akeley run across such a thing yet in any of his adventures? No. Akeley had not ventured that far yet. Nor did he have plans to do so anytime soon. It was a completely different terrain, the Congo, and under Belgian rule besides.

Well, in that case, Boyce wondered what Akeley might think about trying to make a little side trip? Elephants were all well and good, but the mountain gorillas—no other mystery *even compared*. Since Akeley was here, already on the continent, that being half the shove, maybe he'd like to see whether he couldn't locate these mountain apes? Surely permission from the Belgians could be obtained. If he could capture them on film, it would fetch quite a wad of green. Especially if these apes were half as "demonlike" and "murderous" as du Chaillu had reported after killing several himself for sport. Moving pictures. That's what the public wanted. Not some dirty old skins! One needed modern sensibilities for modern times. That's why he himself, W. D. Boyce, would be *filming* the very animals Mr. Roosevelt was now slaughtering. With his camera-armed balloons, he would capture herds of wildebeests and zebras splayed out across the plains; stunning close-ups of beasts in their natural habitats—scenes otherwise far too dangerous to try to photograph on the ground, and far less brutal than Teddy Roosevelt's methods. Yes, indeed. TR's skins would decay a thousand years before his own cinematic contributions ever did. There was only one way to preserve the past for the future now.

"Pictures will live," he said, "when hides will rot."

Carl had to wonder. Considering the alarming number of nickelodeon fires each year, really, what were the chances a movie made with nitrate cellulose film was going to outlast his or TR's arsenic-plated skins?

Regardless, if Akeley was interested, Boyce was prepared to commission such an expedition. After all, Akeley had a motion picture camera himself; why shouldn't he put it to use? And honestly, about the most sensational "wildlife" film done to date was the footage Edison had made of Topsy the elephant being electrocuted at Luna Park. Now, *that* had been a success in the nickelodeons. Even more fun than feeding Topsy lit cigarettes (the alleged reason he'd gone and killed three of his handlers). Akeley had to admit the idea was intriguing, especially since he was pretty sure he'd be broke before he'd be able to complete his elephant expedition for the AMNH. Maybe he'd shot himself in the foot by insisting on coming to New York as a free agent, as a contractor, rather than as a member of the museum's staff. The last year had been spent lecturing and fund-raising for this trip; there was no denying his new connections in New York had helped, but he was still basically working on spec. He agreed to accept Boyce's commission. Needless to say, he couldn't do it right away. First he would have to get the elephants.

For the umpteenth time that morning, he felt the telegram in his pocket. He could have taken it out and read it again to convince himself it was real, but it would have brought too much unwanted attention if noticed, especially by present company, so he had to remain content to feel it there in his pocket. It had been waiting for him when they'd first arrived at the Norfolk Hotel; the manager had delivered it to him with a great deal of ceremony, a great show of discretion that in the end was so indiscreet as to be almost comical. The telegram was from Teddy Roosevelt.

The Akeleys had only been in Nairobi for four days, but Carl was impatient to get going. He was ready to be done with the foolish balloon rides. It was already nearing the end of September. The Roosevelt safari had been in British East Africa since late April, TR having left the United States just three short weeks after he'd left the White House and William Taft, his handpicked successor, had been inaugurated. In the telegram, the president—or, rather, *the colonel*, as he preferred to be addressed now that he was out of office, as he had during his famous charge at San Juan Hill—suggested their respective safaris attempt a rendezvous near Mount Elgon in mid-November. He was now hunting lions somewhere in the Sotik, an area bordering German East Africa.

The plan was still for TR to bag one or two elephants for his group— for a total of five or six—which he knew his masters in New York were counting on to lend that much more prestige to the Hall of Elephants. The idea had first been broached at the White House dinner, back when TR had been seeking counsel from various authorities on Africa, big-game hunters, and other explorers. How blown over Akeley had been upon receiving the invitation, to finally meet his hero, and in such a fashion! And then come that crisp November evening, stepping out of the cold into the stately vestibule of the Entrance Hall of the White House, newly refurbished by the architect Charles McKim, and the long corridor of crimson carpet beckoning them onward. More dazzling still to look down the table and see Mickie, surrounded by a shimmer of china and crystal, talking to Mrs. Roosevelt, and Congressman James Robert Mann, the senator from Illinois who'd joined them, and who, by one of those funny coincidences in life, had beat out that milksop W. D. Boyce in his own ill-starred bid for the seat.

Carl had to smile to himself, looking at his wife, candlelight dancing on her silver bracelets as she demurely told the story of how she had slain the biggest bull elephant ever taken on Mount Kenya. She was still just a girl at heart. How he must have already missed the thrill of going into battle with her, standing shoulder to shoulder, rifles blazing—the way her eyes went cool as she stalked, the erotic lethal game of hide-and-seek. Back in Chicago, nearly every day she'd come into his studio, bringing him lunch, and watching as he worked on *her* elephant. The giant white clay manikin suspended there like something they'd dredged from a fossil pit. When she arrived, Carl would come down from his ladder, where he'd been spackling the giant in his silk vest, a dank handkerchief tucked in his back pocket.

As fetching as Mickie was that night, he was entirely cast under the spell of the minor divinity at the head of the table, with the glinting pince-nez and aggressively mirthful laugh. Beneath the glazed eyes of a moose and a forest canopy of antlers, TR bent forward, listening to Carl with the rapt attention of a schoolboy. For it was his counsel he sought at the moment, and together they were creating a vision of a great adventure. Teddy and his second-oldest son, Kermit, wanted to hunt the first few months in BEA and German East Africa, then up to Uganda, and from there onward up the Nile to Khartoum, where TR hoped to shoot a white rhinoceros. He would be donating most of his specimens to the Smithsonian, which in turn would underwrite his adventure.

He also agreed it might be possible to donate an elephant or two to the New York museum as well; after all, his father had been one of its founders. He sought Carl's opinion on every last detail, and Carl wanted to give him everything he knew and more. He would arrange for his former headman, R. J. Cuninghame, to lead Roosevelt's safari. He also recommended a new outfitter in Nairobi, Newland & Tarlton, which would manage his supply line. They talked about guns and lions. For long range he'd want to use the penetrating .256; at close range, some sort of nine-millimeter would be advisable; at closer range still a .475 cordite. For elephants he recommended the British-manufactured double-barreled .500-.450 Holland & Holland, a rifle Akeley himself couldn't afford. As a personal touch, he would also end up recommending to him his favorite gun boy, Bill, the most trustworthy African he had ever known. That night, before they'd gone out to their waiting carriage, and a quick ride back to their hotel in the cold autumn night, Roosevelt had said to him, "It's my last chance for something in the nature of a Great Adventure."

✼

BEFORE MICKIE'S ASCENT in the balloon, the first to go up had been Fred Stephenson. Fred was a big-game hunter from Minnesota, an old friend of Carl's, whom he'd brought along as a member of his safari. At six foot five and 230 pounds, Fred was quite a sight stuffed into the little wicker basket. Everyone got a good laugh when he'd climbed in and the balloon wouldn't lift off. Even after all the ballast had gone over, it still refused to budge. But then, on a lark, Fred had taken off his heavy boots and tossed them overboard, one at a time, and to everyone's pleasure this little joke had worked and the basket at last had lifted slowly off the ground. There it remained, levitating, twenty feet overhead, the big lug looking down at them with a crazy grin, until they'd winched him back to earth.

After Fred, Carl's other American companion, the cartoonist from the *Chicago Tribune*, J. T. McCutcheon, had gone up. He was of much slighter build than Fred, and had floated off like an animated thought bubble. A cartoonist may have seemed an odd choice for a safari companion, but Akeley had met McCutcheon at one of the lectures he'd given while raising funds for the upcoming trip, and they'd hit it off so well, and J.T. was so riveted by his adventures, that Carl had invited him on the spot to join him and Mickie on their next expedition. Besides, Carl had never met anyone who wanted to kill a lion so badly in his life. The *Tribune* had been happy to let him go along given the prospect of following the goings-on of the former president's safari up close, especially since TR had all but banned reporters from the continent.

When Mickie finally went up—the first female volunteer—some of the women in the crowd seemed stunned that one of their own would do such a thing, but they cheered and waved their silk umbrellas. There were many duchesses and ladies in this crowd—wives of the growing number of Lord Cranworths and Earls of Warwick and Count Coudenhoves and a motley assortment of marquises and marchionesses—and even a goodly number of American industrial tycoons—and presidents!— all here to quench their unquenchable bloodlust.

When Mickie came back down, Boyce noisily congratulated her on being the first woman to soar above the plains of British East Africa. Oh, it had been lovely, Mickie said, still dizzy. She'd been able to look down on the new clock tower of the train station, and the stone and red-tiled buildings that were replacing all the old tin shanties, gardens splotched with Nandi flame trees, jacaranda and bougainvillea, and blue gum trees that lined the streets. How busy Nairobi looked from above! How it had changed! The macadamized roads. The electric streetlights. The big stone edifice of the Bank of India looked like a dollhouse! From up there she could see down onto the polo fields, and the concrete tennis courts, and even a few fielders in white outfits running about a sandy cricket pitch. She could see out over the Athi Plains, and she could see Mount Kenya to the north and Mount Kilimanjaro all the way down in German East Africa. It was like looking down on Africa from a sky-scraper! She and J.T. tried to persuade Carl to go up himself, but he had a telegram burning a hole in his pocket and was eager to get back down to the Norfolk, where the porters had already gathered and were now ready to depart for the Tana Valley.

CHAPTER FIFTEEN

THE SAFARISTS WERE VERGING ON BOREDOM, GOING FIVE weeks now in the Lower Tana River Valley, but it was too soon to move on to the Uasin Gishu Plateau as their rendezvous with Roosevelt was still a while off. During the mornings Fred and J.T. hunted meat for the party, but come midday, to avoid the broiling sun, they loafed in their tents, reading or smoking, while Carl experimented with his motion picture machine, an Urban Bioscope, and Mickie explored along the banks of the river with her tent boy, observing the queer little monkeys that frolicked in the fever trees. Evenings were spent picking ticks from their puttees and flicking them into the popping fire.

This was their sixth campsite since departing Nairobi. Things had been much more exciting at the last camp, where a windstorm had come along and blown over the cook's tent, setting the whole veldt ablaze in the middle of the night. It had taken a hundred men, including the cook himself, who, as it happened, had the distressing habit of preparing meals in a polka-dot apron without benefit of pants, an hour to stamp out the flames.

For a while they tried hunting lions, which Fred and J.T. were hell-bent to shoot, but the Lower Tana wasn't good lion country. Otherwise, there was an abundance of big game, and the valley resembled a lovely park more than anything, with rolling lawns and pleasant tree-shaded knolls, dotted with zebras and giraffes and an exotic diversity of antelopes. For dinner they ate *kongoni* steaks, impala liver, heart of waterbuck.

Akeley tried to film some of the fast-moving animals, but it was like trying to track shooting stars with a child's telescope. For a while, to bide their time, he'd also tried to get rhinos to charge his motion picture camera, with Fred and J.T. ready to blast one to kingdom come in the final take if things got too hairy, but the rhinos refused to charge. The most one might do was trot toward the camera briefly enough to get their scent, but it always turned tail well before anyone got sweaty palms. Apparently, rhinos were not as furious as imagined.

One day over their second breakfast the hunting companions got into an argument about the cleanliness of wild animals versus captives in zoos. Both President Osborn, of the American Museum, and Teddy Roosevelt had been instrumental in founding the Bronx Zoological Gardens, and so given the circuitous nature of conversation, especially now when the interlocutors were looking for reasons to avoid the heat, plus the imminent rendezvous with Roosevelt, it was only natural the subject had come up in the first place. They were discussing monkeys in particular. Mickie felt it was a sin to cage animals in such confined spaces. McCutcheon disagreed. Stephenson was inclined to agree with McCutcheon. Akeley, wisely, stayed out of it.

"Monkeys are uncannily fascinating," J.T. said, cutting up the bushbuck liver on his plate with a fork and knife, "but offensively smelly." Though he might enjoy drawing cartoons of them—monkeys *were* fun to draw—he held no love for the actual species per se.

They sat at a low table sunk in the surrounding high grass, inside a triangle of shade beneath the mess tent veranda. Both J.T. and Fred had accessorized their pith helmets with parrot and guinea fowl feathers, which twittered as they ate their oatmeal and eggs, whiffling as they turned their heads this way or that to greet each next item of food brought out by their servants in waiting. The blue silk puggaree wrapped around Mickie's own white sun helmet fluttered like a pennant in the grassy breeze, and from the nearby bank of the river they could hear the rattle of seedpods in the stirring bulrushes.

Mickie agreed that animals in zoos were filthy. But only because they were demoralized and incapable of keeping themselves clean as they did in the wild. The zoo broke the wild creature's spirit. Corrupted its *morale*. In such conditions it lost the will to live and no longer bothered to care for itself. Naturally it was a common prejudice for people who only saw them at zoos to believe monkeys were unkempt beasts. But surely Mr.

McCutcheon must realize that the monkeys he saw at the zoo—and judged so severely for their lack of hygiene—only seemed that way because of the unnatural and cruel conditions in which they were kept?

No, he said, chewing briskly. He didn't exactly see it that way. Here Stephenson chimed in to say how he too found monkeys repellent; just look at their cages—they were obviously vile creatures.

Carl creaked back in his cane chair, grinning, happy to remain safely neutral.

And besides—Stephenson continued—surely, monkeys were far better off in captivity than in the jungle; in the zoo they didn't have to grub for food or live in constant fear of being eaten themselves!

"When people say that," Mickie said, "they are trying to make us believe that man knows better than their Maker what is best for these wild creatures! Anyway, I doubt if there lives a normal person who would not prefer the sporting chance of fighting for his existence to a life of idleness and slow torture behind prison bars."

The men appeared to contemplate this.

Outside their triangle of peaceful shade was an infinite, endless pyramid of sun. Over the chatter of insects they could hear their syces, or animal groomers, singing as they went about the meticulous work of picking off the horses those ticks that had accumulated during the morning's lion hunt. You saw the ticks in great swags on the rhinos, gathered in the folds and crevices of their thick, platelike skin, like barnacles on a ship's hull. Large colonies clustered in the warm regions, growing like tumors around the groin and under the neck. Feasting upon these insects were the symbiotic oxpeckers, which rode on the rhinos' backs. Their beaks spattered red with blood and flecks of carapace.

After a while, J.T. said, dissecting a papaya, "You know, if anyone were to ask me now, *Is it hot enough for you?* I would answer without hesitation, *Yes.*"

Mickie held her coffee cup to her mouth, but she was not going to allow the subject to be changed. Because it just so happened that she had been spending much of her time, lately, out in the forest observing the very monkeys she was now defending. With nothing more than binoculars and the company of a shy gun bearer, she had lain on her back on the forest floor, camouflaged beneath bits of foliage, waiting with astounding patience, until at last the monkeys' own inquisitive nature won out over their prudence and they came closer to examine the intruder. Once they realized she was only a harmless voyeur, they went about their business indifferent to her presence.

In this way she had been able to observe their natural habits. She had watched them groom and mate and care for their young. The mother and babies were very close, and would spend many hours grooming and cuddling, but the fathers were not as attentive and seemed to spend most of their time competing for the best napping spots. The siblings also seemed very close. She had learned much about their society. How the monkeys competed for food and intimacy. She'd seen how alert and curious they were in the wild. Constantly on the move, ceaselessly foraging for bugs, pawing at the earth, searching the underside of leaves for spider eggs. They scurried about on hands and knees on the forest floor, and the gray fur on their backs shone greenly as they gnawed at the dropped smooth pods from the fever trees above. They ate with spare, nervous movements. Constantly turning their heads from side to side. She told Carl how she had witnessed them playing what looked like hide-and-seek, and how she'd even tagged along with her monkey bandits as they raided native farmers' crops and pilfered crocodile eggs buried in the sand along the riverbank. In fact, once they'd grown accustomed to her presence, she had managed to carry on rudimentary sorts of conversation with them by imitation—scratching under her arms, making the same grunts and coughs, and trying to mimic their peculiar purring noise, which was more like a *wrrrr*—and in this way, despite the amusement it no doubt gave her gun bearer, she had begun to learn something of their language. But most of all she emphasized to her companions how exquisitely clean and wholesome she found the monkeys to be in their natural habitat.

"Much of their time is spent picking the fur clean of each tiny particle of dust," she said, brushing away crumbs with the side of her hand. "Mother Nature provides shower baths and the tropic sunshine dries them." She smiled scoldingly at J. T. McCutcheon. "It's *confinement* that teaches them the offensive habits."

Impressed that she'd been able to get so close, the men laughed amiably, but they still believed monkeys were foul and degenerate vermin. Stephenson made a gesture for Carl to pass the evaporated cream.

In the end, rather than exasperate herself by arguing anymore, Mickie declared that she would prove her point by going down to the river to trap one and bring it back to camp. They would see for themselves then just how wholesome the monkey was in its natural state. She would prove that a wild African monkey was perhaps the cleanest animal in existence! And then, of course, she would set it free again.

With the help of one of the younger boys, trapping a monkey proved surprisingly easy. They set out a basket baited with corn and the next day returned to find an indignant little vervet. It was just an infant. A small gray-furred fuzzball, with a white breast, and orangish potbelly, and a tiny black gremlin face. It had nimble little fingers that grasped hold of the basket as she lifted it up to her face. It had the most delightfully woodsy smell! Its breath smelled as sweet and clean as a human baby's. There was just something so dear about its face—oh, that little goblin face!—and how petrified the poor thing was! How could such a helpless creature survive in the wilderness? It was hard to imagine, really, and in truth she just wanted to protect it.

When she brought it back, the men of course were surprised, and laughed when Mickie joshed McCutcheon by saying that she had named it J.T. Jr. Carl guessed it was no more than six or eight months old. It had tiny razor teeth and hazel eyes, and it squealed at them pitifully. Even after a few days in camp it remained skeptical of Mickie's attempts to befriend it, but it accepted the hand mirror she let it play with, and after a while lay down on her cot with it, falling asleep with the mirror pressed to its face.

Although she had fully intended on letting it go after a few days, after she proved her point, she quickly fell in love with the monkey and, apparently forgetting any qualms she'd had against the evils of captivity, decided to keep it. She justified her decision by saying that she intended to conduct more "scientific" observations about its wild nature before letting it go. But in truth it was just so pretty and had such a saucy little personality she couldn't dream of letting it go. So when they left the Tana River camp a few days later, the monkey had joined their safari.

At first it rode on a porter's load, but Mickie soon saw that the heat had a dwindling effect on the monkey's spirit. It was used to the clement woodland shade along the Tana. She called forward her tent boy, Ali, and gave him an umbrella, and instructed that he was to let J.T. Jr. ride on his shoulder from now on, and to shield the monkey from the fiercesome sun. At the next camp, she made him trade in his beads for a khaki suit and a brand-new fez, the better to serve as J.T. Jr.'s personal valet.

As such, in addition to his primary duty as umbrella bearer, Ali was to bring the monkey's breakfast to her tent every morning. Banana, papaya, and, if available, J.T. Jr.'s favorite dish, fresh figs. Then, every afternoon at three P.M. he was instructed to give the monkey a steaming hot bath. In the afternoon, when there were no other chores to be done, he would go off and pick J.T. Jr. bouquets of wildflowers, which the monkey considered a delectation, especially wild gladiolus.

Ali, who was a round-faced and sweet-natured child, took to his new role cheerfully, despite the taunting he got from the older porters who thought the whole thing beyond ridiculous.

It soon became clear how sensitive the monkey really was—especially to anything like taunting. When Ali, for instance, himself tried to play a harmless joke on J.T. Jr. by making the bath too cold, the monkey bit him on the arm, and from then on Ali learned not to trifle with J.T. Jr.'s feelings.

The first time J.T. Jr. bit Mickie—in the moment before it happened she had just begun to take note (scientifically) of the odd expression forming on its face, and how its ears had flattened out, and its tiny little chin jutted out almost patriotically—without warning it sank its teeth into the fleshy part of her hand.

When Akeley saw the wound he suggested the monkey ought to be punished. For a moment she may have considered this sensible-sounding advice. But not for very long. Because it was then and there that she vowed that she would never punish J.T. Jr., no matter how badly the monkey acted out. Nor would she let anyone else lay a hand on her pet. She wanted her observations to be pure and therefore felt the monkey should exist in as natural a state as possible, unfettered by consequences its captors might arbitrarily impose on its behavior.

No matter how many innocent bystanders got bit.

No matter whose peach-silk undergarments it stole and flaunted from the roof of the tent while its mistress was indisposed in her bath. No matter how many times it tore apart the kitchen tent, broke eggs, pitched plates, smashed teacups, tossed pots and pans, or defecated wherever it damn well pleased. No one was to lay a hand on the animal. It would join them for meals at the table perched on the soup tureen, if it wanted, its skinny tail draped across the freshly cut fruit, and eat as many fresh figs as its heart desired—or lamb, chicken, and veal for that matter—and if it threw a tantrum or turned over a scalding pot of tea, that was all data Mickie could use as well.

There was no question it was a petulant little animal full of cunning. It continued to raid the porters' tents and steal their belongings—it had a fondness for tobacco, pipes, and matches—and if they complained or scolded the monkey or, God forbid, tried to offer it the burning end of a stick in retribution, the monkey would flash its tiny fangs and chase after the men until their ankles bled. Mickie only laughed at its madcap antics. Almost as if it were an accomplice, part of her inner mischief let loose. A surrogate for a saboteur secretly harbored in her heart. Truly, she would have let it get away with murder if she could.

After a while it did become necessary to tie the monkey to the tent pole on occasion. But even from there it had a wide ambit in order to chase chickens, or to climb on top of the tent with its mirror to make faces at the porters, or fling projectiles at the tent boys while they boiled water and filled the canteens each evening.

The monkey, she said, was just a frightened child. And, after all, she still felt guilty for keeping it her prisoner. Instead of punishing J.T. Jr., she would hold the little orphan in her lap, running her fingers through its fur, to soothe the furry tempest. There was no question that she had spoiled it rotten. She doted on it hopelessly, practically never letting it out of her sight. When the monkey was sick she played nurse and gave it medicine, putting ointment in its tiny nostrils with a dropper, rinsing its stinging swollen eyes of the campfire smoke. Sometimes she missed J.T. Jr. so badly when she went out hunting that she would return early for fear the monkey might have grown lonely. The attachment seemed mutual. In fact, she had long since allowed J.T. Jr. to sleep in her cot— originally for the purpose of studying how the monkey reacted to "night sounds"—and now if anyone intruded after they had dressed for bed and lowered the mosquito net J.T. Jr. would lash out viciously. Naturally, Carl was not happy to find that since the monkey had joined them, he was more or less barred from his wife's tent.

As the safari moved deeper into the bush, sometimes, in the middle of the night, Mickie would wake to find the vervet crouched by her head, with its small hand clamped over her nose, making a strange and unsettling hissing-purring noise with its tongue. It seemed on these occasions that the monkey was trying to alert its mistress to the presence of some danger lurking outside that, no matter how she listened, she could never hear for herself.

CHAPTER SIXTEEN

FROM THE TANA VALLEY THE SAFARISTS RETURNED TO NAIROBI and next made their way by rail to Londiani, a dusty little military backwash of three corrugated shacks and one telegraph station, and from here they began an overland march to reach the elephant country of the Uasin Gishu Plateau. After eleven days on foot, heading north and then west across the plateau, they arrived at Sergoi, the farthest-flung outpost of the protectorate. There, in a dim iron bungalow, manned by a malarial official from Derbyshire, Carl found a letter awaiting him from Teddy Roosevelt.

The letter confirmed that Roosevelt was still on the plateau, encamped somewhere along the Nzoia River. He recommended that Akeley get a runner to help lead the way from Sergoi. But from the date on the letter it was evident it had been waiting a number of days, so there was no way of knowing for sure whether the Roosevelt party had moved on in the meantime, nor were they able to find any runners who knew the way exactly.

It was possible TR had already learned what they were now discovering for themselves, namely that there did not seem to be any elephants on the plateau. In eleven days, they had not seen a single one. If Akeley wasn't able to get an elephant bagged by TR, he knew it would disappoint the trustees at the museum.

Another depressing thought knocking around his mind was that if the colonel hadn't already found any elephants himself, he may have decided not to wait any longer and gone on to Mount Elgon, or even

Uganda, instead. The latter seemed even likelier after Akeley met two hunters in Sergoi who had just spent six weeks on Mount Elgon and who told him not to expect any luck on its northern slopes. There were plenty of cows and calves, they said, but all the bulls had been hunted off. For the time being, without any runners who knew the way, and without any definite clues as to TR's whereabouts, all they could do was continue across the plateau and hope for the best.

They were moving west, toward the hazy distant outline of Mount Elgon, with one wary eye on the mountains to the north, a boundary marked on the map with "natives probably treacherous." Near Nyeu, at the equator, they saw a sign: 6,058 MILES TO SELFRIDGE'S OXFORD ST. LONDON. The numerous outfitters that had cropped up in the last couple of years were advertising in the middle of what used to be nowhere. Such was the expanding speed of the safari craze. As they rode their ponies onward through the high copper grass, J. T. McCutcheon, wearing guinea fowl feathers in his helmet, attempted to sketch his namesake riding on Ali's shoulder, wincing nervously at the surrounding grass.

There had been as few signs of lions as elephants. Only a plenitude of carefree antelopes, safe now at least from the safarists who rarely hunted between encampments. It was too much trouble to stop the machine once they'd gotten it started. The ever-present entourage of porters struggled onward, wading through the grass with trunks, chop boxes, and furniture overhead like house servants saving the valuables from a flood.

The monkey irritated Carl. The way Mickie had taken to it almost as if it were a child. Not to say necessarily that he was worried what this meant, if it meant anything. He would not say he was jealous. But he could not have been happy, either, the first night she told him he couldn't stay in her tent because there was not enough room for three. They were in the highlands now, the plateau being around seven thousand feet, and, despite their proximity to the equator, it was impossible to keep warm at night without three or four blankets. Hailing from the Tana Valley, J.T. Jr. had never been exposed to such harsh cold temperatures. He didn't expect her to let the poor thing freeze to death, did he?

During the day, the safari crossed paths with a few Boer settlers trekking behind caravans of ox- and mule-wagons, and then one afternoon shortly after coming upon the Nzoia River, they ran across the Duke of Peñaranda of Spain, whose party was hunting lions, though without luck. Nor had they seen any elephants, nor any former presidents of the

United States. Though the duke had crossed paths with the prince of Liechtenstein, who was also hunting on the plateau. It was no wonder the elephants were in hiding.

It was the following afternoon when a runner showed at camp. At first, they thought he must have been sent by the colonel. It didn't make sense, considering he was coming from the direction of Sergoi, but it turned out that he was in fact *looking* for Roosevelt, though without any more specific directions as to the whereabouts of the former president's camp than they had themselves. Carl had to wonder if this was just another mistake and whether the message the man carried was not in fact *from* the colonel, for Carl's own behalf, but the native had instructions to divulge the contents of his message only to its intended recipient, and there not being any *mzungus* (white men) here resembling the former chief executive of the United States of America, Carl could only guess. In any event, it could not have been all that urgent; as soon as the messenger realized he had the wrong safari, he quickly called it quits and fell in with the porters, evidently seeing no point in trying to track down a customer on his own when they were looking for the same man. He spent the next few days tagging along, sharing his new companions' cigarettes and gossip, and clearly enjoying his impromptu holiday. Whatever the message, the colonel would have to wait.

The next morning they set out with the truant messenger in tow, but no clearer idea where or how much farther except that they should continue along the meandering papyrus-banks of the river. How was one to coordinate a rendezvous in such a vast unmarked territory with nothing but fickle, naked savages to carry the news?

Barring a message of their progress, Roosevelt would surely assume Akeley hadn't received his message, or had otherwise been detained, and with no elephants on the plateau he would simply get impatient and move on to Uganda, and then they would never meet at all.

But then, on the eleventh day, the steady plainsong of the rustling grass was broken by the abrupt descant of scattered gunfire. The shots came from the west. Carl's gun bearer quickly handed him his field glasses and he scanned over the hazy outline of Mount Elgon and then trolled farther down the horizon until he skipped across a blur of movement. A break in the monotony of metal-yellow grass. There was a wagon, the blue-tint horns of oxen, and several blurry Africans with ivory tusks cantilevered on their shoulders. He turned the wheel with his thumb and cast forward and backward from the ivory bearers, and his eye stuttered across a flotilla of portmanteaus and kitchen chairs, barrels of dishes, glinting tin boxes, a writing desk, all bobbing above the grass. A long procession of porters snaked through his lens; the ivory bearers were far from alone. The line virtually disappeared out of sight. He glassed hastily up the line, losing them momentarily in the sea of grass, then pinning them down again and chasing to the head, where he focused tightly on three khaki figures on horseback. They were far enough away that he could not make out any faces, though one of the figures, without doubt, had a more rotund and executive aura than the others. The safari was far too big to be the Spaniards. Four hundred porters at least. It was more like an armada. He waited for the flick of rifle smoke. Several heartbeats passed before the audible reports. At the least they were a mile away.

It absolutely had to be Roosevelt's party. There was nobody else it could be. No operation of this size had ever stepped foot on the continent. And yet it was now headed away, in the direction from which they had just come. If further corroboration was needed, he had it when the flag bearer came into view, near the head of the expedition: the forty-six stars and twisting stripes flapped gigantically. Carl sent off a runner immediately. A short while later, still waiting on his pony with eyes glued to binoculars, when a report came from the headman that a recently evacuated camp along the river had been found, Carl ordered the safari to turn in to await more news.

When his runner returned to say that the colonel had turned back and was now on his way—that it was in fact Roosevelt's party—Akeley set out at once to meet him en route. He raced his pony at full clip across the plain, plunging through the tall grass, risking potholes and invisible grass-clad ant-bear burrows—at this speed, they would send his horse into a somersault—and now, when he came upon the approaching horsemen, he heard the distinctive high-pitched voice that any American who had ever passed within earshot of a whistle-stop knew as well as they knew the sound of their own ears ringing. Roosevelt was calling out to him. Here was the great man, in the flesh, waving his helmet, grinning, a terrific biscuit box of flashing teeth.

When he came to a respectful distance, Akeley dismounted, and at the same time the colonel practically leaped from his horse to greet him with a handshake that could have pulled down an elephant tusks first.

"If I could have seen you an hour and a half ago, I could have got you the elephants you want for your group," Roosevelt said, tugging his riding gloves off by the fingers. "We passed within only a few yards of a herd of ten this morning. Kermit got within thirty yards to make some photographs." The colonel's son stood by with the two other white men, beaming. Behind them rested the great multitude of porters, a ragamuffin army of Minyamwezi, Swahili, Kikuyu, Baganda, Kavirondo, and Lumbwa—the language barrier of mixed tribes discouraged mutiny— like a silent Greek chorus massed behind the wandering hero-king. Since he had not known Akeley's whereabouts, the colonel said, they had left the elephants be.

The other two white men were Edmund Heller, one of three naturalists accompanying Roosevelt from the Smithsonian, and Leslie Tarlton, coproprietor of the Nairobi outfitter Newland & Tarlton. A red-headed Australian with a deeply cleft chin, Tarlton was R. J. Cuninghame's "adjutant," and their guide and professional hunter for now, since, as TR explained, Cuninghame had gone ahead to Uganda to prepare the next leg of their safari. Under his florid hair, the man was sallow. He looked diminished in his clothes and possessed a lingering air of sickness—being on the mend, as it were, from a fever he'd picked up guiding the Roosevelts through the tick-plagued Guaso Nyero.

Their meeting was uncanny good luck. A day later, and Roosevelt would have been gone. It was promising, too, that the colonel had seen ten elephants when Carl had not seen a single one in as many days. Still, it was too late to start after the herd now. So Roosevelt suggested they return to their camp and let the members of their respective safaris get acquainted over a midafternoon luncheon. Tarlton nodded weakly and said they could try to track the elephants the next morning.

Back at camp, everybody gathered about, excited to have pulled off the rendezvous, laughing at their good luck, hardly believing that here among them stood the twenty-sixth president of the United States, only eight months out of office. The encampment was immense. There were thirteen large tents, among them the dining hall, a laboratory for the various doings of the naturalists sent by the Smithsonian, one for the horses, a skinning tent, and another Kermit kept as a darkroom for developing pictures. Several tents were required just to store the salt (four tons of the stuff for preserving skins); out of 260 porters, 200 were required just to carry the scientific impedimenta of the Roosevelt expedition. TR said he had offered to give the natives more tents, practically begged them, but they preferred to sleep huddled together and not alone as the white man chose. TR was especially glad to lay eyes on other Americans and to hear any news they might have brought from home of life after his reign.

The little news he had heard, how Taft was bungling affairs in his wake, was disheartening. Oddly enough, the Akeley safari was the only one he'd crossed paths with since being in Africa. It went to show to what lengths the British had gone to shelter his privacy. After a while somebody remembered the messenger who had been looking for the colonel and went and fetched him so he could deliver whatever news he bore. Really, it was a miracle anyone ever got a message delivered via "bush telegraph"; a true mystery how the modern world could reach them out here in the middle of nowhere. Using his penknife, the colonel casually opened the telegram and, after a startled moment, reread the message aloud to the others. It was from America.

REPORTED HERE YOU HAVE BEEN KILLED. MRS. ROOSEVELT WORRIED. CABLE DENIAL AMERICAN EMBASSY, ROME.

The telegram was dated eight days earlier—November 6, 1909.

After arranging to send a runner back to Sergoi to reassure his wife that he had not been eaten by lions—yet—the colonel ceased to worry and then joked at the premature report of his demise. Everybody else had a good laugh, too, all being in firm agreement on how unimpeachably alive he looked.

After the tent boys had finished laying out the table—crisp white linens set aglint with silver and china—everyone settled down for the luncheon feast. Mrs. Akeley had changed into a long khaki skirt and a fetchingly cut hunting jacket with a few cartridges tucked into the breast pocket. J.T. Jr. balanced on the upturned crook of her arm while she fed it a spear of tinned asparagus. When she asked about her old tent boy, Bill, expecting him to be one of Roosevelt's servers, she learned how he had got into a wild fight with some of the other porters and got himself expelled from the president's party. She had known him to be extremely willful, but it was disappointing to think she would probably never see him again.

The sun was at high noon, but in the shade of the dining tent it was comfortable. With the canvas sides rolled up, the companions could enjoy the breezy view, while awaiting each course, brought out one at a time by the white-gloved tent boys: rhino tail soup, roast guinea fowl, eland marrow spread on toast, roasted francolin, the last being a type of local duck whose grating calls they could hear from the nearby swamp as they dined.

Eminently present for every savory morsel was the legendary appetite of Teddy Roosevelt. For his voracity and expansive physique, his porters had given him the nickname "Bwana Tumbo," which meant Mister Stomach in Swahili. They called Kermit—who wore a fetching cork sun helmet lined with green silk—"Bwana Merodadi." Dandy Master. The Harvard freshman was taking a year off to join the safari, and despite any prior misgivings his father may have had about the boy's mettle, or lack thereof, the only concern now was that his son was too reckless. In Africa, he had hurled himself at any and every danger, seemingly only to prove that he could be just as strenuous as his fearless father. He was forever tearing off alone into the bush after cheetahs, boars, and lions he had wounded or missed.

TR was eager to regale his companions with their adventures. When they'd first arrived, just to warm up, they'd gone hunting on the estate of Sir Alfred Pease, where Bwana Tumbo had made his first acquisition for the nation's museum: two lion cubs. Kermit had shot a crocodile there, too, and when they'd cut it open they had found chewed-up eland bones, rocks, an assortment of hooves, and the claws of a cheetah—items all duly noted down and recorded by TR, who intended to miss nothing in his role as professional naturalist. After Pease's, they had also hunted a bit on the twenty-two-thousand-acre ranch of the American millionaire William Northrup McMillan—his fortune was made in rubber—where Kermit had wounded a leopard with his impetuous riflework, getting a porter severely mauled in the process. The man was only one of several casualties of the Roosevelt safari.

On the Kapiti Plains they went after lions in the company of the legendary white hunter Frederick Courteney Selous, shot hippos on Lake Naivasha, where TR suffered a recurrence of the Cuban fever he'd contracted four years earlier hunting grizzlies in the Colorado Rockies, and had then gone to Mount Kenya for *Loxodonta africana*, better known as the African elephant—the president was a veritable Linnaeus of Latin terms for the quarry he set in his sites. When he spoke now of his first elephant kill, he looked down the sun-filled goblets and tureens with an expression of sheer rapture, describing how the night following this kill he had toasted on a stick and then eaten slices of the leviathan's heart.

In all, he'd killed four elephants on Mount Kenya. Between father and son they had shot seventeen lions, six giraffes, four buffalos, five rhinos, four hippos, and, give or take, about a thousand birds—all in all a lucrative contribution of data for the museum in Washington. So lucrative, in fact, that Edmund Heller had complained in a letter home to his wife that keeping up with the Roosevelts had given him and the other taxidermists a severe case of "rhinoceritis."

The Roosevelts had also been down hunting five weeks along the Sotik, a desertlike plateau bordering German East Africa, which, when brought up in conversation, naturally steered it toward the gloomier topic of international relations. There had been a lot of talk these days about war between England and Germany. It was just a matter of time, it seemed.

The Akeley party themselves noted how the German and English passengers had hardly spoken a word to one another during the voyage from Naples to Mombasa.

"Each went his way without so much as a good morning or a *guten abend*," McCutcheon said.

TR smiled and wagged a finger deliberately. "If England ever has trouble with Germany," he said, "I think it will come from some unreasonable panic which will inspire each to attack the other for fear of being attacked itself." He said that Kaiser Wilhelm II—whom he called the "little Kaiser"—was an irrational and nervous man, and one whom, quite frankly, he had found to be an exasperating nettle. Take, for instance, the nuisance he'd made of things during the Moroccan crisis, when he'd tried to undermine the authority of France and nearly brought *those* two European powers to war!

Germany's emperor had delusions of omnipotence, he said. That was essentially the problem. TR had picked up an eland bone from his plate and begun to work out the marrow with a pickle fork. "It thinks it is a match for England and France combined in war, and would probably be less reluctant to fight both those powers together than they would be together to fight it." Britain was paranoid that Germany had "designs on [its] homeland," and Germany was paranoid that Britain (and France) were trying to lock it out of North Africa.

On the other hand, he felt a great affinity for Japan. (He had turned the bone around and was now attacking it from the other end.) Its rise to power was a phenomenon that had made the world take notice. Like the United States, it was young and aggressive, and he believed it had beaten old mother Russia to a frazzle because, in part, the Japanese had greater *morale*. By morale, he meant purpose and courage—that particular aspect of character so essential to the survival of civilization. Russia was an antiquated empire, and one, he didn't mind saying, which he could not trust—its people truly did possess a bewildering mendacity! But just as England had grown a bit flabby, Russia had lost its force as an empire. Not, of course, that England had lost *its* edge completely; look at the marvelous work the British were doing here in Africa, by George! They had brought civilization where there had only been savagery. Freedom where there was slavery, health where there was disease.

They all stopped eating when a bird call suddenly caught the colonel's ear. A sort of bubbling cluck. Was that a honeyguide? He stood up from the table and reached for his telescope, which he used in lieu of binoculars, and scanned the swamp, looking very much like a sea pirate. His friend John Burroughs—the famous conservationist—had insisted that while in Africa he must look into the mystery of the honeyguide: whether or not it existed, and whether its purported habit of guiding honey badgers and even human beings to beehives was real or fiction. Once the hive was broken, the story went, the bird would rip apart the honeycomb to gorge on the wax.

"Burroughs charged me to look personally into this extraordinary habit, a habit so extraordinary that he was inclined to disbelieve the reality of its existence." TR winced down the brass tube, his teeth bared in a studious grimace. "But it unquestionably does exist. Kermit was led by one to honey in a rock near Lake Hannington." He had seen it himself now several times as well. The honey on the table, in fact, entombed as it was with dead bees, had come thanks to one of these fantastic birds.

In any event, what had he been saying? Yes, the British. Their stand against barbarism. Of course, to do so effectively, firmness was essential. It was necessary to stamp out resistance mercifully, but when dealing with natives the greatest crime was to show weakness. This was something the United States had learned in the Philippines when it had defeated the Spanish and the native rebels there. It took *courage* to build up a civilization and to fight barbarism. This was the one thing all great powers had in common. It was the central work and responsibility of all civilized nations.

But, of course, the bittersweet irony was that the very excesses of a civilization were what often led to its downfall. The problem was over-specialization. The overspecialized citizen became overcivilized and had a tendency to fall prey to the wiles of prosperity.

"The growth in luxury, in love of ease, in taste for vapid and frivolous excitement, is both evident and unhealthy," he said.

Worst of all, the natural will to survive withered. The modern man lost his fighting edge, became unfit for the struggle of national life. In the end this sort—this rarefied dummy—was nothing but a figment of a true man.

"Rome fell by attack from without only because the ills within her own borders had grown incurable," he said. By now he had exhausted his eland bone, having mined it for every last quid of marrow, and his fist was now clenched in the air. The antidote, he was sure, for this dilemma was what he liked to call the strenuous life. It was why he hunted, why he advocated the rugged virtues, why he sought out hard and dangerous endeavors, and why every now and then he felt the need to immerse himself in the wilderness to replenish his morale.

"Oversentimentality, oversoftness, in fact, washiness and mushiness are the great dangers of this age and of this people." He bit off his words with a snap. It was the same brand of sentimental hogwash that said wild animals should not be killed even when they presented an imminent danger to the existence of man. The elephant, for example, which could rampage at any moment, put the settlers' crops in constant peril.

"It would be not merely silly, but worse than silly, to try to stop all killing of elephants." Of course, no other creature compared in grandeur. They were the mighty monarchs of the wild. Every king, every great man, identified with this intelligent, most noble of beasts. It would be a misfortune to allow the elephant to vanish from the face of the earth. Still, where they obstructed the advance of civilization, it was imperative to kill off as many as necessary.

Besides, when you thought about it, as hunters they were merely doing nature a favor. "Death by violence, death by cold, death by starvation—these are the normal endings of the stately and beautiful creatures of the wilderness. The sentimentalists who prattle about the peaceful life of nature do not realize its utter mercilessness." In this way, the hunter was a benefactor—a merciful angel of death. It was all a part of the White Man's Burden. Something the craven mugwumps of the world could never understand. He had left off pounding the table like a lectern, and his fist wavered in the air now like a petrel floating above the choppy waters of his monologue.

All listened rapturously. Each and every bit of it was fascinating. He was brilliant. Courageous. A centripetal force. He spoke in torrents, flying from one subject to the next, seizing each with utmost concentration, biting off each word with his boxy teeth, dominating with enthusiasm and candor, and twiddling his dessert spoon like a tiny silver gavel. The guava jelly had been served up now in little bowls. Looking to the future, some of his admirers felt he should be president of Harvard. Others thought he should be a bishop. The naturalists from the Smithsonian were convinced he could still be a great scientist. He extruded possibility like a meat grinder. He wanted to get to the bottom of things, and he wanted to know the sincere thoughts of others around him, to get a feel at the ticking inside.

Toward the end of lunch Carl brought out a bottle of expensive brandy. It was a gift meant for the colonel from Oscar Straus, TR's former secretary of commerce and labor, who, coincidentally, had been on the same steamer as the Akeleys, on his way to his new post as ambassador to Turkey. Despite accusations by his enemies that he was a drunk (not to mention an opium fiend and/or insane), Roosevelt was not much of a drinker and the bottle stood unopened.

But oh, his enemies! The plutocrats despised him, of course, for putting the brakes on laissez-faire. For throwing a brick into the overoiled machine of free enterprise. They accused him of wanting to burn the Constitution, of being a socialist, for wanting to kill off the railroads. Not to mention for giving too much to the poor, for taking sides with the coal miner, the child worker, the Negro, et cetera. But mainly they despised him for being a traitor to his own class. That was a velvet line one did not cross. But his cause was never sentimentalism, and it was more than mere conscience. He thumped the table. Did these gilded idiots not understand that if there was not a redistribution of wealth there would be revolution plain and simple? Did they not understand the *unrest* in American society? The battle verging between the haves and have-nots?

"It tires me to talk to rich men," he said. "You expect a man of millions, the head of a great industry, to be a man worth hearing. But as a rule they don't know anything outside their own businesses." Did they know that when he was leaving for this great adventure, J. P. Morgan himself, that carbuncled ugliferous half-rotten old Midas, stuffed to the gills with his rotten wealth, had said, *"Wall Street expects every lion to do its duty!"*

Well, by gosh, he'd already given the lions a sporting chance or two at his executive corpus, hadn't he! In any event, he said, draining his coffee and giving J.T. Jr. a tickle under the chin, he would pass the brandy on to Cuninghame, who he was sure would accept it with just appreciation.

Suddenly, he brisked his palms together almost salaciously. "Now, if there aren't any objections, I wonder if I might inflict upon you my pigskin library?"

This particular curiosity was kept inside the colonel's tent, where everyone crowded now with reverent excitement and, with the host's encouragement, took a seat on box and crate or chop box, Mrs. Akeley sitting on the edge of his cot, and TR himself sitting on the floor, cross-legged, passing around a few choice selections from his portable library. Outside, the oversized American flag that marked the colonel's tent slapped and shook like the absentminded fin of some sluggish fish, casting broken shadows on the pitched canvas ceiling. They passed around the books, held them in their hands, turning the pages with attitudes bordering on piety. Roosevelt had packed about fifty volumes, each book having been trimmed down to pocket size and rebound in leather, to better endure the grim hardships of safari life. The entire library weighed in at just under sixty pounds, the legal limit of what could be carried by a single porter. Some were already oilstained, bloodstained, covered in soot and dirt. Among the volumes packed into this aluminum-and-oilcloth crate were *Paradise Lost, Pilgrim's Progress, Don Quixote,* and *Alice in Wonderland*; Dante's *Inferno* in Latin, Montaigne, Molière, and Voltaire in French, and Homer in Greek; Gregorovius's history of Rome, a history of Frederick the Great by Carlyle, the Bible, and four or five Sir Walter Scott novels, including *A Legend of Montrose.* There were books by Goethe and Marlowe and Euripides. Browning, Emerson, Keats. Twain, Dickens, and Shelley. Longfellow, Lowell, Thackeray, and Poe. He did not care a bit for Henry James, who was a "miserable little snob." As un-American as they got, a perfect example of the sort of effete cosmopolitanism poisoning America. (James, for his part, called TR an "ominous jingo.") As for Tolstoy: "The man has a diseased mind. He is not wholesome. He is not sane."

But Shakespeare. He had never really appreciated Shakespeare before, but something about being in Africa, being in the wilderness for such a long time, had revealed the essence of the poet to him at last. Though he had to admit he liked Macbeth better than Hamlet, who was too introspective for his taste—not enough of a man of action. But oh, that Shakespeare was bully! Far more permanent than any other writer. He flensed you cold with your blood running hot.

For every possible idle moment he carried a book in his pocket or saddlebag. He could not bear to waste a single minute. His mind was like a muscular furnace. It needed constant stoking, a steady supply of syntactic calories. He was also reading his friend Henry Fairfield Osborn's latest book, *Age of Mammals*. Oh, what was the line, what was it? A sentiment regarding King Alfred the Great, that fender-off of Viking hordes. Ah, yes. *He loved the great game as if he were their father.* Osborn had taken the quote from the *Anglo-Saxon Chronicle*. TR was thinking he might use it himself as an epigraph for the book he was going to write about his adventures in Africa. Perhaps Akeley would do him the privilege of writing the foreword? Really, would he then? That was bully too!

⁊

IT WAS GETTING to be dusk now, and they moved to the fire, where a tin of cigars was passed around, and Kermit strummed a mandolin, while Tarlton laid out his plan to follow the elephant herd Roosevelt's party had seen that morning. Since everyone could not go on the hunt, obviously, it was decided that TR, Kermit, the naturalists from the Smithsonian, and Akeley would go in the morning, with one tent and forty porters. They planned to be gone three days at most. The colonel wanted to keep on schedule, as he had already planned to be back in Sergoi by November 17.

CHAPTER SEVENTEEN

IN THE EARLY MORNING THEY WENT AHEAD WITH THEIR GUN bearers, an hour or so ahead of the headman and porters, who followed at a discreet distance. TR rode toward the front, behind Tarlton, with the tall skinny figure of Kermit taking up the rear on a horse curiously named Zebra-shape.

The colonel, perched on a sorrel, was dressed in khakis, a sun helmet, and breeches with leather-faced knees buttoned snug to the ankle in lieu of puttees. Slung around his waist was an ammo belt brimming with brass .450 Holland & Holland cartridges, shells capable of cracking the eardrums of a man a quarter mile away. Both suspenders and leather belt worked in tandem to reign in the gibbous presidential gut. When TR had inquired what *Bwana Tumbo* meant, he had discovered a sample of native sarcasm when told that his Swahili nickname could be loosely translated as "the man with unerring aim." The colonel's eyesight by this point was poor: not only did he suffer from severe astigmatism, but he was blind in his left eye, the result of a boxing injury six years prior with his son Ted. At all times he kept eight or nine extra pairs of spectacles tucked in among his saddlebags.

It did not take long for Tarlton to find the path of the herd they had seen the day before, and for a while, they followed the trail of trampled grass still pebbled with dew in the quiet morning sunlight. Tarlton could tell the elephants were nervous and moving quickly to evade their pursuers. They were not even stopping to feed. He could tell this by the lay of the grass, could read each refracted blade like a sundial which told the hour in elephant time. They might go forty, fifty miles before they would want to settle down and feed again. The men knew that a hunter cannot rush. They were prepared for a long slog if it came to it.

They could only keep to the trail and be thankful that the wind stayed in their favor. Even if it took a couple of days, eventually, the herd would have to rest. So they went along at a comfortable gait: down and up the dusty ravines the horses ambled, clambering over stony ridges, swaying unevenly beneath the riders. Here and there the monotony of the endless grasslands was thickened with scrub, an occasional scabbing of brambles along a watercourse, a valley, or thorn trees upon a hilltop. The faint fragrance of heliotrope sweetened the air as the grass crunched softly beneath the horses' unshod hooves.

At one point climbing over a hill, passing under a giant wild fig, an unmanaged many-tentacled thing, the colonel pointed out a brilliant woodpecker on its trunk and then turned to explain the fig itself, how the tree was really a parasite; it began as a simple but deadly vine growing up the *mahogo* tree, until gradually the fig strangled the life out of its host, expanding around the trunk, taking it branch by branch, completely enveloping it, and sending out its own new prolific limbs until the *mahogo* beneath was dead.

"Finally nothing remains but the fig, which grows to be a huge tree," Roosevelt said. If you looked through cracks in its outer bark, you could sometimes make out the skeleton entombed within.

They were headed east, away from the river. West of the Nzoia River was totally uninhabited, and you could march for a straight eternity with nothing but the monotonous whisk of grass and horse in everlasting friction. A steady dry susurrus. By midmorning the heavy pith helmets and red-lined padded spine protectors were laden with sun. As they went along, the colonel scanned the surrounding clumps of brush with his telescope. He called out birds he saw like a relentless pupil: Yellow-billed hornbill! Ross's turaco! Lilac-breasted roller! Firefinch! Mosque swallow! Golden palm weaver! Olive thrush! Sunbird! Bee-eater! Hartlaub's bustard!

The naturalists said again what a formidable scientist he would have made if politics had not gotten him first. TR replied maybe, except that the way science was going these days—toward overspecialization, the same as everything else—he couldn't stand to be cooped up in a laboratory like a bull moose in a china shop. He'd rather work in the field with a gun than a microscope any day. This led the others to share a few anecdotes about their own fieldwork. The ornithologist, Edgar Mearns, whose gray walrus mustache made him look a bit like William Taft, TR's regrettable successor, recalled a battle with the Moros when he was a conscript in the Philippines. At one point the Americans had gotten hemmed in by a large group of native rebels and they had taken refuge in a stockade on a hilltop.

"The Moros advanced time and again with the greatest gallantry," he said, but as they fell, piling up around the walls, he admitted he had felt sorry for them. Even so, as a scientist, he'd seen an opportunity. "I slipped out of the stockade that night and collected a most interesting series of skulls," he said. "They're in the Smithsonian today."

The others chuckled. Now there was a real collector.

Regarding his own amateur legacy as a naturalist, TR so happened to be rather occupied with a lecture he'd been invited to deliver at Oxford on his return trip through Europe, after the African expedition had come to its end.

The gist of his lecture, he explained, would be to make a few remarks on some of the Darwinian parallels that could be observed between the evolution of species and the evolution of civilizations as he saw it. "Of course, there is no exact parallelism between the birth, growth, and death of species in the animal world, and the birth, growth, and death of societies in the world of man. Yet there is a certain parallelism. There are strange analogies; it may be that there are homologies."

He rode with one hand on the pommel.

For example, he said, consider the sudden emergence of a new species or civilization. Even though, of course, there could really be no such thing as an entirely "new" species any more than there could be an entirely "new" nation; just as all species were connected from the beginning of time through common ancestors, so did human societies mutate, so to speak, from earlier historic lineages. As a new species might be born of such transformation, so might a new nation blossom out of mutant barbarity.

But, certainly, for both societies and organisms, competition was essential. That's what was wrong when the oil trust and the coal trust and the steel trust and the beef trust and the six great railroads and even the sugar trust excluded competition; when they excluded competition they acted against nature and imperiled the very health of the nation. It was no more healthy than the tendency toward overspecialization, a tendency equally fatal for species as for civilizations.

"There are questions which we of the great civilized nations are ever tempted to ask of the future. Is our time of growth drawing to an end?" He took a swig from his canteen and wiped his lips with the back of his hand. "Are we as nations soon to come under the rule of that great law of death which is itself but part of the great law of life? None can tell. Forces that we can see, and other forces that are hidden or that can but dimly be apprehended, are at work all around us, both for good and for evil."

If America wasn't careful of what it had achieved, as one of the greatest and most powerful nations in history, it would be just another in a series of expired kingdoms. America was like Rome with a fresh coat of paint. *Tyrannosaurus rex* with a new skin. But paint chipped, skin withered. Civilization was nothing but a thin membrane to keep out the hungry wolves of barbarism. That was always the case. But it was especially true in these times. "Anarchy is now, as it always has been, the handmaiden and forerunner of tyranny," he said. Never mind that it had been the providential bullet from an anarchist's pistol that had put him into office.

※

THEY HAD NOT been going that long when Tarlton raised a hand for silence and slid off his horse. The colonel's thoughts fell short. They had come to a copse of spindly mimosas and convoluted scrub from which there came a heavy thrashing about. A ponderous freight shifting in the trees, a guttural rumbling, and the listless snapping of branches. The red-haired guide sent a tracker ahead, and they waited.

After a little while the porters, who were meant to lag a good distance behind, could be heard approaching, the loudest of them laughing and talking at full voice, and Carl could have turned and shot the man dead but a severe look conveyed to the headman instead seemed sufficient. After a moment the tracker returned with a head count. There were elephants up ahead, all right. Half a dozen or more. To keep the wind in their favor, then, Tarlton had the men remount and led them off the trail at a sharp right turn, cutting out into the untrampled grass, to bypass the grove whose thicket concealed the elephants but for their dark loamy scent.

When they got to the other side of the spindly sanctuary, they could see the elephants in a cluster, nibbling at the thorny tops of the mimosas. They were ensconced within the grove, in a clearing of sorts. A group of ten in all, eight cows and two calves.

"By George!" TR whispered. "It makes one's blood tingle."

It was not even lunchtime, and yet here they were, not eight miles east of camp, face-to-face with the entire herd. It seemed the whole adventure was about to be finished before it had even begun. There were no bulls. That was fine. But there were several good cows that Carl would be very pleased to have the colonel shoot for him now. If they could get the biggest one, it would be a grand acquisition.

The men had dismounted and stood silent, watching the elephants feed, stripping the leaves from the branches, then ushering them via their trunks to their waiting mouths. Their ears flapped lazily, and the fair breeze that blew through the open grove raised the scant hairs on their thick brows and mountainous rumps. The totos scampered beneath their mothers' legs, playing with a dug-out rootball, nudging it along with their little goblin faces.

The hunters were concealed behind a large anthill, and the cows had yet to detect the men. Akeley studied the scene for a while, and when he pointed out the cow he had in mind to the colonel, he moved aside to make room for him to aim, assuming he was going to shoot from the cover of the anthill, but the colonel simply adjusted the spring-clasp of his pince-nez and walked out into the open straight ahead toward the cow.

It was true that it was best to get as close as possible when hunting elephants, but Carl wondered if TR intended to take this one alive, or maybe even climb up its trunk and shoot it point-blank between the eyes. They were already sixty yards inside the grove. If the elephants charged, there would not be much room to maneuver. You could not very well let the former leader of the free world stroll out alone into a herd of mama elephants and their suckling calves. So Carl signaled to Kermit, and the two quickly moved in behind the colonel, flanking him on either side, respectfully abaft, treading at a cool unhurried pace out into the open, but of course right away the cows blared and the totos took shelter behind their mothers' sequoia-like legs. Still, the colonel did not stop. The head cow turned its great heavy face, and wagged its trunk, and sounded a final warning. But TR just shifted the rifle in his hands and moved closer and then only came to a full stop when the elephant at last charged.

TR stood his ground, his gun bearer kneeling behind him, the extra rifle at the ready and pressed to the colonel's leg. He put the walnut butt against his shoulder and aimed with his one good eye and braced himself against the recoil like a lumberjack. When he fired, the cow juked and went down with a great puff of dust and scattered grass seeds. It lay there panting for a few moments, its trunk spewing dirt, as TR rechambered, but then with a squeal it twisted itself back up onto its feet and resumed the charge, but this time with the seven other cows thundering behind.

The ground quaked and the men winced at the blaring trumpets, but all three stood their ground as the colonel took aim. When he fired the second shot—a direct brain shot—the cow went down solid, but it was too late to serve as a deterrent to the other seven, who failed to veer off, and for an earsplitting instant there was chaos and the shattering scrum of gunfire, amid shrieks of panicked totos, and when it was all over there were three dead elephants spraddled heavily on the ground. The totos, neither of which had been harmed, were running in circles screaming. Akeley quickly pointed out the one he wanted to Kermit, who stepped forward, took aim, and shot the calf dead at the side of its mother.

Indeed the excitement was over much more quickly than anticipated. It was not yet lunch, and they had killed four elephants. Kermit went around them, taking snapshots with his Graflex, searching for the best light. TR, already, was anticipating his next leg of the trip. He would be going up into Uganda now, and then from there, he planned to hunt the rare white rhinoceros in the eastern Belgian Congo, before embarking on a riverboat and heading down the White Nile on to Khartoum.

"Going back by the Nile is a long and hard trip," Roosevelt said. "For the first twelve days we will not fire a shot, probably." One could see him struggling against the specter of that boredom. Akeley, for his part, would not have the luxury of boredom for some time to come now, given the work he'd been left courtesy of the Roosevelts.

❦

ONCE KERMIT AND Tarlton set back to go fetch the skinners, Akeley and TR were left alone to guard the corpses. They sat under the shade of a mimosa while they waited, listening to the grass chattering with insects in the broiling sun.

Roosevelt kicked back his feet and took a deep satisfied breath. The scenery seemed to demand the taking of expansive breaths.

"I do not know any man who has had as happy a fifty years as I have had," he said, sighing. "I have had about as good a run for my money as any human being possibly could. Whatever happens now I am ahead of the game." He looked at Akeley and gave him a frank, melancholic smile. He only regretted his children would never experience the great outdoors in the way he had as a young man.

"I was just in time to see the last of the real wilderness life," he said, gouging at the sole of his boot with a twig, scraping dirt from around the hobnails, "and real wilderness hunting." He had seen the wilderness disappearing—when he had lived out West and seen the barren deserts left over from where the timbermen had skinned the country before moving on. It was why he'd left a splendor of wildlife refuges, petrified forests, crater lakes, wind caves, a grand canyon—eighteen national monuments and five national parks in all. An entire *fifth* of the nation preserved under federal protection. Fifty-one bird sanctuaries. Otherwise, the hucksters and pawnbrokers of Wall Street would take everything, higgledy-piggledy, and leave nothing for the future.

TR took off his pince-nez and polished them with a handkerchief before nudging them back up the bridge of his nose. Even if he was sorry that his sons would not experience nature as he had, he was still a profoundly happy man. Deeply grateful for what life had granted him, his children most of all. There was no greater satisfaction. Having children was the most pleasurable of the patriotic duties. In fact he thought it was a sin—a cardinal sin against civilization—to commit willful sterility in marriage. He poked an emphatic finger into the palm of his hand. Look at the marked decline in the birth rate among the higher races. At the rate things were going, they would extinguish themselves! And then, perhaps recognizing the possibility that Mr. Akeley, who had no children, might not have had a choice in the matter, he let it drop.

It was funny. A few years ago, Kermit would not even pick up a rifle. He had four boys in all, plus two daughters. Quentin was only twelve—his birthday was three days from now, it just so happened. His son Ted was fond of boxing and football and fighting other boys, and his son Archie was fond of sailing and had won several silver cups racing his dory and was absolutely bent on joining the navy. But Kermit had had water on the knee as a child, and it had held him back from physical pursuits, much as TR himself had been held back by boyhood asthma, that is, until he had outgrown the weakling, confronted his imperfect nature, and dedicated himself to building up his physique and recasting his very being into the strenuous old Viking that he was today.

But Kermit had always been a bit *timid*. He had never been able to teach him to box. He did not skate. He was no good at running. Swimming had not come naturally. He preferred bicycle riding to horses. And nothing, nothing, could interest him in shooting, even though by the time he was nine his brother Ted had already owned a small-caliber rifle. But now, well, TR guessed he was making up for lost time, overcompensating to prove himself to his old man, sure, and maybe he *was* worried that Kermit was too reckless, but in the main he was proud that the boy was now "tougher than whipcord."

It was just as he had always taught his children. It was just as he had always preached to America. It was his essential sermon: nature must be confronted, and it must be confronted *head-on*.

He flicked a tick off his pant leg. The breeze in the tree set the shadows on the ground aquiver, like the surface of some thorny and inedible aspic.

For Carl, just to be in this man's presence was to awaken fully. He could not help but feel like some dingy savage that had been lifted up and dusted off. One would hate to quail in front of this man. It was impossible not to sense, knowing Roosevelt, that one had been recruited into a great struggle between light and dark. Nothing could be worse than to be regarded by this man as one of the world's "cold timid souls."

After a while, the colonel stopped talking and took out a book from his saddlebag and began to quietly read. It was a copy of Macaulay's *Essays*. If Carl wanted to read, there was a copy of the *Nibelungenlied* in TR's cartridge bag, though it was smeared with snake blood. The puff adder had met its end at the point of TR's knife, not entirely unlike the end the dragon had met at the sword of Siegfried in that very same epic.

Akeley was not in the least put off when the colonel lapsed into silence until the skinners arrived. To just sit in his shadow, that was enough. You would have to be half-dead to not love this man. Akeley lit his pipe and watched the clouds. It was going on sunset, and the animals still grazing in the distance appeared bronze, as if a metallurgist had just cast the entire scene for posterity. It was quiet now on the veldt but for the distant, intermittent bark of a zebra and the thoughtful turning of pages.

❧

ALL THAT NIGHT the lions and hyenas could be heard in the ragged dark outside their campfire. But come morning, before the skinners had reappeared, when the colonel went out at dawn in hopes of catching one of the lions sniffing around the carcasses, Akeley heard him exclaim. He came out to find TR looking at one of the elephants, which was as stiff now as if it were already a manikin covered in plaster. TR held his rifle, chuckling and shaking his head, and when Carl saw the wild dog the colonel had discovered he took an involuntary step back.

It was protruding from the side, from the elephant's stomach. A dismaying sight that made little sense. It was stuck at the neck, with a deranged look in its eyes, the rest of its body trapped inside the elephant. All that was visible was its gory face—the ogreish head of a hyena—as if mounted to the tavern wall of the elephant's bloated stomach.

The captive bared its long teeth and shrieked and snapped its head furiously. You had to feel pity for it. But at the same time the sight was utterly revolting, obscenely comical. It had obviously burrowed inside during the middle of the night when the carrion was still pliant and warm. But once it had chewed its way down into the deep viscous recesses of the corpse, and gorged itself, it must have gotten turned around, and failing to worm its way back the way it had come, had to gnaw its way out with a full stomach, chewing through the side, through muscle and dermis, until it had breached the surface, broken through the outer skin, but then the heavy dermis and rigored muscle had seized around its neck like a dog locked in the stocks. The membranes had contracted around its throat. The hyena howled piteously, snapping its exhausted jaws. The usurped head writhed pointlessly. The fur on the nape had been worn raw from trying to escape. *It was literally tied up in the thing it loved best*: this was the thought that floated unbidden through Akeley's mind. The two men stood there in their pajamas, the rising sun witness to this cruel absurdity. When Carl saw the colonel pull back the bolt of his rifle he did not think it necessary. But then the gun exploded, and the head hung silent from the elephant's side. It was nothing now but a ghost trapped inside another ghost.

CHAPTER EIGHTEEN

THE ROMANCE OF SAFARI LIFE HAD GONE PUTRID. IT FESTERED like the big toe Mrs. Akeley was now hunkered over, gingerly tending to the itchy, pustulated skin where a colony of chiggers had hatched their brood. Sitting cross-legged on the floor of her tent, stripped down to her sweat-mottled peach silk brassiere and scanties, the afflicted foot yanked up over a thigh for inspection, she scratched a safety pin under the nail before dousing the whole foot with kerosene.

An icy rain pattered against the canvas and slopped in the trough dug around the outside of her tent, while the wind off the mountain's glacier swatted at the tied-back door. In the draft, the lamp sputtered, revealing in ghoulish fragments the sullen monkey in the corner, feasting daintily on the stream of white ants that boiled up under the tent floor. The tent reeked of the odor of human female mingled with the peculiar aroma of vervet. The combined mammalian smell—of woman and monkey—many months bottled, was as rank as if they were trapped in the dank interior of a cave.

She slid the medicine chest closer and flipped open the tin lid, which was now covered with a fine coating of rust and mold. She rifled through the vials, chinking them together as she turned each small bottle to view its label until she found the iodine. For an intense moment the toe burned, cooling to amber-blue. A cigarette smoldered beside her, sloughing off a long ash in its tray like the casting of an earthworm. After a moment, she carefully tipped the cigarette into her palm, pressing pinches of ash into the toe. It seemed to control the itching better than anything else.

She spent countless hours in her tent tending to insect bites. Rinsing her measled-looking skin with peroxide and carbolic. Whenever there was water and time the natives bathed, but for some reason they didn't particularly believe in washing their clothes, what little of them they owned, and only rubbed their rags in the dirt, believing it somehow more antiseptic than water—or else they left them out to cook in the sun, with the end result being that the natives looked as filthy as if they had dug up their wardrobes from a hole in the ground. She washed the bites as best she could, but knew it was hopeless as long as her belongings were handled by the same men with whom she was fated to share an entire order of parasites.

The little beasties one could not see—the invisible animals in the blood—had turned out to be much more terrifying than the ones they had come to hunt and against whom they at least stood a fighting chance. She had seen enough exotic disease over the past seven months, since saying good-bye to Roosevelt, to last a dozen lifetimes. She had had her fair share of fever, but it was not her that they went after with something like vengeance. No, it was Carl who had proven the more porous. Microbes seeped through him like a square of Florentine silk.

Spirillum, meningitis, malaria. She had actually lost track of how many times he'd nearly died on her now. You would not think that a person could grow ill for want of elephants, but in the case of Carl it seemed very much to be the truth. Mickie for one did not doubt that the stress of this failure was the cause of his deteriorating health. It was a vicious circle. The longer he spent incapacitated on his cot, taking Bovril injections and chewing grains of quinine, the less able he was to hunt, and the longer they stayed in Africa. She tried to persuade him to go home, to seek medical attention, but he refused to discuss it. When she nearly had him over malaria he would contract spirillum. Then meningitis. Then dysentery again. His eyes would turn yellow-brown, the color of rotten yolks. Almost the same muddy brown tint of the urine left in the bedpan on the floor, blackwater fever having set in once malaria had sufficiently poached his kidneys.* And, as if anyone needed

---

*The pressure required for the proboscis of the female *Anopheles* to penetrate human skin is a force of roughly 0.1 ounce per square inch. Enough, then, to reach the lush undergrowth of arterioles one millimeter beneath the epidermis, and for the malaria-carrying mosquito to extract its blood

reminding of what a martyr he had become for the cause, open ulcers blossomed on his hands and refused to heal. It would have been impossible with such sores, even if the fever did not keep him bedridden, to hold a rifle. In Uganda she had pulled him back over and over again from the brink. This in spite of the fact that she, herself, felt as if she were losing her mind. She had grown so exhausted, from nursing Carl, from the thick oppressive gloom of the country, that at one point, while they had been deep in the Budongo Forest, surrounded for what seemed like days on end of never-ending elephant trumpeting, she had begun to suffer from hallucinations and panic attacks. Every time she closed her eyes a parade of screaming elephants bore down on her, charging at her through her mind, in a tangle of trunks and trunklike vines. When she opened her eyes it went away. But as soon as she closed her eyes, the vines and trunks grew up around her, swollen and twisting, growing over her brain as if it were a bloody trellis. And all the while the even more berserk elephants would not stop screaming. Why did the elephants scream so ceaselessly? Perhaps the forest had driven them mad as well. She could not sleep, and she could not go on, she could not leave her tent. The worst of it was that the ordeal had entered her body too, in that she felt that her own limbs were swollen to the size of elephant legs. She could not shake that illusion, whether her eyes were closed or shut. J.T. Jr. lay beside her, grooming her hair and stroking her neck, and in a way this had kept her from going completely mad.

At last, when they left the forest, the hallucinations ceased, and she was able to take care of her quivering, chill-racked husband again. She read to him, cleansed his wounds, and at night pointlessly tried to translate the Sanskrit ravings of his febrile mind.

The responsibility of keeping him alive felt heavy, but she did not trust the natives to care for him, so she did everything herself. Still, there was a certain distance; she did not, would not, completely give herself to him. As if she did not trust that he would pull through in the end. And as she relied more on the company of J.T. Jr., Carl grew jealous

---

meal, inject a trace amount of plasmodium from its own infected salivary glands, and dispatch a hunting expedition of sporozoites into the bloodstream toward its host's liver. Setting up base camp in the liver cells, the rapidly reproducing parasites soon rupture the borders of their new homeland. From there, they prepare to invade the red blood cells, undetected, by cloaking themselves in the plundered membranes of their colonized liver cells. The host by now is feeling light-headed, tachycardic, short of breath, and ever on the verge of vomiting. Verily, as if his cell membranes were being peeled off, skinned alive one at a time.

of the monkey. He did not understand how alone she really was. All the same she kept him alive so he could continue trying to kill himself.

It was his drive—his unhealthy obsessions—that had worn him down. Of this she was sure. There was nothing wholesome about this line of work; it only stood to reason that after so long it would make him sick. That the psychological and physical stress of failing, again and again, to find the perfect bull for the museum had peeled away his immunity. It was going to do him in if he didn't go insane first. But Carl was "elephant mad," as he had put it himself in a letter to President Osborn. Ahab gone buggy on the veldt. Theseus lost in the maze.

Though it would be difficult for one to say where, exactly, he had lost his way. Had it been on the Uasin Gishu Plateau with Roosevelt, or later in what had become the harrowing nightmare of Uganda? Or sometime between on Mount Elgon?

He had been gone now for over two weeks, exploring the upper regions of Mount Kenya, near the glaciers, and once again she had been left alone. They were back where she had shot her first elephant—a beast that, in hindsight, had died with a fantastic degree of cooperation.

He had taken a small party of porters to search the ice fields, above the tree line, to see whether any of the great ancient tuskers could be found at such preposterous altitudes. He did not know how high they really ventured. Yet there were rumors of bulls that had preserved themselves for so long, at such heights, that saplings grew from their mossy backsides, and whose behemoth tusks dragged on the forest floor. Elephants that had become, literally, part of the mountain.

She would have joined him—she *had* joined him at the beginning—but the climb had turned out to be too much for poor J.T. Jr. He'd gotten altitude sickness. Once above the tundra the monkey's eyes had gone a bit off, he'd begun stumbling about haphazardly, and then gone Nile-green beneath the fur.

The only thing to do, of course, was return down the mountain at once, taking half the porters with her to set up base camp at a more tolerable altitude. She did not know what she would do if anything were ever to happen to J.T. Jr. She had meant to set him free in the wild before, but hadn't been able to do it. Always in the end she'd broken her promises. Whereas Carl had set out to observe all of Africa's wildlife, Mickie had found in the pitiful little vervet a more intimate microcosm.

A loose knock of sorts came at the canvas door, followed by the head of her Kikuyu tent boy. *Good ole Bill.* In spite of having disgraced himself with the Roosevelt expedition, he had picked up again with the Akeleys, in Nairobi. They were happy to take him back. Though he still didn't get along any better with the Swahili porters—who felt superior to the Kikuyu—by now he'd become an invaluable member of the safari. It wasn't altogether surprising the others had a problem with him; his favorable standing with Bwana and Memsahib was a source of envy and irritation—how many times now had Mickie saved him from the *kiboko,* the dreaded rhino-skin whip?—and there was no question he could be a bit cocky. Mickie liked to keep him dressed in clean white button-up shirts and khaki shorts, and had even gotten him to wear lace-up boots. He smelled of Sapolio soap. A young teenager, with loose kinky hair, he was handsome now in an almost ravished sort of way.

She motioned him to enter, and he slipped in out of the rain, carrying a plate of crackers and jam for her supper. Cantilevered from the saucer in his hand was a steaming cup of tea. This was all she was in the mood to eat. It was coming on dusk now; not that it made any difference in the persistent gloom of the rain.

Oddly enough, this was actually the *second* time Bill had taken back up with them. Even after they'd let him rejoin their safari, after he'd botched things with Roosevelt, there had been another incident on the Uasin Gishu Plateau, while filming a group of Nandi warriors spearing lions. (Carl had failed, or his camera had failed, to actually capture the moment of truth. A moment of truth he had tried for repeatedly, insisting that the spearmen continue, until in the end the savanna was littered with the corpses of ten dead lions, like so many bad takes on the cutting room floor.) Several of the Somalis had accused Bill of stealing—it was not just the Swahili who hated him—and there'd been no choice but to insist he open his belongings for inspection. But Bill had refused and then run away. When an *askari* was sent to chase after him, Bill came back at the man with a knife, and had looked mighty intent on using it. Ultimately, there'd been no choice but to hand him over to the authorities at the nearest *boma,* or colonial government office, where he was thrown in jail. The safari had then moved on to Mount Kenya.

Several weeks later, they'd been up on the mountain, at around ten thousand feet, high into the bamboo, when they'd come across a mystery deep in an elephant pit. At the center of the hole was a neatly piled mound of dirt, evidently excavated from the sides and piled up by some animal who'd made its escape after falling in. It was hard to figure what could have accomplished such a feat, though the longer they stood around the pit, speculating, the more Carl began to favor the theory of a warthog. It could have used its curved tusks to scoop the earth. Anyway, it was just at this point, in the midst of tossing out hypotheses, when Carl heard a voice behind him say, "Jambo Bwana."

It was as if he'd materialized out of nowhere. But there Bill was, in the flesh, coming up the trail, grinning like a fool. He looked a filthy mess, in utter rags, his shoes barely shreds. He had not fared well in prison, clearly, but he looked jolly enough now. It was almost beyond belief. How, after somehow getting free, Bill had walked several hundred miles, found their trail on the edge of the second-largest mountain in Africa, and then located them here high in the bamboo forest, at this somewhat baffling elephant pit. Stranger still that Akeley had been thinking about Bill that very morning. Wishing he were there on the mountain. The boy could track anything.

Now, as he entered Mickie's tent, he wore his usual expression of servility and mulish angst. It was just as likely as not that he really was a thief and, who knew, had even escaped from jail to rejoin them—perhaps doing unknown harm to his captors in the process if he'd managed to get his hands on another knife—but he was forgiven now.

Carl had been less forgiving with the others. He had not spared the *kiboko* for a number of dubious infractions by this point. Frustrated by the elusiveness of his giant bull, worn down by illness, Akeley had grown unpredictable, his mood dark when it was not downright evil. He had punished one porter for mistreating chickens. The man had carelessly packed the live birds in a pail of meat, tying them together at the neck and feet for transport, and when Carl saw the man dump out the pail at the next camp and the chickens tumbled out, one dead, the other half suffocated, the sight of this cavalier inhumanity had driven Carl to nearly kill the man. After the punishment, with the man left prostrate on the ground, Carl stepped away, mumbling to himself how it was a marvel he even bothered to let the man live. On another occasion Carl had given out ten lashes each to several porters who'd filched hairs from an elephant skin to make their coats warmer.

That incident had fallen on Christmas Day.

There was no question the natives could try one's patience.

Compared to the rest, though, Bill had been a brick. Mickie had taught him English and even how to do a bit of sewing. And he learned how to keep himself presentable: how to clean his shirts, to pare his nails. If you gave the other natives soap, they sold it for cigarettes or khat, that repellent-smelling weed that turned them into zombies. Several of the gun bearers were bona fide dope fiends—passing around tins of the stuff all day long—and a number of the men had been whipped for smoking "bong."

No, they were a bad lot compared to the ones they'd had back on the Uasin Gishu Plateau. Worse even than the ones they'd taken up with in Uganda. They were careless, and sometimes they seemed heartless as well. Even after one of their own had jumped in the river and been devoured by a crocodile in front of their very eyes, they had laughed about it the same night, as if it had all been a great prank the victim had staged for their pleasure.

That incident, too, had triggered a relapse for Carl. While the men hooted it up and took turns pantomiming the poor boy's death throes around the campfire, it was all she could do to coax his fever down, piling him high with every blanket she could find in camp, hot water bottles, and endless cups of hot tea until his teeth ceased to chatter. You would have thought it had been he who had fallen into the river.

When she finally went to bed that night and held J.T. Jr. tightly— with the boy's scream still in her ears—she'd decided she would never leave her pet in this place. She would not exile him to the cruel wilderness. She would never let him go.

Of course, it had been their own fault. For pushing too hard. For pushing the men. For always needing to hurry on to the next failure.

But the natives simply did not comprehend the importance of the work. There was no question Carl was a perfectionist and that it caused him to suffer. She worried about him now, up on the mountain alone, and it terrified her that he would get sick again. Over and over he had sacrificed his health. All for the sake of his art. Of course other sacrifices had been made as well. When J. T. McCutcheon had secured at least the one young bull Carl needed, it had come at the expense of two more innocent cows who'd recklessly charged into their gunfire. Out of the four elephants Roosevelt had shot, Carl had scrapped two for not meeting his increasingly elusive standards. One right away, which he'd left without bothering to skin; the second after TR left, for being too puny.

Others he'd shot and abandoned for inadequate or imperfect tusks. They lacked symmetry. One tusk was longer or larger than the other. One hadn't made the final cut for a tumor on its face. There did not seem to be one worthy elephant on the entire continent. The elephants— mostly cows and juveniles—were all "inferior grade," Carl said, because most of the good-sized tuskers had been killed off by the ivory hunters and big-game hunters, which of course now meant that the survivors were apt to be more violent, aggressive, and therefore that much less fun to hunt.

On one occasion—after she and Carl had battled what seemed like an unkillable bull in Uganda, collectively putting twenty or thirty steel-jacketed bullets into it before it dropped—she had fallen to her knees and declared miserably, "I want to go home and keep house for the rest of my life." That one, too, they had left to rot, since by the end of the ordeal Carl was too sick to even skin it.

❦

NOW, ONCE AGAIN, she'd been left behind, a lone white woman in charge of seventy-odd filthy savages. All she had now was J.T. Jr. But even the monkey had caused her to endure heartbreak and a few sleepless nights. In one instance he'd got off his leash and run away, and she'd made everyone in camp go out and search in the darkness, scouring the trees and grass with lanterns and firebrands; not until daybreak, when she'd thrown herself on her cot in tears, convinced he was dead, did the truant finally drag himself in after a night spent in the hidey-hole of a tree. But, truly, she had come to feel that nobody had ever understood her as deeply. Or understood her loneliness at any rate. Of course, she knew the monkey was lonely as well. She knew that she had taken him away from his own kind. But she hated the idea of letting him loose into the world, where he would only end up in a crocodile's jaws. She would never let him go, no matter how crazy the natives must have thought her for treating a monkey like a human child. For appointing him his own personal valet. For giving him his own toilet. His own umbrella bearer. For the way she refused to discipline him no matter how badly he behaved.

This trip was not as pleasant as their first trip—their honeymoon—had it been four or was it five years earlier? Many things, maybe everything, had gone wrong. She was always afraid now. Always.

After TR left, they had continued the hunt on the plateau for several weeks, but despite the colonel's incredible luck—four cows slain before lunch that first day—the Akeleys' own luck had quickly run out. There had been no other choice but to move up onto Mount Elgon, to get the two large bulls Carl still needed to complete the group. They would simply have to ignore the rumor of unfriendlies on the southern slope; ivory hunters, they knew, had already decimated the northern slope. They had no guides, no maps, but for twelve days they hunted the tangled maze of old elephant trails that crisscrossed the mountain—the fourth-largest in Africa—but all in vain. Finally, with food supplies dwindling, they were forced to begin their descent in order to reprovision the men.

She remembered the day they came out into a small clearing which looked suspiciously man-made. No one was in sight, which made the party all the more nervous. After a quick search, they soon found a fragile-looking hut tucked between two large trees. It looked like something a Wandorobo would build. Like the dried husk of a sea creature washed up on shore. Inside was a smoking fire, gourds of milk, and three moronic-looking sheep ogling back at the explorers.

That the inhabitants had only just fled in panic from their party—it was not possible for 150 humans hacking blindly through a forest to make a discreet entrance—was soon enough confirmed by the eerie cries of a human baby. It was somewhere out in the woods.

Carl had the headman send a man out to look for it, and after a little while, the porter came back with a small infant which he had found hidden away under a bed of ferns.

It was a little girl, no more than three months old. Surely, when the Wandorobo fled, its mother had hidden it in the ferns to protect it, or perhaps to protect themselves from being discovered by its cries. But what were they to do with it now? There was no telling when, or if, the parents were going to return. In the meantime, while they continued to search for the inhabitants, the porter brought the screaming infant to Mickie. She took the child in her arms and then sent the porter to fetch a bath towel for her to swaddle it. While Carl and the others debated what to do, Mickie and J.T. Jr. cuddled and hugged the infant, and tried to rub warmth back into its tiny freezing limbs.

By now they had sent several of their men to the edge of the woods to try to lure the family back—calling out that they were friends and would do them no harm and had food and gifts. They would have gone on if not for the baby. The sun would not stay in the sky forever. Perhaps they would have even left it in the hut with the sheep, trusting that as soon as they left, the parents would return. But the situation had become more complicated. Mickie was rapidly bonding with the infant and already discussing how she might arrange things so that she and J.T. Jr. could share their space with the baby. This set off a panic, and Carl ordered the porters to redouble their efforts to find the parents. One Kavirondo with an exceptionally deep and booming voice was put at the edge of the forest to hark their goodwill. The more time that passed, the more likely it seemed that she would keep the orphan. Carl would never be able to persuade her to simply leave the baby and trust that its parents would return once they had left. She was convinced that she had saved it already. In fact, she had already started coming up with names for the little nomen nudum.

But then, at last, a man as naked and terrified as Adam emerged from the trees. After a moment, two women and a child came out and stood trembling behind the man as if they expected to be butchered. One woman looked at Mickie holding her baby until Bill managed to coax it away and handed it back to the mother. Once the infant was safely returned, the man spoke to his women, and they went back inside the hut with the infant. He next gestured for the lost *mzungu* to follow him and then led them back into the forest and on down the mountain. After a while, however, they came to a point where he refused to take them any farther, claiming he did not dare go onward out of fear of his enemies, the Karingo, who he said would "blood their spears" just for the simple pleasure of killing one of his kind. They had already come and killed his brother, and that was why he now had to care for his own family plus the dead man's wife and child. And so he too vanished, leaving them to make the rest of the way on their own.

❧

MICKIE CLOSED UP the medicine chest and smoked the end of her cigarette before gingerly drawing the sock back over her afflicted foot. Africa may have been evil with chiggers, but at least there was no Sullivan Ordinance prohibiting women from smoking cigarettes like there was in New York. She didn't know what she had been thinking when she'd wanted to keep the Wandorobo baby. Had she actually *really* intended on keeping it? It was not as if she'd meant to *collect* it. It had only been a moment of misguided biology, surely. The baby was forsaken; they were lost; her instinct to save it was only natural, wasn't it?

When she heard a commotion outside, she pulled aside the flap of her tent to see what was going on, and saw that two of Carl's runners had arrived. The men were at the mess tent talking to some of the others. They had arrived just before dusk.

She called to Bill and had him go over to see what news the messengers bore from Carl. Then she went back to labeling the land shells she'd been collecting in his absence, tagging some of the fossilized little mollusks and snails that could be found in the Afromontane forest, and which the museum would be eager to have for its collection, but when she hadn't heard back after five minutes, she looked out again and saw that more men were gathering around the mess tent. Despite the informal way that Bill and the runner were still chatting, as if swapping notes on the weather, she now felt she had reason to worry.

She set aside her pen and decided to go see for herself what was going on. Exiting the tent, she had to step over the trough filled with icy water; the bludgeoning rains had only just momentarily ceased. An invalid light in the oncoming dusk. By the cook's tent one of the kitchen boys hacking firewood with a dull-bladed panga paused to look up at her. In fact, all the men were looking her way now.

They were a motley bunch: dressed in crazy outfits, those who were not naked, dressed in rags or their loins covered in dingy barkcloth. They wore bizarre headdresses. Hats of zebra skin, straw hats trimmed with ostrich feathers, hats garnished with tin cans and other rubbish. Some had cattails dangling from their waists. All the pomp of savages: monkey skins, empty cartridge belts, some of the Kikuyu swabbed in rusty-colored mud for protection against the weather—it reminded Mickie of the widows she had seen in Uganda who painted themselves with red mud as a sign of mourning. Wailing and yelling.

They were all staring at her now. Wincing against the glacial wind that blasted off the mountain, their faces looked forlorn and cruel. When Bill started back now, coming toward her, his eyes were visibly bothered. But even so, when he passed on the message the runners had brought, he did so in the most casual manner imaginable:

Memsahib. Tembo piga bwana.

They all waited for her reaction. The cook stood holding a dishcloth. Others were crouched about eating, scooping gooey clumps of bean mash from their rude wooden bowls, indifferent whether or not she believed it; it was no great concern to them. Elephant hit master. *Tembo piga bwana.*

It was as if she'd just come to from a daydream, or woken from an afternoon nap, only to find that she and all the belongings of her world had been violently displaced. And yet—*and yet*—there was something about this sensation, the rush of fear itself, that had become so familiar, in a way it was also like finding one's way back to center. The place she had come to know best. After so many months living on the brink, in perpetual terror, and having grown accustomed to expect the worst— after a while one learned to set one's watch by dread.

Like anything, even terror had an order of business. In this case the first order of business was to write a letter. She would address it to Mr. Brown, the commissioner at Nyeri, requesting a doctor at once. Even if she had no way of knowing yet whether a doctor would be absolutely necessary. She suppressed the morbid thought and went back to her tent, found the stationery in her portable desk, dashed off the letter, read it over once before tucking it haphazardly into an envelope, and then called back Bill to bring her two runners whom she promised a great reward if they delivered it to the nearest white official before day- break. The chances, of course, were next to nil. Given how afraid most natives were of the dark. They would most likely stop at the nearest vil- lage and wait till morning. And who could blame them?

It was only after watching the messengers slip into the jungle that she felt the first real tremor of panic creep up from the ground and into her limbs. No matter how she denied it—this absurd story—the impos- sibility of it all pushed deeper into her like a tusk between the ribs.

Come dark, as it began to rain again, and with the campfire more difficult to keep going, the men were beginning to turn in. How could this really be happening? How could it be that these men were now going to go to bed and abandon her? She had to act.

She had to act now.

She called to Bill again but then went outside and called the men out of their tents. As they stood before her, irritable and grumbling in the drizzling rain, she disregarded their mood and quickly chose twenty of the strongest who she thought could make the trip under such conditions. Then she told them to pack a light load and to be ready to leave in several hours. In the meantime, they should try to sleep. They would need their energy for the climb.

It was after nine o'clock now, pitch-dark, and from her tent she could hear the yowl of hyenas through the rain. The campfire was wet and nearly useless, but she called out to the *askari* guarding her tent to take all the dry wood from the mess tent and keep up a roaring blaze.

She busied herself throwing things together. Whatever she thought she might need for such a rescue. She packed up the medicine kit, of course. Bandages. Splints. Extra clothing. Then Bill brought her the two extra tent poles she had demanded and the cotton fabric they sometimes used to trade with villagers. She would need to make a stretcher. It was agony to delay a single moment, but rare had been the time she'd come to her husband's rescue when he did not require a stretcher.

She turned up the lantern bright until the wick smoked. Tearing off strips of the fabric somehow sounded sharply electrical—like the sound of a trolley scraping the wire. As she stitched, her fingers trembled, and the shadows on the canvas bilged and fled. The rain outside had grown deafeningly frantic. She had to focus. No time could be wasted crying now. Not yet. She fixed the fabric to the poles with a running stitch, hastily reinforcing every third or fourth with a backstitch. J.T. Jr. watched, pupils squeezed to pinpricks in the blazing lamp.

Maybe it was not true. Maybe none of this was really happening. Maybe all the natives nestled under their ratty blankets knew something she did not. Maybe she had just gotten the message wrong, or maybe the messengers had only scrambled Carl's message? Of course, it *could* have been the other way around, couldn't it have? A simple matter of botched syntax? *Tembo piga bwana. Bwana piga tembo.* You really could not trust them to get anything right. Certainly the messengers had only meant Carl had bagged an elephant. *At long last!* Could it have finally been the big one? At this flash of hopeful delusion, her heart would have rallied. At long last, able to go home. The insanity come to an end. Imagine the homecoming dinner their friends and colleagues would throw for them back in New York! No doubt somewhere fabulous like the Blackstone. All their friends would be there to celebrate their safe and triumphant return. All the bigwigs from the museum. Even their dear friends from Chicago would take the train, just to be there to fete them in their glory. She could see all the men in sharp tuxedos now, the gals in their swankiest dresses.

The disbelief came over her in jolting gusts, like a faulty switch. Catching a glimpse of herself in the small mirror that hung from the ridgepole, she saw an old woman staring back. Her white hair pulled up in a bun. Adventure was supposed to make you feel young, but it had done nothing but age her prematurely. Her heart had no more need of adventure. Adventure was lunacy. She doubted somehow that she would survive the night. The ghost in the glass stared back. An old woman, thirty-four years old, with needle and thread, sewing a stretcher or a shroud?

Once again they had fallen into their ordained roles. The wounded explorer and the savior nurse. The dragon slayer and his faire Queene. Isolde nursing Tristan back to life after he's fallen on Morholt's poisoned sword. Not that it eased her panic in any way. But, still, there was comfort in fulfilling one's purpose.

How many times could you resurrect a dead man?

But this time it was no mere relapse of blackwater fever. It wasn't just another fit of dysentery that would leave him quaking and perspiring for days on end, cot-bound and clutching a chipped bedpan. This was not just the spirillum microbe come back to stitch more worms into the lining of his stomach. No, her husband had been in some sort of bodily collision with the largest land mammal on the planet. If she knew how to bargain with God, surely she would have. But which one? With her Catholic oaf of a father's grim prairie deity, the one who doled out His judgments in windstorms and weevils, or with Ngai, the Kikuyu god who lived at the peak of this very mountain—his throne planted in the summit's grit and ice? Of course, the ones she really needed to bargain with now were the Africans outside her tent in the rain. It was not going to be easy to persuade them to brave the mountain—to face their Supreme Creator—just to rescue a dead white man.

When Bill came in next she told him it was time to wake the men. The loads were ready and waiting. But he only stood there, wringing his hands with a foolish look on his face. Perhaps, he said, struggling to speak, it would be best to wait for dawn. He did not think the men would go willingly up the mountain in the dark. They were too scared. They were scared of evil spirits. There were leopards and elephant pits. The mountain in the dark was not a safe place, and the men—he lowered his voice to a whisper—they were in a "very ugly mood."

She double-checked her rifle and threw it on the cot. Then she turned and gave her Kikuyu friend a cold stare.

His face was full of anguish. He began to plead with her. *Memsahib did not understand!* Most of the other men were Swahili, from the coast, not Kikuyu, like him, and because of this they were not as accustomed to such extreme weather. The rain, even as he spoke, battered the tent and muted his words. It was freezing cold, Memsahib.

Mickie was impatient with the way Bill was trying to manipulate her, as if she were in a position to put off rescuing her husband until morning. She said if that were the case, perhaps while she and the others went, he would like to stay behind and babysit J.T. Jr.?

He looked as if he were going to cry. Then he broke down and told her that he had overheard some of the men plotting against her. "*Pagazi* [porters] very, very bad," he whispered. Meaning what exactly? What on earth was he trying to say? The boy looked terrified. Spit it out, for Lord's sake!

So he told her exactly what he had overheard: some of the men were planning to kill Memsahib if she forced them to go up the mountain in the dark. He'd heard them saying how they could leave her corpse so hyenas would hide the evidence.

She tried to conceal her trembling hands. Of course, the boy could be lying. It was not as if Bill were entirely trustworthy.

She shouted for the guard to rouse the men at once.

Alone in the tent, she waited a few minutes to collect herself. Then she picked up her rifle off the cot and, as she stepped outside, ordered Ali, J.T. Jr.'s young valet, who'd been huddled out of the rain under the fly of her tent, to go inside and stay with the monkey.

But the men had still not come out of their tents. She ordered the *askari* to throw more wood on the fire and then went around clapping her hands and shouting, until, finally, one at a time, the men emerged from their tents like hesitant animals.

They crowded around the fire, getting as close as possible, squatting on their heels, shivering under threadbare blankets. Cowering from the rain, they held their hands between their knees, hypnotized by the wood streaming away in blue and orange ribbons of loosed electrons. The coals ticked like bits of molten glass.

The firelight licked at their scowling faces. Black hatred furrowed and pooled in the swarming shadows. Their defiance seemed to be a dare, a threat. But she could not back down now.

"It is time to be off!" She pointed at the loads under the fly of her tent. Then she shouted again, saying that everything was ready for the climb. "*Tayari!*"

Not one of them budged.

She had given the order, but there they remained, fixed to their heels. Standing over them, she could have kicked hot coals in their faces if she weren't so frightened. Bill stood behind her holding a smoking lantern. The rain was starting to fall harder. She shouted again—ignoring the mood—that it was time to line up, mount their loads, and prepare to climb the mountain. She was not going to let her husband die because a bunch of savages were frightened silly. No one could blame them for not wanting to leave the warmth of their beds for a midnight hike in the freezing rain. But she herself, a pitiful lone woman, she was ready to take on this mountain now, wasn't she? What were they, she screamed, a bunch of babies? Infants? *Watoto?* As her fear now turned to anger, she found her voice. They thought she was crazy? Fine, then. She would show them crazy. They were wild men, she said. *Shenzies!* Stupid *shenzies* who ate ants and chased rats around camp with her butterfly nets. No, in truth, they were worse. They were a bunch of toothless old women. Disgusting useless women. Had they grown breasts? Look at them huddled around the fire like scared little girls. Little children who couldn't find their mamas. She pouted her face and let out a colicky squeal. *Mama! Mama! Mama!* Pathetic little babies, she screamed, pacing back and forth. She found herself slowly losing control and being taken over by a kind of wild and profane spirit, but she could not stop. She bunched up her fists and wrung out her eyes, pretending to cry. She sucked her thumb. *Waaaaa,* she cried. *Waaaaaa!* She stamped her feet and waddled around the men, who recoiled from her as if she were a deranged imbecile. She would have made fun of their childish god and superstitions if she thought they wouldn't have hacked her up and roasted her right then and there. But after a while the grudging looks began to dissolve. They could not help it. She was too much. This crazy white woman who slept with a monkey. Who made love to a *tumbili.*

Despite themselves, the men grinned. And then she knew that she had won. Even if it had come at the expense of her dignity.

She approached the big Swahili whom she took to be the ringleader and whose eyes were still perched somewhere between a smirk and murder. But when she put her hand on his shoulder and gently pushed him toward the loads, he moved forward. As expected, the others followed.

CHAPTER NINETEEN

IT WAS ONLY WHEN SHE HAD WON HER DUBIOUS VICTORY, AND they were ready to move out, that she discovered to her horror that the guides had gone missing. The two runners who had brought the terrible news from down the mountain were her only possible means of finding Carl. They had run away. Vanished into thin air. Why, damn it all, why did their guides always go missing at the most critical moments?

Before any of the other men could change their minds, she quickly marched them down the muddy path to the nearby Kikuyu *shambas*. They headed down the narrow muddy path with Bill at the lead with the smoking lantern, and Mickie bringing up the tail with her rifle to cut off deserters. There was not a moment to lose.

It was not hard to guess where the guides had gone. Whenever possible the safari had always recruited its guides from the nearest village. Because of the rain the villagers did not hear them coming, not until they were right upon them, and by the screams and terrified faces that greeted the intruders as they stormed one hut after another—tearing the inhabitants from their beds to subject them to the midnight inquest of a now quite berserk white woman—it was clear that they had been taken completely by surprise and were convinced that their enemies had come to kill them in their sleep.

Soon enough, with Bill acting as translator, the hut of one of the guides was found. The guide was not there himself, and so Mickie seized the man's wife and told her that if she did not reveal the whereabouts of her husband Mickie would drag her up the mountain in his place.

At once, the woman led her to a kind of passage cut out of the thick vegetation behind her hut. The men, she confessed, were hiding within. Without hesitation, Mickie took the lantern and crawled back into the tunnel on hands and knees, followed by Bill and one of the *askari*, with the rain clattering on the thorny roof. At the back, hiding inside a kind of secret cellar in the brambles, she found the guides huddled asleep. Using one of the ropes she had brought for the stretcher, they tied the two men together and dragged them out yelping and cursing. When told they could either lead her back to where Bwana Carl had been injured or be handed over directly to the authorities to face the penalty for abandoning a white woman, it did not take long for them to decide which was the better option.

※

But of course, the moment she had turned her back, half of the others had fled. How could it be possible that she was still here—when she so desperately needed to be at the top of the mountain *now*? Not here, but *there*. She would have given anything for the power of time travel, more so because of the way it almost seemed that, if anything, time itself were moving in the opposite direction in which she needed it to move. It was after midnight, and they had not even begun. That's what made this latest turn in the night's dark and pitiless comedy resemble even more something that could not really be happening. But it had. While she had gone to fetch the guides, half of her party had stolen off, taken half the provisions with them, and had now joined some of the villagers.

She could have shot every one of them dead.

Immediately, and without letting anybody know—before anyone else could abscond—she slipped away and ran as quickly as her feet would carry her back down the narrow path in the pelting rain. Running out of blind memory, she headed back toward the last *shamba*. Overhead a spear of lightning lit across the sky, and the surrounding jungle surged incandescent.

But then, dropped back in blackness, she was suddenly grabbed by the front of her coat. Jerked off the path and toward the woods. So, this was to be her killer, waiting for her on a muddy path at midnight. Dragging her off to be butchered, her parts strewn for the hyenas. But as she fought back and pushed away she felt herself suddenly freed as the buttons of her coat gave—the feeble threads that had so needed mending!—and with it the grasp of her unseen assailant. In a split second, without thinking, she struck out with the butt of her gun. It landed square, but when the body gave, it felt as if she had just stove in something more pliant than a man. It crumpled without protest. Only the sound of it falling to the path sent a thudding chill through her even as she was running again; she did not know if the assailant had been one of her own men or one of the villagers who were now possibly harboring the deserters.

But she didn't have time to linger over the possibility of just having killed a faceless man—or of very nearly being murdered herself.

It must have been the sight of her appearing at the *shamba,* in the stern firelight, and the flint edge in her eye, the absolute look of conviction, that had brought the men back. Who would want to fight this insane woman now? They were ready to follow, just so long as they did not have to face her wrath. And so once she had collected all of her men, and everything was once again ready, they set off, following the two truant guides, whom she kept tied together for the first leg of the climb.

Once on the trail, they were immediately engulfed by the mountain. Besieged by the downpour. The forest seethed around them in utter blackness except for the faint shaky mark of the lantern that Bill carried ahead of the tethered guides.

The impossibility of the climb before them was at once cruel and obvious. As she brought up the rear with the rifle, it was a struggle just to stay on her feet. Torrents of flooding rain rushed underneath like an undertow, as she crashed through the dense soaking foliage, blundering forward blindly, stumbling over fallen trees. She coughed up mouthfuls of wet earth each time she fell, all the while trying to fend off images of hidden elephant pits and poisoned spears nocked in the dark.

⁊

IT WAS APPROACHING dawn when the guides finally admitted they were lost. They had stopped in a clearing in the forest and now stood shrugging and looking about themselves as if they had just come to from a daydream. The rain had lightened to almost nothing, just a faint precipitation, and the bamboo trees slinked in and out of a thick fog.

They had climbed all night, for six or seven hours straight, in pitch-black and the maddening rain, and now it was over. The rescue had failed.

At this very bad news, that they were lost, Mickie dropped to the ground, unable to bear another moment of the nightmare, and like a madwoman searching for a lost ring, she began combing through the dead leaves, prying apart vines, scouring the ground for the lost trail, searching for any sign that her husband had passed in this direction. A bootprint. Even the single divot of a hobnail.

She just knelt there, on hands and knees, like a wounded animal, unable to go on. She could contain herself no longer and began to sob wretchedly. The others sank to the ground too, and tried to sleep, waiting for her to decide her future. It was hopeless. Why should she not just take the rifle from her gun boy and end it all now? Was there any reason to stay alive in this godforsaken country one more minute?

It was over. Carl was dead. Her husband was dead, and now, somehow she would probably die too, and in the end they would both be dead on this same sinister mountain. Or worse, she would have to return to America and keep house alone.

But after a few long minutes a faint sound broke through her despair. Had it been a distant falling tree or truly a gunshot? No, clearly it was a rifle! Over that way. Distant, but clear enough that it brought the entire group to full attention. The men cowered when she jumped to her feet and fired off three return shots. In the cold, damp air each sounded as sudden as a hot slab of metal plunged in a slack tub. Then silence. After an excruciating fifteen minutes she heard another shot. They were still far enough apart, and Carl's rifle was bigger and louder than hers, it was possible he could not hear hers at this distance. The shots were paced fifteen minutes apart. She listened for the next one and then hurried in that direction. In two hours they found themselves at her husband's elephant camp.

There, they found a few of Carl's porters sitting around a sooty fire, finishing their breakfast, huddled together as if the smoke itself carried a chill. And then there was the waterlogged tent, pitched on the edge of the bamboo, in a patch of shy morning light.

She went to the tent immediately. When she saw him, she put her hands over her face and tried not to scream. There, inside, without a blanket, was Carl. He was covered in blood and ants. The ants were moving over his face. Or what appeared to be left of it. When she knelt beside him she discovered that he was breathing but unconscious. Blood trickled steadily from the corners of his mouth, and the sight of the blood and the way his stoved-in chest looked filled her with dread, but he was alive! At least for now. Holding back her tears, in the sour tent, she touched him gently. His left eye was black and swollen shut. His nose gashed open. It was a struggle not to lose her poise at the ghastly sight of his face, but she brushed away the bloody ants as best she could. The right half of his face, his entire right cheek, had been violently peeled back and dangled gruesomely, exposing his teeth in a monstrous grimace. His forehead was crusted and oozing from where it looked as if he had been imperfectly scalped. Beside him on the ground was an empty bottle of Stearns brandy.

After doing her best to tend to his wounds, and splinting his chest where the elephant had broken several ribs, she had the porters carefully lift him onto the makeshift stretcher. Then, with Bill leading the way, clearing a path before them with his tireless machete arm, the rescue party slowly made its way back down the mountain.

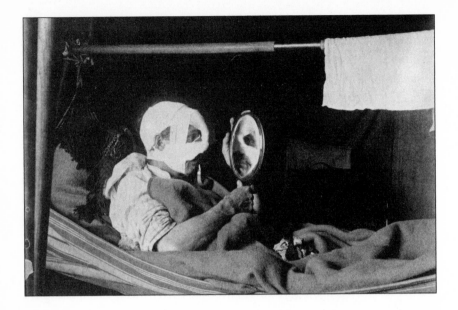

CHAPTER TWENTY

H E FELT AS IF HE HAD NO SKIN.

Or worse—as if he had stitched it on himself, in his sleep perhaps. He had been fading in and out of consciousness for weeks. Coming to, now, he didn't bother to lift his hand to swat away the flies that buzzed his head, crawling over the bandages that concealed the rude, oozing scars of his mangled face. He would have put an animal in his condition out of its misery. He would never have mounted such an ugly specimen.

As his wounds slowly healed over the next three months—the expedition would not return, against all better judgment, to America—he lay on his cot, in and out of delirium, only half aware of the gentle ministrations of his wife. She wasn't there now, however, when he woke. It was midafternoon, and the sun blazed through the crack of the canvas flap. He was alone. Or so he thought until he picked up the shaving mirror on the nightstand to inspect his mummified head and noticed the vervet tied behind him to the bedpost, trying to catch a glimpse of its own bemused reflection.

The only part of his face visible through the cocoon of bandages was one grim, bloodshot eyeball. It stared back almost lasciviously. The monkey, enchanted by its own mirror image, now caught his eye with an inquisitive sparkle. *What did it feel like? Like being used for an elephant's prayer rug.* He stared at the monkey, as if waiting for it to comment. *Like being hit by a motor truck.* That's what it had felt like.

He wouldn't have minded talking to the monkey, which was actually turning out to be not the worst companion in the world, especially with Mickie gone all day, hunting or tending to the many administrative errands of keeping the safari afloat, even if formal operations had been semi-suspended during his convalescence.

He tried to lift his head, decided against it, fell back against his pillows, and reached for his pipe on the bedstand. The smoke seeped through the bandages plastered over his cheek. After a while, he closed the eye, and then, letting the work sounds of camp dissolve around him, took a stroll through the property he had begun to construct in secrecy behind his eyelids.

The marble floor was cool on his stockinged feet, and the echo of his two canes tapped across the monumental navelike space. Gradually, his eyes adjusted to the dim lighting. The numinous panes of glass, each the size of a motion picture screen, reflected faintly on the dark tiles. Everything was as he had left it. The raised bronze lettering identifying the tenant of each exquisite lair. The hall was as grand as one of McKim, Mead & White's soaring spaces. Penn Station with the lights turned low. Up on the mezzanine gallery, the half-finished chimpanzees looked down from their canopy of wax leaves.

He'd begun to build the great thing in his mind over the weeks and months he'd been confined to his cot. There, between fits of delirium and fever, he had become sole witness to this slowly unfolding vision. A vision of such sublime and splendid design, such a radiant blueprint for what his future now held before him, in a way he had to feel sincerely grateful to the elephant.

Even if he had barely seen the creature before it had crushed him down into the rucksack of oblivion. The last thing he remembered was tracking just below the ice fields, trying to determine how high up the elephants really went. He and his trackers had found spoor higher than he ever would have guessed, above the timberline, at fourteen thousand feet, and a little higher in the sphagnum marshes where the air was thin as plasma and sulfur-cold. It amazed him how the elephant could adapt to such diverse and extreme conditions. But how else would it have ever survived the millennia?

But then after Mickie and her altitude-sick monkey had left him for base camp, he and his remaining porters had dropped down several thousand feet, to the upper bamboo forest, where they'd stumbled across the tracks of three very large bulls. By the looks of one in particular, by its footprints, Carl immediately knew he had found the trail of the largest elephant he'd ever come across. A colossal mound of droppings readily affirmed his hunch.

On the other hand, the droppings were four days old at least, a crumbled hive of stubby maggots, but the trackers were still able to single out this large bull's path and to follow it for quite a while unhindered.

The trail itself was a kind of maze. A series of interconnected passageways, blazed over time, that traversed the elephants' feeding grounds high in the bamboo forest. Deep in the maze, though, as Carl tried to follow the bull's tracks, he only ended by circling back around to the same place from which he'd started, almost as if he'd fallen victim to a ruse.

Finally, after deciding to try to find the exit to the maze, Carl was going along the bamboo perimeter when he found another pile of dung. It was just as massive as the four-day-old spoor, but fresh, still steaming in the freezing June mist. He poked at the humid ziggurat with the machete he'd been using to cut a path.

It was then he began to have a distinct sense about this elephant. It came over him gradually. The feeling was he had finally found a bull worthy of bringing back to New York. The one he'd been chasing after for the last long difficult year. As if it had only been one individual bull all along that had evaded him and set up this contest. But now he felt it—this was *the* one.

Even stranger, as Carl and the trackers kept walking through the maze, he started getting the sense that the elephant truly was waiting for him. The feeling was strong. That he was being hunted as well, and was now engaged in a mortal contest with this bull. In fact, he felt it right up until the moment when they came to a small clearing in the tinsel-green bamboo and heard a loud crash in the woods fifty yards straight ahead.

The trackers were already twenty yards forward, on the path, and now braced against the unknown. The porters behind him had run off, shedding their bundles. Carl calmly took his .475 double rifle, while his gun bearer went through the patient ritual of taking out and holding up for Carl's inspection every single bullet from the bandolier. The last thing he needed at a critical moment like this was to load the wrong caliber. Meanwhile, he unwrapped the handkerchief from his hand, trying to rub feeling back into his numbed fingers, and waiting for the trackers to give him a sight line, when, with no more fanfare than a dust mote entering a Victorian drawing room on a ray of midafternoon sunlight, the bull was suddenly upon him. Out of nowhere, a tusk was at his chest. As if the elephant had only been standing there, hidden behind the bamboo curtain, waiting for its cue to enter.

What he remembered now was that the safety on his rifle had caught; though later his porters would remember that he had got off one shot. He did not remember the splintering of wood or an explosion of leaves or whether he got a shot off or not. What he did remember was the odd overwhelming sensation of homesickness, struggling for a moment with the safety, and then he had done the unimaginable: he had thrown the rifle aside and actually reached out to grab hold of the tusk as it lanced past him with the force of a sharpened swinging log. A completely mad thing to do! To climb aboard a charging elephant, as if it were a speeding boxcar. It had been almost automatic, like something he had rehearsed in his mind a thousand times before. Lifted off his feet, lurched skyward, somehow in the next split second managing to get himself between the two tusks, grabbing the other as well, so he had a grip on both like the handlebars of a gargantuan bicycle. Here he was now riding the face of a giant bull, a massive *tembo*, overlord of the forest. Pressed against the thick ridged bridge of its trunk, close enough to see his own terrified reflection jiggling in the piggish gelatin of its cornea, he knew to expect no mercy.

Attempting to scrape the gymnast off its face, the elephant thrust its tusks into the earth. It plowed him into the ground. Thanks to a thwarting stubborn undersoil—a root, a rock—Carl was not killed instantly but remained between the tusks, holding on for bitter life. As the elephant changed its footing, Carl felt the chilled breeze of its nicked, batwing ears and took one last breath of the animal's creosote musk. The smell of hot coal tar. Then a shuddering blackness. Ten hours later, his runners would arrive at base camp to bring Mickie the bad news.

❧

WHEN HE FIRST came to, a heaviness filled his lungs, like iron vapor. He was aware of lying in the mud, and the cold rain, and he could also make out what he took to be his porters, a little distance off, warming their hands around a blaze. He could only see this through one blurry eye. When he tried to get up, he discovered that he was not able to move his legs. And so he lay there, tasting the blood that trickled out the corners of his mouth like a slow burbling spring, convinced that his back was broken. He did not dare touch the side of his face. He had to wonder why his men had not put him inside the tent, leaving him here instead on the wet ground, or not at least set him nearer the fire; then he arrived at the only possible conclusion, which was that they thought him dead.

Nothing could compel a Kikuyu to lay hands on a corpse.

He tried to get their attention several times before they looked over, startled to discover him moaning, but as soon as they seemed persuaded that he was not bluffing, they came along and dragged him into the tent. Then he went unconscious again.

WHEN HE CAME to again, he felt a tickling sensation on his face and hands and under his shirt as well. It was all over his body. Ants, come to feast on his leaking carcass. He was covered with them, but there was little he could do about it. After a while he managed to get one of the porters to bring him some quinine and a bottle of brandy, which the man helped him to down, though a good half of its contents was lost out the trench in the side of his face. But after the bottle was emptied he found he could move his toes. He was not paralyzed after all. Then, again, much relieved, he slept.

WHEN HE WOKE again, the ants were still there, so he lay there like that, like a human anthill, until the rain outside stopped and it was quiet and gradually the monochrome of dawn began to crowbar its way into the tent. It was then he began to feel certain about Mickie being near. It was just a feeling. As much as he had felt the elephant had been waiting for him in the woods. So when the men reemerged at dawn, and he could hear the crackle of fire starting, he told the gun bearer to take his rifle and fire a signal shot every fifteen minutes. Between the explosions he faded in and out.

✌

WHEN HE NEXT opened his eyes Mickie was already there. By the way she covered her face, he knew how bad he must have looked. Then they tied him to a stretcher, and he was lopsidedly carried along by two of Mickie's porters who looked as if they had not slept for a week. It was strange, but he could have sworn he'd seen one of the Africans actually crying over him. It was Bill, the one he'd tried to put in jail, but who'd somehow got free and followed them back up the mountain.

✌

A FEW WEEKS into his convalescence, he started building his museum in the sky. Like a shirker slipping into a nickelodeon in the middle of the afternoon, he could sneak in whenever he felt like it. Each time, there were new details to notice, like the panels depicting the primeval hunters in bas-relief above each alcove. Details he must not forget. He walked around slowly, passing the giant coffin-shaped dais upon which the frozen elephants stood like great bronze statues, estimating the dimensions of the hall in his mind. The overall layout revealed itself more clearly with each visit. The elephants would still be the centerpiece. This was not anything like the original purpose for which he had been sent to Africa, but once he shared his vision with the trustees back in New York, he knew, they would have no choice but to build it.

Carl stood with his fists in the pockets of his bathrobe, mesmerized by the perfection of the vision. All the charmed, fabular beasts caught as if under a spell. Twenty on the first floor and twenty on the gallery. It would be like a giant movie theater where the viewer could walk from one silent screen to the next, but with no reels, no moving parts, no chintzy special effects, no dinky piano playing in the dark pit.

Ticket buyers would be able to stop and enter the illusion, move from window to window, one artificial wilderness to the next, and behold each vivid fragment of Nature for as long as their disbelief could be sustained. Maybe more than the movies, it was like a silent, glittering mausoleum: each scene hermetically sealed for eternity. In the mossy shadows of the rain forest, a leopard, its hide like silk damask, stalking some unseen prey. A rhinoceros making love to its Nile mud. Here were five gemsbok, faces painted like hoofers for the Ziegfeld Follies. A gerenuk on tiptoes, entwined in a thorn tree, hipping away the tender leaves. In one diorama alone an entire grassland ensphered: zebras, giraffes, wildebeests, stampeding across the plains. He could practically taste the rising dust.

Of course he had not yet accounted for every detail. In some, the backgrounds were merely sketched out. Behind one pane a raging brush fire but no animals. Some of the dioramas were still vacant altogether: empty dark compartments, as of yet unimagined.

This vision in his fevered mind would be his true work. He understood that now. To look inside this beautiful forgery, he felt sure, one would almost ache to get on the other side of the glass, to enter the sealed chambers where life and death seemed held in suspension. Here was asylum from the ravages of decay and oblivion. And here was the same paradox, to a degree, that every artist faced: to immortalize time, one must kill it a little bit first. What better way to understand the cosmos than to flense it, bleed it, and then build it back up again to spec. All just so that it might be possible—bearable even—to look directly upon the naked mystery of Nature unveiled.

CHAPTER TWENTY-ONE

WHEN THE BANDAGES FINALLY CAME OFF, WHAT WAS LEFT beneath was an entirely more timid creature, as raw and traumatized as a newborn. Rawer yet after Mickie helped him to shave, using the Gillette safety razor he'd bought in London. And now he was on his feet. The first time he'd been out in three months. They were on the hunt, wading through the waist-high grass. Indeed, just the simplicity of the air against his face had a certain unsettling newness. The act of walking—now that he no longer required the aid of two canes—did not come altogether second-nature either. Though thinner, he still looked the part with his rolled puttees wound tight, boots double-laced, pith helmet brushed just that morning by Dudo, his effervescent new tent boy. The porters were excited and full of anticipation. He could hear them up ahead. The trackers had found spoor in the morning going this direction. Gingerly conscious of every step he took, he was eager to face the day's trial.

Awake to every smell, every sound, every sharp swish of grass, everything vivid and tenuous and wistful in the new way that only a convalescent can apprehend the drab old world after prolonged illness. The smell of primrose. Hibiscus. Acacia blossoms and the halo of bees buzzing the thorny crowns. The sweet scent had to remind him of sitting under the acacia tree with TR, and what would TR think of him now, he had to wonder, hobbling along like a frail old man, eyes strained with uncertainty, like an animal kept too long in captivity suddenly thrust back into the wild to fend for itself? There was no telling how durable his nerves would prove on this first hunt back.

He limped along beside his quietly encouraging wife, trying to stay light and jokey, trying his best to hide the grimaces of pain, as stoic as his brand of manhood required, but mainly focused ahead on the difficulty of the trail. All the porters, hooting and singing, came up behind, trailing the revenant, as if he were a traveling magus who had promised a holy spectacle. Then there was motion toward the front, and the trackers signaled frantically for quiet. He looked to the woods where they pointed, and saw nothing. Next hearing the crunch of wood pulp followed by that strangest of almost infrasonic rumbles. Then he saw it: the fleeting mosaic of corrugated hide shifting inward the trees.

His gun boy was holding out the rifle for him to take. Here was his chance to settle the lingering question of his rickety morale. The stock felt new-familiar in his hands. He would step forward now and conclude this craven chapter of his life. Just because a piece of bad luck had come your way did not mean you needed to continue to live as if it would own you forever. You moved on as bravely as if you had not even taken notice of the interruption. You could not be held captive by such cowardice.

But then once he heard the bellow and trumpet, a strange thing happened to the ground beneath his feet. An emasculated feeling seized his legs, as if the tendons behind his knees had been injected with Novocain, and when he tried to get off the ground he began to quake so that he could not even push himself up by the arms. Hornbills and squabbling vervet monkeys fumbled overhead in the suddenly skewed canopy of leaves and tilted sky. The scene went sideways, and the next thing he knew he was being helped onto a blanket and carried off the field like a conscript overcome by battle hysteria.

THE ELEVATOR LET him off onto the gallery, where he stopped to rest in front of the colobus display. Half concealed in the leaves with which they stuffed their cheeks, the monkeys enjoyed a lofty view over the green and purple valley. He was endlessly revising the floor plan in his mind now. Moving a zebra here, a background there, a celluloid cactus over here—obviously it made sense to place the tree-dwelling creatures up here on the mezzanine. He looked down on the elephants. It was always a bit mysterious the way animals were able to telegraph their fear to one another—how many times he'd been in the forest when all went abruptly silent. The herd below him was poised tensely. The massive old bull's head raised, ears pitched, trunk out feeling the breeze, and the small young bull at the rear spun round to face ambush from behind. The cow and calf clinging to each other in frozen alarm. As if they had just now sensed the presence of the intruder, heard the tap of his cane, gone still with fear.

❧

THE RED-TAILED MONKEYS were cheeping at them from the trees. They were looking right down at them, cheeping like crazy. But so far the elephants hadn't noticed Carl and his gun bearer hidden in their blind of brambles. They were crouched in the undergrowth, not twenty yards away, staked out on the forest edge. It was hot and itchy in the makeshift lair, and, truth be told, it felt a bit like watching elephants from the vantage of a field mouse.

It had been like this for hours, the better part of a day. Bill was stripped down to the waist, squatting with the giant rifle slung across his lap, bits of grass poking from his hair. To bide the time he scratched at the ground impatiently with a stick.

The sun came in on them in scattered blebs, as if they were hidden under a pile of broken venetian blinds. In the sallow light Carl's skin still looked a bit seedy from the last bout of spirillum, which he hadn't quite completely licked. He still felt swampy, and every few hours he swallowed another grain of quinine. By this point they had seen at least twenty elephants, but so far none were good enough for the taxidermist.

Two groups of five or six each had come to the watering hole in just the last few hours, taking their time, easy targets, but Carl remained unpersuaded. There was nothing he'd seen yet worth wasting a bullet. The giants took turns wading in, slopping and squirting themselves with mud, then stood glistening and slick in the bright early morning, shining like nickel and tungsten. They strigiled the water from their bodies with their long trunks, fanning themselves with their giant dripping stingray ears. Just the night before Carl had sat on an anthill until well after dark watching one herd after another come into view, and he had let each of those pass unharmed as well. Now each time a new elephant appeared, Bill looked at Carl, to see whether this time he would make his move. Whether this time—the thought couldn't be helped—he would have the nerve.

Carl wanted to peek out and see if there wasn't any ivory in this latest group. At the moment, the herd's position only afforded a partial glimpse of their legs, and the hunters could only hear the elephants' intestinal grumbling, and the ripping and munching of grass as they slowly fed. Carl tried craning his head to look through the interstices of their blind, and saw that another bull had arrived. It had joined the four others, and together they were just loafing about in the tall hoarding of grass, their mud-bronzed flanks working like bellows.

But then the elephants were starting to move off and back into the forest, back down the trail, so he and Bill waited until they thought the last one had passed, and now with the wind in their favor, but still treading as stealthily as possible, they crept out of their hiding place and down the trail in pursuit.

Quickly, they lost sight of the elephants. At a sort of crossing, an intersection of paths in the woods, they stopped to strain their ears for any sign. The forest remained silent except for the distant *cheep cheep cheep* of the red-tailed monkeys. But then Carl saw the bull—its gigantic muddy rear not twenty feet away. With Bill frozen in place just an inch or two behind him, they stood together motionless—facing off against the hind end. After a moment, Carl tried craning his neck to peer around the massive elephant's behind to see if he could judge its ivory, and it was about then when he saw the cow appear beside the bull. It was staring straight at him, though he could not be sure whether the cow was actually seeing him. Its eyes looked fuzzy. It was not out of the question that it mistook him for a very still, very sallow tree.

He did not dare move. However fuzzy, its eyes were fixed on him, and he remained in a kind of paralysis. Even once the cow was moving toward him he could not bring himself to swing his rifle around, and for some reason could only look on at whatever was about to transpire as if he were an innocent bystander, when just to his immediate right came an explosion as Bill stepped forward and fired straight into the face of the charging cow.

Without thinking, Carl turned, *wheeled*, and struck Bill across the face. A hard quick slap. The kind you might give an infuriating child. Especially one prone to calling out your faults. Under the circumstances it had been the only thing to do to preserve his dignity—his dignity as a white man, naturally—but it surprised him as much as anything to feel, tingling in the palm of his hand, the sting of regret.

❧

AT FIRST IT seemed there was nothing he could do to persuade Bill to not quit the safari and return to Nairobi. However, it came as some relief that Bill's decision had nothing to do with the humiliations of the day before. Or so he said. Carl was prepared to accept his excuses. That he just couldn't take the pace of the safari anymore. That he was tired and scared of the elephants. Bill blamed himself. He blamed his own nerves. His decision to leave had nothing whatsoever to do with the fact that he had been rewarded with a slap in the face for trying to save his employer's life. Of course, Carl thought, Bill had been foolish to think he hadn't seen the elephant. Of course he'd seen the elephant. He just hadn't interpreted its motions the same way Bill had. Still, he did recognize that he had been wrong, to a minor degree, for striking Bill. The boy clearly believed in all sincerity—in his overly excitable way—that he had taken justifiable action to save his life, and so Carl had apologized profusely and *as humbly as the dignity of a white man would permit.*

As shameful as the entire episode had been, he still couldn't stand for Bill to leave. He was by far the keenest tracker Carl had ever met, black or white. And damned reliable compared to the others. He had more than proven himself before this little row; without him, poor Mickie would have been helpless against the mutiny that night after his smash-up on Mount Kenya.

Still, Bill had broken the golden rule. No black man was ever to fire a white man's rifle unless his master was at the direct mercy of a beast. But this could be forgiven. In the end he was able to persuade Bill to stay. Hell, he didn't even have to join him out on hunts for a week if he didn't want. He'd rather Bill stay behind in camp, loaf around, get the rest he needed, recover his strained nerves. There'd be plenty adventure later. Even so, when he went out the next day, Bill insisted on going as well, but only after confiding to Memsahib that he was "not afraid for himself but was afraid for his Bwana."

❧

SHE WAS RUNNING through the forest in the fog. No one could find where he'd gone. Once again he'd vanished from her sight. Each time he got into danger or it seemed she would lose him again it sent off the old panic. The sour-electric current in blood and belly. She ran through the woods like a panicked mother. But then she came around the next bend, and there he was, sitting on the ground, disoriented-looking, like a pitiful old man. His rifle lay on the ground beside him like a toy with mud on its barrel. His hands pale against the earth as he tried to prop himself up to a sitting position. Rocking woozily, he looked infuriated, as if he were just now in the middle of a great quarrel with himself, but the way he looked at Mickie you would have thought the quarrel was with her, but perhaps only because she had become witness to his unmanly demise. Something had broken, had failed to heal, while he'd been hidden away under the bandages. She would have done anything to save him again, to rescue him from this plight over the "question of his morale," as he put it. She knew his repeated nervous collapses and the recurrent fevers were all due to the psychological strain he had suffered from the elephant attack. Just the sound of their trumpets could curl him into a trembling ball. What little strength he had left had dribbled away, and his mind sought the sanctuary of his fever world. All in all, this latest version of her husband resembled a teacup on a rattled shelf. She would have gone out and hunted down the bull for him if it meant she could save his life, if it meant they'd be able to go home at last, but she realized that if he did not overcome this, settle the question for himself, he would never be the same man again. All that remained now was the hard hot coal of obsession, and it smoldered impotently. But for the time being she could do little more than call back the boys to fetch the hammock, clapping her hands sharply, as if anything here could be hurried, ever, by a simple act of will, and then stay with him, watching him suffer, until at last the men arrived with the *tepoi*—were they trying to conceal their smirks, or did they smirk openly now?—to carry bwana back out of the woods and to the humiliating safety of his sour cot.

※

THE RUMBLE FROM the chasm was immense. He was perched practically dangling overhead, from the skinny crag. The torrent of elephants rushing below dodged and stumbled through the narrow gulch. Bill knelt beside him, clutching the backup rifle. They watched in amazement at the elephants charging beneath like ice floes crashing the fjord, and for the time being they were pinned to this fingerhold of dirt. The forest boiled with elephants. The din of trumpets shrieking and snapping branches escalating until the forest itself felt as if it might give under the gaining thunder of pachyderms hurtling through the narrow lane.

He had never experienced anything like it in his life. There had to be nearly a thousand of them. You could hear the marauding echoes for a mile in either direction. His spot on this little hill overlooking the ravine was like being stranded on the last bit of high ground above a flood. Helplessly suspended only feet above the mob, he fought the feeling that he was dreaming up the entire thing.

But here was the odd, just as dreamlike thing. All at once, as if on cue, the elephants went silent. As if he had suddenly gone deaf. Or as if a wall had come down, cutting him off from the noise of the stampede. Though he could see they were still on the move. Nothing had stopped. They had just gone eerily quiet.

If such a thing were possible, they now stampeded in a muted hush, the only sound throughout the forest being a kind of tumultuous rustle that swept behind in their wake like a giant broom. But in fact it was only the dry leaves of the forest floor scruffing underfoot, stirred and agitated into a steady and brittle susurrus. After a while the noise became hypnotic. Nothing could compare to the sound in strangeness. It had the feel of a final moment, an ultimatum.

❧

HOW MANY MORE times could he fail to act? How long would it take to mend his shattered nerves? How many weeks and months had it been now since the traumatizing event? How many months since the bandages had come off? How many more times could Mickie save him before he saved himself?

The elephants had brought them here, to this small cluster of beehive-shaped huts. The two bulls were just seventy-five yards off, but barely visible in the merging gray of dusk and fog, their tusks pulsing, visible then not. Carl and Mickie had taken position in the dooryard near one of the huts. Like other villages in the region, this one appeared abandoned and had a wild and lonely air to it. The greenish-gray fog drifted like mustard gas across a battlefield. Not so much as a grindstone was left in the yard.

Carl was trying to set up his shot in the crotch of a tree, and Mickie braced herself near the hut, by the vacant door, her clothes still drenched from crawling through the wet jungle. They had been on the chase since early that morning. Passing through areas that looked like they'd been hit by a cyclone from where elephants had stampeded villages, plowing over huts, tearing up crops, and flattening banana trees as if the elephants and humans were at war. Then they'd come upon these two bulls, so thick with dried mud that as they ran—crushing everything that stood in their way—the dust shook off their bodies in great choking clouds.

Mickie looked over at Carl and saw that he was having trouble setting up his shot. She had the one bull they had agreed would be hers locked in her sights and now waited for his signal. Fortunately, the elephants had yet to see them. She could see he was becoming impatient with himself, trying to get it just right. He looked tired and pale as the fog that was conspiring with the dusk to lose this shot for good.

As she waited, her elephant dissolved behind a veil of fog. They had been going hard all day, through terrible terrain, and Carl had kept a bully attitude all the way, but now she could see that he was near his end. His hair was longish around the ears, which made him look older. It was a terrible thing to watch her husband so consumed by fear and fatigue. But she could not help but feel, selfishly, a little afraid that his condition would endanger her own safety. If his courage ever deserted him in the face of battle—now—it could be Mickie herself who paid the final price. But she would stand by him no matter the cost. That was not really a question.

When the fog slid back and her elephant materialized again, she saw that it had seen her as well. It turned its great heavy face to her, caked in dry ashen mud, and as it slowly wagged its trunk and shook out its leathery ears, a cloudburst of dust unloosed. A moment before it trumpeted she knew it was going to charge. But before it did—and before Carl had fully gotten himself into position—his own elephant, startled, took off and vanished in the fog. Now there was only the one. And as it came down on them, its trunk slashing like a scythe, at twenty yards Mickie hit at it as fast as she could work her gun. Even under this barrage the elephant did not stop; spurts of dust flashed off its hide like drops of rain pecking at a parched garden. That was when she felt the small hand against her leg. Terrified, she looked down to see the face of a small girl holding an infant in the doorway. A third girl cowered inside the hut. They huddled beneath her legs, petrified. In confusion and horror all she could do was turn back to the elephant bearing down on them and pull the trigger—she and her wraithlike husband firing a final volley in unison—and in an instant the elephant crashed to the ground and came to a dreadful halt not ten feet from where she stood in the doorway.

She had not yet recovered from her shock over the children when out of the forest the hiding villagers emerged in a mob, shouting and running, bearing torches in the dusk and fog, closing in on the fallen elephant, knives out, ready to do their part for a share of this unexpected feast. She flinched when Carl went up to the elephant and fired three last shots. It seemed he did not trust that it was dead. Then she felt the heaves of adrenaline. That abominable excitement—like poured tin—in the stomach. She dropped her rifle and then found that she could not pull herself free from her buckled knees. She remained like that, stuck to the ground, looking at the woozy scene framing her now, at her husband setting up his camera. She could see from his expression, and the way he had taken possession of the corpse, that at last he had resolved the question of his morale. He strode proudly around the fallen bull whose mud-corrugated hide was streaked with the deep heme of its blood. Fear was over. There was no fear. He had conquered it. It had died here, even if the memory of how—or who—had been rescued would fade from memory soon enough.

PART THREE

~∾

Life in the City

CHAPTER TWENTY-TWO

BEETHOVEN'S MINUET IN G, LONG FINISHED, WAS STILL SCRATCHing on the record player. Mickie was sitting in the middle of her living room, watching blood from the two tiny puncture wounds just above her heel trickle over her shoe and onto the cashmere carpet. It wasn't all that much blood, but something essential, a nerve or tendon, something important to the business of standing, had been nipped. Late afternoon sunlight streamed into the apartment from Central Park West, and from where she sat, unable to get up, she could hear children playing around the reservoir in the park, launching toy boats, chasing dogs, though soon, surely, they would be gathered up by mothers and governesses for supper and evening baths and storytime.

The floor provided her a novel view of the apartment, looking down the end of the hall toward the butler's pantry, and J.T. Jr.'s private bedroom, the general open layout, and the familiar objects of her habitat. The elephant ear table in the library; the Kodiak skin on the dining room floor; the walls decorated with some of Carl's photographs; the corner of a leopard skin peeking into view from her wardrobe. The apartment looked as if it had been ransacked. It was all a shambles, despite their new maid's best efforts. No wonder nobody came to visit anymore. The furniture was a disgrace. The curtains hung in tatters. Dark smudge marks scuffed the walls and tracked over the picture molding. And now blood on the cashmere carpet.

J.T. Jr. was up on the windowsill, his favorite retreat, just as the top of her tent had been on safari, watching the needle of the Victrola scratching in the dead space like a persistent but dull-minded creature digging for insects that it would never find. When the sunlight caught the little silver collar, engraved with his name, the monkey's rapid eyes tracked the slippery silvery bleb across the room until the spot of light hesitated in the foyer, nagging the black-and-white framed lions frozen on the wall.

After a while, somehow, she managed to drag herself into the bathroom and dab some permanganate on the wound, and then crawled her way to the bedroom. The maid was not here today. When the telephone started, she just lay there listening to it ring. She must have known it was Carl, calling to say he wouldn't be home till later, which of course always meant very possibly not at all. He would fall asleep on the couch in the elephant studio, and she might not see him for a day or more. In fact, two days later she was still in bed, and the leg was starting to look pretty wicked. Red streaks radiated up her calf. The leg was swollen and distorted to twice its size, almost the way it had looked when she'd been in the Budongo Forest and she'd hallucinated her arms and legs were turning into elephant limbs. The pain was excruciating. She was all alone. J.T. rarely left the window ledge.

When Carl finally wandered home, plaster flaked in his eyebrows and his wool suit, he called the doctor immediately. The doctor, upon seeing the leg, wanted her to go straight to the hospital for surgery. Either that or lose the leg. At this point it was the leg or her life. But she refused to go to the hospital if they would not let her bring J.T. Jr. She would not leave the poor monkey alone in the apartment. She knew how confused and upset and contrite he was already, and she would not add to his torment by abandoning him here all alone (with the maid). She placed no blame on him whatsoever.

Finally, the doctor agreed to perform the emergency surgery there, lancing a pus sac that had formed above the wound, and operating on what turned out to be a partially severed tendon. Deep infection had set in, and she was lucky the doctor didn't have to amputate. During surgery, J.T. remained locked in the bedroom. But when it was all over, Carl forced the monkey to come out and witness what he had done, yanking back the bedsheet to reveal Mickie's leg. You could see the monkey's fur give a shudder. Then, in a flash, he leaped at Carl, fangs bared, and Carl jumped back. He would have taken the vermin by the neck and disposed of it then and there in the basement incinerator if he'd had his way. But Mickie came to J.T.'s defense. None of it was the monkey's fault. She wished he could understand that. But by then her husband had left the room, gotten his hat, and was already on his way back to the museum.

So this time it was Mickie who was confined to bed for three months. The only difference being that Carl was not there to nurse her back to health. For three months she was laid up, the leg that had nearly cost her her life elevated on pillows. To pass the time she fondled her rosary beads, or read snatches of magazines, or brushed out her hair, listening to records on the Victrola, and letting J.T. amuse her with his endless gravity-flouting laps about the apartment. Since she had given up any semblance of a social life to devote herself to the monkey, he was all she had now, so she watched J.T. bounce wall to wall and mantel over chandelier. Over and over again he ricocheted around the apartment like a wind-up fair prize. Then he would disappear into his bedroom, for hours at a time, sitting in the big window that overlooked the park, watching squirrels run arabesques in the tupelo trees by the fountain.

The few remaining friends who bothered to visit could barely wait to ask, unabashedly, why on earth had she kept the monkey? "Why don't you get rid of the little beast? What did you *do to him* when he bit you?"

No one seemed to understand. But she felt no resentment toward J.T. at all, only pity, for he was her *poor little prisoner*. She had no idea what might have driven him to bite her in the first place. She only blamed herself. Perhaps her foot had grazed one of J.T.'s precious dolls. More likely, it had been the stern tone she'd taken just moments before he'd attacked. She had been distracted by some house errand, and when he'd gotten in the way, wanting attention, she'd snapped, "Go to bed, J.T., I can't play with you now."

That's really all she had said.

Things hadn't always been so terrible. When they'd first come back to New York and moved into the apartment overlooking Central Park they were just like any other happy family. Carl was fully rehabilitated, recovered from the last leg of their trip after he'd come down with a final bout of blackwater in Mombasa, where their return home had been delayed an extra two months, two more months with Carl on the brink of death, too weak even to manage the final tedious business of preparing their collection to pass through customs.

When they finally got to New York it took some getting used to not having tent boys to fetch this or that, or take care of the oddments of the day, but they made do. Each night when Carl came home from the museum, J.T. would bounce around in circles, and they would play hide-and-seek before dinner, and Carl would let him pretend to smoke his pipe. In the evening they didn't need for entertainment, with J.T. there to perform his acrobatics about the apartment. Zipping round and round the eighteen-by-eighteen-foot living room like a Sopwith Camel, the flying monkey would start from his perch above the door, caroming off one wall, banking to hurl himself off another, performing little midflight tricks, a midair roll and yaw, then a quick horizontal scurry above the picture molding, strafing the walls with his dirty paws, a dive-bomb off the elephant ear table and then up and across the mantel and one more spin around the room before resuming his perch over the door, where he sat with his usual reflective expression, as if each flight were a proof of some whimsical theorem.

He even helped Carl get ready for work in the mornings. Perched on the lip of the bathroom sink, eagerly waiting for him to finish lathering his face with shaving cream, J.T. leaped up onto his shoulder and took the ivory handle of the razor—Carl speaking in a calm voice, *Careful now, J.T.*, as the trembling monkey scraped the stubble from his rugged cheek. Helping his master shave seemed to give the animal almost inexplicable pleasure.

The family ate breakfast together in the sunny dining room, which overlooked the park, before Carl left for the museum—dressed in a suit and tie to play with plaster and clay—and then Mickie and her pet would begin their marvelous days together.

J.T. enjoyed lounging on the couch, flipping through illustrated magazines, looking at pictures in *Outlook, Saturday Evening Post*, and reading the latest articles about his mother and father's adventures in Temboland. Sometimes he would sit in Mickie's lap and allow her to give him a manicure, while he lazily flipped through a magazine with one free paw. He sucked at baby bottles filled with milk and ate figs Mickie ordered specially shipped from California. They sewed together, Mickie demonstrating for J.T. how to hold the needle and thread between thumb and forefinger, and how to pull it through the fabric, so that if she left the room for a few moments she would return to find the monkey had added his own erratic embellishments to Mickie's finished work. Ripping the stitches out, however, was just as much fun. He loved to rip anything that had stitches. Lace from the window curtains. Bead trimming. Fine-motor destruction was his specialty.

Each night, before going to bed, J.T. sat sleepily on the edge of Mickie's dressing table and helped unfasten her dress, then plucked out her hairpins one at a time with his buffed and polished tiny nails. Then he would retire to his room and watch the fountain. It rose and fell, falling like ash on the still green water. Eventually he would go to sleep hugging the hand mirror he'd had since Africa. Mickie found him most nights with his face pressed to his reflection, a pulse of vapor on the glass, and she would watch his rising and falling chest for a moment or two, for reassurance, before picking him up and tucking him into his box.

In warmer months, he would play out on the fire escape with his dolls, attracting the attention of neighbors who watched his antics with opera glasses; once, after breaking free of his leash, he quickly made his way down the escape and into the apartment on the first floor, where he then crept into the bathroom to find the lady of the house half submerged beneath a great custard of soapsuds. When she saw the intruder, she sat petrified in the tub, until J.T. had slinked forward and snatched a pawful of the custard before fleeing the premises, never to be seen again.

Mickie had had to bribe the landlord by appealing to his sense as a family man to let her keep J.T. She also promised to pay for any molested furniture.

She knew that the monkey was her prisoner, and that New York was hell on his already jumpy nerves. She felt guilty, ultimately, for bringing the creature across the ocean, for throwing him into the midst of this artificial wilderness of steel and smoke. He could not handle the sounds of the city, the blaring commotion. Subways and automobiles threw him into a panic. Only once had Mickie dared to take J.T. on the subway—she herself had not ridden it many times—and during the whole ride he huddled in his little basket, clinging to her finger as if he would pull it off. In the end she decided that it was easier not to go out at all. So she and the monkey would not leave the house for weeks at a time.

On the few occasions she went out by herself she was overcome with feelings of guilt, even if she'd left him with the maid (who on occasion had to lock herself in the bathroom to get away from the monkey's assaults). Images would come to her of J.T. alone, sad as an orphan, clutching his doll, and spoil any pleasure she might have had from her outings. She was too distracted by these lonesome images to be much of a luncheon companion. Often she would leave early in order to go home and assure herself that the monkey had not fallen prey to the worst-case scenarios she could not stop herself from imagining.

Besides, the monkey had fairly well guaranteed she couldn't go to social outings by demolishing every decent piece of clothing in her possession, tearing apart hats, dresses, scarves. Anything with sequins or beads was defenseless. But Mickie could not say, by this point, that she altogether cared. Nor whether, consciously or unconsciously, she had left out the hats and dresses on purpose. It was not as if she was eager to go out. After two years living in the bush, living like a savage herself, J.T. was not the only one who must have felt misplaced. Considering the pace of modern life and how quickly everything tended to change now— overnight it seemed—it was almost impossible for her to readjust to city life. It was easier in the end to project her failure on the monkey.

She still refused to punish the creature. No matter how many dresses he liberated of sequins. No matter how many hats and hatboxes he deconstructed. No matter how often he hid under the tables and pinched the maid's calves. He was free to explore the apartment and open table drawers, rifle through desks, sit on tables, do what he would. After all, she told herself, her scientific observations of the monkey's behavior in the civilized world had not ceased. She was learning much about his reactions in the laboratory of the city. For instance, that when she played *Pagliacci* he would inevitably exhibit his extreme dislike for Caruso on the window shades. No, there was far too much data left to collect for her to have time to go out to meaningless social functions now. She had also begun to feel affronted anytime people came to visit now—they claimed the monkey smelled. She would rather live without said acquaintances, interruptions.

By now people only very rarely stopped by to see her. Mickie could always sense the unspoken thoughts of the few guests they had. The furtive bemused glances. The raised eyebrows. The surreptitious sniffs that said as plainly as words, *Do you detect an odor of monkeys in this house?*

As if J.T. were nothing but a filthy zoo monkey. As if he didn't get a daily bath. The extent of human prejudice was overwhelming.

Entirely unfair, too, because her house was spick-and-span. She had a good Irish maid. On the other hand there were incidents, and it did seem that J.T. went out of his way to antagonize visitors. When guests did come, J.T. rifled through handbags and pockets, and if someone were foolish enough to hold Mickie's hand for too long, he would give them a vicious bite. J.T. did not like loudmouths, and guests who spoke in a sing-songy voice were imminently in danger of a smack. On one occasion when she bothered to sequester J.T. before a party, she consented to let her curious guests see him, only to open the bedroom door to be met by a gust of down feathers and the sight of J.T. jumping up and down on the bed with a gutted pillow in one clenched fist, his other spewing handfuls of feathers swirling overhead, which in a matter of seconds had covered the dark serge frocks of the astonished women standing in the doorway as if they'd stepped directly into a blizzard.

They never called again.

As the animal grew more stir-crazy, the other tenants increasingly complained to the landlord. The monkey was always bombing about the house, raising Cain in the middle of the night, throwing objects to the street below at innocent pedestrians. He flew from sill to mantel to wall to wall to elephant ear table to wall. His circumnavigations had become like an elaborate tic. Like the ritualized motions of a maniac, smashing around the apartment in his interminable attempts to demonstrate the very falsity of gravity.

❧

ONE EARLY SUMMER morning Mickie heard J.T. let out a dismal wail from his room. When she went in to see what was the matter, he was in his window, his attention fixed on the green sward of the park with the most apprehensive of expressions. Mickie herself had not heard the hubbub until J.T. had drawn her to the window, and she saw the cattle running across the park. It appeared they'd got loose from a boxcar and were making a break for it, followed by a number of policemen and neighborhood boys in pursuit.

J.T. was working his mouth awkwardly and scratching irritably at his stomach in a way she'd seen him do before when overly excited or afraid. She stood behind him and watched the cattle lumbering across the grass past the lawn tennis courts. Several of the policemen were carrying rifles. The sound of the shouting men and boys, and the lowing cows, came through the window in muted tones. One of the officers knelt to brace an elbow on his upright knee to steady his rifle, and then the first cow dropped; she felt J.T. go tense. As the chase continued and another cow went down, he began to scream, his eyes bulged with dread. But she could not pull him away from the window. He was trembling violently and would not stop screaming. She did not know what to do to calm him, except to put on the Mischa Elman recording of Beethoven's Minuet in G, which always had a soothing effect on his high-strung nerves, but no effect whatsoever today. Neither was it loud enough to mask the gunshots or the cattle's lows of terror or J.T.'s desperate cries, but merely became the soundtrack for the monkey's unraveling.

He gasped and wailed, shrieking like a child with night terrors who could not be brought around.

Later, that afternoon, she was surprised to receive several callers, among them a physician, but Mickie admonished them to speak quietly because J.T. had suffered an "attack of hysteria" and was resting. The callers exchanged glances in the way Mickie by now had grown accustomed to. Then the doctor, playing along as much to amuse the other now awkward but equally amused visitors, asked if he might have a look at the monkey.

Several hours had passed since the awful spectacle, but J.T. was still lying prostrate on the couch, limp and shivering, still racked by the most pitiful of drawn-out sobs, and a terribly grieved look in his eyes. The doctor knelt beside the couch, tugging the knees of his trousers as he lowered himself, taking J.T.'s frail wrist to note his pulse, and gently palpating his heaving abdomen with a broad pink hand. The women looked on silently.

After a moment he carefully set down the monkey's paw.

"By Jove, you are right," he said. The doctor's sarcastic expression had vanished, and he stroked the monkey's face, which was turned aside now, his traumatized gaze turned inward, still whimpering, far too gone for consolation. "It's a genuine case of hysteria!"

CHAPTER TWENTY-THREE

FROM THE START THE TRUSTEES HAD MORE OR LESS GIVEN AKE-
ley carte blanche. Osborn had immediately fallen in love with his
vision and wanted to erect a whole new hall to accommodate it on the
east side of the building. In the center of this great "faunistic" hall, on a
coffin-shaped pedestal, the elephants would tower eighteen feet over
visitors to the museum. Nothing on a scale even approaching what Akeley proposed had ever been conceived—let alone attempted. It would be
the Sistine Chapel of the natural history world. A three-dimensional
Lascaux of the twentieth century. For the past two years he'd done nothing else, holed up in his elephant studio in one of the old North American mammal halls on the second floor, working with museum architects
on ground and wall plans, supervising the construction of a plaster
scale model, fretting over every detail.

There would be four large corner groups, depicting in composite the
fauna of different topological regions. The Tana River, rife with hippos
and crocodiles. The Serengeti Plains and its embarrassment of ungulates.
A jungle forest scene—maybe with chimpanzees as the focal group—
plus a desert water hole tableau with zebras, oryxes, gazelles, baboons, a
giraffe or two, all gathered as if for an old-time baptism. In addition to
the four large corner groups there would be thirty-six other dioramas.
All in all forty panoramic groups. Forty seasons under glass. Of course,
he'd have to get a lot of animals to occupy all the niches for which he
was now preparing in mock miniature. The water hole group alone

would probably have at least a dozen different species. And that was just one corner group.

All would be hermetically sealed, shut off from the slightest of atmospheric changes. He would use a combination of electric lights and filtered skylights—a series of shutters and colored glass ray-filters—to eliminate the fading powers of the sun. Everything under automatic controls to maintain uniform lighting, temperature, humidity. Of course, given the darkness of the hall itself, where the viewer would stand, the exhibits themselves would not require much light. The viewer would look inward to the source of illumination. The effect being that one was looking out through a great open window. Each diorama capturing a single and unique moment in the hour of the day. He had it all planned to the last inch of artificial sunbeam.

Give him ten years, easy, he figured, to collect all the species he'd need to fill it.

He envisioned having the elephant group flanked by a group of black rhinos on one end and on the other a group of white rhinos, and he was also thinking of throwing in a couple of fountains at either entrance to the hall. Also maybe some life-size bronze figures of natives for perspective. He would cast those himself. One maybe drinking out of a leaf. Another with a spear. He would hire the best landscape artists in the world to do the backgrounds.

Yes, he had accounted for every detail right down to the silver tones for the bas-reliefs over each diorama unit. Each clay figurine sculpted and placed exactly as he envisioned the final life-size menagerie. The model itself was a kind of epic in miniature. It sat on a table in his studio, and trustees and potential backers passed through to view it almost daily. Construction of the hall itself was set to begin September 1, 1914.* He worked around the clock now, already having begun preliminary work on the elephants, the idea being to get it started right away to inspire more backers, though that was clearly not going to be a problem. Subscriptions to pay for the first twenty-five thousand dollars had been secured through J. P. Morgan Jr. It was really going to happen. The transmission of his fever-racked imagination to the concrete world. *Scribner's* had sent over a reporter to do a story on plans

---

*The same date, incidentally, on which Martha, the world's last passenger pigeon, would expire at the Cincinnati Zoo.

for the hall, about the "factitious immortality" that Mr. Akeley was about to bestow upon the mammalia of the dark continent. That was in July of 1914. President Osborn had even prepared a paragraph for the article.

> Africa is the only continent which preserves entire the life of the earth before man entered it as the destroying angel. It is still a living picture of the "great age of mammals," to use the telling phrase of Louis Agassiz, as it existed in all its grandeur before the age of man . . . While still in Africa, Mr. Akeley conceived the idea of a permanent exhibition of all phases of African life, which has since taken form as the project of the African Hall. In Mr. Akeley's hands, taxidermy has entered into the realm of sculpture and art. To collect and prepare the series for the African Hall is a vast undertaking which will extend over a number of years. When complete, it will form an enduring monument to the life of the Ancient World—a monument which twenty-five years hence, and even a less period, it will be impossible to erect. Carl E. Akeley is the leader of the new movement, the first sculptor of this art, the first taxidermist to approach the art from the standpoint of a sculptor instead of from the standpoint of simply filling out the skin, and his great contribution, that which I am sure will make his name endure, is that every one of his animals is first modeled as if the model were to be the completed *thing itself.*

Osborn had also added that this whole endeavor of Akeley's hall was not just to divert and amuse, but to "fix a reality for time to come, and *to extend the actual experience of consciousness.*" What higher scientific aim could there be?

❦

WITH JUST ONE month before construction was set to begin, war broke out in Europe. The museum had put a halt to all unnecessary projects. There would be no hunting expeditions to Africa anytime soon; only soldiers hunting soldiers for the colonies. The world had let Akeley down, had killed his vision with its barbaric stupidity, and he was alone now in his studio, left to his own devices, and his great head-less white elephant, incomplete.

And yet no war could go on forever, so he kept working on the ele-phants, though admittedly with depressed enthusiasm.

As meaningless as his work might have suddenly become, he still spent most of his time confined to his studio. There was, after all, no sense in going home. Especially after the incident with J.T. Jr. He could not bear to look at Mickie hobbling about on her cane. Of course, it was no surprise what had happened. She'd never learned to discipline the monkey, and an incident like this was inevitable. The creature had already maimed their home life. Never mind the fur on the lampshades, the marked-up furniture, the smell. Never mind the smudged foot-prints all over the walls and ceiling, the daily disasters of broken pots, pillaged wardrobes, torn window shades. There was a deeper sickness to it all. The way she had cut herself off from the world in order to pro-tect the monkey from it all, or maybe it was vice versa. Living in virtual confinement, in her own private zoo, had undone his wife's soundness of mind. The whole thing was farcical. A martyr's theatrics.

Mickie's little experiment—introducing the monkey to civilization—had turned J.T. into an agent of demolition. There was no keeping up with the damage and filth. The monkey got into every damned thing. He had figured out how to unlock doors and unscrew bottles. Once Carl had come home to find J.T. had dismantled his binoculars. His good Zeiss glasses! Mickie had tried to take on the task of fixing the bedroom wallpaper herself after months of J.T. impulsively peeling each little loose end he could snag, picking at the tiny printed flowers. Like a compulsive child, wherever he found a tear, he would inflict another rip. The room looked like a maniac's den. Of course, rather than let in a stranger to do the job, Mickie had ordered up glue and brushes and rolls of wallpaper to do it herself. But then, halfway through the job, she'd left the monkey alone in the room to answer the phone—she claimed she'd tied him safely out of reach—and was gone just a second, when she heard the crash and the cat howling and when she ran back found J.T. up on the sill with the gloopy dripping brush, the pastepot knocked over, the cat besmirched and entangled in a sheaf of wallpaper, mewing its poor glue-stuck head off.

In the end, they'd had to hire a proper paperhanger to fix the job.

One damned thing after another.

If Carl scoffed at her ridiculous pretensions, about making a study of J.T.'s primal response to civilization—never mind, for the moment, that she thought the monkey could talk—she bristled. "No caged animal or stuffed *museum* specimen," she sneered, "with its distorted bodies and horrid glass eyes can tell us the fascinating life histories of the wild free creatures!"

Yes, he might say, but J.T. wasn't free now, was he? He was her "poor little prisoner." And then Carl would grab his coat and hat and be out the door.

She really was lucky she hadn't lost her leg. Oh, what a wretched tragedy they had averted, dear Lord. But just barely. The way she blamed herself was pathetic. On the other hand he must have known she blamed him for not being around to take care of her while she'd been confined to bed those three months. After all the times she'd nursed him back to health in Africa. He understood that. He understood the potential for resentment here. Still, he could not go home.

He stayed late at the studio night after night. Far preferring the vapors of arsenic and phenol over the stink of monkey. With the aid of his new assistants, he had figured out how to transfer his methods to the larger canvas of an elephant. Building up an armature—the great undercarriage—with its own leg bones and supporting steel rods, leaving aside the heavy skull till the end. He built it up with clay, following the diagram of his countless measurements, taken by caliper and steel tape in the immediate moments following death. Taped to the wall it looked like a subway map, a confusion of coefficients that just so happened to take the pattern of an elephant. The manikin stood center stage under the heavy-beamed A-frame scaffold, feet propped on pallets, like a bride-to-be patiently waiting on the gown maker's stool.

To get at its more fundamental dimensions, beyond the biomechanical givens, he watched the films he'd made in the interior, but always there seemed there was more to see, too much was lost. It frustrated him beyond all ends that he'd had to make do with such an awkward cumbersome instrument that wouldn't even allow him to turn the camera where he'd wanted.

Since the war had put a stop to his plans, it only depressed him to look at the model of this hall to which he had dedicated so much time. It was already falling apart, the figurines gathering dust. As he slapped clay to the elephant's growing mass, his mind wandered in the way the bothered mind will to other bothersome things, worry seeking worry, and in this way got to thinking about his botched filmmaking efforts in Africa—the failure of the Nandi lion-spearing ritual only being the most vexing.

The camera simply hadn't been nimble enough to capture the action and essence of the hunt. He had lost the lion as soon as it had sprung out of the marsh, so he'd only managed to get the end of the actual spearing. What he had were the preliminary panning shots of the self-conscious warriors; a skittering blur of uninhabited grass; then the camera arriving late to the final act, at sixteen frames per second, the lion already flipped on its back, like an oversized pincushion, limp and spindled by a dozen javelins. The charge and chase had slipped out of frame. It was all jump cut and nothing between. He had lost his narrative.

As a sculptor, as a taxidermist, he had counted on the camera to record the animal's behavior, the better to bring it back to life; the camera was just another tool in his arsenal, right alongside the brain spoon and lip tucker. Motion pictures were superior to memory, at least in theory, for recollecting how the breathing animal had truly existed. In practice, however, the machine was a sorry piece of business that had let him down miserably. The blasted thing jammed every chance it got. The images were unsteady and many worthless. The boxy wooden design leaked light. It was a nightmare to swap out film in the field. Difficult to maneuver, clunky, unreliable, especially whenever anything of interest started running or thinking fast on its feet.

The frustration, no doubt, was compounded whenever he saw what passed for some of the wildlife pictures that were so popular nowadays. The stuff people like Bill Selig were making. *The Leopard's Foundling. Alone in the Jungle.* Paul Rainey's *African Hunt* alone had run for a straight fifteen months and earned MGM a fortune. It was the biggest box office–grossing film made to date. People were wild for this kind of stuff now. For Akeley's taste, there was too much fakery in these pictures; they were not genuine but staged and hokey. Primarily he desired a better machine to aid in his fieldwork. But as he began to imagine what a better naturalist's camera might look like, the fact that there were fourteen thousand nickelodeons out there across the country clamoring for decent wildlife pictures could not have been far from his mind.

In his spare time he had already dissected his Urban Bioscope to try to assess its fundamental flaws. While he continued to sculpt his mammoth elephant manikin, he thought about it in a drifting inconsequential way, the way the mind tinkers elsewhere while the hands are busy. Every once in a while something would come to him while he was up on the stepladder, adding definition to the elephant's trapezius, or shaving its belly, and he'd have to climb down and make a sketch.

A promising glimpse surfaced here and there.

If you could only aim the camera more readily. That was the basic problem he'd had with the lions. He'd been unable to follow the object (the lion) in the lens. The action of the camera was too damned stiff. What this camera needed was greater—what was the word?—fluidity, to be able to follow unfolding events as the eye did. If you could only move it! If you could only follow the action!

So why not, for starters, put the whole camera itself on a better hinge? A universal contraption. Like the eye itself. The best inventions, it seemed, depended on a superior hinge. He began looking into different types of gyroscopic joints, and to design a type of ball-and-socket mount that could fit into the tripod head itself.

Even better, what if he were to add a single handle to control both pan and tilt? Why have two cranks—one for panning and one for tilting—when both functions could easily be incorporated into a single rod? Use a single handle—like a broom handle—to operate *both* the pan and the tilt. Simultaneously. Making it possible to follow an object in any direction. Vertical. Horizontal. Diagonal. Total panoramic flexibility. He had set aside his clay spatula and was sketching again madly. Give it a vertical tilt that would let you gain perfect zenith—zoom in on an eagle directly overhead and then drop it 140 degrees to look at an ant crawling over the toe of your shoe. You would be able to zip from point to point, here to there, as quickly as possible, all the while keeping your eye comfortably pressed to the viewfinder. (To allow this, he could put the finding tube on a kind of ratchet.) It would be as flexible as the user's instincts. A single handle would also make it easier for one man to operate the thing—a single operator to crank, pan, and tilt at the same time. This would allow a steady movement and keep the object in the frame at all times. The mechanism might work similarly to a swivel gun. And like a gun—a swift flash of genius—he would make his camera of *metal*. For fieldwork—for his kind of work—he needed it to be as durable as possible. There was no reason he couldn't make it with lightweight aluminum. Why make it of wood? Everything was metal now. You could mold things into any shape.

One other far-fetched idea had come to him about the shape of the camera while he was inside the hardened hull of his elephant, an electric fan going to blow the vapors of glue and arsenic out the neck hole. Why not round instead of square?

After all, the basic components of the motion picture camera were round. Round lens. Round crank. Round spools of film. Circumferential focal-plane shutters. And yet the exterior design—the compartment—was square. A wooden box filled with useless corners there only to collect sharp motes of film-scratching dust.

So he made a sketch of a round camera. At first it looked laughable. There was no such thing as a round camera. But the more he tinkered with it, and thought about what needed to fit inside the compartment, the more sense it made. Fewer corners to leak light. Less wind resistance. Once again he climbed down out of the elephant and made another series of sketches.

✿

EVENTUALLY HE MOVED beyond the phase of daydreaming and sketching and began to send out one of his assistants, Jimmy Clark, the one who had come to steal his ideas in Chicago fifteen years earlier, to get the actual parts made. The components of the camera were only revealed to him one piece at a time, and so whenever a particular piece was revealed, and he had a sketch, he would have Jimmy find a machinist to do the work, and in this gradual way the parts accumulated, the camera evolved, and was at last assembled into a machine like no one had ever seen. Once he had something close enough to a working model he began to seek backers, and once he had backers, he had more models built, more tests conducted, and then he rented a shop space on Forty-ninth Street to begin building these contraptions in earnest under the supervision of Clark.

Then he would go back to his elephants until he would be interrupted by new ideas for improving his camera.

It was not just during the lion spearing where he'd had trouble, but deep in the forest, it had been too gloomy to get good pictures. To solve this problem, then, he designed a new shutter. One allowing for a maximum of light. Thirty percent more in fact. With more light he could add a greater range of lenses to his arsenal, all the way from a 2-inch "Tessar" f 3.5 up to a 17-inch Dallmeyer "Dallon" Telephoto f 5.6. He corresponded frequently with the people at Bausch-Lomb. The lenses could be swapped out quickly and thanks to a thumbscrew rod he'd mounted within easy reach you could simultaneously focus while following your target. He was especially keen to make the telephoto work, all the better to film natives or wild animals without their knowing.

He had made the camera as lightweight as possible, even redesigning the magazines themselves to carry only two hundred feet—as compared to the usual four hundred feet of film per magazine—though you could switch it out in a skinny ten seconds, three times faster than you could thread and load any other camera on the market. Loaded, it weighed the same—twenty-two pounds—as the unloaded Pathé Professional. Each part was designed with absolute simplicity in mind. He did not want it to have any extra parts. Nothing to break down in the field. It was a feat of artistic engineering. Light-tight. Virtually indestructible.

Just as Étienne-Jules Marey had invented the chronophotographic gun to record birds in flight, and Eadweard Muybridge had built his Zoopraxiscope to film horses, and long before either the Cro-Magnon had shimmied back into his dark-chambered camera obscura to scratch out woolly mammoths and Ice Age bears, so Akeley had designed yet the next tool in a long line of instruments meant to capture the ephemeral presence of the animal spirit. The Akeley Camera would reinvent the oldest of rituals. *Extending the actual experience of consciousness.* In the end it resembled nothing more than a machine gun.

Appropriate, because he had his camera nearly perfected just as the country had entered the war. He had begun looking for someone to sell his new invention. After having failed to persuade Eastman Kodak, whose engineers had borrowed an Akeley long enough to test it out in their laboratories in Rochester, New York, but who decided in the end that they preferred to stick to film and "leave the mechanical end of the motion picture business to others," the War Department had gotten wind of the new camera and ordered all the units the newly formed Akeley Camera, Inc., could manufacture. The Signal Corps would use it to film the war abroad. Given the excellent range of tilt, it was thought ideal for aerial reconnaissance.

Unfortunately, Mickie was unable or unwilling to celebrate his accomplishments with him, and by now he'd tired of making excuses for why she could not join him for this or that function or dinner. She'd already forfeited a good bit of the limelight they'd earned from their adventures together. He'd had to bask in the attendant social glories alone. It was awkward explaining that his wife could not join him at the Century Club because she was cooped up at home with a jealous and psychotic monkey.

All sorts of fabulous people came to visit him at his studio. Italian princes planning future safaris. Publishers eager to print his stories. Famous explorers. Movie actors. Famous himself now, he kept a higher caliber of company. On weekends he went to Oyster Bay for beefsteak picnics with Archie Roosevelt and his young wife, Grace, with whom he'd become close friends. Orville Wright had traveled from Ohio to see him after taking an interest in his camera and its aerial possibilities. The inventor of modern flight and his sister, Katharine, had spent the day together in Carl's studio and then gone out for dinner, though Orville, now an old man, was strain-faced during the meal due to a bad case of sciatica. Akeley had even sat for Lady Scott, wife of the polar explorer, who made a bronze bust of the taxidermist. Invitations poured in for prestigious dinners and weekend getaways to elite resorts where he could hobnob with industrial greats like George Eastman, Harvey Firestone, even Thomas Edison himself.

Not everyone, however, thought his career so heroic. One letter the Akeleys received upon their return from Africa had this to say:

> As I read in the press the account of your exploits in the African hunt, invading the homes of Nature's children, who have never done or wished you ill, and bringing to them pain and death, my heart grew sick that people could be found in a civilized community capable of such work. How do you justify for the paltry object of "scientific collection" the slaughter of our brothers who have the same right to life and the pleasures of earth as ourselves? Who gave you and others the right to maltreat my brothers whom, with us, one great Spirit of Life has created? How can one ever expect mercy and forbearance who show none to their defenseless fellow beings? And for a woman

who is supposed to typify gentleness and compassion, to be
a leader in such work! Bloodsport is one of the basest relics
of a barbarous past; and even when it is given the back-
ground of a nominal "scientific" purpose, it poorly excuses
the blunting of the mind's higher instincts and the viola-
tion of the long-suffering spirit of Justice. Above all, it is a
sad lesson to hold up to the young in this age when already
the love of greed, graft and conquest has blighted to a
deplorable extent the struggling germs of a broader human-
ity; and nearly obliterated the faint traces of charity and
brotherhood in the human line.
Sincerely Yours, J. M. Greene.
Los Angeles, California

People had been just as critical of Carl's now somewhat tarnished hero, Teddy Roosevelt, who had been accused in the papers of shooting lions that had been chained to trees first to minimize his own personal risk. These were patently untrue stories, but the excess of his killing could not be refuted. When denied official permission in British East Africa to shoot a white rhinoceros—an animal already teetering on the brink of extinction—he got it from the Belgians to shoot one of theirs. Here was a creature as endangered as your average Mugwump, and yet TR had gone and shot *nine* dead. This despite the fact that he had once likened the extinction of a species to the destruction of "all the works of some great writer." Since he'd acquired all the species he really needed for the Smithsonian in the first three months of his trip, with seven months left to kill before his voyage home, it was likely boredom that brought up the final tally. Including fish, small mammals, amphibians, et cetera, the death toll reached 11,397.

"I can be condemned only if the existence of the Smithsonian, the American Museum of Natural History, and all similar zoological collections are to be condemned," he fumed at his critics.

Since the United States had finally joined the war in Europe, though, what the former president was really itching to shoot was Germans. For years, TR had publicly been calling Woodrow Wilson a coward for not entering the conflict, but now that the United States had finally joined the Armageddon, TR hoped to gain back a bit of his tarnished glory, further eroded by his failed presidential bid in 1912 on the Bull Moose ticket, by leading a division of volunteer troops into France. But Wilson would have his final revenge by turning down the ex-president's request, saying that he was far too old for such vain heroics.

※

RIGHT ABOUT THE time the American Expeditionary Forces were going overseas, the monkey had lashed out again. Mickie was not yet off her cane when J.T. Jr. had gone and bit his mistress after leaping on her from his hiding place above the door. This time was not as bad, a superficial scratch on the neck; his teeth had missed their mark. But then, only a few weeks later, he bit her for a third and final time on the wrist. It happened while she'd been drawing the monkey a bath—had she neglected to make it piping hot enough for him?—and this time his jagged little fangs had not only punctured the skin but severed a nerve and nearly sliced open an artery.

Carl himself arranged to have J.T. sent away to the Rock Creek Park Zoo in Washington, D.C. At last, the monkey would live in a cage. Mickie did not put up a fight. There was no arguing this time. She stayed alone during the day, never leaving the apartment, in virtual mourning. And then one day Carl returned home to find that she was gone. She had left a note saying that she had volunteered to follow the American Expeditionary Forces to the Western Front. She was on her way to a hospital in Nancy, France. Except for the relentless barrage of German artillery, the work would be similiar to that which she had endured in Africa, often calling upon her to sit through the night at the bedsides of dying, incoherent young men.

He was devastated. Enraged that she had deserted him this way. Even if he didn't know it yet, his muse was gone.

He soon discovered that she had sold her tusks to the museum—to Director Lucas, behind his back—for $1,500 to pay for her getaway. He could not have been happy with the museum for helping fund his wife's escape. They were the tusks she had gotten on Mount Kenya on their honeymoon safari.

He had the apartment patched up to erase all signs of the monkey, pulling down the leopard skin that Mickie had once kept over her wardrobe in a futile effort to scare off J.T. from ransacking her dresses. He could no longer concentrate on his work at the museum and focused instead on fulfilling his contract to deliver his cameras to the army. It was strange to imagine them scouring the bombed-out French countryside from the air, as if he were subconsciously building the cameras to go in search for his estranged wife.

When the war was over he waited for her return. He listened to Wilson's victory speeches on the radio, and there were ticker-tape parades right outside his window. Everyone was in a high mood celebrating the Allied victory, but still she did not come home. He waited for her helplessly, thinking the worst, and then, after several months passed and he had still not heard from his wife, after months of not knowing, came the most gut-wrenching shock of all when he got word through mutual friends that, in fact, she was back in the United States. She had been back for several months.

It gave him such a dread, broken feeling. To realize that she was not coming home at all. That she made no effort to contact him whatsoever. The first visit she'd made was to see J.T. Jr. in his zoo. It was damned poor form.

❧

IT WAS ALMOST impossible for him to go back to his elephants and the plans for the African Hall, which the museum was eager to recommence now that the war was over. President Osborn tried to convince possible donors that Akeley had resumed his work "with great vigor," but the truth was, since Mickie had deserted him he could not summon much enthusiasm for taxidermy, nor for working on the elephants which they, as husband and wife, had gone to such terrible lengths to butcher.

As keen as Osborn was to see the African Hall move forward— especially as it would be connected to the whole new wing of the museum which he now hoped to erect as a memorial for TR, who'd died shortly after the war—he was more focused for the time being on his own pet project: an expedition to the Central Asian Plateau, where, despite any real evidence, he hoped to find relics of his Aryan Dawn Men. The Central Asiatic Expedition would be led by the dashing Roy Chapman Andrews, for whom countless charity balls had been thrown, and gilt doors opened, to raise the necessary fortune for what would be the museum's largest expedition to date. Indeed, among wealthy New Yorkers, sponsorship of the trip had become fashionable, a definite social obligation among those rooting that the Cradle of Mankind would at last be found in the mysterious and alluringly unthreatening

Gobi Desert, which just meant for Akeley that the usual backers—the Fricks, Vanderbilts, Goulds, Sturges, Dodges, Morgans, Colgates, War- burgs, Bowdoins, Harrimans, Rockefellers, and Roosevelts—had already been tapped, making it harder for him to scrape up money for a hall meant to showcase a continent where the origins of civilized man were a clear impossibility in the mind of its president.

Ideally, Carl wanted the security of a single sponsor. A great man who wanted nothing more than to see his name carved in stone, a patron saint he could rely on to foot the bill so he wouldn't have to run around endlessly cadging support from every available corner. Some- one who would just cough up the million dollars Akeley estimated the hall was going to cost—twice as much as the half million he'd originally estimated. Briefly, he thought he had his man, someone he had been promised would be like a godfather to the hall, but then that financier had grown gravely ill or gone insane, it was never really clear which, and Akeley was once again on his own.

To raise money he sold articles and photographs about his erstwhile life of jungle adventure to magazines like the *Mentor, Outlook,* and *World's Work,* and, more and more, went out on the lecture circuit, traveling with his lantern slides and his now well-worn tales. He put on his show for everyone and everywhere, lecturing to the American Geo- graphical Society, the Presbyterian Union, the Ladies' Auxiliary of the New York Zoological Society, private audiences at the home of Mrs. Vanderbilt, and for the brim-fidgeting drummers of the Travelers Insur- ance Company. With no one to go home to he toured far and wide, playing his motion picture footage, speaking till he was hoarse as a muezzin, delighting audiences at the Boston City Club, the Canadian Camp Fire Club, going from pimple-faced boys at the Hotchkiss School in Lakeville, Connecticut, to Dr. John Harvey Kellogg's wealthy hypo- chondriacs at the Battle Creek Sanitarium in Michigan. He went as far as Council Bluffs, Iowa, and secured a contract with the Coit-Alber Lyceum Bureau. By now he could perform in his sleep: for the Boy Scouts of America, the Glencoe Men's Club, Boone and Crockett, the Algonquin Club, the Buffalo Club, Camp Fire Club of America. Over and over again he told the same stories. Reliving his past. Showing off his thrilling scars.

By now he had an idea who he might like to be his ideal backer, and that particular individual happened to be George Eastman, the Kodak

King. Perhaps he could eventually work his way into his favor through the museum trustee Daniel E. Pomeroy—he knew Pomeroy and Eastman were close—but he also knew that it was not quite the right psychological moment to approach Eastman.

When it finally sank in that Mickie wasn't coming home, that she had deserted him for good and for real, he chose to keep the apartment anyway. The last time he'd been separated from her was when he would be gone for a week or more on the trail of an elephant, and when she was back holding down the camp, but at least then he had had Bill to keep him company.

So, instead, he invited a pal from the museum to move in, the arctic explorer Vilhjalmur Stefansson. Stefansson's claim to fame (aside from the fact that his men had nearly mutinied on him on one trip) had been stumbling upon a previously unknown group of people near Victoria Island whom he would dub the Copper Inuit (for their use of copper harpoons, snow knives, and other tools). Many of the Eskimos he also discovered had blue eyes and European features, a fact which led him to develop the theory, over the four years he lived with them, that they had crossbred with early Norse explorers. President Osborn, always queasy about mixed races, and a proud and untainted Norseman himself, had little appetite for Stefansson's theory. He didn't care if they had blue eyes. (He had already ruled out Eskimos—along with Africans—as the missing link.)

Soon enough another colleague, Herbert Spinden, a curator of Mayan archaeology from the Department of Ethnology, moved in too. Stefansson and Spinden were both forty years old to Carl's fifty-five. Life seemed to be moving along at a friskier pace. There were more parties now. More last-minute capers. More distractions from the steady grind. New people to meet. Most of all, there were always more women. Plenty plenty *plenty* more fun to be had. It was 1920. In a sudden splurge of youthful spontaneity Carl went out and bought a new Buick. Now he could take last-minute rides out to the country anytime he wished. He could escape the city on a moment's notice. Being behind the wheel put him in a pixilated mood. Especially when he could install a nice young thing in the passenger's seat to talk his ear off about the latest movies and the latest dance craze or the new hat with the mauve ostrich plume she'd seen that morning in a window at Lex and Sixty-third. It was up to Maine with his secretary in October to a log cabin on the lake, even if her kid brother was tagging along, and it rained the entire time, and the little brother bothered them nonstop with stupid questions. He took her next to the Catskills to gather accessories—this time without the little brother—for a corner diorama he was trying to fix up to lure backers, or at least give the impression that he was trying to lure backers. But it wasn't just flings with his secretary. Young women were coming out of the woodwork, maybe because so many young men had been lost in the war. There were Dorothys and Marthas and Elizabeths and Marys and Camilles to keep up with now. More trips to the country on the weekend in the Buick. Adirondacks, Poconos, Long Island. He invited them all to visit him at his studio first. "Come if possible at about eleven o'clock. That will give us a little time in the studio and from there to my apartment for lunch.—Carl."

Even if the studio had become a place for little more than liaisons. Annoyed that his chief taxidermist seemed to have abandoned his elephants, Osborn, more and more now like a cranky father trying to impose curfew, tried nailing him down with revised contracts, but first a year passed, and then another, and still he had not completed the work. It was ten years since he'd shot the damn things, and only three were partially finished. Akeley seemed to have put off anything to do with the hall until he was convinced he had found his patron saint. In the meantime, he would pursue more immediate gratification.

CHAPTER TWENTY-FOUR

IT WAS WHEN HE MET THE YOUNG ADVENTURER-FILMMAKERS Martin and Osa Johnson that Carl would hatch one of the most brazen ideas of his career. An idea that would propel him directly into the twentieth century. That would, in fact, propel the twentieth century into itself. The scheme was to put movies to work for their older taxidermic cousin. It was a totally unconventional way to finance a major museum project—namely, construction of his African Hall—but then again, his other options were limited.

Right away Martin Johnson liked Akeley's idea. It was just risky enough to sound plausible. Best of all, it would mutually benefit both men's careers. In a nutshell the idea was this: get the museum to back a series of commercial films featuring African wildlife in exchange for the publicity it would generate for the hall. The Johnsons' films—like *Naked Man vs. Beast*—were wildly popular. Famous the world over. If Akeley could persuade the museum to endorse the films, it would boost Johnson's credibility and the reciprocal attention would undoubtedly help draw more philanthropic support to Carl's own mothballed vision.

The Johnsons had just returned from Borneo, where they'd filmed their latest picture, *Jungle Adventures*. This was their third trip together, as husband and wife, and they were as rich and famous as anyone ever hoped. However, one could not turn down the priceless stamp of scientific legitimacy the AMNH would lend. Martin was a rugged lug of a fellow who'd had an auspicious start as a young man working as cook on Jack London's 1907 round-the-world ocean voyage. After London and his cameramen had fallen ill with malaria in the Solomon Islands, Johnson was the only one left to take over filming the natives. Upon his return to his hometown of Independence, Kansas, with a copy of the short film he'd helped make, he had opened a theater to show it off, along with lantern slides of his adventures with Jack London. Included in his revue were several male-only matinees when Martin showed pictures of naked female natives and shared salacious details he'd picked up about the sex habits of cannibals.

Sitting in the audience one day was a sixteen-year-old girl named Osa, who would soon marry the twenty-eight-year-old Martin, after a brief and acerbic courtship, and then spend the next seven years as his partner, traveling on the Orpheum Vaudeville Circuit. Martin evolved into a regular showman, clicking through the slides of the wild men night after night, town after town, elaborating his tales of worldly derring-do, and showing that abbreviated and wilted silent movie strip, during which Osa performed on stage Hawaiian song-and-dance bits that Martin had made up and taught her on the fly.

At last they saved up enough money to fulfill Martin's dream of returning to the South Seas in order to make the great film that London had failed to do, and in 1917 set off for the Solomon Islands, where they were nearly thrown in the pot themselves by a clan of headhunters called the Big Nambas. The result was an instant hit called *Among the Cannibal Isles of the South Pacific*. What people seemed to love as much as anything else was the presence of Osa, on-screen, trying to befriend the fiercesome-looking men with a sweet smile that did not always give the lie to the wild fear in her eyes.

On their second trip back a year later to film the same headhunters who'd tried to abduct them, Osa became the starlet in the jungle, beauty to the beast. This time, instead of offering them beads and bolts of calico, they brought the film that had packed the Capitol Theater on Broadway in order to give the Big Nambas a private showing come nightfall. "The savages liked a five-hundred-foot piece of Armistice Day in New York City better than any of the other films," Martin wrote in a letter to the president of the Pathescope Company. "It shows hundreds of thousands of people on the streets. These cannibals never dreamed that there were so many people on earth!" Then he filmed them *watching themselves* on the silent screen for the first time. Osa sat on the ground beside the chief, trying to put him at ease with her sleepover smile. Each time one of them appeared they shouted and laughed with astonishment. When a man who had been dead nearly a year materialized before them, though, they burst out in terrible dismay and anxiety. Johnson then showed a pie-throwing reel that Charlie Chaplin had given him along with fake mustaches to distribute to the headhunters. The Big Nambas soundly approved of both gifts.

Cannibals of the South Seas, the Johnsons' next film—which included this movie-within-a-movie footage—was a box-office sensation.

Even if he himself wouldn't be joining them on their first African expedition, Akeley didn't have a hard time persuading the Johnsons to go there. When Carl brought the idea of using movies to finance the hall to Osborn, the president immediately saw the potential. They couldn't support the filmmakers directly, however, given the thorny complications of crossing mass entertainment with an institution of serious science. Instead, to help the Johnsons raise funds for what would be an extensive two-year cinematic safari, an independent entity was formed, called the Martin Johnson African Expedition Corporation. It would be presided over by museum trustee Daniel E. Pomeroy, who would not only supervise the expedition but help bring in donors from the Explorers Club and the AMNH, just as Osborn had done for Roy Chapman Andrews and the Central Asiatic Expedition. ("Dan Pomeroy is a peach," Carl confided to Martin.) Part of the deal was that in exchange for the museum's official endorsement, the Johnsons would provide a complete set of negatives for educational purposes and private scientific lectures.

Martin was visiting Carl at his studio almost daily now to help dope out their plans, and the couple had the older single explorer over for dinner often at the suite of rooms they kept for themselves and their menagerie of monkeys and exotic birds at the Hotel Astor. While Martin and Carl discussed the details of their upcoming collaboration, Osa listened with her pet gibbon, Kalawat, draped around her neck; when he thought no one was looking, Kalawat would dip one long fuzzy finger into her cocktail, which he would then slurp loudly. Osa had adopted the ape in Borneo while filming *Headhunters of the South Seas*. Whenever Carl showed up—just as he had years ago when he'd first got home and played with J.T. Jr.—he would get down on the floor to roughhouse with Kalawat. The ape, who wore a child's sweater purchased at

Selfridge's in London, would bounce on Akeley's chest, his silver fur changing colors in the blinking lights from Times Square. One blazing advertisement—a dazzling spectacular for Wrigley's Gum that stretched two hundred feet across Broadway between Forty-third and Forty-fourth—was of a dozen giant electric spearmen who stood nearly a hundred feet each, going through their spasmodic motions over and over against the night sky, as repetitive and mindless as the act of chewing gum itself.

Carl wished he were going with the Johnsons to Africa, but he still had his work cut out for him at the museum. Getting the elephants finished, talking to investors, raising more money for the hall. But before they knew it they were giving the Johnsons a send-off of sorts at the Explorers Club—or was this one at the Waldorf? The Century? These kind of fetes all blurred together nowadays the more jungly and jazzy things were getting—and Osa had to leave Kalawat back home with a sitter.

Martin was already gloating about their impending box-office smash. "There is no limit to the money it can make," he was saying, standing in a circle of admirers. "My knowledge of showmanship, mixed with the scientific knowledge I have absorbed lately, and the wonderful photographic equipment"—here nodding to Akeley, whose cameras he would be using—"make me certain that this feature is going to be the biggest money maker ever placed on the market."

Osa snuggled beside him in what had become her familiar screen costume: white shirtwaist and slender man's tie, her oval face partly eclipsed by an enormous hat with a sweeping brim and giant willowy ostrich plume that cleared her shoulder.

"The public will pay for good stuff when the producers and distributors wake up to the fact that men like you are producing good stuff," Akeley said. "The public is sick and tired of the junk they've been fed."

Akeley despised the fakery that went into some of the wildlife pictures you saw nowadays—even if it was partly due to the popularity of those movies that he had come up with the idea to put the Johnsons to work for him in the first place.

"It will set us up for life," Johnson said, his eyes merrily taking in the surrounding guests through his cloud of cigar smoke.

Carl's roommates, Stefansson and Spinden, were at the party too.

Stefansson admitted the last one Johnson made was a real corker, before meandering off to the bar to freshen his tumbler.

"There's no bunk," Akeley said. "That's what I like about your films."

He liked the straight-up approach Johnson had taken in his films about his subject matter like *Captured by Cannibals*. Martin was a bit hammy now and then but a hell of a sight more factual than most of the other commercial operators. The main thing was that Martin get over to Africa as soon as possible. He had no time to lose if he was going to get a look at the wildlife there and put it on film. Carl had pressed the urgency of it all from the beginning. The way things were vanishing. Hell, he himself was dying to get back over. Now that things were moving again, he predicted it would take ten years, minimum, to finish collecting his ark. His own next trip, Akeley hoped, was going to be to the Congo to get himself a look at the mountain gorilla.

Osa was describing for Akeley's roommates the business of shrinking heads. How the Big Nambas cut the head off when still fresh and first soaked it in some concoction before impaling the head on a stick and slowly smoking it over a fire.

"Naturally," Osa said, "only the heads of friends and relatives are given this amount of care and time." She let Spinden light a cigarette for her. The actual cannibalism they had witnessed there involved a whole head roasting in a bed of coals with the eye sockets stuffed with herbs. She said with a twinkle how closely they themselves had escaped being the next evening's main course.

Martin winked at Osa. "Well, she's good enough to eat, I'll say that for her."

She quirked her head to one side and wagged her hips, the way she was always doing in the movies just before coquettishly turning and blowing away a charging rhino.

Spinden was himself heading off soon for the Yucatán to explore the ruins of a series of seven ancient cities he had discovered a few years earlier in the jungle—a vast Mayan empire of pyramids and viaducts and great plazas he believed had collapsed due to something he called "climate changes." Stefansson, for his part, was setting off for Siberia. Ernest Shackleton, the Explorers Club's great star, though not in present company, was about to set off again too, on a last expedition to the Antarctic—and Shack was ten years younger than Akeley! Everyone seemed to be going off somewhere. Carl started talking about the mountain gorillas. He was quite serious about wanting to get over to film them. He still hadn't tested out his own camera in the field—the purpose for which he'd built it in the first place. Did they know that the gorilla not thirty years ago had been firmly held as a figmentary creature? Of the same genus as the unicorn or leprechaun?

"An actual study should be made before these animals have all been slaughtered," he said. "If we don't watch out the gorilla will be exterminated before we've learned anything about him." He was speaking to a small group near the burning logs in the fireplace. Outside it was snowing. "Slaughtered with no facts in regard to their life and habits."

Boy, did he feel passionate about this all of a sudden. What was so vexing, though, to his mind, was not only the unnecessary slaughter, but that there were no real facts or data about them, that they were being slaughtered without having first been properly and scientifically understood. That was the real tragedy.

The only one Akeley had ever seen with his own eyes was the skin of something purporting to be a gorilla back at Ward's when he was a kid. Well, he'd also seen a lowland gorilla years earlier at the London Zoological Park. "It was very young and its chief aim in life seemed a desire to be loved," he said, wobbling the glass in his hand. In his opinion it looked to have an affectionate disposition.

Even though he had never seen as much as a photograph of a living mountain gorilla, he still felt a stray intuitive knowledge of the animal— at least enough to believe that the popular stories of its ferocity were greatly exaggerated. He was confident the animal had been maligned, and that reports of mountain gorillas biting people in two and turning Springfields into pretzels were greatly exaggerated. He believed in all likelihood that they were probably quite tame. And he intended to prove it, though, of course, he'd probably have to finish the elephant business first before he went on any new expeditions.

Akeley's other roommate, Stefansson, drew Akeley's attention now across the room to a hearty-looking woman who looked like she was dressed in a canvas tent and an upside-down trout basket for a hat.

"Mount Jobe," Stefansson said. And then by way of explanation said that the Canadian government had named a peak after her in the Canadian Rockies.

Her name was Mary Lenore Jobe, and for the peak she had conquered the Royal Geographical Society had made her a fellow, but
Canadians were progressive that way. You could eat a whole mountain,
and the Explorers Club still wouldn't make you a member if you happened to be of the female sex. Certainly she looked stout enough herself
for a good hike. Broad-hipped, and a bit pinch-faced, a bit of tundra in
the general atmosphere of her aura, a bit schoolmarmish when you got
right down to it. When she wasn't conquering mountaintops, she ran a
camp for girls somewhere up in Connecticut, Stefansson said. He'd
apparently made her acquaintance after visiting the camp and dazzling
the little girls with stories of seals and Eskimos, and now he was introducing the two explorers, and Carl found himself listening to Miss
Jobe, who was talking to him, a bit passionately, about the importance
of girls finding health and happiness in the out-of-doors and how young
children couldn't expect to develop without getting away from the
"artificialities of towns and cities for the joyous realities of the wooded
hills and seashore." Stefansson had momentarily disappeared. Carl
couldn't help but notice something vaguely dour around the mouth
that would probably not improve with age. She was already over forty, if
he had to guess. On the other hand, she was still a good fourteen years
younger than he. She was no Mary Pickford, but unlike the other women
he'd been flinging around with, Mary Jobe knew a thing or two about
altimeters and rugged outdoor living—something, to be quite frank, he
missed. She was as refreshing as if a glacial wind blew down off her
dowdy hat. A competent woman. A competent woman who after a little
while he could even imagine himself learning to adore. You could not
deny she had a bit of dash and originality. Even if, right now, she was telling him how when she was a little girl she was "always dreaming dreams,"
whatever that meant. How she had tromped all over the backwoods of
Ohio as a half-pint, getting her button boots clotted with mud. She
went on about the benefits of canoeing and backpacking with the fer-
vor of a suffragist. And yet there was something about her soft crags
that made him think there were worse places where one might pitch
his tent.

"When *I* was a boy," Carl said, interrupting, "I was so afraid of girls
that I hardly dared look at one. But I am getting over that now." As he
said so his own gaze bored into Mary Jobe as if he were hammering in
a piton.

Mary Jobe is the only white woman who's ever witnessed the Carrier Indians having a potlatch, Stefansson offered now that he was back.

"And photographed their totem poles," Jobe said, somewhat flushed.

She had over a hundred hand-tinted lantern slides of her travels that Akeley might be interested in, she said. She too had a passion for photography. She had made extensive records of the native Sekani marriage ceremonies.

They'd nicknamed her Dene-Sezaki, Stefansson said, or "man-woman."

"All very weird and intensely interesting," Mary allowed.

Martin Johnson, still talking brazenly about the wheelbarrows of cash they were going to make in animal pictures, was crossing the room with Osa. A small claque was attached to the auteur. "Five years ago I landed at Sydney after a cruise in the New Hebrides, where I had made what I considered the best pictures I had ever taken of savage peoples. If anyone had asked me as I stepped from the ship, 'What are you going to do with the rest of your life?' I should have answered: 'Just what I have been doing for the last fifteen years. I am going to roam among the black peoples and take motion-pictures that will give them a kind of immortality after they have all been killed off by civilization." He took a drag on his cigarette and exhaled with suave theatricality. Then, putting a florid hand on Akeley's shoulder—Akeley had heard this story before—he said he got a cable from the company that was marketing his films. It said: THE PUBLIC IS TIRED OF SAVAGES. GET SOME ANIMAL PICTURES.

Nothing, Martin said, had delighted Osa more.

Glowing on his arm, she confided, "I was really *very* tired of savages and the way they smelled."

Mary Jobe giggled.

But then fate had intervened in the person of Carl Akeley, and now they were off to the last great stronghold of the fast-vanishing wildlife.

Martin was going to be taking along with his cinematic arsenal several of Akeley's cheese boxes. Well, that's what they looked like! Had Mary Jobe heard the story about the lieutenant in the Signal Corps who'd stopped to get a shot of a burning village somewhere in France— they filmed every damn thing they could, didn't they?—and around the corner here come seven German soldiers, and you know what happened, they threw up their hands 'cause they thought it was some newfangled Yankee machine gun! A hell of a camera. He was going to use three himself in Africa.

FADING AWAY FROM the party, momentarily, and into his regrets, Carl found himself thinking of Mickie as the merriment grew distant around him. There had been one baffling episode in particular. Back when Mickie had begun to think that she could truly communicate with J.T. Jr. The first time it had happened Carl was at home. He remembered how she had asked J.T. if he wanted to go out onto the roof deck for an airing out. The monkey evidently had made some audible response.

Yes.

Mickie claimed she had heard it clear as day.

My Lord, did you hear that? Why that's absolutely remarkable! I heard it quite distinctly. She seemed to take it for granted that Carl had heard it as well.

It was the first day of spring, and they had both agreed it might be nice to go out and give the monkey a fresh airing. She put it to him again. The monkey was sitting in her lap. "J.T., do you want to go up on the roof?" *Yes.* That time he had even answered quite cheerily, hadn't he? He just looked me directly in the eyes and said, "Yes." It's really quite remarkable, Carl, isn't it? I mean honestly.

To her credit she never insisted that J.T.'s diction contained more than this one word. But she persisted in claiming the monkey was answering her questions. For days she followed after the monkey asking him things. Do you want to go to your room and sit in the window and look at the moon with me? *Yes.* Do you like figs? *Yes.* Do you want your doll now? *Yes.* Do you remember where you came from on the river? *Yes.* And you remember good ole Bill? *Yes.* Do you want another fig? *Yes.* Shall I play the Minuet in G again? *Yes.* Do you like bananas? *Yes.* Do you wish you still lived in Africa? *Yes.*

Oh dear, oh dear.

Maybe Carl had let her believe he'd heard it as well. Maybe he had played along, maybe he had heard the monkey make an indistinct noise in response, or he had been afraid not to play along. Considering how much time the two spent alone, one had to assume something like this would happen sooner or later. He only hoped it would just be a passing fancy. Such childish beliefs had a tendency to flare up from time to time. But this one kept on.

What had become of his wife? Did he blame the war? What had they all seen over there? How strange it had been to learn after the war that she was back in New York, had been for months, and yet hadn't come back home. After a while he had to admit to himself that she had left him. That she was not coming back. He had absolutely no idea who she was anymore, what she was doing, or what had happened to her in the war.

Maybe half a year had passed since she'd been back, since the war had ended, when he'd received a strange call one day from a psychiatrist. A Dr. Leon Pierce Clark, requesting an interview. Said it concerned his wife, and so he'd gone over to see the man, to the address in Brooklyn. He did not know why he was being summoned, but then the doctor began to tell him how he had received a visit, a rather hostile one in fact, the week before from Carl's estranged wife. That is, if he was the husband of a Delia Akeley? *Yes.*

Mrs. Akeley, evidently under the false impression that Carl had already sought the psychiatrist's services, had barged into Dr. Clark's office demanding to know whether her husband had paid him money in regards to herself. There seemed to be some confusion. Neither Mrs. Akeley nor Mr. Akeley had ever secured his services before. They had never met. Once she found out that Carl had not been to see the psychiatrist, she sneered at him, apparently disbelieving the man. Who knows where she had come up with the idea? Perhaps she had imagined it all after seeing one of the psychiatrist's books around. He was, after all, a prominent doctor who had authored psychobiographies on Napoleon and Lincoln. But before she could leave he managed to persuade her to sit down for a talk. A consultation.

Among the confessions she'd made were several the doctor now shared with Carl. It was disconcerting information, to say the least. Namely, that his estranged wife desired to kill him. She wanted to murder her husband—or at least this was the conclusion that Dr. Leon Pierce Clark had arrived at after his accidental interview with her. It was, he explained calmly, how she intended to have her revenge.

He waited for Carl to absorb that information and then continued.

Why she felt it necessary to have revenge was not exactly clear to him, nor was he entirely sure it was clear to Mickie either. What was clear was that it was not for money, and what was additionally clear to the psychiatrist, at least insofar as he could interpret Mickie's motives, was that there was no one else in the world who interested her except for Carl; although she had decided they could no longer be together, subconsciously she had become fixated to his person and, almost to a certainty, would try to kill both him and herself. Only in this way, the psychiatrist said, according to his wife's deranged way of thinking, or in the subconscious recesses of that mind, would they both enter into the afterworld together where she could have him to herself exclusively. It was, perhaps, a matter of sexual jealousy.

It was horrifying and inexplicable. And yet the doctor's arguments all seemed sound. The things Mickie had confessed to this complete stranger were entirely mad; they pierced him to the core, and yet . . . Carl felt as the doctor explained the situation that his mind had never been clearer. That suddenly everything made sense. The doctor reassured him that there need not be any publicity attached to Mickie being committed—a course of action which, he recommended, should be done at once. He said Bloomingdale would be a very good place. Several prominent men's wives were hospitalized there. There would be no attendant negative press. He said that once there, she would suffer a mental and physical collapse, and then through a process of reeducation come back to fairly normal. As the psychiatrist explained his situation, putting a shape to it, Akeley tried on this disquieting new skin, tugging gently here, a little slubbing there, seeing if it didn't fit the contortions of his own suspicions after all, even if it might need a little extra glue under the forehead. Carl listened and began to feel that the doctor was right. He agreed. The only solution was to have her committed. Not out of spite. But because if he didn't she would never recover and would bring them both down in catastrophe. Akeley left the doctor's after saying he would contact his lawyer and her physician soon to make the necessary arrangements.

❧

MARTIN JOHNSON WAS still talking about cameras.

Did they know that after the newsreel boys had gone and filmed Man o' War at the Kentucky Derby—the first "civilian" use of the Akeley— that audiences were convinced, *absolutely dead certain*, the camera had been attached to an automobile speeding around the track or somehow

attached to an airplane? Of course it was just two operators with Akeleys stationed on either side of the track so they could take in the whole
race.

You know, somebody said, speaking of Man o' War, old August Bel-
mont Jr. joined the army to go fight in Europe when he was *sixty-five
years old*. It was his wife who'd named the foal in his honor while he
was off killing huns.

Now, that was something.

"I dimly remember the time when I was only fifty," Carl said. "However, I want to say . . . I want to say that I find that the older one grows
the more fun one has because soon after fifty one ceases to take anyone
else or anything seriously. The world considered as a joke must be the
funniest thing in the whole solar system."

"Adventure is a mark of incompetence," Stefansson mumbled.

Look who's talking, Akeley shot back. Stefannson almost had a
mutiny on his last polar expedition. He was lucky he hadn't been cannibalized.

Was the booze getting stronger or was it just prohibition that made
it seem so?

⁊

LESS THAN A year after the Johnsons had left for Africa, Carl stood on
the deck of the *Baltic* as the steamer pulled out into the dark Hudson. It
was July 1921. The harbor breeze clapped at the tarp covering a nearby
lifeboat, where Carl stood by the rail, facing the sideways receding skyline under the summer night. Faintly, he could hear music and drunken
laughter winding its way onto the upper deck from the piano bar below.
The pungent heat of oil and brackish water roiled under his nostrils. It
was a good forty-foot drop to the darkly churning water. As the piers
crept slowly by he could see the Flatiron Building moving away like the
dark prow of another ghostly ship going the opposite direction. The view
of the shrinking city, like a bristling steel panorama rolling by, was
magnificent and gloomy. There was nothing to keep him here now. The
elephants were finished. He had sold his Buick. There was nothing
really that couldn't wait until his return. When he'd told Osborn he was
finally ready to go find the mountain gorillas, it hadn't been hard to get
the museum to pony up ten thousand dollars for the trip. Nothing else
was going to lure investors like that. An acquisition that mysterious

would pay itself back with sponsors in no time. Carl's plans for the African Hall were moving in tandem now with Osborn's plans for the Roosevelt memorial wing. From where he stood everything looked more and more like fulfillment. Against the chalky black haze of the night sky he watched spasms of colored motion over Times Square: the twelve giant spearmen caught in their never-ending war dance, unloosing spears on the invisible enemy. This frantic beacon served for Akeley's departing gaze, until at last the city shrank to a white speck, and the ship turned out into the pitch-black rolling Atlantic.

CHAPTER TWENTY-FIVE

BELGIAN CONGO, 1921

A KELEY COULD HEAR THE FILM PURRING THROUGH THE GATE
as he slowly panned, working from left to right, south to north, the
beauty of the outlook searing his brain. The crank had a steady, satisfying
grip. The viewfinder's rubber seal made a good hermetic pressure around
the eye. He could feel the extra weight in his lungs from the altitude, but
for once it had stopped raining. The mist and fog had parted, and the blue
sky was brocaded with bizarre silks. Hawks rolled above the soaring
treetops far below like specks of ash caught in an updraft. He was just
inside the mountain forest, a dense and boggy womb, looking out over
the breathtaking view. In the air was the faint odor of carbon disulfide—
that volatile ether from the volcanoes which was so oddly familiar.

He panned up from the northern blue tip of Lake Kivu, far below,
and the little kingdom of Rwanda, and then across the basin valley
bumped over with the tiny forested conical hills and here and there
the wisp of smoke from a village nestled below the miniature banana
groves. After Versailles, the Belgians had taken it all from the Germans,
and their White Fathers had impregnated the country like chigger eggs,
but what did that matter now?

He lingered on the first volcano and its massive ashen plume of
steam and then panned northward—blurring out briefly over the white
snag tree that framed the vista between its dead branches—to the more

distant Nyamlagira, twenty miles to the west, above which hovered a crimson-stained cloud revealing the cauldron beneath. He was not close enough to feel its heat, but he might as well have been holding his face directly over the pit. His head felt like a giant burning blister. His fever was only getting worse by the day.

He had begun getting sick well before he'd even reached the White Fathers, around the night there'd been a row among the porters. They were camped south along Lake Kivu, at Lulenga, and earlier in the day one of the men had evidently shot another in the forehead with an arrow after an antelope hunt gone bad. The man's friends blamed the assailant for deliberately attempting murder, and dragged him back to camp in a rage. Carl had ordered the headman to detain the porter until they could hand him over to the administrator at Kivu, four days later. That night, as he lay on his cot, shivering and delirious, he could hear the man screaming between claps of thunder over the lake. Maybe he'd thought he was dreaming the whole thing. But come morning there was no sign of the man. Although the natives pretended he had escaped, a frightened child confessed that the men had killed the prisoner and eaten the corpse.

But children said fantastic things.

Twiddling with the thumbscrew focus he tilted across the lava plains, and the undulating blues and greens, until he cranked upward to the otherworldly jagged peak of Mount Mikeno. Golden moss on the naked rock face—*Mikeno* meaning "the Naked One"—sparkled weirdly. Could the sky have blazed a more forcible blue? He stood on the saddle now, between Karisimbi and Mikeno. Here would be, must be, the background to his mountain gorilla diorama. The place looked so absolutely confected, like a fairyland—as if the clusters of orchids were just spun glass, the drooping moss unspooled strands of celluloid, make-believe trees covered in molded wax leaves and colored crepe paper. An illusion just for the benefit of his fever-cooked brain.

He steered the camera back to the bleached snag—a long expired mahogany—before dropping the vertical pan and bringing the great bestilled gorilla into view. It lay facedown at the foot of the tree. He filmed it for a while. Its silver and black hairs stirred softly. A trail of blood led from where it had tried to drag itself to safety before a final slug in the neck had put it to rest beneath the dead tree. It had tried to run away too, as undefiant as all the others.

The forest smelled of catnip and raspberries and chervil.

He had the guides prop the body up against the tree so he could film it better. With his pipe clenched in his teeth, Akeley crawled over to examine the gorilla. Taking up one of its great hands—it was not a paw but *a hand*—he tested the flex of its wrist. Pulled back its rubbery lips to see the daunting fangs. He spread its toes, touched its swollen belly, fingered the bullet hole in its broad and unsettlingly manlike chest. As wide as Dempsey's. The old king had already survived one attempt on its life: a badly healed bullet wound on its shaggy hip. Its fur shone metallic black, the same shiny black as the camera he had used to steal its soul, click by click, vacuuming up its demonic aura right along with its massive shoulders and weirdly foreshortened legs. The guides stretched out its arms so he could measure—a reach of ninety-seven inches— before he returned to investigating the fingers, the black fingernails, again lifting one of its big hands, a true giant's hand, you had to marvel at its heft, the great creases still warm and soft to the touch. He knelt in the springy foliage, the trampled ferns and *cusso* tree leaves of the gorilla beds. Lingering in the air was the pungent glandular odor of fear released by the others who'd fled quickly when the shooting had begun. Lobes of dung scattered the ground, speckled with blackberry seeds, nettles, bits of bark.

Now, he looked into its face. More than anything its gray eyes seemed to signal an acceptance of the course of things, that its peace-able reign had come to an end.

With his guides looking on, Carl took his pipe and placed it between the gorilla's lips. It dangled there, foolishly, smoke trickling up over its noble mien. Then he took off his glasses and, bending the stems, fit them over its eyes and comically small ears. Behind the scratched lens its gaze offered nothing except the same look it had offered when Akeley first saw it; not that it was indifferent, exactly, to his presence, but almost as if Carl did not exist, and not only as if it were pretending he did not exist. Oh, but his mind was melting like a wax cylinder. He felt on the verge of extinction himself. The urge, of course, was to laugh at the des-ecration he had made. A horrible laughter—his own sickly guffaw—was muffled by the forest.

CHAPTER TWENTY-SIX

IT CAME TUMBLING DOWN JUST EXACTLY AS THE FIRST. AS IF the whole thing was nothing but a déjà vu arranged courtesy of his fever. It was crazy, really, how similar it all was. This tumbling gorilla so much like the first he'd shot and then watched come tumbling down just a few days earlier in such a frenzy of grief. This time it was a fiasco from the start. They'd been going up along the slope when they'd spotted a band of gorillas, five or six, with several young, and he'd seen a large and desirable female grazing. He aimed, pulled the trigger, and misfired. When the female heard the dry metal click, it looked down at him, pausing only momentarily before returning to the fistful of bamboo shoots it had been carefully stripping with its teeth. The rifle misfired a second time, and then, cursing Springfields in general, Carl gestured for the Austrian elephant gun. But just as his gun bearer was leaning out to pass him the .475, the female was replaced by a big male (who made the strangest tempest on its breast with its fists), and he'd fired too quickly and missed and the explosion had set the whole band of them into a frenzy, the gorillas all running off into the woods, the pups hightailing it, and it was an hour or so before he'd caught up and found the female again.

However now the quality of déjà vu had begun. His relative position to the female was the same as it had been the first time—right down to the detail of once again being on the brink of a two-hundred-foot dropoff. Except, this time, without a tree to prop himself against for the shot. Instead, he'd entwined himself as best he could in a shrub—the only hope he had of not blasting himself off the mountain—and when he pulled the trigger it was like he'd disengaged a chock under the ape.

It came tumbling down just exactly as the first.

With his legs bound in the shrub, he lost his balance momentarily from the recoil. Unable to extricate himself quickly enough when he saw that the gorilla was set on a direct collision course with him, he could do nothing but hurl himself facedown and pray that it didn't crush him or rip him over the canyon edge with it, shrub and all.

He felt its breeze before the actual impact. And then it was over. The ape had bowled right over him, but he was still alive and still safely pressed to the mountain. He'd barely felt it and, when he sat up, was surprised to find himself in one piece, with no pain except for a throbbing on the back of his head. But before he had a chance to give his skull a proper inspection he saw that the avalanche was not yet finished—now being face-to-face with a smaller platoon of shaggy black bounders streaming down the slope, a second wave of three furry tumbleweeds that scurried and swept around him—one touching his leg in passing—as they followed their mother, for what else could this be but the panicked youngsters chasing after the runaway parent, down over the canyon edge too. He'd taken a shot at one and missed, and then all were gone.

After assuring himself that he remained in the majority unscathed, except for a nasty welt on the back of his head, he began planning how to get down the canyon to retrieve his quarry. His men leaned on their spears to peer over the fog-blown ledge, looking at Carl like they could not believe he'd fallen for such a thing twice.

The fog settling in now made it impossible to tell where the gorilla had even landed. The guides shook their heads and said it was a lost cause. There was no way. Going straight down such a steep drop was out of the question. Even if they could find the gorilla, it would be smashed to bits. But then before anyone could stop him, or even realized what he was doing, Carl had taken hold of an overhanging vine and swung down into the gloomy fog. The old man did a vanishing act. He was lucky the jump hadn't yanked his arms out of their sockets. But once he landed safely on the shelf below, his guides had no choice but to follow.

If they left him now to die here, they would have to answer to the White Fathers.

Better to die with the *mzungu*.

They worked their way first along the ledge and then zigzagged down the near-vertical slope beside the cliff, working haltingly along the steep vegetation like human flies, switchbacking down the impossible grade.

Halfway down the chasm, the fog was replaced by a cold heavy rain. They had come to another narrow ledge, and with nowhere to go now, his men had fallen into a kind of paralysis. They stood there on the short ledge, trembling and shivering, looking helpless, until at last he'd thrown open his Burberry and let them in under the raincoat. The ones who couldn't fit beneath the slicker huddled under the upturned root of a dead tree.

Above and below them was sheer cliff. The gorilla was somewhere down there. Under the clatter of gabardine fending off the rain he could hear his guides arguing among themselves, how it was pointless to follow this bwana any farther. Why were they risking their necks for this crazy old *mzungu*? Even if he didn't get the exact words, he gathered the tone, and understood that they might well refuse to go any farther. It would be a sensible thing to refuse.

He sat pressed up between one whose head was shaved like a Fabergé egg and another man called Muguru who poked at the muddy ground with a squared-off chopper. He had never been this close to any man, let alone seven naked, shivering Negroes. For the time being, they had fallen silent and just sat shivering and stinking, preserving their energy, looking out at the dismal rain and fog.

When the rain let up a bit, he packed the raincoat, and they continued their ludicrous descent. As he groped for footholds, clinging to wet clumps of burdock and wild celery with the feeble strength of his numb hands, the welt on his head throbbed so he couldn't tell which was from the blow he'd taken from the runaway ape and which the headache from the fever that blurred everything else. He caught glimpses of the female below through snatches of fog. A twisted black shape splayed on an outcropping, near the tail end of a waterfall. My God, what had he done? It was as if he'd shoved some decrepit old woman over a cliff.

As he made his way farther down he felt himself growing weaker still, and doubted whether he'd be able to climb back out, as if he were not sure he'd be able to carry out the burden of his conscience. Each inch down was won more and more by faith than by any reality adhering to the laws of gravity. Not to mention that his entire body was on fire from the stinging nettles that grew everywhere. It was easily shaping up to be the hardest day of his life.

He could hear the gritty stabbing sound above him as the guides drove their spears into the mud for leverage. He had begun to feel pity for these men whom he'd bid follow him down into the chasm. To think, he was paying the lot of them less than what he'd end up paying Mickie per month in alimony. It was criminal. They were all risking their lives, and for what? So he could bring back a few dead apes to America? So spoiled New York women would have something to do on a Wednesday afternoon? If only they could know what he'd gone through to get it.

That he'd had to lie in his cot and listen to one of his porters be murdered and cannibalized and that he hadn't done a damn thing to stop it.

He hardly knew his own mind anymore. What if all of what Mickie had accused him was true? That he'd tried to strangle her. That he'd pulled a razor and threatened to cut her throat. Or was she really willing to say anything just to drag him and his reputation through the mud? Even though he'd made it perfectly clear through his lawyers that he'd give her the divorce by simply failing to show in court. That's all it took. He would not get in her way. But she wanted the world to think he was a madman. It would be all over the papers. But what if it were true? *When did all this happen?* When she was sick. When she was bedridden after the monkey had bitten her leg. It was easy enough to imagine himself finding some rope and tying her to the bed. Just as the porters had tied up the man at Lulenga. Tight, so that her circulation was cut off. Then, doing his best to ignore her protests, patiently taking care of a few last-minute things, maybe writing a letter to explain why he was about to do what he had in mind, going into the kitchen, turning on the gas. Standing there a minute listening to the valve hiss, but not dawdling. Then going into her room and calmly lying down on the bed beside her and waiting. He would have tried to lie still while she struggled beside him. Even though he would have felt impatient, waiting to taste the first whiff of gas. Eager to get on with it. Enough thinking. But then somebody had begun knocking on the door—or so she'd alleged. They'd either heard Mickie screaming or smelled the gas, and then they'd knocked down the door.

Unlike himself at Lulenga, where he'd lain on his cot and listened to the whole thing. Too weak, too sick, too frightened to interfere.

Did he really know if he had tried to destroy them both? Or was what the shrink said true? That it was Mickie who wanted him dead? Who the hell knew anymore? Maybe it was she who'd persuaded him to turn on the gas. Was that so far out of the question? No, it was not. Why wouldn't he have wanted to join her in the afterlife?

She was charging him with desertion, but it was she who had abandoned him. Gone off to serve in a war that didn't belong to her when she couldn't take the absurdity of her own life trapped in a New York City apartment with a monkey all day. Really, he should have had her committed to Bloomingdale when he'd had the chance.

But, of course, he hadn't. In the end he couldn't do it. Probably because deep down—whether or not he'd tried to kill her—he knew it was he who'd abandoned Mickie. He'd cut himself off from her. Even after she'd given everything to help him, working her fingers to the bone, putting her own life second to his from the first day they'd met, barely taking an ounce of credit, saving his life when the pursuit of his murderous art threatened to kill him (to kill them both). He could not count the times she'd risked her own neck for his sake. His glory, his obsessions. But then somehow she'd become like his mother. Back in New York City. It was the air of melancholy, the suffocating stench of depression that he'd grown up with as a child that had probably made it impossible for him to reach out to her, that kept him away. It hardly mattered that he was susceptible to those same moods! The ones that pulled the stuffing out of you, as if someone had found a rip in your seam, was slowly unwinding you. He could have helped her through it. He could have been there for her. But he'd been too selfish, too weak.

He had practically acted as if she'd had it coming when the monkey had bitten her, when what he should have done all along was just get rid of the damn varmint. Done her a favor. He should have been a better husband and made sure nothing like that could have ever happened to her in the first place. He should have got her mind right. She'd given him everything, he had taken it all, then left her behind like one of the hundreds of other animals whose skins he'd tossed aside after realizing they didn't fit his dread vision.

On the other hand, who knew? Maybe the psychiatrist was crazy too. Maybe she didn't want to kill him at all. Maybe it was all just a twisted perverted lie. But even he could recall at least one time in Africa after they'd argued—over what no longer mattered—when she'd deliberately tried to spark an elephant stampede in his direction with a stray shot. She'd admitted as much, that she was that angry. What man really knows whether or not his wife is capable of murder, with or without benefit of an elephant herd to do her bidding?

He had now come even with the gorilla, but only to realize belatedly that it was on the opposite side of the river just below the waterfall. He'd come down the wrong way. He could see it, just across the plunging stream, twisted and broken on its small ledge overlooking yet another steep falloff. He'd been lucky. It could easily have fallen another two hundred feet.

Unable to cross here, he and his men had to descend yet another tortuous forty feet before they could find a crossing place and clamber back up, with the water tumbling down on them. When he reached the gorilla the first thing he did was tie it to a tree with rope. Then he tied himself to the tree as well. Now, perched on the lip of this fog-concealed chasm, they were bound to each other, no matter what happened.

He had just begun to jot down a few measurements when he heard a squeal above and looked up to see one of the guides approaching with his spear wriggling. Dangling from its tip was one of the young gorillas that had followed the mother partway down. Possibly the one he'd taken a shot at himself.

It was still alive, and looked piteous when the guide dropped it at Carl's feet. A trickle of peony-tinted rain dribbled off the slender iron blade of the man's spear.

The hairs on the back of the baby gorilla's neck stood like quills. Its gray eyes were ringed yellow with terror. It was more pitiful than words could express, no less because of the curious expression of pleading intelligence that Carl read as somehow human. Carl sensed that the dying animal would have let him hold it in his arms. Though, of course, he couldn't bring himself to do so in front of these men. If he were alone, maybe he would have been more likely to pick it up and hold it, to try to comfort it as the life and trembly fear ebbed slowly out the gash in its side.

Perhaps he sensed the perversity of comforting the child of the mother whom he not only had just killed but was now lashed to as if by an umbilicus. Instead, he only knelt there, his knife limply in hand, and stared as it whimpered and then died.

There was no data, no amount of scientific righteousness, that could rub away the feeling now that he was the aggressor and savage. *A cold-blooded murderer.* That was the way he put it to himself. The feeling was keen. But for what purpose was all this bloody effort? Was this really the only way—*but it was, wasn't it?*—to obtain the necessary data, because without the data, you would have no understanding, no facts, and if you didn't have that, then what would you have? What would civilization be without its accumulation of facts?

As the fog closed in around them, sealed them shut inside together, he began to have the same thoughts that had vaguely begun to nag at him since he'd slaughtered the first gorilla. Those thoughts started up again now as he returned to the weary business of skinning the female—he would preserve the baby later back at camp, intact, not having the heart to dismantle it—and then when they were done, and they were climbing back out of the chasm, with the bones rattling in the guides' baskets, he was already making maps in his mind, drawing boundary lines, suddenly filled with a different sense of purpose than the one with which he'd come.

A purpose to which he now avowed himself. That is, if he made it out of the jungle alive.

After all, it was death touching him that had made it possible to see things anew. And there were no guarantees yet that he would avoid extinction himself.

But if he did, this is what he pledged: that he would return. Not to kill another single gorilla—he had a license for five more, for a total of ten, which he would not be claiming—but to build something that had never been built before, at least not here, and not an actual edifice, because it would not require a single brick, yet something formidable enough that it would still keep out the princes and the hunters and the men like himself, men of dubious purpose, men with guns. He would build a sanctuary. The kind Roosevelt had created all over America, and of which none yet existed in Africa. It was every bit as visionary as his hall. Even if the sanctuary he now had in mind was in every way unlike his hall, which was nothing if not partitions, compartment separated from compartment, cell from cell—in fact this one had only occurred now because some sort of partition had fallen, as if the little ape had come forward and pushed over the pane separating them, so that all the poison air rushed out and awoke him to his better nature.

He felt the cold rain on his naked face. If he could have held up his

Burberry and stretched it out to shield all the gorillas from the down-pour of bullets, if he thought it could redeem at least a part of what he'd done, he would have done so now. As they hiked out, he was as weak as he had ever been. Soon enough a daydream would come to him where he imagined himself inside the gorilla's skin. Trapped, he had to cut himself free, tearing open the skin from the inside, pushing back the face like a hood, and wriggling out, like a man sloughing off a wet sleep-ing bag. Like a man waking in the forest, in the jungle, and then seeing himself naked, half-emerged from the skin of an ape, the one surface he had never thought to peel away.

CHAPTER TWENTY-SEVEN

MARCH 23, 1925. HE WAS ON THE NIGHT TRAIN TO ROCHESTER. Sitting beside him, in a blue suit and with rather spare and stern features, was Daniel Eleazer Pomeroy, museum trustee and president of the Martin Johnson African Expedition Corporation, that intermediary arm of the American Museum whose job it was to launder money (so to speak) from Johnson's wildlife movies into funding for the African Hall. At last—fifteen years since Carl first glimpsed its cryptic dimensions from behind a veil of bandages—his vision was finally on the verge of coming true.

The two men were in the smoking car. They were close to the same age—Carl would be sixty-one in May, and Pomeroy was just a couple years behind. A retired vice president of the Bankers Trust Company, Pomeroy (who still retained a directorship) had already vowed to put up enough to finance one corner group. With his long beak, lipless mouth, and wrinkled little slits for eyes, the banker looked bony and chilly, but the truth was he was a warm and kindhearted man. At the moment he was trying to calm Carl's nerves. The following morning, at exactly 7:30 A.M., they were scheduled to have breakfast with George Eastman. Since Eastman had retired, and was, as he put it, "seeking a somewhat more detached position in respect to human affairs," he had already given away sixty-eight million dollars—to MIT, the University of Rochester, as well as the music school named in his honor—and seemed bent on giving away every penny of his vast fortune. His only desire, for the time being, was to go big-game hunting in Africa, to make himself "scarce," as he put it. He had let it be known that he wanted to go with the famous taxidermist from the American Museum, and Carl hoped to persuade the man to pay handsomely for the privilege. With Eastman writing the checks, the hall would become a reality in no time. Everything seemed stacked in Akeley's favor. But the closer they got to Rochester, the more he fidgeted and seemed about ready to jump out the window.

Pomeroy tried distracting him by talking of other things. Carl was still due enormous praise for his phenomenal success in convincing the Belgian government to take up his proposal for a mountain gorilla sanctuary, for instance. It was natural to keep congratulating him, especially considering how recently it had all come to fruition, and it certainly helped to turn the mood, at least for a few minutes.

Carl had begun writing letters to various officials before he'd even left the Kivu, urging measures be taken before the opportunity to save the gorilla was lost forever. Back in the United States, the prominent scientist John C. Merriam, from the Carnegie Institution in Washington, D.C., had helped get Carl's proposal into the hands of James Gustavus Whiteley, consul of Belgium, who had then pushed it up to His Excellency Baron Émile de Cartier de Marchienne, Belgian ambassador to the United States, until at last, through the nimble hands of Count d'Arschot, His Majesty's *chef du cabinet*, it had found its way to King Albert himself.

Curiously enough, the king had already entertained a desire to create a sort of wilderness preserve. He had even made a trip to the United States, in 1919, to tour Yosemite and the Grand Canyon, with Merriam and Henry Fairfield Osborn for tour guides, both of whom hoped to impress upon the king the "immense scientific value" of such preserves. The only problem was that his own country, like most of Europe, no longer had much left in the way of wilderness. Then again, there *was* his colony in Africa, the mighty Congo, but the shape of what sort of preserve exactly to make there had remained foggy until the taxidermist's proposal had arrived at the castle. Perhaps the king's desire to create something—this sanctuary for the jungle's lesser denizens—could even be seen as a small gesture of atonement against all the suffering caused there at the hands of his father, the late Leopold II.

And so on March 2, 1925—less than a month before Carl's visit to

George Eastman—King Albert had issued a royal decree protecting a zone of twenty-four thousand hectares for the mountain gorillas to be called Parc National Albert. In addition, a game reserve, under less restrictive conditions, would protect another two hundred thousand hectares running down to the shores of Lake Kivu. Upon the announcement, the Belgian consul, James Gustavus Whiteley, had written to Akeley to give him the good news, saying, "Our cousins, the gorillas, ought to hold a Thanksgiving meeting in your honor."

It would be the first preserve of its kind in Africa.

And, truly, it could not have happened soon enough. Ironically, given the publicity Carl had stirred up in his campaign to save the mountain gorilla, big-game hunters were now clamoring more than ever for the chance to bag this most exotic of trophies. Even the gorillas' closest neighbors, the White Fathers, had been no help, insisting as they did that the apes existed in the "safe thousands." Akeley had told Ambassador Marchienne that he doubted there were more than fifty total in the Congo. Guiltily, he had also confided to a friend that "if this thing did not succeed it would mean that the last gorilla was going to be killed off within the next two years, and all because of this attempt to preserve them!" But since the king's decree, he had enormous reason to be proud. "Every decent thing that I have ever had get across," Carl said to Pomeroy with a look of pained satisfaction, "I had to force."

But then he started thinking about his meeting with Eastman again, and he began wringing his hands and puffing at his pipe nervously.

"By heaven, Dan! If Mr. Eastman only can see how important—how necessary this is . . ." Then he trailed off and resumed stewing in silence, staring out through the gaunt face floating over the blacked-out woods swimming by outside at terrifying speed.

He was afraid of jinxing himself; he would not let himself believe that anything might come of this meeting. That the outcome of his greatest dream might lie in the fickle hands of one rich man. A rich man who could just as easily make Carl's dream come true as a child could operate one of Eastman's cameras. PUSH THE BUTTON, WE DO THE REST.

It was easy to understand Carl's feelings. The African Hall had been put off for so long. There had been so many holdups and obstacles.

But he had only to keep in mind how well things had been going. And not just the gorilla sanctuary. The first Martin Johnson film under their arrangement, *Trailing African Wild Animals* (Metro Pictures, 1923), had been a box-office hit. Fifty percent of those profits were going directly to the hall, and the Johnsons were now already back in Africa making their second film.

Funnily enough, it had probably been the Johnsons who'd first really planted the idea of going to Africa in Eastman's mind. Strapped with the same burden as Akeley to raise capital for their own expeditions, the Johnsons had visited Eastman themselves before returning to Africa for what Martin said would be an intensive four-year filming safari. But within five minutes of hearing Johnson's fumbled pitch, Eastman had shown Martin and Osa the door. It wasn't until the young filmmakers had reached Albany, on the return trip to New York, when Osa suddenly sprang to her feet and forced her dejected husband off the train.

"We're going back to Rochester," she said. "Mr. Eastman isn't going to pass this thing up until he knows what he's passing up."

Several hours later, back in Eastman's mahogany-paneled office, Osa was cooing, "Naturally, we know you have plenty of ways of just making money without suggestions from us."

Martin reprimed his motor: "What I wanted to do was interest you in *the idea* and not a mere business deal." With a boldness usually reserved by the director for dealing with headhunters, Martin unbotched his pitch as best he could, going for frankness over deference, while Osa sat back in her terai hat and skinny little man's tie draped across her adorable potbelly, smirking at Eastman, who returned her gaze across his desk with ice-blue eyes.

In the end they left with a check for ten thousand dollars. No doubt, it had been this unusual visit—and possibly the appeal of seeing the cheeky flapper again—that had first put the idea of a trip to Africa in the old man's head.

Now Carl was going to Rochester on the same errand. The truth was that many of the museum's usual donors—and the museum's own coffers—had already been tapped for what was turning into the museum's biggest expedition ever, the Central Asiatic Expedition to Mongolia, in search of the missing link.

Even if so far—at a cost of $600,000—they had only dug up what turned out to be dinosaur eggs, and absolutely no evidence of Osborn's Dawn Men. The dinosaur eggs were interesting enough, but then the journal *Nature* had published an article about the discovery of something altogether more curious: a fossilized skull that had been blasted out of a cliff, in South Africa, during a mining explosion. At first the skull had been mistaken for a species of cercopithecid, a type of Old World monkey. But then the author of the article, Professor Raymond Dart, who had come into possession of the skull, had quickly realized that it bore a much greater resemblance to earlier hominids. He had dubbed the new species *Australopithecus africanus*. "The specimen is of importance because it exhibits an extinct race of apes *intermediate between living anthropoids and man*," Professor Dart wrote. "Unlike *Pithecanthropus* [a fossil discovered in 1891, aka "Java Man"], it does not represent an ape-like man, a caricature of precocious hominid failure, but a creature well advanced beyond modern anthropoids in just those characters, facial and cerebral, which are to be anticipated in an extinct link between man and his simian ancestor . . . vindicating the Darwinian claim that Africa would prove to be the cradle of mankind."

Akeley, of course, was looking forward to returning to Africa and wrote to a close friend how he would probably end his days there. Everything in his life up to this point now felt as if it had all been preparation. A long period of incubation. This upcoming trip felt like it would signify the true beginning of all the planning behind the African Hall. Finally, he felt he was really getting to work.

Once again, he had finished his business at home. He had finished mounting the gorilla group, including the child ape. He'd been eager to finish the gorillas to woo potential investors. He'd also used them, after a manner, to woo his new wife. It had happened one day during their courtship, when Mary Jobe had come to visit Carl at his studio. While he was busily working on one of the manikins, his black-and-white movie footage of gorillas clambering in the branches of a tree played silently on the wall. Carl used it as a study aid while sculpting. Mary inspected the clay model of the silverback he was working on, which he told her he called the Old Man of Mikeno. It was the first one he'd shot. The one that had snagged at the last instant before a near plummet over the cliff.

Mary laughed at the pups as they dashed out onto the precarious limbs, thick with moss, then dangled acrobatically while the mother ape below tried to have a moment of peace, occasionally swatting one that got into its way as petals and twigs fell about her.

It was the only motion picture ever taken of the species, of which

Carl had gotten a good three hundred feet of film. Watching beside her, Carl said, "I suppose I could have easily killed every one that I saw."

Then, like a boy trying to scare or impress a girl with a frog, he took her over to the preserved corpse of the young gorilla which he kept intact in a large jar of formaldehyde. It was curled up like an embryo. Skinned, its flesh was the pale color of drowned worms.

Removing it from the jar, and holding up the reeking peeled infant, Carl told her he had named it Clarence, after his own childhood name. Something, quite likely, he had never told anybody else before. Honestly, the poor pathetic ape looked no worse than she had in August, after Carl had gone up to visit her at the girls' camp in Mystic, Connecticut, and she'd been so stricken with poison ivy that their rendezvous had been a miserable failure. But she wasn't put off by this display and listened as Carl explained how its fingers could not flex as ours unless its wrist was bent. "When the wrist is straight, as in the act of walking, the fingers automatically close like the claw of a bird when it settles on a perch." He demonstrated this by showing how the dead fingers clasped a stick. He lifted the stick and the apeling hung grotesquely. Verily, as if for dear life. "Even in its present condition," Carl said, lightly touching the fingers, "the weight of the body is not sufficient to loosen their grasp. A legacy of his arboreal life—probably a great aid to him as he grasps roots and branches in the tortuous ascent of a steep hillside."

The smell of this poor dangling thing was enough to bring tears to her eyes—as if Carl were showing her a too-intimate or forbidden part of himself—but, then again, it might have just been the sting of formaldehyde.

Soon enough Carl had a ring on Mary Jobe's own pink finger, and he was excited to bring his new bride to Africa. Mary would be a wonderful asset, as camp manager, especially given her experience running the girls' camp. Though managing ten-year-old girls from Darien, Connecticut, and managing African porters were not exactly the same thing. They were married on October 18, 1924. Coincidentally—or possibly not so coincidentally—just a few days after his ex-wife arrived in Mombasa on behalf of the Brooklyn Institute of Arts and Sciences.

The press would make much ado about this expedition, being led as it were by a fifty-year-old white woman who looked "more like a school teacher than an African explorer." Mickie would be the first woman to lead such an expedition—and without benefit of any companions, save the Swahili porters she hired to travel with her across Kenya, Uganda, and the Congo. The primary purpose of her safari was to "get as far from civilization as possible," as she put it to the *Saturday Evening Post,* and to make studies and photographs of native women and their babies.

Sometime after the New Year, Mickie had gone missing. The *Brooklyn Eagle* had reported that she hadn't been heard from in over two months, but then she had reemerged in the Ituri Forest, in the Congo, where she was said to be living among Pygmies. There, she had taken ill, and, according to her own later accounts, each day her cook would come and ask if she was going to die that day. Delirious with fever, she often heard the cook and her porter discussing how they would prepare her body when she died.* In the end she reached Boma on September 3, 1925, becoming the first white woman to cross the continent of Africa by foot. She was forty pounds lighter, but full of many touching stories about her sometimes oddball ways of getting on with the churlish Pygmies, though she would keep most of her most chilling observations confined to her diaries—that is, of the brutality she had witnessed, native laborers being whipped, beaten, and kept in heavy iron chains while they built roads for the Belgians, for whom perhaps a gorilla sanctuary was not yet atonement enough.

In an interview with the *New York World,* after her return, Mickie had spoken of lighter moments such as teaching Pygmy children to play jump rope with jungle vines. "Mrs. Akeley probably knows more of the customs of these people than any living white woman. Yet she speaks of it all not as a student or an investigator but as one human being of another, telling with a quiet humor of the African widow who dons mourning for her deceased spouse by having her black body painted with a coat of white clay, and when the clay begins to wear considers herself in half-mourning and begins to attend the dances and look around for a new husband, for life must go on even though husbands go the way of all flesh."

☙

WHEN THEY ARRIVED at Eastman's the next morning, Akeley and Pomeroy were greeted by a butler who took their coats and hats, and

---

* She turned out to be sick from ptomaine poisoning, making her the near victim of tinned Franco-American, rather than the anopheles mosquito or overeager cannibals.

then escorted them through the house, which they could not help but notice, as they followed along through the byzantine hallways, was filled with the quake and tremor of organ music. They were shown into the conservatory, a great bright open space of marble, square Doric columns, wicker furniture, and giant potted palms. More than anything else, it was reminiscent of the lobby of an opulent hotel. The entire east wall was window, looking out on the terrace gardens, where sixteen full-time gardeners were employed by Eastman.

A man sitting at a small round table laid for breakfast was introduced to them as Dr. Audley Stewart, Eastman's personal physician. Stewart gestured for Akeley and Pomeroy to have a seat, as coffee was poured, and said that Mr. Eastman would be down shortly. The table was set with Minton china plates monogrammed with Eastman's initials, filigreed stemware with fresh grapefruit juice, and a pile of the day's newspapers, as well as a green pack of Lucky Strikes, sitting at Eastman's place. For a moment they sat, smoking and chatting amiably, even if it was necessary to raise their voices slightly on account of the organ that was being played not twenty feet away, on a giant instrument whose pipes rose thirty feet to the ceiling above. A young man in a starched collar and unfailing posture was at the console, with his back to the men, pushing and prodding at the keyboard and stops.

When Mr. Eastman was announced, they saw him descending the gleaming mahogany stairs, behind a coppice of organ pipes, dressed in a dark gray business suit and plum scarf.

Akeley must have been surprised, after the initial round of niceties, and once Eastman was seated, that the organist did not stop playing. To say the least, it was a distracting accompaniment to a breakfast meeting—especially in a room of marble and glass. The guests enjoyed the fresh cream and butter and eggs, much of which was produced on Eastman's estate, where he kept cows and chickens. He abhorred the new unwholesome foods like margarine, and in part it was the duty of his personal physician to make sure he reduced his intake of gravies and other rich items. Carl mentioned his recent lecture at the Battle Creek Sanitarium, and the kind of diet promulgated by Dr. Kellogg, and how everybody there had been delighted to learn the gorilla was a natural vegetarian. "The gorilla kills no animals for food," Carl said, "and he hasn't progressed sufficiently along the paths of man to enjoy killing as a sport."

Eastman smiled, fitting a Lucky Strike into a slender onyx cigarette holder, but he wasn't interested in gorillas. He wanted to hunt the truly dangerous beasts. Lions. Buffalo. Needless to say, even if he had craved gorilla blood, it was out of the question now.

Eastman listened with a heavenly expression to the stentorian blare of the organ—some awful march or pavane—while Carl talked of his success filming the gorillas, and how people had responded, at the Explorers Club and other private scientific venues, to the footage. Eastman was more interested in the Akeley Camera than gorillas, and had in fact followed the career of this odd-looking machine which was being used now with more frequency by Hollywood for more demanding action sequences. Robert Flaherty had used it to film *Nanook of the North*, and as a testimonial, the director had written: "Various of my Eskimo companions, during the extreme cold weather, operated the camera at times and loaded the retorts. This says a great deal for the camera's simplicity, does it not?"*

Most recently, it had been used to film the Dempsey-Carpentier fight. Still, despite what Carl took in from his patent, the camera itself would not crank out enough money to build his hall. He needed Eastman's kind of money.

Pomeroy and Eastman briefly talked trout—Pomeroy having just returned from a fishing trip he'd taken to Alaska with a mutual friend—before turning to the more serious subject of guns, raincoats, and the best place to get good maps of Africa. (Unlike Eastman, Pomeroy had also already made one trip to Africa to go big-game hunting.) They spoke of Abercrombie & Fitch mattresses, and how Akeley used a Jeffries elephant gun, but Eastman, being in a better position to afford one, might prefer a Holland & Holland. Pomeroy averred that the Springfield .30 was a "great killing weapon." The two guests went about seducing their host with the differences between soft- and steel-nosed bullets, and how they would equip him like a sultan. Akeley recommended they go

---

*Another testimonial came from a Fox News cameraman, Russell Muth, after an incident while filming directly over Vesuvius early in 1922: "We no sooner had entered the smoke when the bottom seemed to drop out of the plane. The motor stopped and we commenced to descend very fast. We just managed to straighten out at about thirty feet from the ground and were heading for a tree. I threw the Akeley out of the plane and then we hit the tree. Fesneau, who was taking ground shots, came up soon after and found the Akeley O.K. He then took pictures of the wreck with it. [Muth suffered only a broken arm.] If I had had any other camera, it would have been smashed to bits, and we would have had no pictures. Hats off to the Akeley."

during the rainy season since there would be fewer safaris in the country at that time, "resulting in less congestion all along the line. If the rains are fairly normal the country will be more attractive than in the dry season."

Pomeroy brought out a few pictures that Martin Johnson had recently sent back, sharing the director's story about running into the safari of Prince Youssouf Kamal of Egypt, and also how they had run into the Duke and Duchess of York, and how Osa and the duchess had spent the day fishing.

Eastman glowed at the prospect of hooking Osa's bait in Africa.

Akeley was quieter about the letters he'd received from Martin, as he found much of the news dispiriting. Johnson complained that the government was so busy exterminating elephants he didn't know whether there were going to be enough left for him to make another movie. Uganda alone planned to trim back the population by ten thousand, Martin reported he had read in the papers. You could hear the panic in his letters as he encouraged Carl to get over there as quickly as possible. "Motor cars are coming in so fast that the railway from Mombasa can hardly handle the freight—five special trains brought in Fords and Durants a few days ago. The streets of Nairobi are absolutely full of motor cars during the day. It's almost like Fifth Avenue. Roads are being built everywhere . . . Half the safaris slaughter from motor cars," he wrote. "Taxi drivers advertise a trip around Kenya in three days."

It was too bad they couldn't make a sanctuary of the entire continent.

After, of course, they had got what they needed for the dioramas.

One of the things Carl would be doing on this trip beside filling in the groups would be helping a surveyor from Brussels who was going to meet him in the Congo to map out the gorilla sanctuary. Carl was also planning to bring along a group of artists, the best landscape painters he could secure, to do real-life studies for the backgrounds. He wanted to leave nothing to imagination.

Musing on this, Eastman recommended that Carl consider a painter he personally knew, by the name of Ezra Winter. Winter had done the murals for Eastman Theatre, one of Eastman's great musical contributions to Rochester. Carl said that he would gladly follow up, and took Winter's information.

The massive electric gold-leaf sconces blazed on the walls—walls which were themselves steel-reinforced concrete, on account of East-man's great fear of fire. A sensible fear, given the amount of nitrate film stock stored in his on-site vaults. Not to mention the original Van Dycks and Rembrandts hanging in various rooms.

As the dishes were cleared, the pipe organ bleated and voxed humana.

By now the moment of truth had arrived, when Akeley had to press upon Eastman the business he had come all the way to Rochester to ask. The pressure he'd been feeling to get back over to Africa before every animal he wanted for his hall was either exterminated or run over by a car—a pressure which had been building up inside like an overheated bellows—came out now in such an explosion that he must have sur-prised himself as well. With the hot bowl of his pipe clenched in his fist, stem jabbing the air in the direction of the Kodak King's chest, Carl blurted to be heard over the music. *"To hunt with me in Africa will cost you a million dollars!"*

Pomeroy tried not to let his tea slop over into his saucer. Dr. Stewart inspected his box of matches. Eastman only looked mildly startled, however, maybe even amused, as he stamped out his cigarette, set down his coffee, before standing to exit the room, with Pomeroy following, to discuss the matter privately in his library.

Left alone—Dr. Stewart having made himself scarce—Carl was stuck staring at the back of the organist's head. He relit his pipe and sat back in the wicker chair. Perhaps noticing the radio in the billiard room—a gold-knobbed Atwater Kent—he idly wondered whether East-man had heard his broadcast, back when he'd given a talk over WEAF on his travels to gorilla country, making his "plea for the preservation of harmless wild life" and offering his ideas on the sanctuary. It had been near Christmas 1923, and he'd spoken into the brass receiver for a quarter of an hour, sealed off alone in the soundproof studio, yet strangely conscious of the thousands of people whom he could not see but who were listening to his every word. The broadcast had evidently touched a chord. He'd received a mountain of correspondence.

One letter came from Jersey City: "We have just listened to your most interesting talk of your experiences in Africa. Our attention was so intense that it was a sort of shock when you had finished, an awaken-ing to our surroundings. Won't you please talk to all of us again? Sin-cerely, Mrs. H. A. Trotman."

A year after the radio broadcast, he had even received a visit from the famous Swiss psychologist Carl Jung. Jung had come to New York in the winter of 1924, and while there had sought out Akeley to discuss the logistics of travel in Africa, as he was preparing his own odyssey, a trip for the purpose of investigating the dreams and subconscious images of the "primitive mind" firsthand. He was planning to go to the area of Mount Elgon, where Mickie had nearly stolen the abandoned Wandorobo child. What was it Jung had said, about modern man suffering from a *profound uncertainty*? They had sat there, in his elephant studio, the two Carls surrounded by the skulls and spears and other fetishes gathered by Akeley over the years. Maybe in a moment of softness, showing the psychologist the death mask he had made of the Old Man of Mikeno, Carl confessed how he sometimes felt he was "really fonder of him than of myself." (He had even taken to signing letters as "The Old Man of the Mikeno.") And then perhaps prodding the great white hunter about his dreams—after all, here was a man who'd been attacked by both a leopard *and* an elephant—Jung had discussed his belief in how dreams revealed certain things about the inner anxieties of man, most especially when a person dreamed of being pursued by a wild animal, as these dream beasts were symbolic of the instinctual self. The more dangerous the animal was in the dream, the more it signified that "an instinct has been split off from the consciousness." As well, Jung said, the more "unconscious is the primitive and instinctual soul of the dreamer—and the more imperative its integration into his life if some irreparable evil is to be forestalled."

Carl sipped his coffee lest the organ music shuffle him off to sleep.

Curiously enough, it was in part the value of so-called psychology— this merciless peeling back and scraping below the mind's layers—that had ensured the success of the gorilla sanctuary. Because Carl had managed to convince his greatest backers, from the National Research Council, to the AMNH, to the likes of John C. Merriam, who had helped to move the whole thing along, that the real value of such a sanctuary was not for the sake of the gorillas, per se, but to keep them around on earth for a while longer for the value they offered science. A centerpiece of the sanctuary was to be a biological research station where scientists—the only visitors who'd be allowed inside the park— could come and observe man's cousin for the purpose of collecting data which would probably not so much interest the gorilla but help illuminate "problems of human behavior," as Merriam stated in a letter to

Henry Fairfield Osborn. Osborn, of course, was much obsessed with questions of human "problems," having only recently hosted the Second International Congress of Eugenics in the august halls of the museum itself, and was eager to consider any new information, especially as it might pertain to improving the condition of society. Obtaining such information was considered important enough that even Akeley conceded how every once in a while "the killing of a reasonable number of specimens [i.e., gorillas] for scientific institutions would be legitimate and necessary."

❦

WHEN EASTMAN AND Pomeroy came back from the library, smelling of leather-bound books, Eastman told Akeley that a million dollars was "quite beyond what [he] had planned to contribute," but that that he was prepared to give $100,000. He would sponsor six out of the forty dioramas. Something in the way he spoke made Akeley feel confident that Eastman intended to give more money, perhaps later on, once they got to Africa and he'd been bitten for real, and so he leaped to his feet and ecstatically shook Eastman's hand. Of course he hadn't really expected a million dollars. It was probably nerves that had made him demand so much. But this was grand; this was wonderful.

So it was agreed: Eastman would join Akeley and Pomeroy in Africa in May of the following year, 1926. Dr. Stewart would join them as well, and they would meet up with the Johnsons to film lions. On the drive back to the train station, as the chauffeur took them down East Avenue, past the whalebone gate that still stood outside Ward's Natural Science Establishment, Carl told Pomeroy, giddy as a child, "This is the most wonderful thing that ever happened. At last I begin to see the realization of my life's dream."

PART FOUR

Under the Volcano

CHAPTER TWENTY-EIGHT

THE MAN CARL HAD SETTLED ON AS HIS HEAD PAINTER HAD not been his first choice. His first choice—Ezra Winter—had turned the offer down flat. The second, Willard L. Metcalf, whose famous, stately landscapes Akeley had very likely seen when he'd visited the White House, had signed on for this trip of a lifetime but then dropped dead, over breakfast, of a whiskey-induced heart attack. With just two months before they set sail, and colored Christmas lights already infesting Central Park, Akeley had hastily arranged to meet another painter, Bill Leigh, the so-called Sagebrush Rembrandt. He'd seen Leigh's illustrations of the Grand Canyon, and his pensive Navajo warriors, on the covers of *Scribner's* and *Collier's*. His panoramic landscapes of the American West were perfectly suited to capture the terrifying, vertiginous grandeur of Africa.

He and his painters and his new bride had arrived in Nairobi in the spring, a couple of months ahead of his new patron saint, George Eastman. Even though Eastman had already given him $100,000, he had strongly implied that he would chip in more toward the $1.5 million Akeley still had to raise, so Carl felt assured that as soon as he had Saint George in Africa, where its charms could work their magic, it would be a fait accompli. Given Eastman's passion for preserving the world, one snapshot at a time, how could he pass up the opportunity to foot the bill for the largest still life of its kind?

While they waited for Eastman, they headed to the Lukenia Hills to work on backgrounds for the klipspringer, a bantam bouncy species of antelope which dwelled in the rocky kopjes. It was one of the big corner dioramas that Eastman's money was going to make possible. Carl was filled with optimism, and their days passed serenely and full of work. He eagerly looked forward to getting to the Congo to get backgrounds for his gorillas as well, which waited back in New York, complete, if in scenery-less limbo.

He had hoped that Mary would be swept away by his Africa, but she did not care for the arid, bleak kopjes of Lukenia. The helter-skelter boulders and slabs of cantilevered rock looked like the tumbled ruins of a temple whose upended granite steeples cast giant shadows on the rolling, stark plains. The only part of the safari that Mary had so far truly enjoyed was *before* they had gotten to Africa, when she and her husband had been received at the Royal Palace in Brussels by His Majesty, King Albert. The gardens and statuary, the oak parquet floors, the bas-reliefs by Rodin in the Throne Room, and the marble and copper walls of the Mirror Room, which Leopold II had built to create an homage to the Congo he'd never set foot in during his sinister reign, were all much more to her liking. Under gilded chandeliers, they had discussed the details of the sanctuary and made plans to meet the young zoologist Dr. Jean M. Derscheid, who was conducting a royal topological survey of the park, and who would meet them there in October.

※

IN LUKENIA, THE nights were filled with laughter around the campfire. In the morning, Leigh and his assistants fixed their easels high on the rocks with views of Mount Kenya to the north, blue and ringed by silver clouds, and the wide plains below where giant purple shadows from passing clouds grazed on the bone-yellow grass. Akeley filmed klipspringers and made tiny clay models of the diminutive gazelles, arranging them in a mock diorama he'd built out of an empty chop box, complete with a miniature backdrop hand-painted by Leigh. At night it was quiet but for the click of the klipspringers' sharp tiny hooves, and the clack of stones being turned over by baboons hunting crickets.

Come April, they returned to Nairobi to greet Eastman and Pomeroy. The banker and the Kodak King were met at the train station as well by Martin Johnson and his wife, Osa, looking like a sturdy Boy Scout in drag. Martin wore a fedora, baggy pants tucked into tall black leather boots, and a thick cardigan with an ascot. In the same slouch terai hat and flared jodhpurs and tie which the always smiling *Homo sapiens* starlet appeared in their silent Movietone features, Osa stood with her plump silver gibbon, Kalawat, draped around her neck, sucking on a fig, his big brown eyes blinking in the rain.

When the Akeleys arrived, the Johnsons had been in Africa going on three years, and still hadn't produced their second film. You couldn't bribe an elephant the same way you could a savage with a handful of beads or cigarettes, especially when it was too busy running away from its exterminators.

"This country is not half as good as it was four years ago," Martin said. "Five years from now it won't be worth a damn."

At first, they'd found the technique of letting Osa wound an animal with a grazing shot dramaturgically justifiable if it incited a furious charge; once safely offscreen, she'd put it out of its misery. They had had several close calls where they'd literally had to run for their lives. On at least one occasion they had to shoot their way out, leaving a wake of dead elephants. This was the collateral damage of making nature pictures. But Johnson didn't like killing as much as his wife did. In hopes of getting more footage of animals acting their peaceable selves he had lately been spending many dull hours stuck in stuffy blinds, reading magazines, and waiting days at a time for something to happen. So far, however, he had had lousy luck with lions. While sitting on his hands might have worked for antelope, baiting a water hole with a dead zebra and waiting passively for the king of beasts yielded nothing. After a year with too few results, and sick of filming animals lapping at water holes, Martin decided that if they were going to get pictures that would satisfy the public they would have to take bigger risks. Like stalking lions out in the open.

Akeley had chartered a private train for Eastman to take the 330-mile trip inland from Mombasa to Nairobi, but when the camera tycoon arrived he was not impressed. He found the city dirty and drab, and was depressed by the endless hovels and ceaseless rain. House servants in flowing white robes went ducking indoors out of the downpour. As they drove to the hotel, on the newly paved roads, an English bobby directed them onto Limuru Road, now lined with department stores, newsstands, and office buildings. The tallest skyscraper in Nairobi stood five stories. It was now a place where one had to be less concerned with lions than getting hit by a car. With nothing else to do, the men sat around the Norfolk Hotel bar in their crisp new puttees and khaki suits, watching the rain streaming against the windows.

Despite his pinched badger's face, Pomeroy got along well with Akeley's crew of rugged artist-hunters. But while they drank at the bar, Eastman was cold and aloof, sitting in a corner by himself in his new Burberry raincoat. As if the rain were Akeley's fault, he complained incessantly that they were wasting precious time that could have been spent hunting. It did not seem like the best time to ask for more money.

In the end, worried that Eastman was becoming unmanageably glum, Akeley hired a white hunter, Philip Percival, to take the party out to the sunnier Kedong Valley, fifty miles west of Nairobi, where his guests could kill time—and if they were lucky, maybe a few lions—until the weather improved.

The night before they left, Martin was in the lobby having a cigar, and Osa was in their room, with the window open, changing into one of the numerous items of lingerie bestowed upon her by Martin, when Kalawat began to chatter at a moth that had flown into the room. The misty halo of an electric streetlight glowed outside the open window; the rain pattered on the pavement below; and then, without warning, the monkey who had once had a bit part in *Among the Cannibal Isles of the South Pacific* suddenly jumped through the curtains into the downpour.

Osa ran to the window, but the monkey was out of reach, scrambling up the clay tiled roof. In a silk peignoir and undone hair, she flurried downstairs to the lobby, where she found Martin. Together, they ran outside, and from the street tried to call down Kalawat, who answered them with his high-pitched chattering taunts. He jumped from the roof to an overhanging tree and then back to the roof. Osa ran back upstairs to try to lure him back into the room, but just as she did so, Kalawat jumped from the roof and landed squarely against the power lines running down Delamere Avenue. The invisible volts clasped the ape without a sound, as Osa stood screaming at the open window. At last, the ape fell to the street below, where its limp, long-armed carcass lay smoking in the rain.

CHAPTER TWENTY-NINE

AFTER A BRIEF FUNERAL FOR THE GIBBON, THE AKELEY AND Eastman parties went their separate ways. The whole thing had put Carl in an agitated mood. He and Eastman had not hit it off, the first bagged game of the expedition was an electrocuted pet ape, and he was certain if Eastman's mood didn't improve it would jeopardize any chances of getting more support for the African Hall. He was also frustrated that he hadn't been able to track down his old Kikuyu friend Bill. He had not joined Akeley on his 1921 gorilla trek to the Congo, but this time Carl was eager to have his trusted friend and tracker along. But he couldn't be located, or did not want to be found, and so finally Carl had to give up and leave without him.

There was nothing left to do but get back to work and hope that eventually things could be repaired with Eastman. So they drove by automobile up to the Northern Frontier in the meantime, and it was here, in the desertlike region of Kenya Colony,* where they began work on the Water Hole Group. But here, too, it seemed as if the land had been evacuated of wildlife. After three days of travel, they saw only half a dozen antelopes, drifting like discarnate spirits. The previously abundant cheetahs, lions, elands, and rhinos were gone. The Masai they met along the way, who wore radiator caps and typewriter wheels in their

---

*British East Africa in 1926 was no longer a protectorate of Britain but a full-fledged colony and had been renamed Kenya Colony.

stretched earlobes, and jewelry twisted out of spare telegraph wire, complained that lions had begun eating their cattle because the lions' natural prey, the antelope, had practically evaporated. Still, to fill the giant
terrarium back in New York, the Akeley party settled in around the
shallow water holes with guns and easels, and bided their time painting
the deserted landscape. As they traveled farther north, along ancient
caravan routes that had served Somali cattle herders, and slave traders
from Abyssinia, they saw the peeling crumpled skeletons of Sopwith
Camels, mired down in the eroding sands like machine-creatures of a
lost age, guns rusted. The land had an almost ego-obscuring theatrical
vastness and reminded Leigh of the Painted Desert in Arizona. In this
region the only vegetation was thorny but in it lived the gentle Samburu,
who carried soft iron spears to defend their sheep against lions, and
who, when she saw them, put Mary Jobe Akeley in mind of Egyptians.

MARY FOUND THE Northern Frontier no less barren and lonely than
the rocks of Lukenia. The entire time she had seen only two flowers: a
yellow rose and something that looked like a pale purple petunia. The
movie people were surely having more fun, flitting about greener
regions of Africa with the multimillionaire Eastman. It was hard not to
feel like she was missing out. But her husband had his work do to: his
endless, never-ending life's labor. He worked so hard, so much of the
time, sometimes it made him seem like a dull man. It was true. But
lately he was at the opposite pole, moodwise, as if something had taken
over his personality. He was in a near craze, consumed by his efforts to
collect the idealized giraffe. She had never seen him like this. He'd been
out every day, all day, for three weeks. She was sure it would have been
easier if he didn't have his heart set so specifically on a *sixteen-foot-tall*
giraffe—sixteen feet *exactly*—as if it were going to stand and be measured for its coffin before Carl shot it.

But lately, he had become more the surly old man. He snapped at his
helpers and carried about him an air of doom, his eyes fixed to some
distant, impossible problem. Tensions in camp ran high. When Akeley
returned yet another day in a foul mood without his giraffe, he found
the morale of the camp falling apart. One of the younger artists had
become so sick with fright over the nightly serenade of lions that he had
fled camp and gone home at the earliest chance. Then the senior painter,

Leigh, and the museum preparator, Richard Raddatz, who also served as the safari's all-around handyman, had been fighting. Apparently Leigh had asked if Raddatz would fix one of his equipment boxes that had broken, and Raddatz had refused. When Leigh asked for the tools to do the job himself, Raddatz locked the toolbox in his tent. When Leigh complained to Akeley, Akeley chewed out Raddatz.

"What's this got to do with me?" Raddatz asked, close enough so Carl could smell the chewing tobacco in his grizzled cheek. For an artist entrusted with the most delicate work of the expedition—preserving the native fragile fronds and gossamer flower petals—he was no less a cowboy than the Sagebrush Rembrandt.

"Everything up to a kick in the pants!" Akeley shouted.

Mary was worried over her husband's increasing irritability, but at the same time it was more peaceful when he was gone, so she was happy to stay behind during the day and keep house. Even if it meant her only company was the natives.

She found the natives childish but almost endearing if "properly managed." For her part, as safari manager, she had to be a stern taskmaster over the tea, sugar, flour, and rations for these overgrown children. It seemed they had an insatiable appetite for sweets. Likewise, she disapproved of the way her tent boy always carried the towel over his shoulder, which she thought was a filthy habit. And yet she didn't like the way they were always begging for soap and then hoarding it. "You boys must eat soap," she said.

On the other hand, Mary was surprised that not all the blacks looked the same, as she'd expected. She was surprised to find that each had their own distinguishing features, just like white people, and that after a while she could tell one individual from another. They even had their own personalities. This pleased her, though she wasn't sure why. All in all, the natives somehow reminded her of the pet collie she'd had as a girl, her only playmate.

One morning, while Carl was out trying to find a custom-tailored giraffe, an envoy from the nearby Samburu tribe came for a visit, led by the favorite wife of their chief. For the last three nights, while the moon seemed to stay full, the Akeleys had been kept awake by the sound of drums which Carl said was the Samburu, who lived nearby in thatched cone-shaped huts made of skin and thorns, celebrating a wedding. At first she'd been frightened by the drums, but then decided they were romantic, and as a newlywed herself, sort of, she was delighted for the company.

This Samburu queen, who was tall and beautiful, arrived in camp with a retinue of girls with shaved scalps glistening with animal fat, and beautiful gold hoop earrings and numerous concentric hoops of red glass bead necklaces above their naked breasts, and a coterie of young male warriors who were as adorned as the women, hair long and twined into fine braids caked red with clay and tied back in loose earthy knots. The young warriors had never seen automobiles and gathered around the machines, inspecting the hood ornaments, peering into the grilles, tapping the wheels gently with their spears, and examining their own funhouse reflections in the chrome and dusty windows.

The Samburu chief's wife was named Billy Billy. Or this, at least, was what Mary decided to call her. She had high cheekbones and around her long throat and hard gleaming clavicles were draped an abundance of beaded necklaces, like an extravagant ruff. She was several heads taller than Mary, and as elegant and graceful as a giraffe, but not nearly as timid. Fiery copper bracelets and anklets wound about her lithe arms and bare smooth legs. Right away, Mary sensed the Samburu queen found something amusing about her own appearance. Her people stood behind their queen and regarded the cooks working for the whites with clear contempt. But, all the same, they had brought gifts of milk mixed with sheep's blood soured in calabashes that smelled of bitter smoke. Mary could not bear to put this to her lips, but instead, while her own porters guzzled it as if it were the finest nectar, she invited her guests to join her for bread and jam.

She fixed them tea with sugar as well. They loved the sugar, and when offered more, took it gladly, licking the crystals off their flattened palms. As they visited, Mary tried not to stare at Billy Billy's exposed breasts, her scantily clad legs, or any other part of that regal beauty not concealed by the soft skins of uncertain dead animals. The giant hoop earrings chimed lightly as she giggled, sucking sugar from her thumb. Mary felt proud for being a successful hostess with such an exotic people. Yet she got the distinct feeling the younger women were making fun of her own peculiar dress. If only they knew that she didn't dress like a man in her own country. She tried to make her own ladylike status clear by explaining that she, too, was married to the chief, of sorts, of their own tribe, the bwana of their safari. She wanted to let her guest know that her husband, also, was a great hunter, but for a greater *scientific* purpose. But Billy Billy stopped her. She and her companions craved more sugar. Mary thought about it. It would be their third or fourth helping. Their safari had only a limited number of provisions, and she knew how the natives were like children when it came to things like this: if you gave them some, they wouldn't stop pestering for more, and so, with as much grace as she could muster, she rested her hand on Billy Billy's wrist and told her, firmly, "No."

Maybe it had come out too firmly.

When she heard the severity of her tone she felt she sounded like a harsh parent, but it was too late, and no amount of explaining would explain away her rudeness.

Nonetheless, the next day Billy Billy and the other women returned. They took Mary by surprise while she was in her bath. They had decided they were willing to sell milk to the safarists for the duration of their stay despite her rude behavior the day before. They stood patiently over her blanched, pear-shaped body lying naked in the lukewarm bath, as if they had only found her knitting. Forced to disembark from the tub and get dressed under their gaze, she could not avoid the insolent mirth they made over her hair. True, limp from the bath, her pageboy cut was even less flattering than usual, but now she was forced to stand naked, portly, and flat-footed as the women crowded around her and, in hysterics, examined the hair on her head, pulling away their hands in gleeful disgust, hooting shrieks of disbelief at such an unbecoming and impractical growth. Finally she managed to get into a robe and began to self-consciously comb her hair, patiently enduring their presence, perhaps out of fear of doing otherwise.

It was then that Billy Billy insisted Mary give her her safari outfit. The queen told her, with a peremptory stare, that she must have it. Mary looked at her field suit hanging above her cot and told her no, but Billy Billy continued to insist. Mary could not help but smile at the image of this Samburu wearing the British khakis, with her bald pate concealed by a pith helmet. When Mary told her that, in truth, she could not give her the suit because even if she wanted to, she could not live without this artificial skin in this inhospitable wilderness, Billy Billy pouted and said that Mary should give it to her anyway. Mary did not fail to see the smirk. Again, she felt like a clod, and maybe not a little sick of being the subject of so much fun.

It was then that their attention shifted to the mirror. It was the first mirror the women had ever seen, or so they claimed. Before she could stop her, Billy Billy snatched away the mirror and darted outside into the sunlight, and then held the glass to her face, staring at her eyes for a long while, batting her eyelashes, and then commencing to explore the rest of her body from every vulgar angle, all the while talking to herself, or the reflection of herself, admiringly, as if she were completely alone. When she came back to Mary she was in near tears, holding the mirror to her heart, clearly grieved at the idea of relinquishing this magic window. Finally, stunned by how taken the woman was with this relative trinket, Mary submitted and gave it to her as a gift. She hoped it would dispel her guilt over the sugar debacle of the previous day.

But her redemption was short-lived. Because as soon as the other women saw how she had favored Billy Billy, they felt sorely neglected. It was unfair that she had not presented them each with a magic window so they could gaze at their own nomadic beauty. They crowded around her, imploring Mary, pressing against her, with their babies fastened to their hips with goatskins, and petulant want filling their eyes. Some of the women had even begun to ransack her tent, unwilling to go away empty-handed. They searched her belongings, rifling through her toilet case, and when they found one smudged mirror tied to the back of her dressing case, they appealed to her sense of decency and fairness. The only thing she could do would be to smash it and give them each their own shard, but that was ridiculous. Besides, the mirror on the back of her dressing case was the only one she had left now. How else would she fix her pitiful hair? She couldn't give it away, or else she herself would be mirrorless—but this excuse elicited little sympathy from the Samburu women.

CHAPTER THIRTY

HAVING FAILED TO BEFRIEND THE NATIVES, MARY WAS HAPPY when Carl finally returned with his giraffe. Amazingly, he had found one within inches of the coveted sixteen-foot mark. Now it lay dead, its long blue tongue unwound on the grass. Looked at in a certain way, with its vestigial nubby horns, like two velvety ball-peen hammers, and its black-and-white webbed skin, the giraffe was almost reminiscent of a very large—if more graceful—banana slug.

That night, with the giant skin stretched in the tree like a grisly sail, its deposed rib cage suspended between its legs, the hyenas came out of their cool dirt earth-holes to feast on the remains left in a heap just out-side camp. The shrieks and barks of the scavengers fighting over the entrails kept the Akeley party awake until dawn. Come morning, Leigh stepped out of his tent, stretching his long limbs, and said, "Did you hear that goddamn cyclone of bestiality last night?" Akeley laughed for the first time in weeks.

✀

SHORTLY AFTERWARD, CARL left for Embu to get supplies and was late returning. He should have been back in the morning, so by lunch-time, Mary began to worry. When he still wasn't back that night, she became frantic.

"Don't worry," Raddatz said. "Carl drives like a bat out of hell. He probably just bottomed out on the Kagio road." It was why he carried extra water and tinned sardines. It wasn't until the next day, late in the afternoon, that he finally reappeared. Raddatz was right. Not exactly following the road, but going overland, using a compass to guide himself back to camp, Carl had been driving too fast on the trackless veldt—pushing it upward of twenty-five miles per hour—when he'd snapped an axle. Stuck, he'd spent the night sipping Scotch and listening to jackals. Though he'd torn cartilage loose from his breastbone when he slammed into the steering column, he didn't mind so much. The Scotch killed the pain. He had the stars for company. He liked the time alone.

A day later—about a month since the Akeley party had arrived at the water hole—they saw a glimmer on the horizon: white silent flashes bouncing in the distance. Sunlight on glass or metal. It was moving toward them, and soon enough they heard the downward shifting whine of truck gears, and the bleat of Klaxons, and they stood there squinting with their hands on their rifles until a dozen or so vehicles with eighty black men piled on the back and hanging off the running boards, some jumping off and now running alongside, came into focus. When he saw who it was, Akeley stuck an arm into the car and began to bleat his own horn back in welcome.

Bringing up the tail end of the Eastman safari—the biggest motorized safari ever—was a touring car piloted by Osa Johnson, her headlights adorned with chaplets of morning glories. Martin stood tall in the back, hat flipped back and cravat fluttering, eye pressed to the viewfinder and grinding away to capture for posterity the belated reunion of the two lost tribes of Kodak Nation.

Since they'd last met, the Eastman party had left the Kedong Valley, where they'd had some luck with lions, and then gone north where they'd been hunting buffalo in Marsabit, but without as much luck. Nonetheless, Eastman was less crabby than he'd been in Nairobi. In fact, he was almost giddy. The cause of his new effervescence quickly became evident: it was all about Osa. The old man—who some suspected was a virgin or worse—was head over heels. He was gaga. He loved the zaftig safari flapper. She teased him like an adoring niece, and he called her his "little big game hunter." They were constantly flirting and giggling, and though she wasn't much of a cook, it turned out that he was, so while the rest of the men mixed cocktails, the tycoon and the ingenue played in the kitchen, making biscuits, huckleberry pies, corn bread, and lemon tarts. (Mary was so excited to have civilized company that she even squandered enough sugar for a nut and raisin cake.) That such sweet and warm smells were capable of being produced by such a cold and fussy man amused the others, yet they were more than happy to enjoy the delights he and his girlfriend cooked up while they gabbed. Meanwhile, the porters cooked their mealy-meal and boiled green bananas in empty petrol tins over the campfires, eating the porridge with their fingers.

A now tanned Pomeroy sat back with his sundowner, smirking at his industrialist friend's new frivolity, and watching as Eastman's personal physician, Dr. Stewart, bandaged Akeley's battered ribs. The scratchy, happy sound of a phonograph playing "The Black Bottom Dance" came from the Johnsons' makeshift tent: an acre of airplane cloth canopied over their automobile.

> *I done shown y'all my black bottom*
> *You ought to learn that dance*

Osa had inadvertently done Carl a great favor. There was renewed opportunity here in the old man's euphoria. The safari romance— though clearly platonic, and Martin was far from threatened—might have softened the curmudgeon enough to allow Carl another chance at hitting him up for more money.

That night around the fire, they shared bits of news and gossip. How the Eastman party had crossed paths near the Kenyan border with Ralph Pulitzer, hunting lions. Martin told Akeley how, just a couple weeks before Eastman had gotten to the Kedong Valley, a Mrs. G. L. Bailey, who had also been hunting lions with her husband, had been mangled by two rhinoceroses. One of the beasts had caught the woman with its horn, and split her up the side, before then stomping the gin out of her with the eager help of its mate. Somehow the woman had survived and was convalescing in Nairobi.

This proved his point—Akeley grimaced as Stewart tightened the gauze—that hunting lions wasn't half as dangerous as most other things. The big-game hunters had grown bored killing them years ago, Akeley said, and had to make a game of it now, like shooting them from horseback or using nothing but revolvers.

But nothing could keep Eastman from regaling the others with the story his companions had already heard a hundred times since the

Kedong: how he had shot his first lion, and how beautiful and monstrously big it was, a giant maned beast that he'd nailed with two soft-nosed rounds—a shot in the crotch followed by a quick shot in the chest—and how the night after this feat the natives had carried him around the fire on their shoulders, chanting their hunting songs in praise of the godlike brave white warrior, et cetera. Akeley certainly felt the sting of regret that he hadn't been able to deliver such a moment for his patron personally. However, he also saw his chance to woo Eastman back. The old man still desperately wanted to kill a buffalo. He seemed addicted to taking increasingly risky chances.

Just a few weeks earlier, Eastman had taken his 16mm Cine Kodak and walked up to a grazing rhino like a patient on laudanum until he was only twenty yards away. Even when the rhino charged, Eastman continued filming, as if the camera gave him protection from danger, like an amulet, and in fact at the last minute he had actually stepped aside and *reached out and brushed his hand against the side of the passing rhino.* When it reared back to charge again, however, Osa had shot it and it fell just six yards from Eastman, who kept grinding away obliviously. It was unclear whether she'd saved his life or merely prevented a suicide.

Killing buffalo was an entirely different thing than killing lions, Akeley said. They were more aggressive and wily than the lion. And where there used to be thousands of buffs in the swamps along the Theba River, now there were fewer than a hundred, so they were smarter. Or wary, at least. They didn't graze in plain sight. They hid in the swamp, where they were much more dangerous to come upon suddenly.

What hunting buffalo came down to in the end, Carl said, was hard work.

"I've done nothing but hard work my entire life," Eastman sneered, fondling in his soft hands the finest British pith helmet money could buy.

And so, by the end of the evening, Akeley and Eastman had hatched a plan for hunting buffalo in the Tinga Tinga. But once there, even if there had been any buffalo, the sound of Eastman's ceaseless slapping at mosquitoes, and his tormented cries and cursing, chased them all away. Disappointed after only a few days of tracking, Eastman suggested that they venture farther down the Theba, but the boggy ground proved so difficult for travel that the springs on his Buick snapped. At wit's end, and without Osa to keep him happy, the camera tycoon decided that hunting buffalo was not his cup of tea after all, and he quit the mosquito-infested swamp to travel south for the hotter plains of the Serengeti. There, he would join the Johnsons filming lions.

CHAPTER THIRTY-ONE

AKELEY WAS OUTRAGED. HE FELT ROBBED. EVEN THOUGH AT this point Eastman had not given the Johnsons a fraction of what he'd promised the museum, he could not help but feel that he was competing against the younger moviemakers. Eastman continued to throw money at the Johnsons—he had just bought their expedition three new Willys-Knight cars: one "big six" and two one-ton trucks.

Still determined to get his way, Akeley quickly juggled the expedition's schedule so he could follow his truant patron down into the Serengeti. Before abandoning his painters in the swamp, he told Leigh, "I'm going down into Tanganyika to get five hundred thousand dollars for this work from Eastman." He had begun to act as obsessed with the tycoon as if he were chasing after some rare, gold-horned antelope.

It was toward the end of July 1926 when Carl and Mary left the swamp. Before leaving, he shot off a telegram to Martin Johnson.

> WE ARE "HEADING IN." . . . PERFECTLY CONVINCED
> THAT IF I CONTINUE TO TAKE MYSELF AND MY
> WORK SO SERIOUSLY IT WILL RESULT IN COMPLETE
> DISASTER. PERHAPS WE'LL HAVE A BIT OF FUN
> WITH THE LIONS. LOVE, AKE.

And then they took the long rutted dusty road down into the heart of lion country in what had formerly been German East Africa but after the war had been renamed Tanganyika by the British. After three days in the car, seeing hardly another soul except the occasional Boer ox-wagon trundling across the prairie, the Akeleys found Eastman's party bivouacked along the lower Grumeti River.

When they arrived, they found the camp in a flurry of activity. Martin was eager to film a lion-spearing ceremony, and his new best friend, George Eastman, had trucked in forty Lumbwa warriors from the nearby town of Narok. The recruits loitered, squatting on their haunches, some holding geometrically decorated cowhide shields and tall, withy leaf-shaped spears all pointed in the air as if they were collectively dowsing for the big cats. Some of them wore robes of skin, but most were naked, their faces and arms painted white and black and their white ostrich-feather headdresses giving them the flair of cabaret dancers. These were the extras for hire. Johnson, who did not exist apart from his camera, was cranking away, taking in the warriors' blank stares. Daniel Pomeroy was not around, having gone into western Tanganyika to hunt greater kudu. Eastman stood akimbo in his tall suede boots, energetically talking to his hired white hunters, potbelly thrust forward, pink turtlish face shining from a fresh shave.

They could truck in Lumbwa spearmen, but it was not so easy to cast the lion. Even once you had a lion there was no promise it would agree to be speared cinematically. A few days earlier, for instance, they had surrounded one lion, but the cat had broken through the circle with a spear sticking out of its head, only to disappear down the nearest *donga,* one of the many dusty gullies that ran through the veldt like a system of grass-concealed canals. The Lumbwa were too afraid to go in after it, and so after an hour or so of listening to the lion's growls of pain, Eastman's hired white hunter, Philip Percival, picked up his gun and stepped toward the lair before the others could stop him. They waited anxiously, staring at the motionless curtain of grass. After a few minutes they heard two shots.

"I was tired of having that beast suffer," Percival said, when he crawled back out. "But don't tell the Missus."

The Lumbwa seemed a little shamed by the incident, and today, upon the Akeleys' arrival, they seemed forlorn and bored. But now word arrived that another lion had been found not too many miles out, and so the Lumbwa were packed aboard the waiting trucks and motored out to the temporary set of yet another *donga,* where a hopefully more docile lion awaited. Spears clattering, they clambered off the trucks, and quickly set up a perimeter, while the cameras began to roll at a slightly safer distance. Wearing a V-neck sweater and wool hat, Carl had set up his own camera on the north side of the lair, while Mary sat smiling behind the wheel, taking it all in like a letterman's sweetheart at an early autumn scrimmage.

Percival's men, who had cornered the lion, now covered it long enough for the Lumbwa to complete their pregame rituals. This pep rally involved forming a circle around their chief and praying loudly to Mungo, the god who would assure them of this victory of a hundred men against one lion. As they gyrated and shook their spears, the ostrich feathers bound to their heads palsied silently and their naked feet pounded on the muted grass.

It did not take long. The headman directed his advance guard to flush out the lion, while the others positioned themselves strategically, if timidly, around the *donga,* and when the thrashers moved through the grass and the lion erupted the swiftest man cast his spear first and the others followed quickly. Some spears cracked like stick insects smacking midflight, falling harmless to the grass, but most found their mark. The lion staggered, bristling with javelins, flipping gruesomely like a harpooned sea animal. Its mane was clotted with blood. Teeth bared pitifully. It was not so different than it had been with the Nandi almost twenty years earlier. The only difference today was they had captured it all in stereoscope.

Cheering on the game, Eastman was clapping and hooting even as the light faded from the lion. When it fell a bugle made out of the horn of some other luckless animal was sounded, and the hunters danced around the corpse.

"Okuri! Okuri!" He is dead! He is dead!

They knelt by the lion to feel its fading power. Even vanquished, the lion still managed to telegraph a kind of reassurance to its killers: that the primeval fears that had troubled them for millennia had been finally laid to rest, tamed once and for all. It was a joy to take turns being photographed holding up its giant lifeless head, smiling at the laborious absurdity of their triumph.

CHAPTER THIRTY-TWO

Two weeks after the lion spearing, Raddatz and Leigh showed up, mosquito-bitten, differences apparently settled, having completed their studies of the Tinga Tinga. Leigh was surprised to find Carl looking fifteen years older than the last time he'd seen him. His skin looked gray, the lines in his face were deeper, and his already stooped shoulders were even more stooped, as if he had been carrying someone around for the last few weeks. Shortly after their arrival, he and Carl went out to scout locations for the background painting for the Plains Group.

Akeley drove, Leigh riding shotgun with a sketch pad in his lap. A short distance from camp they were engulfed by the mind-numbing expanse of lion country, an endless flat veldt where here and there stood mobs of loitering topis, gnus, and waterbucks—devil-horned harte-beests by the thousands. Giant herds grazed between the sinuous tire tracks winding through the grass, and the wildebeests' rumps shone in the afternoon sun, their long weird faces marking the passage of the intruders. More than once the car was brought to a standstill when the crowds of ungulates grew too thick and massed around till it seemed the car itself would be crushed. All they could do was inch forward, caught up in the slow-motion stampede, trapped in a traffic jam of a million uneasy acres of zebra stripes, withers, spiraled and recurvate horn.

"There's probably five million animals on this plain, but a few years ago there were three times that many," Akeley said, waving away the flies, and juking the wheel when a flap of dewlap abruptly mopped the windshield like a flesh squeegee.

It seemed to Leigh they were passing the turnstile of creation.

Once the car emerged, the two men drove in silence. Finally, they came to a range of hills and parked the car, then hiked up to an overlook of the plains and a zagging watercourse below. Akeley still hadn't spoken, so Leigh refrained from talking. The silence was not so unwelcome here, but, still, Akeley seemed like a different man than the one he'd known at the beginning of their adventure, during the easygoing days in Lukenia. They walked out along the tree-lined ridge until they came to a spot where the sunset against a distant cluster of shadowy kopjes gave them pause. The painter took his handkerchief and tied it around a branch so he could find the way again when he returned.

They lingered for a while, silent, looking at, if not enjoying, the sight of one more extinguished day.

"This will make a marvelous group," Leigh finally said. "It should be a corner group in the hall."

Akeley cleared his throat. "It will be," he said.

Adopting a deliberately overflown tone, perhaps trying to make his friend laugh, Leigh framed the view between his broad hands. "It will be a page of natural history that will survive, perhaps, after much of this animal life has been wiped out—a record of something which never can be again—a document of *inestimable* value."

"Exactly." Akeley smiled weakly.

"There is no price too high to pay for such a document!" Leigh said.

After a tense pause, Akeley nodded. "Absolutely none." He was looking at the pith helmet in his hands, grimacing.

Leigh retied the handkerchief unnecessarily. The sky was deepening to lilac. Finally, he got up the nerve to ask.

"Did you, uh, get your five hundred thousand dollars?"

The broken vessels in Carl's eyes flamed. He had, in fact, made his final plea to Eastman. He had tried to rekindle the importance of his work in the old man's mind, gently reminding him that the true time capsule, the work that would be encased in marble and glass, not the more fragile nitrate of Johnson's films, would be his African Hall once it was completed in all its glory. He wanted Eastman to know it was not too late for him to be his Medici. Perhaps it had been a mistake to bring it up while Eastman was baking pies. The old man had been laughing over a nightmare Osa was telling him she'd had back in New York where she'd dreamed a rhinoceros was coming up the fire escape. When Akeley interrupted, Eastman made the face of a man who had just bitten into the brown spot of an apple. He merely paused to shake the flour off his apron, wiped his glasses, then flatly refused Carl. Now, Akeley clenched the brim of his helmet as if he would snap it off. "The old tightwad didn't give me a cent!"

CHAPTER THIRTY-THREE

I T WAS AROUND THE TENTH DAY OF FILMING LIONS WHEN SMOKE was seen on the horizon. It was easy to imagine that the sun itself had set the earth aflame, but it was only grass fires set by the Masai to hurry along the sweet, young shoots for their gentle-teethed cattle. As the safarists drove into the burned-over area, where the ground was still warm but not hot enough to melt their tires, the soot took flight and crunched under their wheels like paper cinders. A flurry of ashes lifted in their wake like black-winged insects.

❧

EVEN AFTER THE ongoing success of the lion filming—they would crank out 4,400 feet of film in less than three weeks—Eastman and Akeley kept their distance. There was no longer any pretense of warmth whatsoever between the two men. Perhaps it was that both were alike—at least in terms of being single-minded obsessives, intent on embalming the world around them. Eastman and Akeley may have occupied the same camp, but they hardly spoke a word, each acting as if the other did not exist. That pretense became easier to maintain the morning Akeley failed to materialize from his tent.

When his tent boy brought Carl a bowl of warm water for shaving, he found that bwana was sick. Carl felt feverish and nauseated and said that the others should set out that day without him; he could not take another day in the field; just the day before, after fourteen hours in the

baking sun and being jostled around in the back of the car with the rattling petrol tins, he had told Mary, "This afternoon has been like living
a year all in one day."

When they returned that evening, he was outside the door to his
tent, wrapped in blankets, where he remained for the rest of the night,
mute. The most he would eat was hot broth and a poached egg. He
looked hollow and melancholy, as if something had gone from him, and
after a few days, it put everyone else in a gloomy and anxious mood.
Days passed without him emerging from his tent. Even though he himself had persuaded the Johnsons to come film in Africa, he must have
realized that it wouldn't matter if he ever came out of his tent again; the
future had been decided, and his own particular contribution, as revo-
lutionary as it once may have been, was already on its way to becoming
obviated. Film left no place for dioramas.

How ironic, though, that he should compete against a medium he
himself had helped to bring into its own.

The only good news, perhaps, was that once again his old friend Bill
had appeared in camp, as mysteriously as ever. Carl had searched for
him back in Nairobi without luck, but now, when he needed him most,
Bill had managed to track them down out of the blue. It seemed like the
boy—the man—had always been able to read his mind.

Bill now helped Mary to nurse Carl night and day, while the others
continued to film and work around him.

At night he groaned and tossed in his cot. Still, nobody knew exactly
what the matter was. Dr. Stewart, Eastman's personal physician, said he
did not think anything at all was the matter, except maybe nerves. Then
one morning, Eastman decided to up and go elephant hunting three
hundred miles away in Meru. The grass fires were growing closer. It only
made sense. He left without bothering to say good-bye to Akeley. The
others could hear Carl in his tent, retching into his bedpan.

At night a fringe of flame burned on the hills, the veldt lit up like
Atlantic City. Raddatz and the others began discussing moving camp
or building a brake. The slow-burning fire moved in a thin line, leaving
a powdery black nothing behind. The smoke whorled, genielike, and
crept under the tent flaps, until finally the choking black soot covered
everything in camp, infested their food so their mouths were full of
ash, blackened their clothes.

When Pomeroy returned from hunting kudu, and saw how bad Carl was, he urged Mary to take him back to Nairobi to seek medical treatment. So the next morning, as the grass fires grew ever closer, and the others who planned to stay prepared to move camp, they set up a cot in the back of one of the trucks. Then with Mary driving and Bill riding in the back by Carl's side, they began the rugged three-hundred-mile trek back to Nairobi. It was September 3. When they were several miles away, Carl could still see the welling plumes of smoke in the receding distance.

❧

MARY TOOK HIM to the hospital in Nairobi, but the doctors could find nothing wrong. There was no sign of malaria or blackwater. A light case of typhoid maybe. Or, more likely, the overwork and strain of the trip had worn him down. The doctors said it was most likely simply a case of "nervous collapse." Regardless, it didn't matter, because there were no beds to offer him. The hospital was full. One of the patients preventing Akeley from getting a bed was Mrs. G. L. Bailey, the white woman who'd been rolled by the two angry rhinoceroses.

With no room left for any more safari casualties—and since the doctors couldn't exactly find anything wrong with Carl anyway—he was sent to the Kenya Nursing Home. There, he could dwindle away with the early settlers in their twilight, and the hoary British consuls with one mosquito boot in the grave. It was difficult to imagine a more ignoble setting, or anticlimactic end to such a life of adventure. But, alas, lives led adventurously or not—most, really—come to mediocre ends all too often. Why should Carl Akeley's have been any different? Life fades to gray, even for the extraordinary. And so the man who had once strangled a leopard with his bare hands—hands on which the tendons now stood visible against his frail skin—lay propped on a pillow, unable to light his own cigarettes, waiting on death while his dowdy wife read to him from a collection of predictably unpredictable O. Henry stories.

CHAPTER THIRTY-FOUR

T HE COLLEAGUES CARL HAD LEFT BEHIND IN THE SERENGETI had given up on him by now. It only seemed a matter of time before their leader would be taken under by his mysterious affliction—or was it just the nonspecific slow blight of age? They had all watched his gradual decline since they'd been in Lukenia.

So imagine their surprise upon returning to Nairobi, in mid-October, having completed their work, to find Carl up and out of bed and engaged in dialogue with a sallow-looking young man with a French accent. A series of large crinkled maps were spread out on Akeley's bed and unfurled on his small writing desk, pinned down with dirty dishes. The maps were aswirl with concentric rings. Only a smattering of unpronounceable village names appeared between the contours and altitudinal numbers. The region of the maps was only half charted; the full extent of its wilderness ungraphed. The young man, not a day over twenty-five, had slicked-back hair and the sunken eyes and woolen suit of an undertaker. He held his own cigarette carefully aloft and away from the map, which he hunched over with a prismatic compass, while Akeley stood beside him like an eager student. The young Belgian, who in fact was to be the administrator-general of Parc National Albert, and who was here to complete a geographic survey of the Kivu, and to make a census of the gorillas, had resuscitated Akeley with his maps. The color had returned to his face; the strength was back in his voice; he was lighting his own cigarettes, one excitedly after another.

He firmly shook Leigh's hand and introduced everybody to the Belgian, whose name was Dr. Jean M. Derscheid, the cartographer and zoologist whom the Akeleys had met previously at the palace in Belgium. With his face almost pressing the map, Carl exhaled a cloud of cigarette smoke that drifted across the creases like mist. "My friends," he said. "It is time to go to where the fairies dance."

⟡

AFTER THEIR MOTORCADE traveled 360 miles to Kabale, Uganda, and arranged with the District Commisioner's Office there for two hundred porters, they began the last 125-mile leg of their trek into the Virungas by foot. Two days' walk past Lake Bunyony, they came to a bamboo region of prehistoric lakes that had turned to blackish bogs, and the muck clung to the porters like tar. Wading across, Derscheid held his oak-and-brass survey tripod above his head, and Leigh did likewise with his easel. The rain had stopped now, and as they passed through the putrescent treeless swamp the sun was brutal. But mostly, as they trudged uphill, higher, along the narrowing grass trails, they were engulfed by a bamboo belt. The light was different in the bamboo: golden-green and slanted. Aside from the murmur of the porters, it was dead silent during the day. There was not even the buzz of insects.

In Kabale, before they had begun by foot, Carl asked Mary if she wanted a chair to be carried in. She said no, that walking had always been one of her chief pleasures in life, but soon enough her romantic notions festered like the blisters on her feet. The first day's hike was the most grueling fifteen miles she'd ever walked. The dense humid forest now felt like being in a leafy oven. As she slogged up the trail, the porters swished past, bumping against her, causing her to lose her footing. Each day was interminable and nerve-racking. Finally, at dusk on the third day, they came into the highland village of Behungi, where they had a god's view across the deep rolling valleys and bottomless gulches of trees and scattered blue lakes, to the volcanoes that stood like smoking anthills along the border between Uganda and the Congo. When the sun set they could see the bloodshot eye of Nyamlagira flaring in the distance—it beckoned them onward. It was so serenely beautiful here, and Mary was so tired, she begged Carl to rest a day, but there was no time, he said, and so the next morning the safari began its slow, steep, mile-long descent.

"When we return over this trail," Carl said, "we'll start at daylight. I'll never climb this hill in the heat of noon again."

❦

THE FIRST DAY after crossing into the Congo things began to go badly. Whereas the roads in Uganda had been broad and shaded by trees, here the upward path was narrow and rocky. They were now in the Kivu, the most primitive region of the Congo. The aura of the place was on an entirely wilder frequency. The vegetation more chaotic. Even the grass huts in the little desolate villages they marched through looked more feral than the huts in Uganda. They were half-alive, with ferns crowning the rooftops. Misshapen pumpkins on witchy-looking vines grew out the sides of the huts like unchecked cancers.

Mary had been watching her husband nervously for the past several days. His pace had slowed. He seemed weaker and more distracted. If she had already expected to lose him in Nairobi, it now became like watching a ghost struggle up the mountain. So when Raddatz cried out for a hammock, and she looked back and saw Carl on the ground, she thought the worst. He had fallen along the worst possible section of trail: a narrow ledge skirting a steep canyon. Mist from a cataract rose up from the chasm too far below to hear. He lay there, on the brink of a thousand-foot drop, mumbling like an idiot, *I have to think what's best to do.*

Given the lethal narrowness of the path, it was nightmarish enough already for the porters given the task of carrying the half-dead white man, but then thunderclouds darkened the mountain. You could hardly hear the men shouting over the downpour as they struggled not to slip on the mud-slicked path, lest they spill the catafalque over the abyss. Finally, they stopped and hastily set up a tent on the trail to take cover.

Bill got Carl's bedding from the rear end. They would have stayed for the night, but being behind the rest of the safari, and without food and water, when the rain slackened they moved on. Carl stared hollowly at the dripping trees. Muted flashes of lightning carved his ragged white face out of the jungle twilight. They hiked three more miles before coming to open country bordering native *shambas* where the rest of the safari had already bivouacked for the night. As soon as they arrived, Bill and Mary set up a tent for Carl, and though he said he felt much better, he collapsed at once and was soon unconscious, still dressed. For the rest of the evening, in her own tent, Mary listened to the storm, watching the rain creep under the sides.

The next day Carl felt good enough to walk on his own. Yet, still unable to keep up with the rest of his party, he kept to the rear, in the company of Bill and his wife. He and Mary walked together, sometimes holding hands, talking little. While the path remained muddy they had to concentrate on each step, but soon the clouds passed and the sun reappeared and would stay broiling above them for the next ten long days. Even more oppressive than the heat, though, which dried and cracked the mud underfoot, was the suffocating monotony of the trail. It was so narrow that at times staring ahead gripped Mary with the claustrophobic illusion of a tunnel closing in on her, and she had to stare at her feet until she could shake the feeling. But then the interminable sight of her own feet marching without end filled her with a different kind of despair.

Carl trudged on solemnly, shoulders stooped, his walking stick jabbing the soft earth. Day after day they swished through the overgrown maze, marching onward, through jungle and humid swamp, mangroves and leprous-looking palm trees. They crossed rivers of alligators and rhinos whose dim, poodlish eyes stared impassively at the passing humans, and ever higher and higher, up into the Kivu mountains. "Just put your head down and go," Carl muttered. "That's the only way to do it."

CHAPTER THIRTY-FIVE

IN THE MORNING IT WAS RAINING AGAIN WHEN SOME OF THE porters began clearing a path upward toward the saddle between Mikeno and Karisimbi—the old site of Carl's gorilla camp. As the men hacked at the dense undergrowth, their breath was chalky in the frigid air. For three days they chopped upward, clearing a path for the artists, and for three days the rain did not cease.

Meanwhile, the rest of the party went about their chores below. Porters not busy moving the camp up to the saddle busied themselves by making charcoal for burning later at higher altitude. Leigh painted studies of the native flora in his tent. Working under the steady patter of rain in his own tarpaulin atelier, Raddatz cast the same delicate fronds and pistils in plaster—preserving samples in vials of formalin— only stopping every few minutes to spit a gob of tobacco juice outside his door. While Derscheid tromped around with his level rod and theodolite, determining the minutes of angle that would encompass the sanctuary (for gorillas now nowhere to be seen), Carl went down to the canyon lip, with Bill carrying his own three-legged instrument, the 16mm motion picture camera, to try to film Nyamlagira between gaps in the fog. He stood waiting in the cold rain for hours, with Bill, forever patient, but the volcano refused to reveal itself.

"I feel just like I did when I was here the first time," Carl said, when Mary came to check on him the next morning, after he had woken, again, with fever and nausea. His eyes were sunken, and his hands trembled on the bedpan, which he held loosely on the blanket covering his lap. Later that day his former gorilla tracker, Muguru, arrived at camp, ready to assist Carl in his search for the location where they had shot the old silverback, the view he had in mind for the background.

It continued raining into the night, and by daybreak sleet covered their tents like wet plaster. It had turned a terrible raw cold. The charcoal fires barely kept the artists' hands warm enough to paint and to collect the icy fronds of foliage. The leaves and wild celery fluttered in the icy mist. More than once an arctic gale uprooted several tents, and they had to scurry to hammer the stakes back down.

For one afternoon Carl felt good enough to get up and work, setting his tripod in the crusty sleet to await a glimpse of the volcano, but on the third day he was bedridden again. And so, two nights later, when the clouds broke for the first time in days, and the beacon of Nyamlagira finally revealed itself, he could only lift himself enough to peer out his tent flap. In the black starless night the volcano looked like a cauldron of angry spitting blood. When an incandescent geyser of lava shot into the heavens, searing the cloud mass above, the molten spume floated on his retinas long afterward.

※

ON THE FOURTH morning Akeley woke saying he hoped to be ready to make the last leg of the climb in the afternoon. He called Leigh into his tent. He had been cot-bound for three days since arriving at the lower camp, and when the painter came and sat beside him, Akeley propped himself up and tried to light a cigarette with a shaky hand. Raddatz and Derscheid had already taken their equipment up to the saddle camp between the peaks of Mikeno and Karisimbi; the rest of them had stayed behind with Akeley. But now, Carl said, he was ready to make the final ascent.

"You had better take your boys and go on up to the saddle ahead of me," he said. He grimaced and dropped his first match and then caught the cigarette with the second. "Mary and I will follow slowly." He lay back heavily on his pillow to smoke, and turned his head to speak to Leigh. "From here to saddle camp it's a three-hour hike—you can be up there today and start looking for my gorilla background as soon as possible. Muguru will be able to take you there. Just keep along the western slope of Karisimbi until you come to the clearing with a perfect view of the volcanoes, with Nyiragongo straight in front of you. Look for the snag tree I told you about. You'll know it when you see it."

※

AT FIRST, DESPITE the treacherously near-vertical grade of the final ascent, Carl climbed on his own for a while. But the altitude was like an extra measure of gravity, and Mary insisted they stop and that he let himself be carried in the hammock. When they continued, with Carl borne aloft by two porters, and clinging to the sides of his palanquin, Mary hiked alongside, making small talk when it was convenient to breathe.

But after a while, Carl said he felt too cold to stay in the hammock. He asked to be let down so he could walk on his own. The landscape had begun to change. The trees grew diminutive. They climbed slowly and stopped frequently to catch their breath and to admire their enchanted surroundings. The clouds were breaking, and they could see jagged glimpses of Mikeno and the snowy dome of Karisimbi. The sun had come out now, and the air was filled with an angelic green light, lacy with chervil and dock. Silver-throated sunbirds were feeding on lobelia between the drooping fronds, and a golden monkey sat perched overhead in one of the gnarled black mahoganies. Bright green and golden moss swagged between the branches of the wild rose trees across which erupted a full spectrum of lurid orchids.

"Mary," Carl said, taking her hand to help her up a rock step. "Do you see now where the fairies dance?"

Though he was visibly weaker the higher they climbed, the light had returned to his eyes. Then, about halfway up, they heard a crash in the woods. Something rushed at them, black and low to the ground. Mary saw a hideously deformed face, wigwagging arms, and bared yellow fangs. When it was almost upon them it slapped at the earth and let out a roar—a guttural heinous bark—then vanished into the trembling ferns. Mary stopped short, petrified, but Carl smiled, taking her hand. His bearers, holding the empty hammock, were frozen in place.

"There is your first gorilla," he said.

After that, they saw no more. The fog crept back in, gradually erasing their magical surroundings, and as it grew darker and colder it grew silent too, as if the mist had put the jungle to sleep. They hiked two more miles in the rain before reaching the top.

By the time they arrived at the saddle camp, near dusk, Derscheid could see that Carl was feverish, and Raddatz tried to persuade him to go inside his work tent to warm himself beside the charcoal fire.

"No," Carl said, his voice shivery. "I want to sit outside." He gazed at the alpenglow on Karisimbi's dome.

"The mercury has fallen to 32 Fahrenheit," Derscheid said.

Raddatz ordered several porters to bring a stove nearer to Carl, and then Bill brought soup. Carl ate it slowly, the steam tickling up around his tired, ragged face. The spoon shook between his fingers, rattling the bowl.

Derscheid sat making corrections to his map with a compass and pencil. "We are a full 2,000 feet higher here," he said. "It's no wonder you feel poorly, Carl." He wiped the fog from the glass face of one of the brass instruments beside him with his sleeve. "We are at 10,627 feet— only 1,000 feet below the timberline."

Carl nodded. Then, for a while, in a quiet voice, he reminisced about the last time he had been here. This was the same place where he'd set base camp five years earlier, when he'd first seen gorillas.

They sat and watched the fire. After a while they heard a hooting sound.

"An owl," Carl said.

"Oh, dear, there are no owls here," Mary said.

They sat in silence. After a minute, it hooted again. Carl cupped his tea.

When it became dark, a freezing wind drifted down into camp, and thunder rumbled distantly. When it looked to storm, Bill led Carl by wobbly lantern-light back to his sleeping quarters, set off a little ways from the others.

"Be sure to keep your lantern burning outside your tent tonight," he told Mary.

"Why must I?" she said.

"*Tui,*" Bill said.

Carl squeezed her hand. "Leopards," he said.

❧

CARL DID NOT sleep that first night at the saddle camp, and in the morning his nausea had returned. Deep down, he must have sensed that the vague black something which he had carried around now for several months was about to rupture. He barely dared eat anything more than a bowl of broth.

Later that day they found leopard tracks outside Carl's tent. When his wife saw them, it seemed to make her fear for her husband all the worse, and she broke down and told the others that she was terrified for her husband's life.

"It is just the altitude," Derscheid said. "He will feel better as soon as he acclimates." He did not think the old man's symptoms were anything grave—no one was expected to feel well in the Congo—and then, when a break in the rain came, the Belgian set off with his surveying equipment.

At the end of the day when Leigh returned to base camp, wet and freezing, he wanted to see Carl. They'd had no luck finding the location of the gorilla background and he hoped to probe him for better clues, but Carl was too sick to see anyone. The mood of the camp was considerably more tense. The porters looked morbid and anxious. Raddatz told him it was dysentery and that Carl had suffered several violent hemorrhages.

The two men stood outside Carl's tent near a sputtering charcoal fire. A bowl and spoon sat outside the tent collecting rainwater. Leigh could hear Carl inside, groaning faintly, and the tender murmur of Mary's soothing, worried voice.

The next morning, in a downpour, Leigh set off again with Muguru. Bill and Derscheid—who was not only a zoologist and cartographer but also a physician, though he'd never formally practiced—stayed behind to watch Carl. They moved swiftly through the woods, Leigh and his gun boy following the trackers' footprints in the melting snow. The rain was unrelenting but did little to cool the painter's hands and arms, which burned from a thousand stinging nettles. When it turned to sleet in the afternoon the muddy ground took on a cold silvery sheen.

After the precipitation finally stopped, the only sound was the ring of machetes against cold stalks. Leigh felt sure they were near now, though the fog was so thick at each clearing they found, at each crag or outlook, the view of the valley was so obscured it was impossible to tell.

Muguru, however, had grown more alert, and silenced Leigh and the others with a harried gesture—warning them suddenly to be quiet and watchful. Leigh moved with extra caution, never taking his eyes off Muguru's creeping figure, even as he flitted in and out of the mist, threatening to vanish with each step. Then, just ahead, they came out into a glade, and the guide turned and beckoned him quickly. When Muguru shouted and turned to face Leigh, though, he was smiling, and the painter saw it right away: the dead tree, as white as marble, clumps of gray moss twisting in the breeze. They had stumbled upon it, Carl's Elysium, seemingly out of nowhere. It was a jungle chapel, a place out of a storybook, an enchanted garden perched on the edge of a precipice of sky. If he could only see the volcanoes he would have known for sure, but where the mountain dropped off was only dense impenetrable fog.

CHAPTER THIRTY-SIX

Leigh was eager to report to Carl that night when he returned, but frightened by how unwell his friend looked. The interior of his tent was stuffy and smelled horrible, like the insides of a man disintegrating. A cotton pad, heavy with dark blood, lay in the chipped bedpan on the chop box by the foot of his cot.

Raddatz had told Leigh that the hemorrhages hadn't stopped. Earlier in the day Carl had suffered one, passing more than a quart of blood, and he had screamed that he could not endure another. Mary was hysterical. Derscheid was perplexed. At a total loss as to what was wrong.

Leigh sat by the cot, watching Carl struggle to breathe. The old man's hands were nothing but tendon and waxen skin. His own hands were bloodstained, scratched and torn from nettles and blackberry thorns. "I believe I found it, Carl," he said. "It was hard to tell for sure. There was a lot of that foggy stuff in the way, so I'm going back tomorrow."

A meager grin twisted the scar on the old man's gaunt cheek. Threads of pain stitched his face. "I wish I could go with you," Carl said. Outside, Karisimbi gleamed in the moonlight. "You must return as soon as possible and let me know if it's the right place. Go as soon as you can and make sure." Leigh promised he would, and said that if it was the place, he would set up camp at the site itself and stay there until he had finished painting. Soon, though, Carl began writhing under his blanket. He grew delirious and ceased making sense. As he tossed and jabbered to himself, the only thing that was clear was something about electrical wiring. Leigh couldn't make out what he meant. As far as he knew, Carl was, in his fevered mind, trapped inside one of his empty dioramas, fussing with the lighting.

The next day the sky was clear, and Leigh's party made it back to the spot without difficulty. He had begun to acclimate to the altitude now, and each return up the mountain was easier. It did not take them long to return to the small clearing. Indeed, it was right on the brink of a dizzying view. Muguru's snaggled teeth shone as he smiled and nodded proudly. With the fog lifted, it was hard to believe they were in the same place. Standing under the snag tree, they were eye-to-eye with the smoking peak of Nyiragongo. They stood for a long time, dazed by the lurching western view, with the downward slope of Karisimbi falling stage right, and Mikeno jutting up like a broken bottle of black glass. Lake Kivu, miles below to the south, shimmered like a coin. It was the most beautiful place the painter had ever seen in his life. He could not wait to tell Carl. But for a little while, though it was getting late, if just for a few moments, he needed to paint to convince himself it was all real. While he painted, his gun boy lay nearby, napping in a patch of sunlit moss. Then he marked the spot to return the next day, weather permitting, to begin his work in earnest.

As soon as he arrived back at camp, overjoyed to tell everyone that he had finally found the location, he knew something was wrong when he was accosted by Bill. It was strange. It seemed as if he were trying to tell him a story—about something that had already happened—something that had happened long ago. Some disjointed story about he and bwana hunting elephants. It came out garbled, however, since the African was sobbing. Still, as Leigh grew more confused, Bill kept pressing him with his story. How bwana hadn't seen the elephant, and only he, Bill, had seen the elephant, but how bwana hadn't believed him. Leigh would have been happy for the intervention of Derscheid, who had come over to interrupt before he'd even set down his easel and paintbox, if Derscheid hadn't also been weeping.

Of course, by now, Leigh realized what had happened.

"When?" he asked.

"This afternoon," Derscheid said. He was bundled in a coat. "Between three and five o'clock."

Leigh ignored the African tugging at his sleeve. "What was the cause?"

"I don't know." The Belgian pinched the bridge of his nose as if to stave off the tears that leaked between his fingers. No one really seemed to know what had happened. Leigh could hear Mary in her tent, wailing pitifully. He saw the others standing outside Carl's tent, and as Leigh approached he could only partly absorb the clinical details that the Belgian imparted, as if angry with himself for having missed some crucial sign.

"I gave him a dose of chlorodyne for the dysentery," Derscheid said, "and then, this morning, at eight o'clock, when his heart began to beat so faintly that it was nearly imperceptible, I gave him a hypodermic of caffeine. His pulse grew stronger, but his respiration was short and noisy." He had then sent for a doctor in Gisenyi, a village on Lake Kivu, and succeeded in getting the dying man to eat several spoonfuls of Bovril. He squeezed his temples and blinked hard as if to summon himself back to reality. "But by eleven o'clock the heart action fell again and I gave him another injection of caffeine, but this time without result. About 11:35 there was no pulse or respiration perceptible ... I made two more injections of caffeine, but in vain."

Standing outside the open tent flap, Leigh lingered with the others, looking inside at the dead man, who lay in his pajamas, mouth agape, eyes wide open, and the wrinkles of his face relaxed into an awful shade of white. The sides of the tent shivered and bellowed unevenly. They took note, absentmindedly, of the lobed pawprint cleanly preserved in the mud outside his tent, though, of course, none of them were foolish enough to believe that the leopard had caused his death.

Leigh could still feel the agitation of the African beside him. Bill stood in the circle of helpless white men and pointed at the corpse. They had been hiding behind some rocks, he said, and Carl had had his sights on a bull. But the thing was, the funny thing was—and here, for the briefest of seconds, a smile without any delight at all twisted his mouth—bwana had not seen the cow that had snuck up on them. He was too focused on the bull. Only Bill, *Gikungu*—his name was Gikungu, *not* Bill—Gikungu had seen the cow. It was hard for him to speak through his choking sobs. But he was insistent that the white men hear his story. He had had no choice, he said. He did not even have to think. The cow was about to charge. And he had aimed the other gun, which was already in his hands, and fired. That's when bwana had swung around and slapped him across the face. When he said so now, his face flinched.

At first, since they had not been paying full attention, it touched the others that Carl's favorite boy was crying real tears for the white man. After all, he had been like a father to him, they thought, but the longer the black man told his story the more his desperation confused them. Eyes swelled with brittle rage, he accosted Raddatz, and then Leigh, again, frantic that they understand. He wanted the world to know that he had saved Carl Akeley from certain death. He stood glaring inside the tent. He, Gikungu, had saved this dead man's life.

The others listened without saying a word. They were left uncertain whether his tears were of grief or out of anger or meant to exalt the dead man. But their minds were elsewhere. The thing they were worried about now was how they were going to give the body a proper Christian burial. For that they would need wood to build a coffin and cement for a tomb. It turned out they already had nails. But for the rest, they would send a team of runners to Kabale—125 miles away—for cement, and another group of runners to a nearby sawmill for planks of mahogany. But then the mutinous runners had gone and dumped half the cement on their return trip. Unbelievably, the white men would send them back on a second trip for more. Because the body had to wait so long, Raddatz had it moved into his makeshift studio, where he himself cut open the veins and drained off his former employer's blood. Then, using the same formalin they had used to preserve hundreds of collected specimens, he embalmed the taxidermist. The first night they sat up with the body, taking turns until dawn. The rain had finally stopped, and the sky was full of stars. They winked above the volcanoes clear and blue. Still, the cold was nearly unbearable, and the eerie rasping of leopards kept them on guard late into the night. Although preserved, they did not want to take any chances that the body of their friend and leader would be dragged off by wild animals. Come morning, they would begin to dig the grave. Taking turns with shovel and ax, they chopped down into the soft volcanic rock that rang against their spades like broken shards.

ON MAY 20, 1936, THE AKELEY HALL OF AFRICAN MAMMALS opened to the public. The day before had been the official dedication—coinciding with what would have been Carl's seventy-second birthday—at which F. Trubee Davison, the museum's new president, spoke of this "living testimony" to the generosity of everyone who had given their time and money to the "realization of Akeley's magnificent vision." (Davison himself had helped by going to Africa to shoot four more elephants for the herd mounted in the center of the hall.) Dr. Harold E. Anthony, curator of the Department of Mammals, then read comments prepared by Carl's widow, Mary, who had been stricken with laryngitis. Then Daniel Pomeroy snipped the white ribbon leading into the African Hall from the new Theodore Roosevelt Rotunda.

The memorial to Roosevelt—a monumental new wing of the museum—had itself been unveiled at a separate dedication four months earlier. Attended by Mayor Fiorello La Guardia and President Franklin Roosevelt, the ceremony had been presided over by the vice chairman of the New York State Theodore Roosevelt Memorial committee, since the chairman, Henry Fairfield Osborn, had died suddenly in November. A late morning heart attack in his study, just a year after traveling to Frankfurt to receive an honorary doctorate from Johann Wolfgang von Goethe University for his part toward a more eugenic world. In his correspondence, Osborn had also expressed approval of Hitler's philosophy of racial purity. After touring Germany and seeing the youth movement there, Osborn had said, "To observe the spirit of the young Germans is to realize that the world will have much to deal with in the not too distant future."

The American public, who now streamed in through the grand new entrance off Central Park West, passing under TR's own quotations on youth chiseled into the granite walls of the rotunda, *I want to see you game, boys, I want to see you brave and manly,* gaped in amazement at the soaring columns, but moved on eagerly to the next inner sanctum where recorded tom-toms played on hidden speakers. As the mob entered the dim jungle hall, blinking and expectant, they were startled to find themselves under a frozen stampede of elephants—and surrounded by a multitude of strange and vivid worlds.

Boys and girls pressed against the glass to see the largest of the four corner groups, the Water Hole, necks craned to the heights of the giraffe, the fierce jaws of the baboon, jockeying for position and waiting out the urge to blink in hopes of seeing whether the zebra would.

What was the trick? So many questions for which their parents had no answer. Were they dead or alive or only frozen somehow? *Was it real?* They went from window to window. The basking lions. Giant sable. The shy forest antelope, emerging out of crepuscular bamboo. The adults were just as overwhelmed, transported by each bewitched tableau, asking their own uneasy questions.

As of opening day, only half the dioramas were complete. Fifteen out of the planned twenty-eight, twelve less than Akeley had originally schemed. Nine were from the Akeley-Eastman-Pomeroy expedition, including the wild dogs and the klipspringer, the only two on the mezzanine.

Some of the groups were only partly done: preliminary backgrounds sketched out on grids on white curved walls, unpainted plaster rocks and trees. Other spaces were still completely vacant, blank waiting rooms. These void compartments were almost as intriguing as the inhabited ones: to think how they were reserved for some creature that might never arrive, that might go extinct first. In which case, would the museum leave the diorama empty?

To complete the job would take at least one more expedition, more sponsors, another few hundred thousand dollars. Financing the hall with movies had not panned out, mainly because Martin Johnson had not really panned out. There had been too much rain, he complained.

Too many car problems. It had grown harder to find animals worth filming. And so those fabulous Johnsons had moved on to other sources of sponsorship—Coca-Cola, Lucky Strike, FAB shampoo. At one point Osa had posed with a village of Africans all wearing "Maxwell House" aprons.

A plaque beside the buffalo diorama informed the visitor that it had been a gift of the late George Eastman. The Kodak King had gone back to Africa in 1928, this time up the White Nile, later filling his Rochester home with elephant foot flower vases and elephant foot spittoons. Then, one March afternoon, in 1932, he had sat down at his desk to write a simple note.

To my friends.
My work is done—
Why wait?
GE

His personal physician, Dr. Stewart, had diagnosed him with an incurable spinal disease that was rapidly robbing Eastman of control over his body. Once, Eastman demanded, "Audley, you're always listening to my heart. Just where is it?" And so after finishing his note, and sending away the witnesses of his new will, written only minutes earlier, he lay on his bed and put a Luger to his chest where Audley had shown him, and that was that.

At some point every visitor was drawn to the gorilla diorama. How much the big one looked like King Kong! Really it was uncanny. But movies were one thing. This was altogether different. Skeptics searched each clump of moss, each blade of grass, for the trick. But nothing gave it away. A person could stand here all day, studying the smoking volcanoes, the seamless backdrop of trees and reeling canyon, until they left in a vertigo of disbelief.

Nothing called the bluff.

But what if, say, somebody had thought to ask the older woman, there in the crowd, with the white hair tucked under a black scarf, and a mournful look about her, what she thought? True, she appeared somewhat distracted, oblivious to the jostle of children. Just to look at her, you'd be forgiven for thinking she was a librarian on her lunch break. Come, like the rest, to escape the real world if only for an hour. But, then again, there was something in the way she regarded the gorillas that made one curious. A sympathetic bystander might have noticed the way her eyes moved over the scenery, making her appear more confused than anything. As if she were searching for something she had lost—misplaced, impossibly, on the other side of the glass. How could anyone have ever guessed that, more than anyone, she knew all the secrets? All the tricks that made this world so unbelievably real. Or, even crazier, that she herself had slain the elephant, the one turned in alarm, and not President Roosevelt as the museum liked to let visitors think? But then, as the crowd moves to the next window, herding round to get a better glimpse, she is gone, lost for a moment in the crush of curiosity seekers, unrecognized, and fleeing this dark chamber and out into the blue of a perfect afternoon, itself trapped in the reflections of a thousand windows rising up above the park.

NOTES

First, a note regarding the methods used to write this book. While some of the techniques I used to construct my narrative may appear unconventional for a work of nonfiction, such as collage and an admittedly near-allergic avoidance of the subjunctive, I believe my commitment to narrative flow forced me to be rigorous when it came to the factual basis for my material. Even though I employed some techniques that are traditionally novelistic, such as describing an individual's thoughts and feelings or re-creating a conversation as I think it may have occurred, in reading the notes below the reader will find that any such narrative liberties are based on actual documentation.

PROLOGUE

Please see notes for chapters 25–27.

CHAPTER ONE

For the early years I read Carl Akeley's autobiography, *In Brightest Africa* (Garden City Publishing, 1920), but perhaps relied much more heavily on his brother Lewis's correspondence with Mary Jobe Akeley (Carl's second wife) for the emotionally turbulent stuff—letters which can be found in the archives at the American Museum of Natural History (AMNH). It's from this correspondence that we know Carl resented his mother for holding down his father, about her own depression following the death of three of Carl's siblings, as well as the disturbing story about one of Carl's aunts who was so offended by his obsession with skinning field mice that she felt it might justify institutionalizing the boy. Mary managed to get these additional, if sad insights from Lewis while writing her own accounts of Akeley's life, *Carl Akeley's Africa* (Dodd, Mead, 1929) and then *The Wilderness Lives Again* (Dodd, Mead, 1943). Both books were extremely helpful to me at every level of my writing, even if Lewis begged Mary to steer clear of the "dreadful years" as it was "probably impossible to tell the truth about the Akeleys and keep within the bounds of good taste." For better or worse, Mary complied. My favorite book by far was Delia Akeley's *Jungle Portraits* (Macmillan, 1930), which I suspect is much more revealing than its author always intended. A great short biography from the point of view of Roy Chapman Andrews, Carl's good friend and fellow adventurer (supposedly the model for Indiana Jones), is *Beyond Adventure: The Lives of Three Explorers* (Duell, Sloan and Pearce, 1954). I must give special thanks to Penelope Bodry-Sanders for writing the only previous and serious biography, *Carl Akeley: Africa's Collector, Africa's Savior* (Paragon House, 1991), which served as a veritable road map for me along the way. I confess that at the beginning of my project, before I was able to gain access to the archives at the AMNH, I attached myself like a barnacle to Bodry-Sanders's own repository of research which she had generously donated to the Explorers Club. If the reader desires a more comprehensive account of Akeley's very full life—including his presidency of the Explorers Club from 1917 to 1918—Bodry-Sanders's book still remains the only true biography, if sadly out of print.

For sections on John Wallace's gloomy dungeon of bird stuffers, I found good material in William Earl Dodge Scott's ironically titled *The Story of a Bird Lover* (MacMillan, 1904), and an exquisite article by Mark V. Barrow Jr. in the Winter 2000 issue of *Journal of the History of Biology*, "The Specimen Dealer: Entrepreneurial Natural History in America's Gilded Age," from which I also gleaned much about Ward's Natural Science Establishment. Ditto "Ward's Natural Science Establishment" by Herman L. Fairchild in the May 1928 issue of the *Scientific Monthly*; Roswell Howell Ward's *Henry A. Ward: Museum Builder to America* (Rochester Historical Society, 1948); Sally Gregory Kohlstedt's "Henry A. Ward: The Merchant Naturalist and American Museum Development" in the *Journal of the Society for the Bibliography of Natural History* (vol. 9, 1980); and *Henry A. Ward: Reminiscence and Appreciation* (Rochester Historical Society, 1921) by Reverend Augustus Hopkins Strong. For the episode of Akeley getting fired from Ward's, and other details covering his tenure there, I relied on the ever-reliable *In Brightest Africa* (henceforth *IBA*), as well as correspondence between Henry L. Ward (son of Augustus Ward, and the foreman who caught Akeley sleeping on the skins) and Mary Jobe Akeley (AMNH archives, February 5, 1940). Material on Carl's apprenticeship under David Bruce also comes from *IBA*, as well as from a biographical sketch on Bruce prepared by Louise Johnston Meyer for the Brockport Historical Club (February 3, 1967).

More general information on curiosity cabinets and the nineteenth-century obsession with nature comes from many books, notable among them Lynn Barber's *The Heyday of Natural History: 1820–1870* (Doubleday, 1980); Hans Huth's *Nature and the American: Three Centuries of Changing Attitudes* (University of California Press, 1957); Edward Lurie's *Nature and the American Mind: Louis Agassiz and the Culture of Science* (Science History Publications, 1974); and Roderick Nash's classic, *Wilderness and the American Mind* (Yale University Press, 2001).

In addition to Carl's own first bible, J. W. P. Jenks's *Taxidermist Manual*, I was able to obtain good information on the old style of taxidermy from Solomon H. Sylvester's *Taxidermist's Manual: Giving Full Instructions in Skinning, Mounting, and Preserving*

Birds, Animals, Reptiles, Fishes, Skeletons, Insects, Eggs, &c (Published by Author, 1865); Leon L. Pray's *The Old Taxidermist* (Joseph E. Bruchac, 1975); and Stephen T. Asma's *Stuffed Animals and Pickled Heads* (Oxford University Press, 2001). The very best academic-theoryish book on the history of taxidermy is undoubtedly Karen Wonders's *Habitat Dioramas: Illusions of Wilderness in Museums of Natural History* (Uppsala, 1993). But there's nothing like actually seeing how it's done, and for me, this meant spending time with the best taxidermists I could find, like David Schwendeman and his father, David Sr., at Schwendeman & Son Taxidermy, in Milltown, New Jersey, and the crème de la crème, John Janelli, of Jersey City. No human alive knows more about Carl Akeley than John Janelli, nor, I believe, understands what it must have been like to *be* Carl Akeley. For the entire time I worked on this book, you could say Janelli was my own personal taxidermist-consigliere, answering hundreds of e-mails, spending countless hours on the phone, studying dioramas with me in person, sending reams of articles and hard-to-find books in the mail, and, most of all, sharing his own passionate appreciation for the true genius of Akeley's methods.

CHAPTER TWO

This chapter—like all the others—relies on *IBA* for the general events of Carl's life during a particular period. Information on the career and paranormal living quarters of Isaac Funk can be found in *Encyclopedia of Occultism and Parapsychology* (Gale Group, 2001); and James H. Hyslop's *Contact with the Other World: The Latest Evidence as to Communication with the Dead* (Century, 1919). For figures on immigration, as well as the attitude by "native" New Yorkers toward that influx of humanity, I consulted Samuel P. Hays, *The Response to Industrialism: 1885–1914* (University of Chicago Press, 1995); and Robert H. Wiebe, *The Search for Order: 1877–1920* (Hill and Wang, 1966). *Flight Maps: Adventures with Nature in Modern America* (Basic Books, 2000) by Jennifer Price, in particular the chapter "When Women Were Women, Men Were Men, and Birds Were Hats," and Robin W. Doughty's *Feather Fashions and Bird Preservation: A Study in Nature Protection* (University of California Press, 1975) were of especial help for sections dealing with the millinery trade. Details regarding the reunion between Henry Ward and Carl Akeley can be found in their correspondence, which is housed in the Rush Rhees Archives, University of Rochester.

CHAPTERS THREE AND FOUR

For the chapters on Jumbo, and his adoption by P. T. Barnum, I relied on a number of excellent sources, including Henry A. Ward, *The Life and Death of Jumbo* (Philadelphia, 1886); Neil Harris, *Humbug: The Art of P. T. Barnum* (Little, Brown, 1973); and Philip B. Kunhardt III, *P. T. Barnum: America's Greatest Showman* (Knopf, 1995). In addition to these books, a number of articles were very helpful in fleshing out Jumbo's long and ultimately tragic tale, including "The Colossus of His Kind" by James L. Haley in the August 1973 issue of *American Heritage Magazine*; "The Life and Death of Jumbo: An Illustrated History of the Greatest, Gentlest and Most Famous and Heroic Beast That Ever Lived," published by the Cleveland Public Library (1927); and Les Harding's *Elephant Story: Jumbo and P. T. Barnum Under the Big Top* (McFarland, 1994), from which I pilfered (p. 11) Barnum's quote, "If I can't have Jumbo living, I'll have Jumbo dead, and Jumbo dead is worth a small herd of ordinary elephants." Details regarding the symptoms of musth (see: green penis) came from Martin Meredith's book *Elephant Destiny: Biography of an Endangered Species in Africa* (Public Affairs, 2001). For the admittedly somewhat digressive footnote on Thomas Jefferson and the American mastodon, I consulted Paul Semonin's *American Monster: How the Nation's First Prehistoric Creature Became a Symbol of National Identity* (New York University Press, 2002), as well as a gripping account via the Academy of Natural Science's Web site: http://www.ansp.org/museum/jefferson/ mastodon/index.php. To re-create Akeley's skinning and mounting of Jumbo, I relied on his article "The Elephant: In Jungle, Zoo and Circus" from the June 1924 issue of the *Mentor,* and Penelope Bodry-Sanders's *Carl Akeley: Africa's Collector, Africa's Savior* (Paragon House, 1991), p. 25, where I got Akeley's quote about Jumbo's rotting corpse when he says, "This stench is enough to gag a maggot." The serious scholar will note (hopefully with a minimum of choler) that I changed the tense from the original "The stench *was* enough to gag a maggot." Details of the unveiling of Jumbo and P. T. Barnum's surprise dessert of tusk jelly can be found in Les Harding's *Elephant Story.*

CHAPTER FIVE

The story of Carl's friendship with William Wheeler was largely gleaned from *IBA*, correspondence between Mary Jobe Akeley and Lewis Akeley (AMNH Archives), Mary Alice Evans's biography, *William Morton Wheeler, Biologist* (Harvard University Press, 1970), and an article in the April 1927 special issue of *Natural History* after Carl's death—dedicated to reminiscences of Akeley—by Wheeler, called "Carl Akeley's Early Work and Environment." The staff at the Milwaukee County Historical Society provided material that gave me a better visual of Milwaukee, circa 1885, including the article by Larry Widen, "Milwaukee's Dime Museums." For the use of taxidermied animals in advertising, I consulted *My Way of Becoming a Hunter* (W. W. Norton, 1955)—see p. 20, authored by one of Akeley's apprentices, Robert H. Rockwell, who in many ways surpassed Akeley at his own game. The bit on Wheeler getting beat up by the "law and order" ruffians was taken from Evans, *William Morton Wheeler, Biologist.* Background for Wheeler and Akeley's discussions about the changing trends/philosophy of museum exhibition came from Steven Conn's deeply fascinating book *Museums and American Intellectual Life, 1876–1926* (University of Chicago Press, 1998), and material on changing religious attitudes toward nature post-Darwin/post–natural theology came from *The Heyday of Natural History.* The source of the joke I put in my characters' mouths about Sears, Roebuck is *Almanacs of American Life, Victorian America: 1876–1913* (Facts on File, 1996, p. 46). Wheeler's line, "Are you really thinking, Carl, or are you just thinking that you're thinking?" is given to us by Wheeler in "Carl Akeley's Early Work."

To learn about the evolution of what would eventually become known as the Akeley Method, I read many accounts, most vividly in the books by another of Carl's apprentices, James L. Clark, *Good Hunting: Fifty Years of Collecting and Preparing Habitat Groups for the American Museum* (University of Oaklahoma Press, 1966), and *In the Steps of the Great Museum Collector, Carl Ethan Akeley* (M. Evans, 1968); Karen Wonders, *Habitat Dioramas: Illusions of Wilderness in Museums of Natural History* (Uppsala, 1993); and a number of articles, notable among them "Masterpieces of American Taxidermy" by William T. Hornaday in *Scribner's* (July 1922); "Preparing Preparators" by M. L. Pindar in *Museum Work* (July 1924); "The Story of Museum Groups" by Frederic A. Lucas in the *American Museum Journal* (January 1914); and (this one takes the cake) James L. Clark's illustrated article—showing the process of constructing the manikins, molds, and clay models—"The Image of Africa" in yet another special issue of *Natural History* dedicated to the African Hall (January 1936). In terms of clarity, Mary Jobe Akeley's description of the method in *Carl Akeley's Africa* (Dodd, Mead, 1929) is a close second to Clark's. I also had my taxidermist pal, John Janelli, explain the whole thing to me about fifty times. Given the many permutations Akeley's method went through, before gradually becoming the *Method*, it was pretty difficult to wrap my head around— but evidently I was not alone, as the museum world itself was kept in the dark until Carl revealed his exact techniques at the annual meeting of the American Association of Museums on May 5, 1908. As for my own techniques, to get the feel for describing Carl working up clay onto the orangutan's skull, I resorted to my own memory of observing a forensic sculptor for a magazine piece I once wrote, where the sculptor, Frank Bender, was attempting to reconstruct the face of a murder victim from a partly crushed-in skull.

CHAPTER SIX

I mainly learned about Carl's megalomaniacal plans—*ambitious* doesn't really capture it—to create a hall encompassing the entirety of mammalian life in Wisconsin from *IBA*, from Mary Alice Evans, *William Morton Wheeler, Biologist* (Harvard University Press, 1970), and from a few conversations I had with a former curator at the Milwaukee Public Museum by the name of Floyd Easterman, who also designed the Akeley Medallion— the veritable Oscar in the world of modern competitive taxidermy, this year's winner (2009) being for a full-size reproduction of a lowland gorilla and its habitat by, coincidences are funny, Wendy Senk, an employee of the Milwaukee Public Museum's Taxidermy Department.

As for Carl and Mickie's early courtship, I must admit to a degree of speculation in the way I tied it to the muskrat hunting trip—since it is not known for certain but seems to be the consensus among the Akeley rhapsodes that he was accompanied on those first collecting trips by Arthur Reiss, his barber and rival in love. (Thus I hope the reader will forgive all the lame "It must have been"s and "the barber could very well have"s and "Akeley in all likelihood"s, and other subjunctive demurring.) So, yes, I groped my way a bit through some of the unspoken swampy stuff to get to what we do know: that Akeley and Mickie were getting it on behind the barber's back.

CHAPTER SEVEN

The whole ordeal of the spotted pony and Carl and Mickie's efforts to get the mounts to the Columbian Exposition in time can be traced through the urgent correspondence between Carl and his contact at the Smithsonian, Edward Earll (AMNH archives). Akeley to Edward Earll, April 11, 1893: "We have failed up to the present time in getting a spotted horse that would fill your order although we have tried Chicago as well as the cities surrounding us, we still hope to get one although we will be a little late with it. We have delayed shipping the white and bay horses so as to ship all together, should we not get the other in a few days will ship the two and the spotted one later." Details on the exposition itself were gleaned mostly from the very hefty and comprehensive four-volume history created by authority of the board of directors, and edited by Rossiter Johnson, *A History of the World's Columbian Exposition Held in Chicago in 1893* (D. Appleton, 1898), and the Field Museum's comprehensive online history of the expo: http://www.fieldmuseum.org/research_collections/library/hist_colexpo.htm. There is also a lovely book by Julie K. Brown called *Contesting Images: Photography and the World's Columbian Exposition* (University of Arizona Press, 1994), and, of course, I read Erik Larson's fabulous *The Devil in the White City* (Vintage, 2003). We know that Mickie, Carl, and Wheeler went to the exposition themselves, shortly before Wheeler departed for Germany, thanks to *IBA*. I discovered their morbid but humorous conversation in front of the sculpture of the bear mauling the Native American inside the Palace of Fine Arts, where they mused on what the physical sensations of such a conundrum must really feel like, thanks to a letter from Akeley to his friend Fred Willoch, April 26, 1923 (Rush Rhees Archives, University of Rochester). Information on the ubiquitous Kodaks comes from Elizabeth Brayer, *George Eastman: A Biography* (Johns Hopkins University Press, 1996). Details on the Kinetoscope can be found in Ray Phillips, *Edison's Kinetoscope and Its Films: A History to 1896* (Greenwood Press, 1997).

CHAPTER EIGHT

We know about Mickie pushing Carl to go to Paris from an interview she gave for the "Woman of the Week" feature in the *News Review* (February 22, 1932), as well as Mickie's account of her running away from home at the age of thirteen and taking up with Arthur Reiss, as well as some of her psychic baggage—details of which can also be found in Elizabeth Fagg Olds, *Women of the Four Winds: The Adventures of Four of America's First Women Explorers* (Houghton Mifflin, 1985).

Details on the Four Seasons are covered in *IBA,* Mary Jobe Akeley's *The Wilderness Lives Again* (Dodd, Mead, 1943), correspondence from the Field Museum archives, and from detailed images provided to me by the photographic archivist there, Nina Cummings, who is a bona fide Akeley freak (highest compliment). While there Tom Gnoske, also a bona fide Akeley freak, went to great lengths to secure a report for me stating that the snow in the winter diorama was actually *sugar*—presumably laced with arsenic.

The best source I had regarding the method that Mickie is using here—patented by Carl Akeley—for making wax leaves is a pamphlet I found at the AMNH archives, by

Laurence Vail Coleman, *Plants of Wax*, AMNH Guide Leaflet Series, no. 54 (1922). Mickie also spoke about the tribulations she went through making all the foliage by hand, after she'd gone on her solo trips to collect sod and foliage in northern Wisconsin, in "Woman of the Week."

Info about how the leftover wonders of the World's Columbian Exposition became the starter collection for what would become the Chicago Field Museum comes from an article by Donald Collier, "Chicago Comes of Age: The World's Columbian Exposition and the Birth of the Field Museum" (*Field Museum of Natural History Bulletin,* May 1969); and Ralph Dexter's article "The Role of F. W. Putnam in the Founding of the Field Museum" in *Curator* (vol. 13, 1970). Carl's stopover in Chicago and Elliot's invitation to Africa are recounted in *IBA,* and details about Elliot's career thus far come from "Daniel Giraud Elliot" in *The Auk: A Quarterly Journal of Ornithology* (January 1917), and "Daniel Giraud Elliot: A Brief Biographical Sketch on the Occasion of His Eightieth Birthday to Emphasize His Long Devotion to Scientific Work and His Services to the Museum" in the *American Museum Journal* (vol. 15, 1915).

CHAPTER NINE

Much of what I learned about the geopolitics of Africa during this period came from the incomparable history by Thomas Pakenham, *The Scramble for Africa* (Random House, 1991), and John Reader's excellent *Africa: A Biography of the Continent* (Vintage, 1997). To get a better idea of the conflict that Akeley and Elliot were skirting unbeknownst to themselves (i.e., the impending war between Emperor Menelik II and the Italian colonists manqué, as led by the tragicomic figure of General Oreste Baratieri), I read Robert L. Hess's *Italian Colonialism in Somaliland* (University of Chicago Press, 1966), as well as A. Donaldson Smith's *Through Unknown African Countries: The First Expedition from Somaliland to Lake Lamu* (Greenwood Press, 1969), the latter since it was Smith who first put Elliot on this course of luckily averted disaster, and because it was also the source of some of the details I got on Akeley's sidekick, Edward Dodson, who'd accompanied Smith on that virgin expedition on behalf of the British Museum. The basic chronology of the trip—from the trouble of obtaining camels, to the surreal encounter with Sultan Nuir and the Habr Yunis—comes from the narratively rich twenty-five-page report Elliot handed in to the Field Museum (1896 Accession no. Z151, Field Museum Archives), Carl's own "Report of the collecting of Beira antelope included in Dr. D. G. Elliot's list of the mammals obtained in Somaliland, 1896," *Field Columbian Museum-Zoology* (vol. 1, 1896–99), the extensively detailed correspondence kept by Elliot (Field Museum Archives), at least when he was healthy enough to write, and Carl's own accounts in *IBA* and subsequent newspaper coverage.

Naturally, the most sensational aspect of the trip was its finale: Akeley strangling the leopard with his bare hands. Incidentally, that was the first piece of information I ever read about Akeley, in the midst of writing a magazine story for *Harper's* about the extinct eastern mountain lion, which led, in the desultory fashion of this sort of research, to reading about other large felines (and the people who throttle them). The details of his fight with the leopard are recorded in *IBA*, and retold in a few dozen newspaper articles, and I was lucky to gain some internal thoughts from that letter Carl wrote to his friend Fred Willoch (cited above in notes to chapter 7), which I excerpt in part here: "As I struggled to wrest my arm from the mouth of the leopard I recalled vividly a bronze at the World's Columbian Exposition in Chicago, depicting the struggle between a man and bear, the man's arm in the mouth of the bear. I had stood in front of this bronze one afternoon with a doctor friend [Wheeler] and we discussed the probable sensations of a man in this predicament, wondering whether or not the man would be sensible to the pain of the chewing and rending of his flesh by the bear. I was thinking as the leopard tore at me that now I knew exactly what the sensations were, but that unfortunately I would not live to tell my doctor friend. I was feeling no pain whatever, just the joy of a good fight, and I did live to tell my dr friend all about it." The sculpture from the Chicago World's Fair is now on the campus of the California School for the Deaf, in Fremont, California, where Douglas Tilden, the artist, had been a student.

CHAPTER TEN

Mention of Carl's streetcar eureka can be found in *IBA*, but surely the reader who goes and checks and then compares it to my version will probably wonder if I'm not guilty of embellishment. How does the author know his sleeves were rolled up? How does he know the little girl was staring at his scars? How does he even know there *was* a little girl? Since Akeley himself didn't provide those details, I suppose you could say that I am guilty. On the other hand, I would argue that I'm only guilty of a very restricted and rigorous sort of embellishment, that being of the inferential sort. For instance I know that it was summer, and I know from photos that Carl often rolled up his sleeves (see *Kingdom Under Glass*, p. 235). I also know that there were little girls in Chicago in 1898, and that little girls stare at gruesome mammal-inflicted scars. This might sound like an awful lot of demurring just to avoid those peevish "it very well may have been"s, but if a given *embellishment* (I prefer the term *develop* or *elaborate*) falls within what I feel to be an acceptable range of inevitability (i.e., logical certainty)—and it doesn't interfere with the known facts—then I stand by its soundness. Regarding the facts surrounding the apotheosis of his technique, please see notes on the Akeley Method from chapter 5.

As for Teddy Roosevelt's visit to see the Four Seasons at the Field Museum on his way back from Colorado in 1901, the source is *IBA*, page 158, where Carl says: "I first met Theodore Roosevelt on my return from Africa in 1906.* Previously, on his visit to Chicago as Vice-President, soon after I had finished the deer groups for the Field Museum of Natural History, he called at the Museum and was so interested in the groups that he asked to see me, but unfortunately I was not there." He also makes mention of it in the foreword he wrote to Theodore Roosevelt's *African Game Trails* (Charles Scribner's Sons,

---

*According to Edmund Morris, in an endnote of his own, p. 734 of *Theodore Rex*, the date of Akeley's dinner is uncertain, but probably happened between October 25 and November 7, 1907—reminding us, once again, that this whole narrative nonfiction thing can be a bit murky, especially if the author relies too exclusively on the principal subject's memories.

1926), p. x. Likewise, when I say that TR was Carl's "personal hero," I'm probably engaging in understatement—one need only read his foreword to *African Game Trails* to feel the *love,* a word which Akeley freely used to express his feelings for the president. In another instance he refers to TR as "Christlike" (Penelope Bodry-Sanders, *Carl Akeley, Africa's Collector, Africa's Savior* [Paragon House, 1991], p. 125). Where it might sound as though I'm putting thoughts into TR's mind, as he gazes at the deer, I am only channeling his own words, in this case from a letter he wrote Frederick Selous about his "melancholy" over the vanishing wilderness and hunting grounds of Africa and America: "I was just in time to see the last of the real wilderness life and real wilderness hunting," *Theodore Roosevelt: Letters and Speeches* (Library of America, 2004), p. 126. I gathered details of that vice presidential stopover in Chicago from newspaper accounts—on his Colorado quarto-centennial address from "Roosevelt Pays West a Tribute" (*Chicago Daily Tribune,* August 3, 1901); his tour of the naval trainer *Dorothea* on Lake Michigan, "Make Roosevelt a Storm Center" (*CDT,* September 1, 1901); his review of the Illinois National Guard, "Chicago Welcomes Roosevelt" (*CDT,* August 31, 1901); and for the panther fight from "Roosevelt Stabs Two Lions in Close Fight" (*CDT,* January 17, 1901).

The description of TR's voice as bearing "more than a suspicion of falsetto" comes from the September 14, 1901, issue of *Forest and Stream,* in a surreal report on the summer outing of the Vermont Fish and Game League, where TR had spoken to the other guests (among them a young Winston Churchill). In making note of the image of a mountain lion (i.e., panther) at the top of the invitation (in Vermont they're called *catamounts*), he went on to joke about hunting panthers the previous winter with the ex-governor of Vermont, Phil Stewart. "Stewart took the hunt less seriously than I did," TR said. "I wanted to shoot the lions, but he wasn't particularly interested in that—he wanted to Kodak them!" Everyone thought that was hilarious. Only moments later, news arrived that President McKinley had been shot. TR's earlier quote about the "tameness and monotony all too common in our lives" comes from that same speech, and the telegram—ABSOLUTELY NO HOPE—is courtesy of *Theodore Rex* (Modern Library, 2001) by Edmund Morris (p. 3).

For the scenes of TR's return to Chicago, April 2, 1903, all details of his agenda and quotations of speeches given while there come from the wonderfully tedious reporting in the *Chicago Daily Tribune,* including details of his reception at the University of Chicago and the business about the pickpocket. As for the alleged plot on his life—a bit I so desperately hoped to blow out into a big action-packed scene with frock-coated walrus-mustachioed Secret Service agents kicking down barn doors, and interrogating anarcho-conspirators, et cetera, that I spent many days kicking down doors myself—figuratively speaking—hounding the gentle dormice at the South Dakota State Historical Society, and pestering the Secret Service itself (whose staff were very nice and always called me sir but who no doubt now have in their own archival possession a sample of my stem cells)—in the end it all boiled down to nothing more than two casual references, a 106-word piece in the *Chicago Daily Tribune* (March 26, 1903) titled "Alleged Plot Against

President"—the article that instigated my chase—and a very dismissive article about the whole thing in the *Watertown Public Opinion* (March 27, 1903)—that's Watertown, South Dakota—headlined "Fremont's Scare: He Deals Out a Bunch of Scare Talk to Congressman Tawney." Congressman Tawney, however, "did not place much reliance in the information, but said he would notify Secretary Shaw and other authorities." I found nothing else on the matter in all the major biographies about TR (see notes to chapter 16), and the sensitive reader might interpret the sudden but threatless appearance of the pickpocket as an avatar for the anticlimax I myself felt at the end of my own manhunt.

The digressive exposition into the growing environmental movement, including the material on John Muir, was largely informed by these books: Kevin Brownlow, *The War, the West, and the Wilderness* (Knopf, 1979); William T. Hornaday, *Our Vanishing Wild Life: Its Extermination and Preservation* (Charles Scribner's Sons, 1913); Benjamin Kline, *First Along the River: A Brief History of the U.S. Environmental Movement* (ACADA Books, 1997); and Philip Shabecoff, *A Fierce Green Fire: The American Environmental Movement* (Hill and Wang, 1993). Muir's quote on the "stupefying effects of the vice of over-industry and the deadly apathy of luxury" comes from Kline's book (p. 50).

One of TR's favorite epithets "goo-goo" comes from *Theodore Roosevelt: Letters and Speeches* (Library of America, 2004), here abridged from "lunatic goo-goos" (p. 210). For Roosevelt's quote on "race suicide" see an article he wrote for *Outlook* (vol. 105, 1913), "A Premium on Race Suicide," as well as Thomas G. Dyer's book *Theodore Roosevelt and the Idea of Race* (Louisiana State University Press, 1980), pp. 142–67. As for the ideas of Roosevelt's friend Henry Fairfield Osborn, please see notes to chapter 13. The connection between Akeley's dioramas and the Cro-Magnon cave painters was inspired after reading Ian Tattersall's highly recommendable *Becoming Human: Evolution and Human Uniqueness* (Harcourt Brace, 1999), in particular the first chapter. The list of contents of the time capsule placed in the cornerstone of the Law School Building were provided to me in an e-mail by David Pavelich, reference librarian, at the Regenstein Library, University of Chicago.

CHAPTER ELEVEN

While writing this book, I had the opportunity to visit the actual continent of Africa only once. That hardly counts as much on-the-ground research, but thanks to Delia "Mickie" Akeley's vivid book *Jungle Portraits* (Macmillan, 1930), I was able to see it much as she did. Additionally, I had the benefit of her diaries and correspondence, from the AMNH archives, as well as from the private collection of Jesse Page, Mickie's step-great-grandson. On several occasions I stayed with Jesse and his girlfriend, Liz, both of whom were generous to a fault—giving over their house for me to search through trunks and boxes of safari memorabilia that still smelled of Mickie's perfume—even letting me sleep on the guest bed in the "Africa Room," where spears and shields hung on the wall, and where I pored over Mickie's field diaries sitting at the elephant ear table Carl made for their apartment on Eighty-ninth Street. One time my pal Janelli met me up there (outside Boston), and Jesse even let us fool around with Mickie's hunting rifle (a 9.5

Mannlicher). General contours of the 1905 expedition come from *IBA, Jungle Portraits*, and Carl's report in the *Annual Report of the Director*, January 1908 (FM Archives), as well as from several in-depth interviews with Mickie, including Helen Hulett Searl's "In the Service of Science" in the *Woman Citizen* (December 1925) and the "Woman of the Week" feature interview with Mickie in the *News Review* (February 22, 1932). When it came to sorting out Mickie, two other books were also especially helpful: Elizabeth Fagg Olds, *Women of the Four Winds: The Adventures of Four of America's First Women Explorers* (Houghton Mifflin, 1985), and Mignon Rittenhouse, *Seven Women Explorers* (Lippincott, 1967). Information about the Uganda Railroad and the settlement of British East Africa comes from Charles Miller's exhaustive *Lunatic Express: An Entertainment in Imperialism* (Penguin, 1971), and Pakenham's *Scramble for Africa*.

Speaking of the train ride they took, here's another example of how I used inference to develop scenes without crossing the boundary into fiction via pure speculation/ invention/embellishment. Neither Carl nor Mickie ever made mention of the dust goggles I describe them as wearing on the train. Nor did I ever see a photograph of them in such goggles. However, from reading Miller, I learned that in addition to all the other discomforts of the train ride (ceaseless thirst, bad food), "dark goggles were also advised . . . as protection against the desert's red dust which penetrated every compartment in billowing red clouds" (p. 510). That certainly doesn't *prove* that the Akeleys wore those goggles too, but they were sensible, well-equipped travelers, and I'm comfortable enough with the likelihood to omit the milksop subjunctives. Not to pick a fight with imaginary agonists, but for anyone who just doesn't buy it, I would have you consider how cognitive scientists like Steven Pinker have repeatedly demonstrated that a 100 percent certainty is never possible anyway when it comes to memory. So even if Carl himself *had* written that he firmly remembered wearing those goggles, it's just as possible he could be confusing his own memory with the interposing memory of all those other passengers wearing goggles.

The cryptic reference to Mickie's brief stay at some sort of health facility in California—for reasons that were unclear—remains a mystery to me, but was discovered in a letter from Akeley to Field Museum Director Skiff, February 8, 1905: "Dear Sir: Feeling the necessity of taking Mrs. Akeley to a milder climate, for a few weeks, at least, and having decided on the Pacific Coast as the most desirable region." And then, in a letter to President Higinbotham, dated March 4, 1905: "Dear Sir. We arrived here Mar 2nd, and the following morning (yesterday) we called at the office of the Drs. Moore where we were cordially received by Miss Ainsworth, to whom you have so kindly introduced us. As a result of Miss Ainsworth's gracious interest in our welfare we are now pleasantly located, and I shall feel, when I leave Mrs. Akeley, that she has a friend here to whom she may freely go in case of need." I was never able to get any closer to the bottom of this.

As for the Akeleys' visit to the London outfitter to get kitted up, I clearly got carried away, but it was much more fun than trying to comprehend all the political tedium of the Scramble for Africa. Technically, the shopping scene is a composite, set at Silver & Edgington, Ltd., where the Akeleys shopped, though many of the actual details come from *Yesterday's Shopping: The Army and Navy Stores Catalogue, 1907* (David and

Charles Reprints, 1969). Other sources consulted to re-create this scene were Michael S. Moss and Alison Turton's *A Legend of Retailing: House of Fraser* (Weidenfeld and Nicolson, 1989); and Nicholas A. Brawer's sumptuous *British Campaign Furniture: Elegance Under Canvas, 1740–1914* (Harry N. Abrams, 2001).

For the fascinating medico-sartorial ideas of the time I consulted a number of sources, including Sir Francis Galton's *The Art of Travel; or Shifts and Contrivances in Wild Countries* (John Murray, 1872), Simon Brett's tongue-in-cheek but factual *Take a Spare Truss: Tips for Nineteenth Century Travelers* (Elm Tree Books, 1983), and then the weirdly not-so-tongue-in-cheek manual put out by the Royal Geographical Society (1911), *Hints on Outfit for Travellers in Tropical Countries* by Charles Forbes Harford, M.A., M.D. A top-notch article on the subject is "The History of the Flannel Binder and Cholera Belt" by E. T. Renbourn, B.Sc., M.D., M.R.C.P., from the *Directorate of Physiological and Biological Research, Clothing and Stores, Experimental Establishment, Ministry of Supply* ("Medical History" vol I, no. 3, July 1957). I must also thank the only expert on colonial headdress whom I've ever met, Douglas Zinn, principal investigator of PITHH (Project Investigating Tropical Headdress History), who suggested many of the great sources listed above, and who also provided most of the gorgeous names for the hats I used in this chapter (my personal favorite: the Lady's Pith Bombay).

To reconstruct the Wild West flavor of Nairobi, circa 1905, I consulted several sources, among the best being by H. K. Binks, *African Rainbow* (Sidgwick and Jackson, 1959); Robert W. Foran, *A Cuckoo in Kenya: The Reminiscences of a Pioneer Police Officer in British East Africa* (Hutchinson, 1936); Jan Hemsing, *Then and Now: Nairobi's Norfolk Hotel* (Queensway House, 1975); Anthony Kirk-Greene, *Symbol of Authority: The British District Officer in Africa* (Tauris, 2006); and Philip H. Percival, *Hunting, Settling and Remembering* (Trophy Room Books, 1997). Mickie's introduction to and "adoption" of Bill come from *Jungle Portraits* ("In a flash I was overwhelmed with a desire to possess that child," p. 135), and the introduction to R. J. Cuninghame comes from *IBA* and *Jungle Portraits*. The sources for the momentary reverie into the fate of Bill Pickering, barkeep, are Foran's *A Cuckoo in Kenya* (p. 250) and Hemsing's *Then and Now* (pp. 45–46). The business about the Kikuyu uprising—and the cause of the safari's delay—comes from Miller's *Lunatic Express*, as does the story of the German settler executed by urine (p. 457). For anyone interested in the multifarious and very legitimate reasons for the Kikuyu not lying down and letting themselves get pissed on by their new white overlords, I recommend reading "Masai and Kikuyu Responses to the Establishment of British Administration in the East Africa Protectorate" in the *Journal of African History* (November 1970).

CHAPTER TWELVE

I reconstructed the scenes on Mount Kenya, and Mickie's first elephant hunt, from *IBA;* Mickie's *Jungle Portraits* (Macmillan, 1930); a photo-essay by Carl, "Elephant Hunting on Mount Kenya: A Woman Wins the Record Pair of Elephant Tusks for a Sportsman's License in East Africa," from the *American Museum Journal* (November 1915); but the most dramatic material by far came from a version Delia (Mickie) wrote for the book *All True! The Record of Actual Adventures That Have Happened to Ten Women of Today* (Brewer, Warren and Putnam, 1931). It is in this chapter, titled "My First Elephant," where we meet their Wandorobo guides, Joey and Julius Caesar, and feel the nausea of Mickie's internal anxiety. It is also where I nabbed much of the dialogue used in chapter 12. "'Feeling all right?'" I fibbed and answered, "Yes" (p. 19). Carl's line, "What a monster," when he first sees the elephant, was exported from his own account of the affair in "Elephant Hunting on Mount Kenya," p. 329.

CHAPTER THIRTEEN

For the general layout of the American Museum of Natural History, I relied on the handy *General Guide to the Exhibition Halls of the American Museum of Natural History*, no. 35, of the Guide Leaflet Series (1911). Additional details—including those of the noisy construction of the new wing—come from *The American Museum of Natural History: Its Origin, Its History, the Growth of Its Departments to December 31, 1909* (Irving Press, 1911), as well as "The State Museum and State Progress" in the October 1912 issue of *Science*, both publications authored by Henry Fairfield Osborn. (He kept close tabs on his building.) For more general reading on the history of the AMNH, I recommend Joseph Wallace's *A Gathering of Wonders* (St. Martin's, 2000), and Geoffrey Hellman's *Bankers, Bones and Beetles: The First Century of the American Museum of Natural History* (Natural History Press, 1969). For additional detailed information on the mounting of *T. rex*, I am lucky to have a bona fide dinosaur hunter for a friend, Dr. Kenneth Lacovara, associate professor of biology at Drexel University, who has spent the last five years of his life digging up the most complete skeleton ever found of a super-massive dinosaur. He's also a frequent expert on shows about ancient life on the Discovery Channel, the History Channel, et cetera. Details about the near-miraculous discovery of the preserved *Trachodon* skin were found in the *New York Times*, "Dinosaur Mummy 3,000,000 Years Old" (March 21, 1909). That it was the "most important acquisition of the year" is acknowledged by Osborn in the *Report of the President* (AMNH archives).

As for Osborn's admiration for Carl, I got the comparison to Phidias in a letter from Osborn to J. P. Morgan Jr., April 28, 1908: "The finest opportunity which offers itself is that of the possibility of securing Mr. Akeley for the great Elephant Group. Akeley's work is really marvelous. It is so far ahead of the work of any other man in his line, that I always compare him in my mind with Phidias." Details about TR's plans to go to Africa and the planned rendezvous with Akeley are covered in *IBA*, as well as in the TR biographies (see notes to chapters 14–17).

I learned about Osborn's somewhat nefarious bent of mind on the issue of race in a dismaying number of sources, but my primary sources would include Ronald Rainger's *An Agenda for Antiquity: Henry Fairfield Osborn and Vertebrate Paleontology at the American Museum of Natural History, 1890–1935* (University of Alabama Press, 1991); and Brian Regal's *Henry Fairfield Osborn: Race, and the Search for the Origins of Man* (Ashgate, 2002); as well as many articles written by Osborn himself, including several doozies such as "The Cavemen Knew," in *Collier's* (May 23, 1925), and "Lo, the Poor Nordic," an editorial he wrote in the *New York Times* (April 8, 1924). His quote about the perils of the melting pot—"Put three races together, and you are as likely to unite the vices as the virtues"—comes from "The Second International Congress of Eugenics Address of Welcome" (p. 312), an affair hosted by Osborn at the AMNH, in *Science* (October 7, 1921). A more boiled-down version of the address was reported in the *New York Times* article "Eugenists Dread Tainted Aliens" (September 25, 1921).

For historical details on Central Park, through the eyes of H. F. Osborn, I consulted Elizabeth Blackmar and Roy Rosenzweig's *The Park and the People: A History of Central Park* (Cornell University Press, 1992), and the always helpful folks at the Milstein Division of United States History, Local History and Genealogy, at the New York Public Library.

CHAPTER FOURTEEN

The material on W. D. Boyce, and his African Balloonograph Expedition, comes from Janice A. Petterchak's *Lone Scout: W. D. Boyce and American Boy Scouting* (Legacy Press, 2003); H. K. Binks's *African Rainbow* (Sidgwick and Jackson, 1959); Charles Miller's *Lunatic Express: An Entertainment in Imperialism* (Penguin, 1971); an article by Harriet Hughes Crowley, "The Great African Safari Bust, or How the Boy Scouts Came to America," in *American Heritage Magazine* (April 1975); and the all-around superb firsthand account of the Akeley expedition, *In Africa* (Bobbs Merrill, 1910) by John T. McCutcheon, who, unbelievably, actually parted company with the Akeleys shortly after Christmas 1909, returned to America, and wrote and published the book before Carl and Mickie had even *left* Africa. One of the most helpful, or lucky, things in general was that practically every person who ever went along on one of Akeley's five expeditions—whether or not they made it into my book as a character—churned out a book. McCutcheon's is definitely one of the best and least flinching.

Some of Boyce's more cockamamie quotes—"I should enjoy greatly being up in a balloon in a thunderstorm wouldn't you?"—come from Petterchak's *Lone Scout* (p. 50). That Boyce was the first to commission Carl to get a mountain gorilla—postponed for reasons that shall become clear soon enough—comes from an article in the *Leader* (Nairobi), "Boyce to Send Expedition to Congo" (November 27, 1909). References to Paul du Chaillu, the first European to lay eyes on a gorilla—in fact, it wasn't a mountain gorilla (*Gorilla gorilla beringei*), but a lowland gorilla (*Gorilla gorilla graueri*)—can be found in his book *Explorations and Adventures in Equatorial Africa: With Accounts of the Manners and Customs of the People, and of the Chase of the Gorilla, the Crocodile, Leopard, Elephant, Hippopotamus, and Other Animals* (Harper, 1861). Boyce's blustery quote "Pictures will live, when hides will rot" is also from Petterchak's *Lone Scout* (p. 51), and Akeley's smug internal response (supposed by author) can be more than aptly justified even after the most cursory read of *This Film Is Dangerous: A Celebration of Nitrate Film*, edited by Roger Smither (Fédération Internationale des Archives du Film, 2002).

For those morbid enough to look, video footage of Thomas Edison's electrocution of Topsy the elephant can be viewed on YouTube. Details of the White House dinner come from Edmund Morris's *Theodore Rex* (Modern Library, 2001) and *IBA*. I should also mention that many of the physical descriptions of Akeley—such as coming down the stepladder from sculpting, with a handkerchief in his back pocket—are informed by the thousands of images I browsed in the photographic archives at the AMNH. TR's line "It's my last chance for something in the nature of a Great Adventure" comes from Joseph Gardner's *Departing Glory: Theodore Roosevelt as ex-President* (Charles Scribner's Sons, 1973), p. 110.

CHAPTER FIFTEEN

The account of Mickie's fateful adoption of the vervet monkey J.T. Jr. comes from the second book she wrote, *J.T., Jr.: Biography of an African Monkey* (Macmillan, 1932). It is, without a doubt, the strangest of all the safari memoirs I consumed. Some of the dialogue in the argument scene over breakfast also comes from J. T. McCutcheon's *In Africa* (Bobbs Kerrul, 1910). Also of use was Mickie's article in the *Saturday Evening Post,* "Monkey Tricks" (September 18, 1926), as well as a few incidental details about vervet monkey behavior which I picked up in *How Monkeys See the World: Inside the Mind of Another Species* by Dorothy L. Cheney and Robert M. Seyfarth (University of Chicago Press, 1990), but truly the best observations were made by Mickie.

CHAPTER SIXTEEN

We find the letter from TR awaiting Carl in Sergoi in *IBA* (p. 160) as well as in J. T. McCutcheon's *In Africa* (Bobbs Merrill, 1910), p. 135, and Akeley's anxiety over having possibly missed the president, believing he'd already gone ahead to Uganda, in Akeley's foreword to *African Game Trails* (Charles Scribner's Sons, 1926), p. xii, the memoir TR wrote about his year spent hunting in Africa. Those two books, plus McCutcheon's *In Africa* were the main sources used to re-create their trek to the rendezvous with TR along the Nzoia River, as well as the entire extended TR cameo. Of additional help were Kermit Roosevelt's *The Happy Hunting-Grounds* (Charles Scribner's Sons, 1921), and Philip H. Percival's *Hunting, Settling and Remembering* (Trophy Room Books, 1997).

We begin to pick up signs that the monkey was increasingly becoming a wedge between Carl and Mickie from their diaries and letters, for instance, when Carl wrote her, while away hunting elephant on Mount Elgon (February 17, 1910): "Dear Mickie I love you . . . I love you dear . . . I want you with me darling so much. Separation is hell for me. I'm jealous of your thoughts. Yes I'm even jealous of the monkey." (After one argument, according to the diaries they kept, Carl went out and shot her a lion as a make-up gift.)

The encounter with the Duke of Peñaranda is mentioned by McCutcheon in *In Africa* (p. 136). The episode with the runner carrying the telegram meant for TR, who ends up bumming along with Akeley's safari, and therefore protracts Mrs. Roosevelt's anxiety regarding reports of her husband's death, is recounted in McCutcheon's *In Africa*, p. 135, and *IBA,* as is the nearly ecstatic rendezvous with Roosevelt, even though TR doesn't mention it himself in *African Game Trails* (which must have hurt Carl's feelings, even if he did get to write the foreword).

I spent a great deal of time reading about Roosevelt in hopes of accurately evoking him in these pages, and, like Akeley, I must admit I fell in love with the man, maybe just as much *for* all his paradoxes. I read several biographical works, including the phenomenal *Theodore Rex* by Edmund Morris (Modern Library, 2001); Joseph Gardner's *Departing Glory: Theodore Roosevelt as Ex-President* (Charles Scribner's Sons, 1973); Patricia O'Toole's *When Trumpets Call: Theodore Roosevelt After the White House* (Simon and Schuster, 2005); *Roosevelt as We Knew Him* by Frederick S. Wood (John C. Winston, 1927); an article by Robert Foran, "With Roosevelt in Africa," in *Field and Stream* (October 1912), which goes a bit into Kermit's recklessness; and a chapter on Roosevelt by his friend H. F. Osborn in *Impressions of Great Naturalists* (Charles Scribner's Sons, 1924). I also steeped myself in TR's letters and speeches—the man's first calling in life, before politics, was to be a writer. His second, surely, was to be a naturalist. The main wellspring of his writing encompasses a twenty-four-volume set, *The Works of Theodore Roosevelt* (Charles Scribner's Sons, 1923–26); these are also selected writings such as *Theodore Roosevelt: An American Mind*, edited by Mario DiNunzio (St. Martin's Press, 1994), and *Theodore Roosevelt: Letters and Speeches,* edited by Louis Auchincloss (Library of America, 2004).

The story of Bill's disgrace within the Roosevelt safari is told in *IBA,* p. 133. Details of TR and Kermit's hunting prior to meeting with the Akeleys come primarily from *African Game Trails.* As for the figure of the death toll—seventeen lions, six giraffes, four buffalos, five rhinos, four hippos, and, give or take, about a thousand birds—it is actually a lowball figure. According to O'Toole, in *When Trumpets Call,* the final take for the Smithsonian, including fish, small mammals, amphibians, et cetera, was 11,397 (p. 72). Heller's line about "rhinoceritis" also comes courtesy of O'Toole (p. 51), as does the business about the natives' nickname for TR, "Bwana Tumbo" (p. 57).

As for reconstructing TR's bloviated monologues, I got a general drift of what TR talked about from remarks made by members of the Akeley party. For instance, McCutcheon wrote in *In Africa* (p. 139) that TR "told many of his experiences in the hunting field, and for three hours, at lunch and afterward, he talked with the freedom of one who was glad to see some American friends in the wilderness and who had no objection to showing his pleasure at such a meeting. He talked about the tariff and about many public men and public questions with a frankness that compels even a newspaper man to regard as being confidential." Basically, that is, he talked about everything. I also know from TR's many interlocutors that this was his style. As his friend Archibald Butt described it (quoted here from Morris's *Theodore Rex,* p. 532): "Roosevelt moved on to discuss the King of Abyssinia, Albert Beveridge's affectations, Shakespeare's 'compressed thought,' and the Book of Common Prayer, with interspersed witticisms that had his listeners roaring with laughter. 'His humour is so elusive, his wit so dashing and his thoughts so incisive that I find he is the hardest man to quote that I have ever heard talk . . . In conversation he is a perfect flying squirrel, and before you have grasped one pungent thought he goes off on another limb whistling for you to follow.'" Among the instances where I took his words—to fill up those three hours around the luncheon table—would include "If I could have seen you an hour and a half ago, I could have got you the elephants you want for your group . . ." (McCutcheon, *In Africa*, p. 138); "If England ever has trouble with Germany . . ." from a letter to Cecil Spring-Rice, British ambassador to the United States, May 13, 1905 (*Letters and Speeches*, p. 386); "Burroughs charged me to look personally into this extraordinary habit" of the honeyguide and its habit of gorging the wax of beehives, from TR's *African Game Trails*, p. 283; "Rome fell by attack . . ." is from the Romanes Lecture given by TR at Oxford University, June 7, 1910, titled "Biological Analogies in History" (p. 97), as is "The growth in luxury, in love of ease, in taste for vapid and frivolous excitement . . ." (p. 98); "Oversentimentality, oversoftness, in fact, washiness and mushiness are the great dangers of this age and of this people . . ." comes from TR's letter to Granville Stanley Hall, November 29, 1899 (*Letters and Speeches*, p. 183); "It would be not merely silly, but worse than silly . . ." is from *African Game Trails*, as is "Death by violence, death by cold . . ." (p. 169) and the stuff about the White Man's Burden can readily be found in the selected writings of *Theodore Roosevelt: An American Mind* (pp. 181–88).

The bit about the bottle of brandy from Oscar Straus, TR's former secretary of commerce and labor, whom Akeley had encountered on the Atlantic crossing (Straus was on his way to his new appointment as U.S. ambassador to the Ottoman Empire) is from *IBA* (p. 160). I found his quote "It tires me to talk to rich men . . ." in Morris's *Theodore Rex* (p. 360). The story about J. P. Morgan's venomous line "Wall Street expects every lion to do its duty!" is taken from O'Toole's *When Trumpets Call*, p. 15. McCutcheon gave TR's invitation to "inflict" (p. 159) his library upon his companions, and the dimensions and contents and construction of said "pigskin library" are thoroughly described in an article TR himself wrote for the *Outlook* (April 30, 1910). His opinion on Henry James ("miserable little snob") comes from a letter to James Brander Matthews, June 29, 1894 (*Letters and Speeches*, p. 165). His low opinion of Tolstoy—"He is not wholesome. He is not sane"—is found in a letter to Robert Grant, September 1, 1904 (*Letters and Speeches*, p. 345). And his newfound appreciation for Shakespeare, save his doubts about Hamlet's lack of courage, comes from a letter to Henry Cabot Lodge, September 10, 1909.

CHAPTER SEVENTEEN

Members of the Akeley party mentioned that while they were on the elephant hunt, TR spoke of his upcoming Oxford lecture, which he was still preparing; I obtained the lecture itself from the Internet Archive and used excerpts as dialogue. TR's line about the wild fig comes from his *African Game Trails* (Charles Scribner's Sons, 1926), p. 122. The bit about the Smithsonian naturalist Mearns chopping off Moros heads comes from Kermit Roosevelt's *The Happy Hunting-Grounds* (Charles Scribner's Sons, 1921), p. 13. It was from Edmund Morris that I learned "By George!" and "It makes one's blood tingle" were expressions used with frequency by TR, and so I took the liberty of having him use them at the sight of the elephants. The whole quick massacre is covered in *IBA*, pp. 160–62.

The scene between TR and Carl waiting with the dead elephants for the skinners has always affected me in a strange way, I suppose because of the tension between a man who wants to talk about his children and a man who we can only presume (as I do) is in a barren marriage. Carl writes about this moment quite emotionally in *IBA* (pp. 162–63). TR's quote "I do not know any man who has had as happy a fifty years as I have had . . ." comes from Joseph Gardner's *Departing Glory: Theodore Roosevelt as Ex-President* (Charles Scribner's Sons, 1973), p. 107. The virulent diatribe on the "patriotic duty" of having children, and the failure to do so being a "cardinal sin against the race and against civilization," comes from his article "Race Decadence" in the *Outlook* (April 8, 1911), a subject which he would return to again in a September 27, 1913, article, again in the *Outlook,* called "A Premium on Race Suicide." The final grotesque image of the hyena trapped inside the elephant comes from *IBA* (p. 163) and *In Africa* (pp. 149–50), which includes an illustration of the situation by McCutcheon.

CHAPTERS EIGHTEEN AND NINETEEN

A number of details for the 1909–11 expedition come from the diary Carl kept, and which Mickie scribbled in occasionally as well, usually when he was sick. Much of it's pretty dull stuff, a running tally of animals killed, problems with equipment, weather, and the tedious day-to-day business of managing the safari. (July 16: "Sat in chair today while M cut my hair.") It's also the source of much that never made it into their books, such as whippings doled out for smoking "bong," and Carl's vicious beating of the porter over the chicken incident. Another frequent topic of the diary is the constant worry over their horses catching rinderpest, and it's where I pick up random details such as that J.T. Jr. liked to snack on ants. It's also where I learned of Mickie's podiatry woes: "It takes me hours to look after the wounds on my feet and other places. My big toe is really worrying me greatly and I am afraid of real trouble." Details of Carl's repeated illnesses are recorded in the diary, in Mickie's *Jungle Portraits* (Macmillan, 1930), and in Mickie's terrified letters to friends, in particular one from October 28, 1910, to Carl's brother, Lewis, where she says: "I am beginning to get desperate. I don't know what to do for him next. I have tried everything and we are a hundred miles from a Dr. I think the sun and terrific nervous strain he is under, when he comes up with elephants effects [sic] his injuries in some way." The detail of the stigmata-like ulcers on his hands comes from *Jungle Portraits* (p. 83). Mickie writes about her own panic attacks and moments of insanity—in particular when she suffers from hallucinations that her limbs are turning into vines and elephant legs (she blames it on the exhaustion from taking care of Carl)—in *J.T., Jr.: Biography of an African Monkey* (Macmillan, 1932), p. 108. Carl's own line about being "elephant mad" is from a letter to Osborn, October 30, 1910. The diary is my source for J.T. Jr.'s altitude sickness, the episode where Bill threatens one of the porters with a knife and Carl has him thrown in jail, and the scene where Carl is standing around trying to figure out what sort of creature had escaped from the elephant pit when Bill suddenly shows up again out of the blue (June 11, 1910). The horrifying crocodile attack and its aftermath are covered in *Jungle Portraits, IBA,* and an article Mickie wrote for the *Saturday Evening Post,* July 28, 1928, called "Crocodiles."

That Carl ditched a couple of the skins of the elephants TR had shot because they were too "puny" is reported by J. T. McCutcheon in *In Africa* (Bobbs Merrill, 1910). Among other elephant skins jettisoned in Akeley's pursuit of perfection was the one killed after the long battle that ended with Mickie collapsing and saying, "I want to go home and keep house for the rest of my life," a line that comes from *IBA*, p. 40. One other article was indispensible: "Elephant Hunting in Equatorial Africa" in the *American Museum Journal*, February, 1912.

The description of the encounter with the abandoned Wandorobo infant, and Mickie's attempted kidnapping, comes from Carl's diary, as well as McCutcheon's *In Africa* (pp. 302–3) and Mickie's *J.T., Jr.,* (p. 39). Photos of the Wandorobo are also in the archives at the AMNH. The lengthy episode where Mickie gets the news that Carl has got in some kind of donnybrook with an elephant—*Tembo piga bwana*—followed by the near mutiny of the porters, and then the amazing midnight rescue, is all grippingly told in *Jungle Portraits* (pp. 230–51) and in an article she wrote called "Jungle Rescue" for *Collier's* (February 11, 1928).

CHAPTER TWENTY

The first image of this chapter, of Carl laid up with the mirror and his face bandaged, comes from a few wonderful photos of him in the AMNH archives. In one he is staring out of one eye through the bandages. In another, you can see J.T. Jr in the background. It's always amazed me—and filled me with a kind of dread respect—that instead of returning to America after being nearly killed by the elephant, he stayed on to finish the job. The internal lines *What did it feel like? Like being used for an elephant's prayer rug. Like being hit by a motor truck* come from "Carl E. Akeley and His Work," the *Mentor*, June 1924. As for Akeley traipsing around inside the hall in his mind, I took the liberty of doing it this way—as literal dream—since Carl himself repeatedly refers to the idea that visited him during his convalescence as a "dream" or "vision." Any details posed as Carl's thought (e.g., "He was endlessly revising the floor plan in his mind now"; he was mystified by "the way animals were able to telegraph their fear to one another") come from his writing.

The account of the smash-up with the elephant, and the Indiana Jones–like save Carl made by grabbing the tusks, appears in many sources: *IBA* (pp. 44–52), and countless articles, including one he wrote for the *Leader,* July 23, 1910, and in correspondence. The letter he wrote to recount the whole episode to Theodore Roosevelt, July 22, 1911, is one of the fresher accounts.

CHAPTER TWENTY-ONE

Carl's first attempts at recovering his morale, lost after the near-fatal encounter with the bull on Mount Kenya, and subsequent failures to reassert his manhood (or where it stood, at any rate, in regard to elephants) are written about by Mickie in *Jungle Portraits* (Macmillan, 1930), pp. 85–87, and additional details of his first pusillanimous elephant hunt are told in *IBA*. *IBA* also covers the second attempt, while out hunting with Bill, which ended even worse with the humiliating slap, the apologies that were *forthcoming and as humble as the dignity of a white man would permit* (pp. 141–42); the ironic bluster of offering to let Bill stay behind in camp for a few weeks to "loaf and rest" in order to recover his nerves (talk about projecting!); and Bill's decision to go back out with Carl after confiding to Mickie that he was "not afraid for himself but was afraid for his Bwana" (p. 143). The fragment of Carl dangling from the kopje as a massive herd of elephants rush underneath comes from his diary and from a letter to J. T. McCutcheon, February 15, 1911.

The finale of this part of the book—in which Carl regains his morale after an ambivalent kill (was it Mickie or Carl?)—is based on Mickie's great chapter "Elephants in the Fog" in *Jungle Portraits* (pp. 87–95), with supporting details from the diary and *IBA*. Indulgence forces me to cop to two allusions in this last paragraph: the appositive "knives out," which refers to the Radiohead song I listened to over and over again while writing this scene; and the last lines, "Fear was over. There was no more fear," a play on the ending of *The Death of Ivan Ilyich*, by Leo Tolstoy, who, as we all know, was not sane.

CHAPTER TWENTY-TWO

Almost all the drama for this chapter was supplied by Mickie's *J.T., Jr.: Biography of an African Monkey* (Macmillan, 1932)—including the episode of the attack that nearly cost Mickie her leg, the monkey's deepening anxiety, and eventual breakdown ("a genuine case of hysteria") following the massacre witnessed from his perch in Central Park.

CHAPTER TWENTY-THREE

Exceptional details of Carl's early models for the African Hall can be found in "The New African Hall Planned by Carl E. Akeley" in the *American Museum Journal* (May 1914). Osborn's quote on fixing reality and extending "the actual experience of consciousness" comes from "The Story of African Hall," the *Mentor* (January 1926, p. 9). The source of Mickie's line "No caged animal or stuffed *museum* specimen . . ." is her article "Monkey Tricks" for the *Saturday Evening Post* (September 18, 1926).

I studied up on the Akeley Camera in a number of books and articles, including: David Bordwell et al., *The Classical Hollywood Cinema: Film Style and Mode of Production to 1960* (Columbia University Press, 1985); Eileen Bowser, *History of the American Cinema: The Transformation of Cinema, 1907–1915* (Charles Scribner's Sons, 1990); Kevin Brownlow's chapter "The Film of Fact" in *The War, the West, and the Wilderness* (Knopf, 1979); Carl Louis Gregory, *Motion Picture Photography* (Falk, 1927); Reese V. Jenkins, *Images and Enterprise: Technology and the American Photographic Industry, 1839–1925* (Johns Hopkins University Press, 1975); Richard Koszarksi, *History of the American Cinema: An Evening's Entertainment: The Age of the Silent Feature Picture, 1915–1928* (Charles Scribner's Sons, 1990); Gregg Mitman's fabulous book *Reel Nature: America's Romance with Wildlife on Film* (Harvard University Press, 1999); and a number of journal articles, among the best being Mark Alvey's "The Cinema as Taxidermy: Carl Akeley and the Preservative Obsession," *Framework* (Spring 2007); "Carl Akeley's Pancake Camera," *American Cinematographer* (February 1987); and, an artifact in itself, the actual operator's manual, *The Akeley Camera: The Camera of Superior Accomplishment* (manufactured by Akeley Camera, Inc., 244-250 West Forty-ninth Street, New York). The source of the quote "leave the mechanical end of the motion picture business to others" is a letter from Eastman Kodak's general manager, Frank Lovejoy, June 2, 1917, who wrote: "I have discussed the matter of your Camera with Mr. Eastman, and after thinking it over carefully our conclusion is that we would not be interested."

The bit about TR having shot nine endangered white rhinos comes from Bartle Bull's *Safari: A Chronicle of Adventure* (Carrol and Graf, 2006), p. 180. TR's defensive quote "I can be condemned only if the existence of the Smithsonian, the American Museum of Natural History, and all similar zoological collections are to be condemned" is from Patricia O'Toole's *When Trumpets Call: Theodore Roosevelt After the White House* (Simon and Schuster, 2005, p. 67).

For the final, near fatal attack on Mickie by J.T. Jr., see her biography, *J.T., Jr.: Biography of an African Monkey* (Macmillan, 1932, p. 241). My source for Mickie's sudden desertion of Carl is Elizabeth Fagg Olds, *Women of the Four Winds: The Adventures of Four of America's First Women Explorers* (Houghton Mifflin, 1985). The Akeleys' divorce proceedings (case no. 22S-377906) were supplied to me by the Office of the Clerk of the Circuit Court of Cook County. The sale of her "honeymoon" tusks to Director Lucas comes from a letter Lucas wrote, May 16, 1918: "The purchase of Mrs. Akeley's elephant tusks is a somewhat delicate matter owing to personal relations, but from a purely impersonal standpoint, I should feel that $1,500 was a very fair price for them."

Osborn's happiness comes from a letter to one of the prospective donors, August 12, 1920: "My dear Mr. Davison: You will be very glad to hear that Mr. Akeley is resuming the work for the African Hall elephant group with great vigor." I learned of Osborn's involvement in the search for his Aryan Dawn Men from Charles Gallenkamp's book *Dragon Hunter: Roy Chapman Andrews and the Central Asiatic Expeditions* (Penguin, 2001), as well as from Roy Chapman Andrews's article "The Third Asiatic Expedition of the American Museum of Natural History" in *Science* (June 2, 1922).

I got to know Carl's new roommate, Vilhjalmur Stefansson, through his autobiography, *My Life with the Eskimo* (Macmillan, 1913). Most of the running around Akeley engaged in, running off to the Catskills and to Maine, and all his various flings were cobbled together from correspondence mainly found at the Rush Rhees Library Archives, University of Rochester.

Osborn's irritation over Akeley's delays is expressed in the Revised Agreement for the Completion of African Elephant Group, December 26, 1918, which states in Article 1: "Beginning January 1, 1919, Mr. Akeley agrees to devote at least one-half of his time to this group, and to do his utmost to complete the work in 1919." They were still talking about it on November 23, 1920, when Akeley himself wrote to Osborn: "I have not given up the African Hall by any means; but I realize that we have to take a fresh start with fresh people if we succeed in doing any thing at all with it. I cannot help hoping that we shall find a man who alone will finance the entire undertaking."

CHAPTER TWENTY-FOUR

The background on Martin and Osa Johnson comes from their numerous books, including several I read by Martin Johnson: *Camera Trails in Africa* (Century, 1924); *Safari: A Saga of the African Blue* (Putnam, 1928); and *Congorilla: Adventures with Pygmies and Gorillas in Africa* (G. G. Harrap, 1932); Osa Johnson's *I Married Adventure* (J. B. Lippincott, 1940); a great chapter in Kevin Brownlow's *The War, the West, and the Wilderness* (Knopf, 1979); and the very fine biography by Eleanor and Pascal Imperato, *They Married Adventure: The Wandering Lives of Martin and Osa Johnson* (Rutgers University Press, 1992). Charlie Chaplin's gift of fake mustaches and pies for the Big Nambas is discussed in Osa's *I Married Adventure* (p. 56). Conrad Froehlich and Jacquelyn Borgeson from the Martin and Osa Johnson Safari Museum, in Chanute, Kansas, fielded dozens of my pestering questions.

As for the scheme of the AMNH and the Johnsons to mutually benefit each other, see the prospectus "Martin Johnson African Expedition Corporation Under the Supervision of The American Museum of Natural History" (AMNH). That 50 percent of the profits would go to the AMNH for the African Hall comes from the document "Subscriptions to Preferred Stock of Martin Johnson African Expedition Corporation." Carl wrote "Dan Pomeroy is a peach" in a letter to Martin Johnson, April 13, 1925. I found the details of the electric spearmen right outside the Johnsons' room at the Hotel Astor from James Traub's book *The Devil's Playground: A Century of Pleasure and Profit in Times Square* (Random House, 2004).

As for the party scene, it's a composite of several parties that took place around the same time—don't all parties blur together anyway?—one where Akeley was introduced to Mary Jobe by Stefansson (which actually took place in Chicago) and the send-off for the Johnsons at the Explorers Club. The technique I used to re-create my dialogue for the party was a composite too or, more precisely, a collage. Martin's line "There is no limit to the money it can make . . ." comes from *I Married Adventure*; Carl's "The public will pay for good stuff . . ." is from a letter to Martin Johnson, June 23, 1922; Martin's "It will set us up for life . . ." from *I Married Adventure*. We know that Akeley respected Johnson's work from a number of sources, including one letter he wrote to Sam Rothapfel, director of production, Capitol Theatre, March 9, 1923: "Mr. Martin Johnson's new African picture is . . . superior to any we have seen from Africa. My keen interest in this picture is due to the fact that, as presented, it is absolutely free from any form of fakery, misrepresentation or disagreeable feature of killing or torturing animals." Osa's bit about shrinking heads comes from *I Married Adventure*, as does Martin's line "Well, she's good enough to eat, I'll say that for her" (p. 105). Carl talks about his intention of going to see the mountain gorillas, "An actual study should be made before these animals have all been slaughtered," in a letter to Sir William Northrup McMillan, December 20, 1920: "You perhaps know that it has been my ambition for some years to make an exhaustive study of the gorilla." Regarding the lowland gorilla he'd seen at the London Zoological Park, whose "chief aim in life seemed a desire to be loved," see Mary Bradley's *On the Gorilla Trail* (Stackpole Books, 2005, p. ix).

I got to know more about Mary Jobe from her numerous books (see notes to chapter 28) and abundant correspondence at the AMNH archives, as well as Patricia Gilmartin's journal article "Mary Jobe Akeley's Explorations in the Canadian Rockies" in the *Geographical Journal* (November 1990), from which I obtained much of MJA's prattle about the "artificialities of towns and cities for the joyous realities of the wooded hills and seashore" (p. 298); and Carl's line "When *I* was a boy I was so afraid of girls . . ." is lifted from a letter he wrote to his nephew, Field Akeley, January 7, 1921. The stuff about Mary Jobe having potlatch with the Carrier Indians and "photograph[ing] their totem poles" likewise comes from Gilmartin's article (p. 299), as does the reference to the Sekani nicknaming Mary Jobe Dene-Sezaki, or "man-woman," as well as Jobe's quote "All very weird and intensely interesting" (p. 299).

Martin Johnson's line "Five years ago I landed at Sydney . . ." (p. 9) is from his *Camera Trails in Africa*; the cable THE PUBLIC IS TIRED OF SAVAGES is quoted in the same source, same page. Osa's follow-up line, "I was really *very* tired of savages and the way they smelled," can be found in *I Married Adventure* (p. 162). The anecdote of the Akeley Camera being mistaken for a machine gun comes from *Photoplay* (January 1919).

The surreal bit about Mickie thinking that J.T. Jr. could speak comes from *J.T., Jr: Biography of an African Monkey* (p. 228). As for the even more surreal visit to the psychiatrist Dr. Leon Pierce Clark, the details are laid out in a solitary letter from Carl to Herbert Bradley, June 11, 1920 (Rush Rhees Archives). Upon finding the letter, I had one of those outer body experiences that come only after poring over archival material for nine hours straight, most of it dull as dust, but then something like this appears and you look around at the two or three other glaze-eyed researchers and want to go around the room and give everyone a high five, but instead you just get up and quietly go to the water fountain, then make a notation for photocopy, and crack the next folder.

CHAPTERS TWENTY-FIVE AND TWENTY-SIX

Surely the most heinous crime of omission in my book concerns Carl's 1921 expedition to the Congo. The omitted being his companions, the illustrious Herbert and Mary Hastings Bradley and their angelic six-year-old daughter, Alice. Such a huge noise was made about his choice of travel mates (the entire party included Alice's nanny, and Akeley's secretary as well), that I don't blame the reader familiar with this part of the Akeley saga if they question my motives. The big deal, of course, was that Carl was bringing *human females*—including a little girl with golden locks of hair—to a barbaric land, in search of the most barbaric of creatures said to have even a sexual appetite for human women (see: ignorant popular imagination). Totally confident—at least before he got there—that the mountain gorilla would be harmless, Carl claimed he was bringing the women to prove the animal was no menace, but of course it also made for great publicity prior to the trip. The problem here is, narratively, once he actually gets to the Virungas, he has second thoughts, wimps out, and leaves them behind with the White Fathers for safekeeping, while he goes it alone. To be quite honest, at first I was frustrated by how it all failed to play out. I desperately wanted to keep the Bradleys in the story, but the fact is, they just weren't around for most of the action—not even good ole Herbert—and I didn't really know how to account for all that time spent idling back at the mission playing cards. In the end, however, I realized it was all for the best to leave the Bradleys on the cutting room floor. Akeley really was quite stuck in his head, disintegrating, and I chose to keep the focus boxed close in around him. Beyond that, even if U.S. newspapers thought it sensational, the more I thought about it, the more the mere presence of the women seemed overblown, especially considering how many human females already lived in Africa! And not only *black* African females, but the many *white* colonists who had lived there for quite some time and who, of course, were raising families there. Mary Bradley points this out herself in *On the Gorilla Trail* (Appleton, 1922), during the Atlantic crossing (p. 11): "Our first discovery was that we were not the only family in the world risking its young . . . The decks were full of children and almost all, we learned, had been born in Africa or had gone out at a tender age and were now returning from leave at Home."*

Regardless, I owe a debt of gratitude to Mary Bradley and her book, for several of the most chilling details, including those involving the episode where the porters allegedly murdered and cannibalized one of their own (p. 70), as well as the detail of their own consumption of gorilla flesh (p. 121): "The natives did not eat the meat. We ourselves had cooked and eaten a little, just for the sake of doing it, and found it perfectly good meat, firm and sweet, but I couldn't get over the family feeling of sampling grand-uncle Africanus!" Mary Bradley also wrote another wonderfully strange book, for children, called *Alice in Jungleland* (Appleton, 1927), wherein the following conversation between Alice and Carl is recorded (p. 100):

> Alice never tired of asking, "Uncle Akeley, how did you feel with a big gorilla going for you?" And when Uncle Akeley said, "I was thankful it wasn't a lady, Alice," Alice said "Why?"
>
> "Because I am more afraid of ladies," said Uncle Akeley gravely, and Alice said, "Because you aren't allowed to shoot them?" and Uncle Akeley said, he expected it was something like that, but certainly the gorillas didn't go for you as hard as the ladies did. Which was a grown person's joke.

At the risk of digressing past the point of plain sense, especially as it concerns a character whose *nonexistence* I've just taken pains to justify, for anyone curious about what happened to dear little Alice, she grew up to join the CIA and then became a famous underground gender/genre-bending science-fiction author, who wrote under a pseudonym. Julie Phillips tells Alice's story in *James Tiptree, Jr.: The Double Life of Alice B. Sheldon* (St. Martin's Press, 2006). Offstage, Herbert Bradley also played a significant role, not only as Carl's friend but as his attorney, providing us with much correspon-

---

*As for other omissions, I may as well here confess that for as much space as I devoted to the invention of Akeley's motion picture camera—see chapter 23—I completely ignored his invention of the cement gun, as well as his many other patents, including a number connected to dentistry equipment, ditto his design for bulletproof spotlights, ditto better tanks during World War I.

dence regarding all the inner fury Carl felt toward Mickie, and the various tawdry details concerning their impending divorce, including the accusations Mickie made about Carl threatening to kill her (AMNH archives), which was also reported in "'Akeley Tied Me, Turned on Gas,' Wife Charges," *Chicago Daily Tribune*, March 23, 1923; and in "Mrs. Akeley Divorces 'Caveman' as Cruel," *New York Times,* March 23, 1923.

As for the general account of Carl's gorilla hunt, and his epiphany, I relied on *IBA* and the endless correspondence he took up with American ambassadors and Belgian officials to advocate for the sanctuary. The metaphor of sloughing off the gorilla skin comes from the ideas that Carl himself would presently imbue into a bronze sculpture, a self-portrait titled *Chrysalis,* of the artist pushing the skin of an ape down around his hips—which in turn became a momentary if flammable symbol for evolution right around the time of the Scopes trial. For Akeley's thoughts on the matter, I read his article "Is the Gorilla Almost a Man?" in *World's Work* (September 1922).

CHAPTER TWENTY-SEVEN

A description of Akeley's nervousness on the train ride to Rochester to meet with George Eastman, including the dialogue I used, and how Carl was constantly lighting and absentmindedly relighting his pipe, was told in a reminiscence by Daniel Pomeroy in "Akeley's Dream Come True," *Natural History: The Journal of the AMNH* (January 1936). The correspondence arranging the meeting can be found in the AMNH Archives. Eastman's quote about "seeking a somewhat more detached position in respect to human affairs" comes from the *Dictionary of American Biography* (vol. 11, supplement 1). To educate myself on the Kodak King, I availed myself mainly of Elizabeth Brayer's *George Eastman: A Biography* (Johns Hopkins University Press, 1996), but also dipped into Carl W. Ackerman's *George Eastman* (A. M. Kelly, 1973).

Most of the information regarding Carl's pursuit and eventual success in persuading the Belgian government to create a mountain gorilla sanctuary in the Virungas can be traced through the correspondence on this subject at the AMNH and the Rush Rhees Library Archives. On King Albert's visit to Yosemite and the Grand Canyon, see *Los Angeles Times,* October 19, 1919, "Queen Goes to Dizzy Heights." (King Albert's wife enjoyed the thrill of having a couple of forest rangers hold her arms while she dangled out over the abyss.) Belgian consul James Gustavus Whitely's letter congratulating Carl upon the news of King Albert's decree, "Our cousins, the gorillas, ought to hold a Thanksgiving meeting in your honor," is undated, but begins "The 'Gorilla Sanctuary' has been fixed," so the approximate date must be March 2, 1925. Specific details of the sanctuary—hectares, et cetera—are provided in another letter from Whitely to Akeley, May 11, 1925, which he sent along with a translation of the king's decree. Carl's relief over the gamble he realized he had inadvertently taken with the gorillas' lives, by stoking the anger of gorilla hunters—"if this thing did not succeed it would mean that the last gorilla was going to be killed off . . ."—comes from a letter to Herbert Bradley, November 13, 1923. The line "Every decent thing that I have ever had get across . . ." is in a letter to Osborn, January 12, 1920.

The story about Martin and Osa Johnson's meeting with Eastman comes from *I Married Adventure* (pp. 267–70). Well worth reading just for its historical significance is Raymond Dart's article about the discovery of *Australopithecus*, "*Australopitecus africanus:* The Man-Ape of South Africa," *Nature* 115 (1925): 195–99.

As for Mary Jobe Akeley's visit to Carl's studio the day he showed her the skinned baby gorilla, my sources are *IBA* and an article by Carl, "Gorillas—Real and Mythical," *Natural History* 23, no. 5 (1923). The film footage of the gorillas on the wall can be viewed at the AMNH. "I suppose I could have easily killed every one that I saw" comes from a letter from Carl to Robert Yerkes, April 31, 1922. As for the lovers' rendezvous being ruined by a case of poison ivy, this arrives via a letter from Carl to his friend William Elizabeth Brooks, August 22, 1922.

Details on Mickie's solo expedition for the Brooklyn Institute of Arts and Sciences can be found in Mickie's book *Jungle Portraits* (Macmillan, 1930); Elizabeth Fagg Olds, *Women of the Four Winds: The Adventures of Four of America's First Women Explorers* (Houghton Mifflin, 1985); correspondence from the aforesaid Brooklyn museum; an article Mickie wrote for the *Saturday Evening Post,* March 3, 1928, called "The Little People"; as well as her diary.

I visited the George Eastman House in August 2008 and was given a personal tour by the curator, Kathy Connor, who supplied me then, and through many follow-up e-mails, with a bounty of atmospheric detail. Additional details were gleaned from a March 18, 1990, article by Kathleen Quigley in the *New York Times,* "Splendor Restored at Eastman House." Carl's mention of his visit to the Battle Creek Sanitarium—"The gorilla kills no animals for food"—comes from the Spring 1925 edition of the *Battle Creek Idea,* in the article "In the Jungles with Akeley." "Various of my Eskimo companions . . ." is from Revillon Frères, February 27, 1922, printed as a testimonial in the operator's manual *The Akeley Camera: The Camera of Superior Accomplishment* (manufactured by Akeley Camera, Inc., 244-250 West Forty-ninth Street, New York), ditto the footnote about the plane crash near Mount Vesuvius. My knowledge of small talk involving trout comes from a letter from Pomeroy to Eastman, July 8, 1925, regarding a fishing expedition on which Pomeroy and some mutual friend of his and Eastman had recently gone: "Bonbright's bag consisted of sixty salmon in three weeks!" The other points of small talk—weather, guns—were similarly pilfered from correspondence between the gentlemen. Eastman suggested Ezra Winter as one of the painters Carl ought to hire in a letter, December 16, 1925. "To hunt with me in Africa will cost you a million dollars . . ." comes from Robert H. Rockwell's *My Way of Becoming a Hunter* (W. W. Norton, 1955, p. 206). I'm pretty sure Carl also mentions it in *IBA.* His recollection of his moment on WEAF radio comes from the fan mail I found at Rush Rhees Library.

Jung's visit to discuss his impending trip to Africa with Carl comes from Penelope Bodry-Sanders's chronology (Explorers Club Archives), augmented by Blake W. Burleson's *Jung in Africa* (Continuum, 2005), p. 19, and Carl Jung's autobiography, *Memories, Dreams, Reflections* (Collins, 1962, p. 254). Carl's expression of being "really fonder of him [the gorilla] than of myself" is from his letter to Mary Bradley, December 12, 1923.

The business about what I took to be the ulterior motives behind the making of the gorilla sanctuary—that is, the real interest being not the fate of gorillas per se but to deal with "human problems"—comes from a letter from John C. Merriam to H. F. Osborn, June 1, 1922: "Referring to our conversation of some days ago regarding the possible development of psychological work bearing directly or indirectly upon problems of human behavior, I wish to express again the hope that in the near future it may be possible to develop a plan by which the studies in animal behavior suggested by Akeley's recent discoveries of gorilla colonies in Africa may be carried out in the most advantageous possible way." Akeley concedes that "the killing of a reasonable number of specimens for scientific institutions would be legitimate and necessary" in a letter he wrote to the Belgian ambassador, Baron Émile de Cartier de Marchienne. Neither man suggests what a reasonable number might be.

CHAPTERS TWENTY-EIGHT TO THIRTY-SIX

The main sources for Akeley's final, 1926, expedition were Mary Jobe Akeley's books *Carl Akeley's Africa* (Dodd, Mead, 1929) and *The Wilderness Lives Again* (Dodd, Mead, 1943), and her diaries; George Eastman's privately printed *Chronicles of an African Trip* (1927); Robert H. Rockwell's *My Way of Becoming a Hunter* (W. W. Norton, 1955);* Martin Johnson's books *Safari: A Saga of the African Blue* (Putnam, 1928), *Congorilla: Adventures with Pygmies and Gorillas in Africa* (G. G. Harrap, 1932), and *Camera Trails in Africa* (Century, 1924); Osa Martin's *I Married Adventure* (J. B. Lippincott, 1940); William Leigh's *Frontiers of Enchantment: An Artist's Adventures in Africa* (Simon and Schuster, 1938); the diary of Audley Stewart, George Eastman's personal physician; the exceptionally helpful journal of Dr. Jean Marie Derscheid; as well as a statement prepared by Carl's assistant, R. C. Raddatz, February 10, 1928, and gossip Raddatz would also later deliver to Mickie Akeley.

Despite Mary Jobe Akeley's stunning descriptions, it's true that she seems to have had a bit of difficulty adjusting to the bleakness of the Athi Plains and then later handling the visit from the Samburu queen, Billy Billy, all of which is recounted wonderfully in *Carl Akeley's Africa* (Dodd, Mead, 1929, pp. 79–83). "This country is not half as good as it was four years ago . . ." comes from a letter from Martin Johnson to Carl, June 25, 1925. The rainy rendezvous with Eastman in Nairobi, and Eastman's cranky attitude, is corroborated by Rockwell in *My Way of Becoming a Hunter*. The tragedy of Kalawat is recounted by Osa Martin in *I Married Adventure*, pp. 294–95. That the Masai had now taken to wearing radiator caps in their earlobes, and jewelry made of spare telegraph wire, comes by way of Martin Johnson's *Camera Trails in Africa*, p. 24. The fight between Leigh and Raddatz and Akeley shouting "Everything up to a kick in the pants!" comes from Rockwell's book (pp. 213–14), as does the premature departure of one of Leigh's painting assistants, who could no longer handle the frightening chorus of lions at night. That the Africans reminded Mary of the pet collie she'd had as a girl is told by the author

*Rockwell was on the expedition, collecting, but does not play a starring role in my book.

herself in *Carl Akeley's Africa*, p. 200. "Did you hear that goddamn cyclone of bestiality last night?" is in *Frontiers of Enchantment*, p. 70. The weird episode of Eastman flirting with disaster when he *reached out and brushed his hand against the side of the passing rhino* was witnessed by Martin Johnson and written down for posterity in his book *Safari*. Details of the lion-spearing scene with the Lumbwa warriors are provided in Johnson's *Safari*, in Eastman's *Chronicles*, as well as in *Carl Akeley's Africa*, where Mary captures Percival's quote "I was tired of having that beast suffer, but don't tell the Missus" (*Carl Akeley's Africa*, p. 132).

The scouting expedition for the Plains Group background is lovingly narrated by Leigh in *Frontiers of Enchantment*. The dialogue here, between Carl and Leigh, is taken verbatim from Leigh's book (p. 131) even if I attempted to tweak Leigh's speech as if it were tinged with a little more irony than Leigh probably intended. (This was achieved through a bit of body language, appropriately subjunctified.) The silent tension between Eastman and Akeley following Eastman's refusal to give Carl more money is acknowledged by Rockwell in his book and is also discussed in a letter from Mickie Akeley to F. Trubee Davison, May 25, 1927, after getting a personal briefing on the trip from a disgruntled Raddatz.

Mary's *Carl Akeley's Africa* (*CAA*) is my source for the following: "This afternoon has been like living a year all in one day" (p. 146); Mary reading Carl O. Henry stories (p. 186); "When we return over this trail . . ." (p. 171); when Carl's strength abandons him on the climb, and he sits mumbling, *I have to think what's best to do* (p. 174); "Just put your head down and go . . ." (p. 174). For Derscheid's period equipment I obtained some nice particulars from the Virtual Museum of Surveying (www.surveyhistory.org). "I feel just like I did when I was here the first time" is from *CAA* (p. 185), as well as Carl's frustrated efforts to film Nyamlagira, despite the cloud cover, which Mary also writes about in her diary. In *Frontiers of Enchantment* Leigh provides the dialogue of Carl telling him, "You had better take your boys and go on up to the saddle ahead of me" (p. 162) and then his instructions for how Leigh should find the location of the gorilla background on the western slope of Karisimbi. "Do you see now where the fairies dance?" and the one sighting of a gorilla they have comes from *CAA* (p. 187). Derscheid's line of dialogue, "The mercury has fallen to 32 Fahrenheit," when Carl finally arrives at the saddle camp, visibly feverish, is also in *CAA* (p. 198), as well as Carl's instruction to Mary "to keep your lantern burning outside your tent tonight" in case of leopards (p. 188).

The account of Leigh's continued search for the gorilla background is from *Frontiers of Enchantment*, including the lengthy bits of dialogue, and some of the details of Carl's worsening condition. Most of the medical details—such as that Carl had "lost more than a quart of blood"—come from Derscheid's journal. It is from Derscheid's journal that we get the awful detail about Carl saying, "I think I shall not be able to support more than another one"; and how he rambled on about wiring and electrical problems (November 16, 1926). Upon returning to camp, and finding out that Carl had died, it is Leigh who notices that Bill is going on about an episode from almost twenty years earlier between himself and the dead man (pp. 176–77). The dialogue between Leigh and Derscheid—

"When?" . . . "This afternoon between three and five o'clock"—comes from *Frontiers of Enchantment* (p. 173). "I gave him a dose of chlorodyne for the dysentery . . ." is from Derscheid's journal. The detail of the leopard print in the mud outside Carl's tent is noted by Leigh in his book (p. 168).

The burial of Carl Akeley—and the trouble of obtaining the necessary provisions—is detailed by Derscheid, who seems to feel badly about the trouble they're causing for the native runners. Mary Jobe Akeley, on the other hand, in a letter to the girls back at Camp Mystic, explains how in addition to sending the natives one hundred miles to Kabale for cement—she had to send them back a second time because they had "spilled nearly all of it"—she was going to have "my natives dig a three foot drain between the steep mountainside and the knoll on which the tomb is. Now we are putting in a surrounding stockade six feet high of young trees. It takes nearly 200, as we are putting them as close as they will stand as a defense against buffalo and elephant. They are set in 2.5 feet in the lava rock. Next summer I want to have the stockade surrounded by a rock wall, and Mr Akeley's old boy, Bill, will come back to do the work." That digging into lava with a shovel sounds like broken glass comes to me from my friend Kenneth Lacovara, a geologist.

EPILOGUE

News of the dedication of the Akeley Hall of African Mammals was reported on in the *New York Times,* May 20, 1936, in the article "Akeley Memorial Dedicated by 2,000" and the same day in the *New York Herald Tribune,* "Akeley Exhibit Opens in New Hall of Museum." That Mary Jobe Akeley had laryngitis comes from the former. Additional sources include another story in the *New York Times,* "Africa Comes to Life in New York," May 17, 1936, and a piece in the *New Yorker* by Morris Markey, "Africa Brought to Town" (May 2, 1936). Details of the Roosevelt Memorial Rotunda—and its own dedication—are provided in the *New York Times,* "President Honors Cousin Here Today" (January 19, 1936).

The death of Henry Fairfield Osborn is reported in the *New York Times,* November 7, 1935, a lengthy obit which mentions his trip to Germany to receive the honorary doctorate, while the story about his tour of the Nazi Youth Movement, and his quote "To observe the spirit of the young Germans is to realize . . ." is from the *New York Times,* September 14, 1934, "Osborn Back After Tour." Osborn's correspondence regarding Hitler is mentioned in several books, including Charles Gallenkamp's book *Dragon Hunter: Roy Chapman Andrews and the Central Asiatic Expeditions* (Penguin, 2001), and Ronald Rainger's *An Agenda for Antiquity: Henry Fairfield Osborn & Vertebrate Paleontology at the American Museum of Natural History, 1890–1935* (University of Alabama Press, 1991), which cites a letter to W. K. Gregory, March 23, 1935, Gregory Papers, box 13; and Gregory to Raymond Pearl, May 6, 1935, Galton Society Folder, Raymond Pearl Papers, American Philosophical Society.

The detail of the tom-toms is mentioned in "Akeley Memorial Dedicated by 2,000," as is the fact that on opening day, 1936, only fifteen out of the planned twenty-eight dioramas were complete. The story of Eastman's suicide is covered in Elizabeth Brayer's *George Eastman: A Biography* (Johns Hopkins University Press, 1996).

That Mickie would have visited the African Hall is beyond a shadow of a doubt, especially considering how we know, through a December 6, 1936, article in the *New York Herald,* that she was preparing a biography about Carl—a project that, sadly, was killed by the efforts of Mary Jobe Akeley and Carl's brother, Lewis. We also know, from a letter Mickie wrote on May 25, 1927, to F. Trubee Davison, that "there is nothing in the world that I would not do to help make this hall the finest exhibition of its kind in the world." That it was Mickie who shot the "rear guard" elephant, and not TR, is acknowledged in correspondence between Mickie and F. Trubee Davison, according to Penelope Bodry-Sanders, *Carl Akeley: Africa's Collector, Africa's Savior* (Paragon House, 1991, p. 151).

ACKNOWLEDGMENTS

My first thanks must go to my editor, Gillian Blake, who for five some-times tumultuous years carried this book. Even when the waves got rough she never tossed it in the sea, and for that I will remain eternally grateful. Without her exquisite editorial gifts, her patience, and clarity, this book would never have been possible. Equal thanks to my agent, Heather Schroder, who first saw the promise of the book, encouraged me to delve headfirst into a few topics I knew absolutely nothing about (taxidermy, the history of Africa, zoology, and presidential biography, just to name a few). Vicki Haire gave the book a vivid and clear-eyed copyedit. I must also give dear thanks to Gregory Djanikian, Al Filreis, and Mingo Reynolds at the University of Pennsylvania, for letting me teach (without so much as a proper license), an experience that has given me immense pleasure. I only wish I could individually thank all of the students I've had who have taught me in return. The research support provided by the always accommodating staff of the Penn libraries was unprecedented. Completing this book likewise would have been impossible without the financial support I received from the Pew Fellowship in the Arts, as well as the Pennsylvania Council on the Arts. I would like to extend personal thanks to Melissa Franklin, director of the Pew Fellowships in the Arts, as well as Sarah Biemiller, Ann Cinque, and Ellen Maher. The MacDowell Colony provided me with one of the most charmed and rewarding months of my life, where I wrote several of this book's earliest chapters.

My research trip to Africa was generously underwritten by *GQ* magazine, even if my editor, Joel Lovell, and his boss, Jim Nelson, were under the impression I was going to Rwanda exclusively to write a story about tourism. Thanks, guys! Thanks also to Roger Hodge, my erstwhile editor at *Harper's*, and to John Jeremiah Sullivan, who gave me the assignment that would, inadvertently, and via the phantasmagoric charms of *Puma concolor,* lead to my discovery of Carl Akeley. Immeasurable thanks must be given to Penelope Bodry-Sanders, who discovered Carl Akeley long before I ever did, and who first wrote of his adventures in the only true and comprehensive biography about him. Not only her fabulous book, but the research trail she so generously left in the archives at the Explorers Club, in New York City, provided me with a veritable and unerring road map. It was at the Explorers Club where I was lucky enough to meet Claire Fleming, Ryan Haley, and Dorthea Sartain, all of whom provided the most welcome of research environments imaginable. Mickie Akeley's step-great-grandson, Jesse Page, and his wife, Liz, welcomed me into their home to pore over old diaries and rifle through trunks of safari memorabilia that still smelled of Mickie's perfume, even letting me sleep in the "Africa Room," where spears and shields hung on the wall. I will never forget their generosity nor Jesse's amazing deep-fried turkey.

I could not possibly thank all of the librarians who helped me, but the list would have to begin with Barbara Mathe, museum archivist and head of Library Special Collections at the American Museum of Natural History, and Tom Baione, acting director. Nina Cummings has been one of my best sources from the very beginning, as well as an excellent host for my visit to the Field Museum in Chicago, probably the most fun I've ever had on a museum field trip. I would also like to thank Kathy Connor, curator of the George Eastman House; Mary Huth, Rare Books and Special Collections, at the Rush Rhees Library, University of Rochester; and Liz Dailey at the Rochester Historical Society. Special thanks to Kate Davis for a very fruitful barter system that left me far the richer—typed transcripts of Carl's and Mickie's diaries. Thanks also to Mark Alvey, Thomas Gnoske, Armand Esai, Christine Giannoni, and Michael Godow at the Field Museum. Stephen Rogers at the Carnegie Museum of Natural History gave me a great deal of guidance at the onset of my project, pointing me in the right directions, and introducing me to My Most Beloved Taxidermist, John Janelli, which is in no way meant to diminish all the other taxidermists who shared their time and wisdom with me, among them Bill Yox, Floyd Easterman, John Matthews, and David Schwendeman.

Special thanks to Stephen Quinn for my first guided tour of the dioramas in the African Hall, for answering numerous and sundry queries, and for his gorgeous book about the habitat dioramas, *Windows on Nature,* which must be bound with Bakelite. Any other coffee-table book would have long ago been demolished by such relentless ogling.

Thanks to Robert Peck at the Philadelphia Academy of Natural Sciences; Susan Otto from the Milwaukee Public Museum; Deirdre Lawrence and Tara Cuthbert of the Brooklyn Museum; Jeanette Polard and Kathy Maher of the Barnum Museum; Mike Sampson of the U.S. Secret Service; Amy Meadows, Marshall Fields archivist; David Ward from the C. G. Jung Foundation; David Pavelich, Regenstein Library, University of Chicago; and Conrad Froelich and Jacquelyn Borgeson at the Safari Museum, in Chanute, Kansas, who were always cheerful and generous with their time to a fault. Many thanks to Lucy McCann at the Bodleian Library at the University of Oxford.

I would also like to thank the New-York Historical Society; Milwaukee Historical Society; Brooklyn Public Library; the Peabody Museum at Yale; Milstein Division of United States History, Local History & Geneaology, at the New York Public Library; Saint Thomas Historical Society, Ontario; Saint Thomas Public Library; Elkins County Railway Museum, West Virginia; Rochester Public Library; National Railway Historical Society; the Audubon Society; and the World Wildlife Fund.

For encouragement, for inspiration, for answering the weirdest of queries, for giving me a boost at some point along the way, countless individuals are to thank, but the briefest of lists would have to include: Lauren Arens, Adam Bates, Jessica Baumgardner, Sven Birkerts, Ward Bowen, Meredith Broussard, Claire Busse, Lisa Carlson, Robert Claus, Susan C. Colby, Jamie Farrell, Bridgetta Bourne-Firl, Virginia Foletta, Walton Ford, Dave Foreman, Sue Frederick, Bob Gallagher (in memoriam), Jack Gantos, Bernard Goffinet, David R. Godine, Joe Greenwald, J. C. Hallman, Jack Hitt, Dick Houston, Melissa Ierlan, Pascal Imperato, Alan Isselhard, Bob Iveson, Bob Jones, Sam Katz, Tim Kirk, Kenneth Lacovara, Lewis Lapham, Bill Lattin, Todd Lester, Darren Mann, Michael Martin, Toby Lester, Michael and Jennifer McGloin, Nicholas Montemarano, Susan Morse, Jason Moser, Ernest Ntagozera (in memoriam),

Emily Nussbaum, David Pearce, Mark Polizzotti, Pamela Polston, Jason Ross, Fred Scherer, Peter Schwartz, Jeff Sharlet, Don Silver, Phil Sirois, Mary E. Smith, Carol Cioffi Smith, Steve Steiger, Zoe Strauss, Thomas Swearingen, Jack Tabor, Alison True, Brendan Vaughan, Greg Veis, Alisa Volkman, Calvin Wang, David Warner, Bill Wasik, Art Winslow, Holly Wofford, Margaret Wood, Sarah Zar, and Douglas Zinn.

Thanks to Quinn Eli for reading chapters, for being the most insightful human being on the planet, for being the dearest of friends; and to Thomas Devaney, for your vision, your poetry, your grace and friendship, for listening to me endlessly plot. To Evan Rossheim and Janet Hoffman, the best neighbors a person could ever dream of having, with special thanks to Janet for reading several chapters and for her thoughtful suggestions. Very special thanks to Beth Kephart for your steadfast friendship, your endless support and enthusiasm for this project, and for your empathy for a fellow writer's anxieties. Thanks too for the glass elephant eye—it has been a most auspicious talisman.

To my loving family, to Nora and Adele, to John and Tina, to my brother Jeff, to uncle Al, to my mother, Judith, and my father, John. Thanks most of all to my daughter, Ruby, whom I promise to take to Africa one day, yes, maybe even on a boat, like Max, and to Julie, for being my first editor, for putting up with me when I couldn't shut up about the plight of Jumbo, for pretending I still existed when I might as well have been far away on top of a mountain hunting elephants, for giving me more love and patience and support than any person could ever possibly deserve. Thanks too—beautiful librarian that you are—for bringing home countless wonderful books and bits, for letting me take you away from your true patrons to find out how many teeth an antelope has or how much pith is really in a pith helmet. For telling me about the Boer War, and looking up the Swahili for *monkey*. Thanks, too, for letting me rant, for not holding my occasional lapses of *morale* against me, and thanks, too, for making me laugh like a hyena sometimes. I would skin a pack of wild dogs for you.

INDEX